Elizabeth Parsons Ware Packard

The Prisoners' Hidden Life or Insane Asylums Unveiled

Elizabeth Parsons Ware Packard

The Prisoners' Hidden Life or Insane Asylums Unveiled

ISBN/EAN: 9783744762687

Printed in Europe, USA, Canada, Australia, Japan

Cover: Foto ©Suzi / pixelio.de

More available books at **www.hansebooks.com**

THE PRISONERS' HIDDEN LIFE,

—OR—

Insane Asylums Unveiled:

AS DEMONSTRATED BY THE

Report of the Investigating Committee of the Legislature of Illinois.

TOGETHER WITH

𝔐𝔯𝔰. 𝔓𝔞𝔠𝔨𝔞𝔯𝔡'𝔰 𝔒𝔬𝔫𝔡𝔧𝔲𝔱𝔬𝔯𝔰' 𝔗𝔢𝔰𝔱𝔦𝔪𝔬𝔫𝔶.

BY

MRS. E. P. W. PACKARD.

"Ye shall know the truth."

CHICAGO:
PUBLISHED BY THE AUTHOR.
A. B. CASE, Printer. 139 Monroe St.
1868.

Entered according to act of Congress A. D., 1868, by
MRS. E. P. W. PACKARD,
in the Clerk's office of the Dist. Court for the Northern Dist. of Illinois.

Preface.

The legalized usurpation of human rights is the great evil underlying our social fabric. From this corrupt center spring the evils of our social system. This corruption has culminated in the Insane Asylums of the nineteenth century. Let the Government but remove this cause of insanity, and the need of such Institutions would be greatly lessened.

So long as the enlightened mothers of the present day are obliged to assert and defend their own identity, simply because the Government fails to do it, so long will their offspring bear the seeds of unbalanced organization, which only waits for circumstances to develop into insanity.

It is one object of the writer in giving her narrative to the world, to fasten the public eye upon this evil, as the great germinating cause of the insanity of the present age.

The great evil of our present Insane Asylum System lies in the fact, that insanity is there treated as a crime, instead of a misfortune, which is indeed a gross act of injustice. Supposing our Government should establish a Charitable Institution for the purpose of taking all who have had the misfortune to lose their property, and imprison them, where they could be punished to any extent, without appeal, for this calamity which had befallen them. Supposing too, the Government forced this class to accept the discipline of this Charitable Institution, without their own consent, on the verdict of a jury, that they had lost their property—would this guardianship of human rights be recognized as humanitarian or just?

But supposing the defenders of such Institutions should contend that it is for "their good," and the good of "society" to thus entomb them; "for, they are no comfort to themselves, nor their families," while saddened by the loss of their fortunes and business reputation; and besides, we do not call this Institution a Prison, but an Asylum, "where they can rest, and be kindly cared for."

But permit me to reply that *calling* it an Asylum, when it is in reality a Prison, where they *are* punished for their misfortune, does not materially help the matter. And besides, whether legalized injustice ever promoted the good of the individual, or society, is a question yet to be settled.

To lose one's property and become poor and dependent is a great misfortune, and such unfortunates ought to receive our commiseration, and be encouraged and helped to rise and retrieve their fortunes, instead of being cast out of society as public nuisances, to be publicly branded as men whose business capacities are henceforth to be regarded with suspicion and distrust. If it would be unreasonable to treat the misfortune of losing property on this principle, how can it be reasonable to treat a greater misfortune—that of losing one's reason—on this same principle?

In disclosing to the blinded public the real character of their Insane Asylums, the author has relied mainly upon her own personal observation, and three years experience, as data from which to draw her own conclusions; and if from this data her conclusions are not legitimate, she asks the reader to be the judge.

And it is to add weight to these conclusions, that she has annexed to her narrative the testimony of several other married women, who have experienced a term of imprisonment in Jacksonville Insane Asylum. Of these five ladies whose statements she has appended, three of them, viz: Mrs. Olsen, Mrs. Minard and Mrs. Shedd, claim that they have never been insane.

Of that part of Mrs. Olsen's thrilling narrative relating to myself, the writer would say that she feels a delicacy in allowing herself to be so lauded in her own book, and that her only apology for so doing lies in the fact, that her confidence in Mrs Olsen's intelligence, christianity and her purity of purpose was so entire, that she consented to publish her narrative before reading it herself.

It may be a satisfaction to the readers of this volume to know, that the facts herein stated have been authenticated and corroborated by the Illinois Investigating Committee, appointed by the Legislature of 1867 to investigate and report the result to the Governor; which they did on the second of December, following. In this Report, the writer, Mrs. Olsen, Mrs. Minard, Mrs. Shedd, and five others, were acknowledged as competent witnesses in the following language, viz:

"In point of intelligence, character and credibility, they are as worthy of belief as other witnesses on whose testimony in courts, the property, character, liberty and lives of suitors daily depend.

"The committee have entire confidence in the belief, that

all these witnesses had a clear understanding, and comprehended, when examined, the obligations of the oath administered to them; and in an unusually intelligent manner testified to matters within their recollection, and were prudent and entirely honest, and testified to facts as they believed them to exist. With one or two, unimportant exceptions, neither of them exhibited any appearance of a disordered intellect, moral obliquity, or defective memory; and, therefore, to reject their testimony, appeared to the Committee as calculated to defeat an investigation after the truth, and possibily subvert the ends of public justice."

Mrs. E. P. W. Packard.

Chicago, May, 1868.

CONTENTS.

Introduction.. 11

CHAPTER I.
Inspiring Sentiments... 13

CHAPTER II.
Result of expressing my Obnoxious views, viz: Free Discussion of Religious Belief----Rights of Private Judgement—"Total Depravity"—The Unlimited Atonement—God's Immutability—What is it to be a Christian—Freedom of Conscience—Spiritual Gifts—Questions for the Class............... 14

CHAPTER III.
My Abduction.. 34

CHAPTER IV.
My Abduction—continued....................................... 44

CHAPTER V.
My Journey.. 51

CHAPTER VI.
My Reception.. 59

CHAPTER VII.
My First Day of Prison Life................................... 61

CHAPTER VIII.
The Parting Scene... 69

CHAPTER IX.
Disappointed Hopes.. 73

CHAPTER X.
The Sunny Side of my Prison Life 77

CHAPTER XI.
My Transition... 85

CHAPTER XII.
Removal from the Best Ward to the Worst...................... 88

CHAPTER XIII.
My Occupation... 93

CHAPTER XIV.
How I Obtained my Papers...................................... 99

CHAPTER XV.
Evidences of My Insanity...................................... 102

CHAPTER XVI.
The Attendant who Abused me................................... 107

CHAPTER XVII.
"Let Dr. McFarland Bear his own Sins"......................... 110

CHAPTER XVIII.
Attempted Reconciliation with Mr. Packard..................... 111

CONTENTS.

CHAPTER XIX.
Letter to My Children sent to the Wash tub..... 116

CHAPTER XX.
How I Obtained my first Writing Paper....................... 119

CHAPTER XXI.
An Honorable Act in Dr. McFarland........................ 121

CHAPTER XXII.
Married Women Unprotected................................ 124

CHAPTER XXIII.
My Life Imperiled... 127

CHAPTER XXIV.
Hope of Dr. McFarland's Repentance...................... 132

CHAPTER XXV.
"You should Return to your Husband"...................... 133

CHAPTER XXVI.
Uncared for... 136

CHAPTER XXVII.
Self-defense—Clandestine Letters.......................... 139

CHAPTER XXVIII.
Miss Mary Tomlin—A Model Attendant 147

CHAPTER XXIX.
Mrs. McFarland—The Matron............................... 150

CHAPTER XXX.
Guilty Husbands... 154

CHAPTER XXXI.
The Sane kept for the Doctor's Benefit..................... 157

CHAPTER XXXII.
An Unpleasant Response.................................... 162

CHAPTER XXXIII.
Is Man the Lord of Creation............................... 163

CHAPTER XXXIV.
Petition to the Trustees Presented September 1861............ 165

CHAPTER XXXV.
The Rights of the Tax Payers.............................. 169

CHAPTER XXXVI.
The Imputation of Insanity a Barrier to Human Progress......... 170

CHAPTER XXXVII.
Mr. James Lyon's Advice................................... 174

CHAPTER XXXVIII.
Record of a Day... 175

CHAPTER XXXIX.
How I Bought and Retained some Paper...................... 179

CHAPTER XL.
The Aristocracy of Jacksonville Rebuked—Another Honorable Act. 183

CHAPTER XLI.
"Love Your Enemies"....................................... 187

CHAPTER XLII.
How Mr. Packard gave me Paper and how I lost it............. 189

CHAPTER XLIII.
Dialogues with Dr. McFarland on the Woman Question.......... 191

CHAPTER XLIV.
My Family Relatives.. 194

CHAPTER XLV.
Old Mrs. Timmons Deserted by her Children.................... 199

CHAPTER XLVI.
Mrs. Chenoworth's Suicide—Medical Abuse..................... 202

CHAPTER XLVII.
Changes and how Brought About................................ 211

CHAPTER XLVIII.
My Battle with Despotism—No Surrender....................... 215

CHAPTER XLIX.
Good comes of Seeming Evil.................................... 219

CHAPTER L.
Reading Books and Papers...................................... 221

CHAPTER LI.
Abusing Mrs. Stanley.. 225

CHAPTER LII.
Subduing a New Prisoner....................................... 228

CHAPTER LIII.
Treatment of the Sick... 232

CHAPTER LIV.
Mrs. Leonard's Visit to her Mother............................ 234

CHAPTER LV.
Mrs. Emeline Bridgman—or Nature's Laws Broken............... 238

CHAPTER LVI.
The Guilt of Folly.. 245

CHAPTER LVII.
Mrs. Watts Driven from off her Sick Bed....................... 249

CHAPTER LVIII.
Dangerous to be a Married Woman in Illinois................... 250

CHAPTER LIX.
Interview with Mr. Wells of Chicago—A Victim of homesickness. 253

CHAPTER LX.
An Asylum Sabbath... 257

CHAPTER LXI.
Letters to Dr. McFarland...................................... 258

CHAPTER LXII.
My Attempt to get an Attendant Discharged.................... 261

CHAPTER LXIII.
A New Attendant Installed—Something New..................... 265

CHAPEER LXIV.
My Protest Deprives me of no Privileges...................... 267

CHAPTER LXV.
Dr. McFarland a Respecter of Persons......................... 269

CHAPTER LXVI.
Kidnapping the Soul... 271

CONTENTS.

CHAPTER LXVII.
Orthodox Heaven and Hell.................................... 274

CHAPTER LXVIII.
A Scene in the Fifth Ward—A Good Omen...................... 276

CHAPTER LXIX.
Every Moral Act Influences the Moral Universe................ 280

CHAPTER LXX.
The Death Penalty to be Annihilated......................... 281

CHAPTER LXXI.
I was Punished for Telling the Truth........................ 284

CHAPTER LXXII.
Wrong Actions are Suicidal.................................. 289

CHAPTER LXXIII.
Mrs Sybil Dole—A Fallen Woman............................... 289

CHATER LXXIV.
Can a Blind Person See...................................... 292

CHAPTER LXXV.
Human Instincts above Human Enactments...................... 294

CHAPTER LXXVI.
The Prisoner who called Himself "Jesus Christ".............. 296

CHAPTER LXXVII.
Letter to Judge Whitlock of Jacksonville.................... 300

CHAPTER LXXVIII.
Difference between Contentment and Patience................. 303

CAAPTER LXXIX.
My Successful attempt to obtain my Freedom.................. 305

CHAPTER LXXX.
The Dawning of a New Dispensation........................... 312

CHAPTER LXXXI.
The Moral Barometer Indicates a Storm—A Hurricane........... 316

CHAPTER LXXXII.
The Clouds Disperse... 323

CHAPTER LXXXIII.
My Oldest Son Obtains my Discharge.......................... 327

CHAPTER LXXXIV.
The Trustees Force me into the Hands of Mr. Packard......... 329

CHAPTER LXXXV.
Jacksonville Insane Asylum a Type of other Insane Asylums... 338

CHAPTER LXXXVI.
A Note of Thanks to the Railroad Companies and the Press of Ill.. 339

CHAPTER LXXXVII.
An Appeal to the People of Illinois for a Redress of my Wrongs.. 340

PART I.

INTRODUCTION.

"A wounded spirit who can bear." Spirit wrongs are the keenest wounds that can be inflicted upon woman. Her nature is so sensitively organized, that an injury to her feelings is felt more keenly than an injury to her person.

The fortitude of her nature enables her to endure physical suffering heroically; but the wound which her spirit feels under a wanton physical abuse, is far more deeply felt, and is harder to be borne than the physical abuse itself.

Her very benevolent, confiding, forgiving nature, renders it a greater crime to abuse her spirit, than to abuse her person. To most men, and some women, this position may appear absurd, yet it is true; neither do we feel disposed to blame this class for not appreciating it, for their coarser organization incapacitates them to understand us.

When woman is brought before our man courts, and our man juries, and has no bruises, or wounds, or marks of violence upon her person to show as a ground of her complaint, it is hard for them to realize that she has any cause for appeal to them for protection; while at the same time her whole physical system may be writhing in agony from spirit wrongs, such as can only be understood by her peers.

Spiritual, sensitive woman, knowing this fact, suffers on in silent anguish without appeal, until death kindly liberates her from her prison-house of unappreciated suffering.

It is to delineate these spiritual wrongs of woman, that I have given my narrative to the public, hoping that my more tangible experiences may draw the attention of the philanthropic public to a more just consideration of married woman's legal disabilities; for since the emancipation of the negro, there is no class of American citizens, who so much need legal protection, and who receive so little, as this class.

As their representative, I do not make complaint of physical abuses, but it is the usurpation of our natural rights of which we complain; and it is our legal position of *nonentity*, which renders us so liable and exposed to suffering and persecution from this source.

In the following narrative of my experiences, the reader will therefore find the interior of woman's life delineated through the exterior surroundings of her bitter experiences. I state facts through which, the reader may look into woman's soul, as through a mirror, that her realm of suffering may be thus portrayed.

I therefore commence my narrative where my persecution commenced, with the marital usurpation of my rights of opinion and conscience, and as I progress, will note such incidents as I can best employ to portray my feelings, rather than the recital of the physical abuses I witnessed; since my Coadjutors and the Committee have so graphically described the exterior life of the prisoner, it is unnecessary for me to enlarge on this feature of prison life in Insane Asylums.

My Asylum journal, delineating my inner life more particularly, is given, of course, in the language in which it was written at the time, and will doubtless, to many appear, for this reason, to be strong language. Allow me to suggest to such critics, that before you harshly, and rashly censure the writer, just place yourselves in her exact position, and then judge whether your real emotions could be clothed in milder language. And let us remember too, that if we speak at all, it is the truth alone we are bound to utter, regardless of the censure or applause of mortals.

I.
Inspiring Sentiments.

Providence hinges mighty events on pivots exceedingly small. What men call accidents, are God's appointed incidents. We are traitors to any truth when we suppress the utterance of it, and allow the opposite error to go unrebuked. High principles must be advanced as real laws. A desire to elevate all mankind to the nobleness for which they are designed, should manifest the depth and purity of our moral convictions. We should meet evil with mildness, yet, with unfaltering firmness. We should aim to bring out a noble spirit into daily intercourse, believing that a holy life is a more precious offering to truth, than retired speculations and writing; for, he who leaves a holy life behind him, bequeaths to the world a richer legacy than any book. The want of moral courage to carry out great principles, and to act upon them at all risks, is fatal to originality, because the faculties slumber within, being weighed down by the chains of custom. This habit of reliance on principle, should give us a buoyant consciousness of superiority to every outward influence. A far higher anticipation of great results from worthy deeds, should make us strenuous in action, and fill us with a cheerful trust. We must be palsied by no fear to offend, no desire to please, no dependence upon the judgment of others. The consciousness of self subsistence, of disinterested conformity to high principles, will command an open freedom to our utterances, and will summon into our service a spiritual force that will resist and overcome all obstacles.

Under the inspiration of such sentiments have I penned the following narrative of my experiences, beneath a dark cloud of adverse events, whose silver lining is yet to be discovered to my physical vision. As the dyer uses mordants to set his colors, so my Heavenly Father has employed the mordant of adversity to individualize my sentiments of morality and virtuous action. And, by my experiences, it would seem, that my Father intended to so capacitate me, that I should be daunted and discouraged by nothing, that true loyalty might be burned into my heart. This loyalty demands that individual reason and conscience be the guide of human actions. It allows no oligarchy of creeds, sects, or customs to be a standard, which ignores the individual as the sovereign over himself. *The God within,* is the monarch of this realm of human freedom.

II.

Result of expressing my Obnoxious views.

I have been Illinois State's Prisoner three years in Jacksonville Insane Asylum, for simply expressing religious opinions in a community who were unprepared to appreciate and understand them. I was incarcerated June 18, 1860, and liberated June 18, 1863. Fortunately for me, all these obnoxious views were presented in writing, and are now in my own possession, although they were secretly taken from me, at the time of my abduction, and retained for years in the hands of my persecutor, Rev. Theophilus Packard, who was at that time the pastor of the Old School Presbyterian Church at Manteno, Kankakee County, Illinois.

He had been my husband for twenty-one years, and was the father of my six children, five of whom are boys, and one girl. At the time he forced me from my dear little ones, my daughter was ten years old and my babe eighteen months. I was in perfect health and of sound mind, and cheerfully and faithfully performing the duties of wife and mother to the entire satisfaction of my family and society, so far as I know. And, since the only plea Mr. Packard makes in defence of this course is, that my religious views were dangerous to the spiritual interests of his children and the community, I feel called upon to present these views, frankly and candidly, that my readers may judge for themselves whether my imprisonment can be justified on this basis.

As an Introduction therefore to my "Hidden Life" in my prison, I shall present these views just as I presented them to the bible class in Manteno, a few weeks before my incarceration. I became connected with this class at the special request of Deacon Abijah Dole, the teacher of the class, and with the full and free consent of my husband. Mr. Dole gave as his reason for wishing me to join his class, that he found it impossible to awaken any interest, and he fondly hoped that I might bring forward some views which might elicit the attention he desired.

I seated myself among his pupils, who then numbered only six men in all, as a sincere seeker after the truth. Mr. Dole allowed his pupils to be regarded as mutual teachers, so that all were allowed to ask questions and offer suggestions. Availing myself of this license, others were encouraged to follow my example, so that our class soon became the place of animating discussions, and as our tolerant teacher allowed both sides of a question to be discussed I found it became to me a great source of pleasure and profit. Indeed, I never can recollect a time when my mind grew into a knowledge of religious truths faster, than under the influence of these free and animated discussions. The effect of these debates was felt throughout the whole community, so that our class of seven soon increased to forty-six, including the most influential members of the community.

About this time a latent suspicion seemed to be aroused, lest the church creed be endangered by this license of free inquiry and fair discussion; and a meeting of some of the leading church-members was called, wherein this bible-class was represented as being a dangerous influence, involving the exposure of the creed to the charge of fallibility. To prevent this, it was agreed that the tolerant Deacon Dole must be exchanged for the intolerant Deacon Smith, in order that free discussion might be effectually put down. And this Deacon Smith suggested, that the way to put down free-discussion was, to *put down Mrs. Packard*. This he engaged to do, in case they would install him as teacher. This being done, the battle commenced, and I found our license had expired, with our kind teacher's resignation. Ignorant as I was of this conspiracy against the right of private opinions, I continued to use this God given right, as my judgment and conscience dictated, until I found, by open opposition, that it was the express object of the change, to abolish all expression of any views which did not harmonize with the Presbyterian Church creed. I knew and felt that it was their determination to fetter me, and bring me into unquestioning acknowledgment of their doctrines, as the sum total of all important truths. Of course I could not do this, and be honest to myself; but from this point, I had the precaution to put into a written form, every idea I uttered in conflict with what Deacon Smith thought orthodox views, so as to avoid being misrepresented, and I almost uniformly read these papers to Mr. Packard, before presenting them to the class, and secured from him his consent to my reading them.

This digested form of presenting my ideas, tended to increase rather than diminish the interest in favor of my new views, so that finally after Mr. Packard had given his consent for my reading my articles, Mr. Smith would refuse to have them read. Up to this point, Mr. Packard acted the man, and the Christian, in his treatment of me. But now came the fatal crisis when evil influences overcame him!

One afternoon Deacon Smith visited him in his study, and held a secret interview with him of two hours length, when he left him a different man. That evening just before retiring to rest, he remarked in a very pleasant tone,

"Wife, I want to talk with you a little while, come here!"

OBNOXIOUS VIEWS. 17

I went into his extended arms, and sat upon his lap, and encircled his neck with my arm, when he remarked in a very mild tone of voice.

"Now wife, hadn't you better give up these bible class discussions? Deacon Smith thinks you had better, and so do some others, and I think you had better too."

"Husband, I should be very glad to get rid of the responsibility if I can do so honorably, but I do not like to yield a natural right to the dictation of bigotry and intolerance, as Deacon Smith demands, but I am willing to say to the class that as Deacon Smith, and Mr. Packard, and others, have expressed a wish that I withdraw my discussions from the class, I do so, at their request, not from any desire to shrink from investigation on my part, but for the sake of peace, as they view it."

"No, wife, that won't do; you must resign yourself."

"Won't that be resigning, and that too on a truthful basis?"

"No, you must tell them it is your choice to give them up."

"But, dear, it is not my choice!"

"But you can make it so, under the circumstances."

"Yes, I can make it so, by stating the truth; but I can't by telling a lie."

"Well, you must do it!"

"O husband! how can you yield to such an evil influence? Only think! Here you have pledged before God and man that you will be my protector, until death part us, and now you are tempted to become my persecutor! Do be a man, and go to the class, in defiance of Deacon Smith, and say to the class, 'my wife has just as good a right to her opinions as you have to yours, and I shall protect her in that right. You need not believe her opinions unless you choose; but she has a right to defend her honest opinions as well as yourselves. I shall not suffer her to be molested in this right.' Then you will be a man—a protector of your wife—and you will deserve honor, and you will have it. But if you become my persecutor and go against me, as Deacon Smith desires, you will deserve dishonor, and you will surely get it. Don't fall into this fatal snare, which the evil one has surely laid for you."

He construed my earnestness into anger, and thrust me from him, determining to risk this result at all hazards. From that fatal time, all good influences seemed to have forsaken him, and he left to pursue his downward way, with no power to resist evil or flee from the tempter. Reason, conscience, judgment, prudence, consistency and affection, all, all directly sunk into the fatal sleep of stupidity or death. From that point, I have never had a protector in my husband. He has only been my persecutor! In a few weeks from that time, he forcibly entombed me within the massive walls of Jacksonville Asylum prison, to rise no more, if he could prevent it. He told me he did this, to give the impression that I was insane, so that my opinions need not be believed, for, said he, "I must protect the cause of Christ!"

The following is a copy of some of the articles I prepared for the class, wherein my most radical opinions are delineated, which led to this unnatural imprisonment.

Free discussion of religious belief.

Free discussion implies that both sides of a subject can be investigated, and allows full liberty to each individual to express his honestly cherished opinions, and also give his reasons in support of them. My classmates, we have nothing to fear in applying the scales of free discussion to our religious belief, for truth will sustain itself; the scales of free-discussion, intelligently used, always preponderate on the side of the truth, that is, the weightiest reasons always bear upon that side, and indicate a balance in its favor. For instance, should we wish to test the existence of a God in the scales of free discussion, what have we to fear in the use of the scales on this point? If we are not prepared to support his existence by such arguments as will make the scales preponderate right, is it not best for us to bestow study upon that point sufficient to defend it with intelligent reason, since this is confidently assumed to be a truth in our creed? Then we shall be prepared to defend, as well as assert our belief. It is not respectful for us to say to **our** opponents on this or any other point, "I know your side is the wrong one, and you ought to take our positive assertion as authority sufficient to condemn you as a heretic, simply because you believe contrary to my honestly cherished opinions." No, my classmates, the religion of authority has had its day—a reasonable religion, such as will bear the infallible tests of truth, based on arguments drawn from God's word and works is the religion for us. Truth should be endorsed by us through our reasoning faculties alone, and therefore should not conflict with our common sense and enlightened reason. And it is my opinion that the religion God sent to man, is so peculiarly adapted to man's nature, as not to conflict with the common sense views of the common mass of minds. And ere the bright millennial day dawns upon us, I believe that theologically sectarian views, will give place to the common sense views of mankind, and that this is to be the way there is to be "but one God, one faith, one baptism."

Now, what can be the harm, dear classmates, in our trying to hasten this day, by bringing our educated belief to this test, by kindly using the scales of free discussion. For myself, I feel willing to have all my opinions tested by these scales, and I am willing to yield any point of belief to a weightier invincible argument in the opposite scale—that is, those views which seem best supported by sound argument and candid reasoning I willingly endorse, although they may conflict with some of my preconceived ideas, or my educated belief, or even with our sectarian creeds. For it is not impossible but that some simple moral truth may have become perverted by educational influences. And candor and honesty, it seems to me, compel us to admit, that there is a mixture of truth and error in the creeds of all denominations of christians, not even excepting the creed of the Presbyterian church; and what can be the harm in thus testing these views, and thereby separating the precious from the vile, rather than by trying to defend our sectarian creeds, by arguments and reasons which are not based in truth for their support, thus perpetuating falsehood or errors.

It is my desire, dear classmates, that this social bible class be employed as a means to fit us to become valiant defenders of our faith—that we here capacitate ourselves to defend all points of our belief by rational and intelligent reasons, that we may be able to meet the common enemy of our holy religion with arguments "such as he can not gainsay or resist." The truth never suffers by agitation and free discussion. It is error alone that fears the light and shrinks before the scales. Let us dare to judge for ourselves what is right, and let us know what right and truth are, by bringing our religious belief to this test of reason and common sense. Let us throw off the blinding influence of prejudice and sectarian zeal, and come up upon the nobler, higher platform of being simple, sincere, charitable, honest seekers after the real, simple, naked truth.

Having obtained permission from our teacher, Deacon Smith, to read the above article before the class, I commenced reading; but finding it to be a defence of what he had determined to stop—free discussion—he interrupted me, by forbidding my reading any farther. Of course I quietly submitted to this mandate with unanswering obedience.

Rights of Private Judgment.

I profess to be no theologian, or to have adopted the creed of any sect or denomination of christians as infallible. But I do profess to take the works and word of God, or facts and revelation as our only infallible guide in our search for truth, and a "thus saith the Lord," as a settling of all controversy. But since I know it to be a fact that equally sincere and honest christians put a very different construction upon the same event of Providence, and the same text of scripture,

I feel that we are compelled to assume the responsibility of private judgment. And in so doing, I believe we are obeying Christ's directions in the 57th verse of the 12th chapter of Luke, viz: "And why, even of yourselves, judge ye not what is right?"

I regard this bible class as having reached that stage of development where God holds us individually responsible for our belief. I therefore esteem it a great privilege to be in a bible class where *our* opinions are called for, rather than the opinions of commentators. Not that I wish to disregard the opinions of commentators, or learned theologians in my search for Bible truth; for I do think that their opinions are entitled to great deference and respect. While I at the same time believe that the Bible is a book so peculiar in its nature, that learning and talent are not indispensable to a correct interpretation of it, any more than experience and education are indispensably necessary to our judging correctly of the wants of nature. For instance, because an adult may choose strong drink to allay his thirst, and the child prefer cold water, I do not think we are justified in concluding that strong drink is the best adapted to meet the wants of nature, simply because a mature man chooses it; for this adult may have perverted his natural appetite, so that his choice may not be so much in accordance with nature as the instincts of the child. As in our physical, so in our moral nature, there may be a liability that a simple moral truth may have been perverted by educational influences. Therefore, I do not think that because a talented and learned theologian advances an opinion, that he is certainly correct; neither because an illiterate layman holds a different opinion, do I think he is certainly wrong. But in both cases we should judge of the opinion upon its own intrinsic merits, independent of the source or medium through which it comes to us.

Now, dear classmates, conscious that I am alone and personally responsible to God for my religious belief, I do not want to embrace an error. Therefore I will be very thankful to be shown wherein my opinions are unsound, or my reasoning inconclusive. Just consider my views, not as those of a theologian, but as one who is searching for truth on the same common plane with yourselves; and I ask you to give my opinions no more credence, than you think truth entitles them to as you view it. For it is the common sense of common men and common women that I so much covet as my tribunal of judgment, rather than learned commentators, or popular theologians, or venerable doctors of divinity.

"Total Depravity."

It is the authority of creeds, echoed by the theologians and ministers of the Presbyterian pulpit, not excepting our own pastor, that human nature is necessarily a sinful nature.

Now I ask the privilege of presenting to our class this question: "If human nature is necessarily a sinful nature, how could Christ take upon himself human nature and know no sin?" This question was referred to their pastor for an answer. Mr. Packard gave it as his opinion that a "Holy God might make a holy human nature for Christ, and a sinful nature for the rest of the human family." Upon this, one of the class inquired, "Can a holy God make sin?"

These questions troubled both our teacher, Deacon Smith, and their pastor. They could not answer them satisfactorily to themselves or the class; and it was to extricate themselves from this unpleasant dilemma, that they at once agreed that this question was the result of a diseased brain, from whence it had emanated, and therefore it was unworthy of their consideration! Thus their reputation for intelligence and ability was placed beyond question, and the infallibility of their creed remained inviolate! And their poor afflicted christian sister must be kindly cared for within the massive walls of a prison, lest her diseased brain communicate its contagion to other brains, and then what will become of our creed! for we cannot afford to follow the example of this "Man of God," and sacrifice our wives and mothers to save our creed!

SPARE THE CREED!

Though the mother's heart do bleed,
Spare, O, spare our trembling creed!
Though her tender infants cry,
Though they pine, and droop, and die,
Though her daily care they need,
Spare, O, spare our trembling creed!

Force the mother from her home!
That once pure and peaceful dome;
Bind her fast with maniacs, where
None will heed her yearning prayer;
Let cold bars and bolts and keys
Fetter mothers such as these!
Iron manacles we need
To protect our darling creed.

What are homes or children's claims?
What a doting mother's aims?
What were life, love, liberty,
If our creed imperilled be!
Nothing in this world we heed,
Like our dear endangered creed.
Thus State power august hath wrought
Fetters for too daring thought!
Souls thus bold, Asylums need,
To protect our precious creed.—Mrs. S. N. B. O.

This was the pivot on which my reputation for sanity was suspended; for I could not be made to confess that God made a bad or sinful article when he made human nature; but on the contrary, I claimed that *all* which God made was "good"—that is, was just as he intended it to be; and I furthermore argued, that to be natural, was to be just as God had made me to be—that to be unnatural, was to be wrong or sinful. I claimed that God's work, as he made it, was perfect—it needed no regeneration to make it right—that regeneration was necessary only when we had become unnatural or different from what God had made us. I willingly acknowledged that our natures in their present state, were perverted or depraved, in many instances to a painful degree; but that none are entirely lost to all traces of the divine image. For example, the drunkard is depraved in his appetite for drink, and the regeneration he needs, is not a new appetite but a restoration of it to its natural, original, unperverted state. Then he would have only a natural appetite for food and drink, which is in itself no sin; but the sin consists in his abuse of a natural instinct, not in the natural use of it. So that the natural exercise of our faculties, as God has made them, is not wrong, but only the unnatural or abusive use of them is wrong or sinful.

The Unlimited Atonement.

The professedly orthodox pulpit says, that "God *intended* all mankind for a life of purity, virtue and happiness." Now I wish to ask, if *God's intentions* can be thwarted? If they can not be thwarted, and God intended all mankind for happiness, will not all men be saved? If God intended it, and does not accomplish it, is he omnipotent? I believe God is omnipotent—that he intends nothing but good—and he will carry out all his intentions. I believe the devil is not omnipotent—that he intends nothing but evil—and he will ultimately fail in all his intentions.

Therefore, God's intention in sending his Son into the world to redeem and save it, can not be defeated; and when he assures us in his word that he "would that all men be saved," I believe that he is sincere, and thereby intends to bring all men ultimately to repentance and faith in Christ. And when he assures us that "death and hell shall be destroyed," I believe it. And therefore there must ultimately be a time when sin and punishment shall cease to be; and as sin and punishment had a beginning, they must have an end. But as God never had a beginning, so will he never have an end, but is destined ultimately, to be the mighty conqueror and head over all.

God's Immutability.

While Deacon Smith was our teacher, I once asked him this question, viz: "Did God change his purpose towards Nineveh, when he said he would destroy Nineveh and afterwards saved it, as Jonah seemed to think he did, and expostulated with him to this effect?"

Deacon Smith replied, "He did not. God never changes his purposes." This I considered as a correct answer; but his attempt to reconcile the two facts, viz: his attribute of unchangeableness, and his change towards Nineveh, was not satisfactory. He simply remarked, "God was not obliged to explain his plans and operations of government to Jonah's satisfaction." This reason seemed to my mind to reflect a degree of dishonor upon the perfect character of our God. I believe we have a right to inquire, like Jonah, into a knowledge of his ways concerning us, and that we can, and ought, so to interpret his providences as not to reflect dishonor upon his character for justice and veracity, either in word or action; and I believe he is willing thus to manifest himself to us, and thereby convict us of our unreasonable complaints against his providences towards us. I say this suggestion from Deacon Smith did not satisfy me, but the suggestion of Mrs. Smith and Mrs. Dixon did fully satisfy me.

They said, "the Ninevites repented, as a reason why God's actions towards them changed." Here was the key which unlocked all the mystery. It is *we* that change, not God. He has unchangeably decreed that sin and sinners shall be punished. And he has unchangeably decreed to extend pardon and forgiveness to the repentant sinner. These two eternal purposes are his unchangeable decrees thus to act in all future time. The Ninevites knew it was so, and therefore they resorted to the only possible way they could resort to and be saved. They repented—God's immutable purpose stood unchanged. They were forgiven, and thus saved.

What is it to be a Christian?

It is not to cease to be a sinner. "No man liveth and sinneth not." All come short of perfect obedience to God's laws. To be a christian is to be like Christ—that is, to live in accordance with the laws of our being, both physical and moral and spiritual; but as our knowledge of these laws is limited, we are liable to transgress ignorantly; but the christian is willing to put on Christ's righteousness, by repenting of his wrong doing, and thus living like him. By obeying God's laws, he becomes like Christ, and thus puts on his righteousness.

It is one part of my christianity, as I view it, to obey the laws of health, and thus live a healthy, natural life, believing that is the best foundation on which to build up my spiritual nature. I can not conceive of a symmetrical spiritual body without a healthy natural body to sustain it, any more than I can expect to build a cupola without a house to rest it upon. "First the natural, then the spiritual," seems to be the order God has established to develop human beings and make them like Christ. The human nature must be sublimated into the divine nature; or in other words, the lower, animal propensities must become only the servants of the higher, spiritual faculties, instead of being their masters as they now are, in their present depraved or unnatural condition.

Freedom of Conscience.

Conscience is God's vicegerent in the soul. To heed the voice of conscience is to heed the voice of God. I never dare to do what I conscientiously believe to be wrong; neither will I be deterred from doing what I conscientiously believe to be right, impossibilities of course excepted, for God never requires of us impossibilities.

I regard my conscience as a safe guide for myself, therefore I allow it so to others; while at the same time I believe it is only safe when it is based upon truth; and to me, the truth must be based upon God's revealed will, as I view it in God's word and works, and is thereby identified with the Bible. But I do not regard my views of truth as a standard for any other human being but myself; therefore I do not feel at liberty to judge any other's conscience than my own. I cheerfully assume the entire responsibility of my own actions, viewed from my own standpoint; but I am not willing to take the responsibility of any other's actions, viewed from their standpoint. We must all stand or fall for ourselves in judgment. Therefore, I claim Freedom of Conscience for all the human family equally with myself.

Spiritual Gifts.

The following article was prepared for the class, but was refused a hearing lest it be found to favor Spiritualism.

I differ from Deacon Merrick in the opinion that those spiritual gifts mentioned in the 12th chapter of 1st Corinthians—viz: the gifts of healing, working of miracles, prophecy, discerning of spirits, interpretation of tongues the word of wisdom, and the word of knowledge, etc., were confined to the apostolic age. But it is my opinion that they are the legitimate fruits of pure christianity, and attendant upon it to the end of time. Christ says, "these signs shall follow them that believe." Faith is evidently the stock on which these gifts are grafted, and I believe this is a kind of faith which it is our duty to cultivate and exercise to the same degree that the apostles did. And my reasons for this belief are supported by facts and revelation, as I view it.

FIRST.—The Bible supports this opinion. Christ instructed us to exercise a kind of faith, which he compares in power to that of "removing mountains," and also, "if ye had faith as a grain of mustard seed ye might say to this sycamore tree, be thou plucked up by the roots, and be thou cast into the sea, and it shall obey you." Now these illustrations evidently seem to teach that in the exercise of this faith we may expect effects to be produced beyond what our reason alone would justify us in expecting. Again, in James it is said, "the prayer of faith shall save the sick." And again, "all things whatsoever ye shall ask in prayer, believing, ye shall receive."

Now will it be uncharitable in me to suggest that the faith of the orthodox churches of the present day may be like unto the faith of the woman who was told she could have whatever she asked for, *believing* she should have it. Shortly after she wanted something very much, and so prayed for it to get it; but it did not come. Chagrined at her failure, she remarked indignantly, "I knew it would not come when I asked for it!" Now may not christians ask like this woman, *dis*believing, instead of believing they shall have them?

SECOND.—The proof of facts that this faith was not confined to the apostles—first, the Bible fact. James directs the churches to call for the elders of the church " to come and anoint the sick man with oil, and to pray over him, and the prayer of faith shall save the sick." These elders who had this power were not the apostles. And Joel prophesies of the last days, "your sons and your daughters shall prophesy." From this it seems there is to be a time in the future when pure, simple christianity, like that which the apostles taught, is to prevail again upon the earth, and then these gifts are to follow as the fruit of this simple faith; thus showing that this faith was not to be confined to the apostles, but was intended to be the natural heritage of the church whenever she became pure enough to produce this vigorous growth of faith required to ensure these manifestations. This faith was taught by Christ and exemplified by himself and the apostles.

Again, all the christian fathers, certainly down to the end of the third century, affirm the continuation of these gifts; and they maintain their assertion by well authenticated facts in church history. But in succeeding ages, when the mass of christians had become corrupted by worldly materialism and carnal-mindedness, these gifts became more and more rarely manifested, and were mostly confined to the humble few who adhered more tenaciously to the primitive faith and practice. Yet instances have occurred among some distinguished teachers of christianity. So late as the year 1821 Rev. Prince Hohenlhe, of Worburg, Germany, a distinguished divine, after preaching to immense crowds, commenced to perform miracles. To the astonishment of the populace, he made the blind to see, the deaf to hear, the lame to walk, and the paralytics to be cured; and in a short time, no less than thirty-six persons were restored to health, from a state of hopeless infirmity. This he did by his prayers and a firm confidence in God's power.

Another fact nearer home. About twenty years since I heard of a woman in Chesterfield, New Hampshire, who exhibited the power of discerning spirits, by telling at first sight the true character of entire strangers, as correctly as if she had always known them. But to come still nearer home. Have we not seen those who could instinctively read persons at first sight? and others who have a kind of prevision of what is about to take place, and they even act upon it with a kind of certainty that it would take place, for their experience had assured them that it could be relied upon as prophetic.

I once heard of a physician who had this foresight to such a degree as enabled him, in many instances, to save life, by acting in accordance with it. For instance, he once, while riding home, felt an impression that he was needed in a certain street; and following the impression, he went directly there, and found a man who had just been thrown from his horse, and in such a situation that unless surgical help were immediately applied, he must have died. And many times had he left his bed at midnight to visit his patients, guided only by these impressions, and thus saved the lives of many of his patients.

This kind of discernment is a gift higher than reason; and may it not be possible that they are of the nature of these spiritual gifts, and are but the incipient developments of a law of our spiritual nature as yet undeveloped, on which these gifts are founded, which is to be the fulfillment of Joel's prophecy?

OBJECTION FIRST.—Mrs. Dixon objected that since the power of working miracles is included among these gifts, she concluded they must be confined to the apostolic age, since the day of miracles is past. I reply, if the term miracle must mean only a suspension of a law of nature, or contrary to nature, I think with her, that the day is past for such manifestations. But, if it may bear the interpretation which men of talent and ability put upon it—viz: that a miracle signifies, and implies a supernatural power, meaning a power acting in harmony with a higher than natural law, I think they may, and still do continue. The law by which these supernatural events takes place, is unknown to us, and may be beyond our present ability to comprehend. For example, had we never seen or known that a caterpillar could be changed into a butterfly, we should call it a miracle. The facts occurring daily on the telegraphic wires would have been considered miracles to past generations. So of eclipses, which were regarded as miracles, until the law of eclipses was discovered. And I think it will continue to be a fact, that supernatural events will continue to take place, because they are the result of laws on a plane of which we are as yet ignorant. I believe these spiritual gifts are all controlled by established laws of our spiritual existence, of which we are at present comparatively ignorant. I fully believe God never acts except in harmony with established laws, and is never compelled to break these laws to bring about his purposes.

OBJECTION SECOND.—Deacon Merrick objected, that if this was the true view, all who believe must have this power; and since none do have it as he thought, therefore there can be no true christianity in the church.

I reply, that I do not think this a legitimate conclusion—that because all do not have this power, therefore none do. Would Deacon Merrick say that because all the blossoms of the apple tree do not perfect into perfect, sound, ripe apples, therefore none do; or that there are no apples at all? Or would **he rather** say, that each blossom has in it the germ of the **mature, sound** apple, which will naturally be developed into fruit, **unless** some accident occurs to prevent it? So all who have **any degree** of saving faith, have that in them which will ultimately perfect into this vigorous faith, and bring forth some of these perfected fruits or spiritual gifts. This faith is the natural outgrowth of human nature—that is, it has that universal principle of human nature, viz: trust or confidence, for its foundation to rest upon. We can no more get faith without this principle of human nature to build it upon, than we can get apples without soil to support the tree; and no more is the soil a sinful article because it is natural, than is human nature sinful because it is natural. Both the nature, and the precious spiritual fruits germinated upon it, are parts of God's well done work, and therefore are both equally good in their places. But for lack of proper cultivation this kind of fruit is rarely brought to perfection in this life.

Another illustration. I once heard the Rev. Mr. Cooper, a Presbyterian minister, of Salem, Iowa, relate the following fact, which took place when he served on board a vessel, on the coast of Norway: His captain found himself utterly unable to navigate his ship through a very dangerous channel between an island and the main land. A pilot on board seeing the very dangerous condition they were in, volunteered his services to the captain, assuring him he could take the ship safely through. The captain accepted the offer, although not without some misgivings as to the ability of this stranger pilot. But confident he could not guide it himself, he felt compelled to accept the offer. Consequently he resigned his ship entirely to this pilot's control, and directed his men to follow all this new pilot's directions.

The pilot accepted his charge, and commenced by reversing all the captain's orders, and headed the ship towards the breakers on shore. This aroused the captain's fears. Still he could do nothing but submit. But very soon his fears became so much aroused, in view of their approach towards the breakers, that he ventured to tell his pilot that they were going into the breakers. "I know it," was his only reply, and still approached the breakers. The captain expostulated with him three times; and each time received the same answer, "I know it!" For a time the captain paced the deck in agony, wringing his hands, until at length becoming desperate, he determined to take the ship into his own hands, confident that his professed pilot was unworthy of confidence, and was just in the act of doing so, when, behold: the pilot turned the ship about, and soon brought it out of all danger.

He afterwards found that the pilot had turned the ship at just the point, and the only point, where it could be done without being wrecked, for there was a narrow channel of rocks beneath, which the pilot knew how to follow; but the least deviation from that course would have been destruction to the ship, and an attempt to turn before the right point was reached would have been not only impossible, but certain destruction.

Now this captain had only just faith enough in his pilot to save him. He did not have that degree of faith needed to raise him entirely above his fears, in view of dangers so apparent to his reason. This degree of faith demanded the exercise of even a higher faculty than his reason, for it apparently conflicted with reason. But gospel faith in its highest exercise, never conflicts with reason, although it sometimes transcends reason. But the different gradations of faith, from the mere saving faith to that all conquering faith, which allays all anxiety and solicitude, under the most adverse circumstances, depends upon the different organizations and surroundings which determine its development and growth. And all these manifold variations and gradations are ultimately to perfect into that sound and vigorous faith which Christ inculcated, and is the stock upon which all these spiritual gifts germinate into natural fruit.

Questions for the Class.

The following are some of the questions I proposed to the class for discussion, some of which were allowed to be discussed, and many were not:

1. Do true christians ever die with unrepented sins upon them?

2. Does death, which is merely a natural law of the body, affect the spirit; or does the extinction of merely animal life produce any change in our spiritual life?

3. Is it not the spirit that repents?

4. Why then cannot the spirit repent when **disconnected** from the body?

5. Does truth ever change?

6. Can people have a difference of opinion on the same subject, and yet all be correct?

7. What causes this diversity of belief?

8. Will all equally good people see the truth in just the same light?

9. How ought we to treat those who we think teach error?

10. Should we accede to the errorist the same right of opinion we do the advocates of truth?

11. Are we to expect new moral truths to be developed at the present day, since the canon of scripture is complete?

12. Does progress in knowledge necessarily imply a change of views?

13. Is not the platform of common sense the platform for a common religion to stand upon?

14. Are bigotry and intolerance confined to any one church, or is this "Great Beast" found in all churches?

15. Can there be "one Lord, one faith, one baptism," without a mutual yielding of sectarian views among all denominations of christians?

16. Have we any reason to expect that a christian farmer, as a christian, will be any more successful in his farming operations than an impenitent sinner? or, in other words, does the motive with which we prosecute our secular business, have anything to do with the pecuniary results? And if not, how is godliness profitable?

If any of my readers would like to see my answer to the sixteenth question, I could refer them to my "Three Years' Imprisonment for Religious Belief," where they will find it on the thirty-third page. In that book the reader will also find a full account of my jury trial before Judge Starr, of Kankakee City, where my sanity was vindicated; and my persecution is there demonstrated to be the triumph of bigotry over the republican principles of free religious toleration.

This trial was not allowed me until after an imprisonment of three years, when, by the decision of the court, it was found that I had not been insane, and thereby had been falsely imprisoned all this time. The way in which my incarceration was secured will be found in the subsequent chapter.

III.

My Abduction.

About three weeks before my incarceration. Mr. Packard came to my room one day, and made me another proposition for withdrawing from the class. Said he, "Wife, wouldn't you like to visit your brother in Batavia?"

"I should like it very well, if it is not running from my post of duty."

"You have not only a perfect right to go, but I think it is your duty to go and get recruited."

"Very well, then I will go with the greatest pleasure. But how long do you think I had better make my visit?"

"Three months."

"Three months! Can you get along without me three months? and what will the children do for their summer clothes without me to make them?"

"I will see to that matter; you must stay three months, or not go at all."

"Well, I am sure I can stand it to rest that length of time, if you can stand it without my services. So I will go. But I must take my baby and daughter with me, as they have not fully recovered from their influenzas, and I should not dare to trust them away from me."

"Yes, you may take them."

"I will then prepare myself and them to go just as soon as you see fit to send us. Another thing, husband. I shall want ten dollars of my patrimony money to take with me for spending money."

"That you can't have."

"Why not? I shall need as much as that, to be absent three months with two sick children. I may need to call a doctor to them; and besides, my brother is poor, and I am rich, comparatively, and I might need some extra food, such as a beefsteak, or something of the kind, and I should not like to ask him for it. And besides, I have your written promise that I may have my own money whenever I want it, and I do want ten dollars of it now; and I think it is no unreasonable amount to take with me."

"I don't think it is best to let you have any. I shan't trust you with money."

"Shan't trust me with money! Why not? Have I ever abused this trust? Do not I always give you an exact account of every cent I spend? And I will this time do so; and besides, if you cannot trust me, I will put it into brother's hands as soon as I get there, and not spend a cent but by his permission."

"No, I shall not consent to that."

"One thing more I will suggest. You know the Batavia people owe you twelve dollars for preaching one sabbath, and you can't get your pay. Now, supposing brother 'duns' and gets it, may I use this money if I should chance to need it in an emergency? and if I should not need any, I won't use a cent of it? Or, I will write home to *you* and ask permission of you before spending a dollar of it."

"No, you shall neither have any money, nor have the control of any, for I can't trust you with any."

"Well, husband, if I can't be trusted with ten dollars of my own money under these circumstances, I should not think I was capable of being trusted with two sick children three months away from home, wholly dependent on a poor brother's charities. Indeed I had rather stay at home and not go at all, than go under such circumstances."

"You shall not go at all," replied he, in a most excited, angry tone of voice. "You shall go into an Asylum!"

"Why, husband, I did **not suspect** *such* **an alternative.** I had rather go to him penniless and clotheless even, than go into an Asylum!"

"You have lost your last chance. You *shall* go into an Asylum!"

Knowing the inflexibility of purpose which characterized my husband, I knew there was no refuge for me in an appeal to his humanity, his reason or his affection, for a commutation of my sentence. I therefore laid my case before our kind neighbor, Mr. Comstock, who professed to be a kind of lawyer, and sought his counsel and advice. Said he, "Mrs. Packard, you have nothing to fear. It is impossible for your husband to get you into any insane asylum; for before he can do this, you must have a jury trial; and I can assure you there is no jury in the country who would pronounce you to be an insane person, for you give every evidence of intelligence that any person can give."

As this Mr. Comstock had been a constant attendant at our bible class for some time past, and had thereby heard and seen all the evidence which could be brought against me; and as he professed to understand the law on this point, this unqualified and positive assertion served to quiet my fears and anxious foreboding to a considerable degree. But had Mr. Comstock known the law as it then was, he could not have made this assertion. He probably took it for granted that the common principles of justice characterized the Illinois statue laws, viz: that all its citizens should be allowed a trial *before* imprisonment; but being mistaken on this point, he blindly led me astray from the truth.

Had I known what Mr. Packard knew, of the legal power which the law gave the husband to control the identity of the wife, I should not have been thus deceived. I did not then know what I now do, that married women and infants were excepted in the application of this principle of common justice. This class were not only allowed to be imprisoned by their husbands or guardians without any trial, or without any chance at self-defence whatever, but they were also expressly licensed to imprison them in an insane asylum *without* evidence of insanity! This legal license reads thus, as found on the Illinois Statute Book, page 96, Session Laws 15, 1851, Section 10: "Married women and infants who, in the judgment of the medical Superintendent (meaning the Superintendent of the Illinois State Hospital for the Insane,) are evidently insane or distracted, may be entered or detained in the hospital on the request of the husband of the woman, or the guardian of the infant, *without* the evidence of insanity required in other cases."

Not knowing that Illinois had legalized this mode of kidnapping the married women of their State, I had no idea that my personal liberty depended entirely upon the will or wishes of my husband. I thereupon returned to my home with a feeling of comparative security, trusting and supposing that upon the principles of our free government of religious toleration, my rights of conscience, and rights of opinion were respected and protected by law, in common with other American citizens. Still, believing that a most strenuous effort would be made to fasten the stigma of insanity upon me, by my opponents in religious belief, I now began to consider what my plea of self-defence must be when arraigned for trial on insanity, based upon what they regarded as heresy.

But while my mind was cogitating my plea, and my hands were busily employed in my domestic duties, I could not help noticing many singular manifestations in Mr. Packard's conduct towards me. One was, from the time my sentence was pronounced, Mr. Packard left my bed without giving me any reason for this singular act, and he seemed peculiarly determined to evade all, and every inquiry into his reasons for so doing. Still I insisted upon knowing whether it was because of anything I had done, which led him thus to forsake me. He assured me it was not—adding, "you have always been kind, and true and faithful to me." While this truthful acknowledgement, afforded a kind of relief to my feelings, it only served to increase the mystery of the affair still more, and even to this day this mystery has never been solved in my mind. The only reason he ever gave me was, "I think it is best!"

Another thing, he removed my medicine box, containing our family herbs and cordials, from my nursery into his sleeping apartment, and when I found it necessary one night to give my little Georgie some lobelia to relieve him from spasmodic croup, I was obliged to seek for it, and finding it under his bed instead of its accustomed place, I inquired why he had made that arrangement, and received the same mysterious reply, "I think it is best!"

Another thing, he seemed unaccountably considerate of my health, insisting upon it that I should have a hired girl to help me. This arrangement surprised me, all the more, because I had so often been refused this favor, when I had asked for it at times when I thought I needed it within a few past years. I however found it very easy and pleasant to concur with this arrangement, which afforded me more uninterrupted time and thought to devote to my plea. But there was one thing about it which I did not like, and that was, to dismiss my girl, just when I had got her well learned how to do my work, without giving any reason whatever, either to me or my girl, for this strange conduct. But I afterwards found out the reason for dismissing her was, because she had remarked to a neighbor of ours that, "I can't see what Mr. Packard does mean by calling his wife insane; for she is the kindest and best woman I ever saw—I never worked for so kind a mistress."

But his summary manner of disposing of my good, kind, faithful French Catholic girl, and supplying her place with one of his own church members, an opponent to me in argument, and she the eldest daughter of the most aristocratic family in the place, was very peculiar. This aristocratic, Miss Sarah Rumsey, was introduced into my family as a dinner guest, on whom I bestowed all the attentions of the hostess until after dinner, when my girl came to the parlor to bid me "good bye," saying with tears, "Mr. Packard has dismissed me." "Dismissed you! For what?"

"I dont know—he simply told me to get my things and

leave, that my services were no longer wanted in his family."

While I was trying to comfort her under this uncivil discharge, Miss Rumsey stepped up and volunteered her services as "my help."

"My help! have you come here to be my hired girl?" said I, in amazement.

"Yes, I am willing to help you."

"But I wish to understand you—has Mr. Packard secured your services as my hired servant?"

"Yes, Mrs. Packard, I have come for that purpose?"

"Very well, then, I will set you to work, and you may look to him for your wages."

She then followed me into the kitchen, where I gave her my instructions, and then I retired to my parlor, leaving her to take her first lesson in practical service in her beloved pastor's kitchen.

During her term of service, which lasted until I was kidnapped, about one week from this time, I frequently caught Mr. Packard and Miss Rumsey and Mrs. Sybil Dole, his sister, in most earnest conversation, which was always carried on in a whisper whenever I was within hearing distance, and my presence seemed always to evoke manifestations of guilt on their part. I think the theme of conversation at these clandestine interviews was, my abduction and how it should be secured.

My children now became almost my only companions and councillors. The three youngest slept with me, so that I had their company both night as well as day. I expressed to them my fears that I might yet be forced away from them, always assuring them that no power but force should separate me from them. They always responded, "they will have to break my arms to get them loose from their grasp upon you. Mother, if they try to steal our dear mamma from us!" But the filial influence Mr. Packard most feared to cope with, was my second son, I. W. Packard, then sixteen years old. My oldest son Theophilus, was then at Mt. Pleasant, Iowa. I. W. communicated to Theophilus the dangers he feared impending over his mother. Theophilus responded, pledging himself that should his dear mother ever be put into an Insane Asylum, he should never rest until he had liberated her. I. W. agreed to this same pledge of untiring devotion to his dear mother's welfare.

During these ominous days of solicitude and painful forebodings, this tender hearted and devoted son would never leave for his work in Mr. Comstock's store, without first coming to my room, and as he would imprint a most loving kiss upon my lips, he would whisper—"dont feel bad, mother! keep up good courage. I shall do all I can for you."

And he did do all he could to stem the rising current, by rallying influences in my defence. Quite a number of volunteers gave him their pledge that his mother never should leave that depot for an Insane Asylum; but unfortunately, his father became acquainted with this fact, and to prevent any co-operation with his mother in the execution of any of his plans for my deliverance, he issued his mandate that I. W. should not speak to his mother for one week. Not knowing that such an injunction had been laid upon him, I accosted him from my window on his return from his store, and, as usual inquired after nis health. He had been my patient for some weeks past, having spit blood several times during this time, and of course I felt a deep solicitude for his health; and now when he answered me only by the pressure of his fore finger upon his closed lips, and a significant shake of his head, I became alarmed, and anxiously inquired, "can't you speak?" A shake of the head was his only response. I rushed to the door to meet him, to ascertain what had happened, where we met my only darling daughter of ten years, whom we all called "Sister," to whom he said, "Sister, I want you should tell mother that father has forbid my speaking to her for one week, and that is the reason I can't answer her questions."

"But how is your breast, my son?"

"Sister, I want you should tell mother it is worse; I have spit more blood to-day."

In this manner, with my daughter for our medium, I administered to his physical wants and spiritual comfort for one week, which term expired one day before my abduction. During this time he never failed to come to my room or to the window, before leaving, to bestow upon my lips his loving kiss of silent, undying affection.

A few days previous to my seizure, Mrs. Dole and Mr. Packard tried to prevail upon me to let her take my darling babe home with her for a few days, to rest me from my night watches with my sick children, to which I foolishly consented, supposing this offer was only dictated by affection and sympathy for me. I soon became impatient for my babe, and Mr. Packard allowed me to go to Mr. Dole's with him to see Arthur, but would not allow me to bring him home with me. They must keep him a day or two longer! I must consent to take a few more nights of good sound sleep before I could embrace my darling babe once more! Alas! this was the final parting with my precious darling infant, weaned from the breast but three months before. His little arms could hardly be unclasped from my neck, to which he seemed to cling instinctively; with the tenderest affection he would press his soft cheek against mine, and say, "dear mamma! dear mamma!" These were the only words he could articulate. O! little did I suspect this was a treacherous act of false affection, to steal from me my darling babe. But so it proved to be.

This was Saturday. On Sabbath they stole from me my only daughter, by a similar act of hypocrisy. After meeting Sabbath evening, the Rumsey carriage called at our door and claimed the privilege of taking my daughter home with them to visit her intimate friend and schoolmate, the youngest Rumsey. They plead that her health needed a change. and she could come home any day I chose; and in answer to my inquiry, "has this anything to do with my being taken off?" they all with united voices, insisted that it had not, adding, "this is not our most distant thought."

I at length reluctantly consented to her going. and we too, parted for the last time before my abduction, little suspecting it to be so. But as we were embracing each other for the last time, she whispered in my ear, "Mother, if there are any signs of taking you away, you will let me know, won't you?"

"Certainly I will, my daughter, you may rely upon your mother's promise in this thing. So set your heart at rest, and enjoy yourself as best you can." And we parted!

That night I had no one to caress but my darling Georgie, of seven years, who was now nearly recovered from his lung fever. But from some unknown cause, sleep was not easily courted that night. Usually my sleep was sound, quiet and refreshing. Sleepless, wakeful nights were unknown to me. But now some evil forebodings assured me all was not right. About midnight I arose and silently sought Mr. Packard's room, to see if I could make any discoveries as to the aspect of things. Here instead of being in his bed, I found him noiselessly searching through all my trunks and bandboxes. What could this mean? Without his observing me, I went back to my bed, there to consider this question.

Before morning my suspicions assumed a tangible form. I summoned I. W. early to my bedside, to tell him I was sure arrangements were being made to carry me off somewhere, and therefore I wished him without delay to go and get "Sister" home, as I had promised to send for her in case of any appearances of this kind. He replied, "Mother, I will do so; but I must first go of an errand on to the prairie for Mr. Comstock, and then I will return to the house and take you to ride with me to Mr. Rumsey's and get Sister."

"Yes, that will do; we will go by brother Dole's too, and get my baby. I will be all ready when you return, to go with you." This was our parting!

Little Georgie, ever ready to serve me, ran out into the dewy grass and picked a saucer of ripe strawberries and brought them to my room, saying as he handed them to me, "I have picked some strawberries for your breakfast, mother;" and he had hardly time to receive his mother's thanks, when his father called him out to the door, and with extended hand said, "Come,

George, won't you go with father to the store and get some sugar-plums?"

Glad as any boy of his age is to get sugar-plums, he of course, readily went with his father to get his plums, and also to get a ride too with his brother off on to the prairie! This was our parting scene!

Thus had my children been abducted, to prepare the way for the mother's abduction, on the morning of the 18th of June, 1860. And now the fatal hour had come that I must be transported into my living tomb. But the better to shield himself in this nefarious work, Mr. Packard tried to avail himself of the law for commitment in other cases, which is to secure the certificate of two physicians that the candidate for the Asylum is insane. Therefore at this late hour I passed an examination made by our two doctors, both members of his church and our bible class, and opponents to me in argument, wherein they decided that I was insane, by simply feeling my pulse!

This scene is so minutely described in the "Introduction to my Three Years Imprisonment," that I shall not detail it here. The doctors were not in my room over three minutes, conducting this examination, and without asking me a single question, both said while feeling my pulse, "she is insane!"

My husband then informed me that the "forms of law" were now all complied with, and he now wished me to dress for a ride to Jacksonville Insane Asylum. I complied, but at the same time entered my protest against being imprisoned without a trial, or some chance at self-defence. I made no physical resistance however, when he ordered two of his church-members to take me up in their arms, and carry me to the wagon and thence to the cars, in spite of my lady-like protests, and regardless of all my entreaties for some sort of trial before commitment.

My husband replied, "I am doing as the laws of Illinois allow me to do—you have no protector in law but myself, and I am protecting you now! it is for your good I am doing this, I want to save your soul—you don't believe in total depravity, and I want to make you right."

"Husband, have I not a right to my opinions?"

"Yes, you have a right to your opinions, if you think right."

"But does not the constitution defend the right of religious toleration to all American citizens?"

"Yes, to all citizens it does defend this right, but you are not a citizen; while a married woman you are a legal nonentity, without even a soul in law. In short, you are dead as to any legal existence while a married woman, and therefore have no legal protection as a married woman." Thus I learned my first lesson in that chapter of common law, which denies to married woman a legal right to her own identity or individuality.

IV.
My Abduction.—Continued.

The scenes transpiring at the parsonage, were circulated like wild-fire throughout the village of Manteno, and crowds of men and boys were rapidly congregating at the depot, about one hundred rods distant from our house, not only to witness the scene, but fully determined to stand by their pledge to my son, I. W., that his mother should never leave Manteno depot for an Insane Asylum.

The long two horse lumber wagon in which I was conveyed from my house to the depot, was filled with strong men as my body guard, including Mr. Packard, his deacons, and Sheriff Burgess, of Kankakee city among their number. When our team arrived at the depot, Mr. Packard said to me, "now, wife, you will get out of the wagon yourself, won't you? You won't compel us to lift you out before such a large crowd, will you?"

"No, Mr. Packard, I shall not help myself into an Asylum. It is *you* who are putting me there. I do not go willingly, nor with my own consent—I am being forced into it against my protests to the contrary. Therefore, I shall let you show yourself to this crowd, just as you are—my persecutor, instead of my protector. I shall make no resistance to your brute force claims upon my personal liberty—I shall simply remain a passive victim, helpless in your power." He then ordered his men to transport me from the wagon to the depot in their arms.

Before this order was executed, I addressed the sheriff in these words, "Mr. Burgess, won't you please have the kindness to see that my person is handled gently, for I am easily hurt, and also see that my clothing is so adjusted as not to expose me immodestly, which with my hoops I fear you will find some difficulty in doing."

"I will heed your requests, Mrs. Packard," he kindly replied. He then ordered two men into the wagon, to lift me from the board seat, which was placed across the top of the wagon, and hand me over the wheel, gently down into the arms of two men, who stood with outstretched arms below to receive me, and transport me into the "Ladies' Room" at the depot. This order was executed in as gentle and gentlemanly a manner as it could be done, while the faithful sheriff carefully adjusted my clothing as best he could, and I was landed upon a seat in the "Ladies' Room." I then thanked Mr. Burgess and my carriers for the kind manner in which they had executed my husband's order; and they left me alone to join the crowd on the platform. I then arose, adjusted my dress and walked to the window, to see who were there assembled. I saw they were my friends and foes both, about equally divided, the countenances of all equally indicating great earnestness and deep emotion.

Soon Mr. Packard came alone into the room, and I resumed my seat when he addressed me as follows: Bending over me, he spoke in tones the most bland and gentle, and said, "Now, wife, my dear! you will not make us carry you into the cars, will you? Do please just walk into them when they come, won't you, to please me! Do now, please me this once; won't you?"

Looking him full in the face, I said, "Mr. Packard, I shall not. It is your own chosen work you are doing. I shall not help you do it. If I am put into the cars, it will not be my act that puts me there." He then left me, and soon returned with Mr. Comstock at his side, when he said, "Now, wife,

Mr. Comstock thinks you had better walk into the cars, and you know you think a good deal of him; you will follow his advice, won't you?"

"Mr. Comstock is too much of a man to advise me to leave my dear little children, to go and be locked up in a prison without any trial. I know he would not advise any such thing," said I.

Mr. Comstock then, without having spoken one word, left the room. While these scenes in the Ladies' Room were being enacted, Deacon Dole was acting his part on the platform outside. Finding the crowd had assembled to defend me, and that they were determined I should never be forced into the cars, his conscience allowed him to be the bearer of a lie from Mr. Packard to the company, on the plea that the interests of his beloved pastor and the cause of the church required it as an act of self-defence. He therefore positively told them that Mr. Packard was pursuing a legal course in putting his wife into an Asylum—that the Sheriff had legal papers with him to defend the proceeding, and if they resisted the Sheriff, they would be liable to imprisonment themselves. The crowd did not know that Deacon Dole was lying to them, when he said the Sheriff had legal papers; for he had none at all, as the Sheriff afterwards confessed—adding, "I went to the Probate Court to take out my legal papers, and they would not give me any, because, as they said, I could not bring forward any proof of insanity which could satisfy them that Mrs. Packard was insane. Therefore I ventured to carry out Mr. Packard's wishes without any papers!"

Thus the "majesty of the law," added to the sacred dignity of the pulpit, so overawed this feeling of manliness in these Mantenoites, that they dared not make a single effort in defence of me. Therefore, when the engine whistle was heard, Deacon Dole found no obstacle in the way of taking me up in his arms, with the help of another man, and carrying me from the depot to my seat in the cars, except the difficulty of knowing how to take hold of me in a modest and gentlemanly manner. I, however, soon solved this difficulty for him, by suggesting that two men make a "saddle-seat" with their four hands so united, that I could sit erect and easily upon it, between them both. This, with my assistance, they promptly did, and I quietly seated myself, while Mr. Burgess kindly arranged my wardrobe for me. While borne along on this human vehicle, by my manly (!) body guard, my elevated position afforded me a fine view of the sea of heads below me; and while I imploringly and silently looked towards them for that protection and help they had so confidently volunteered should be extended to me if needed, I looked in vain! "No man cared for my soul!" although Mrs. Blessing was walking the platform, wringing her hands in agony at the spectacle I presented, and in a loud voice, while the tears were streaming down her cheeks, she was imploring them to extend to me the help I needed, in these expressive words: "Is there no man in this crowd to protect this woman? Will you let this mother be torn from her children and thrust into a prison in this style, with none to help her? O! is there no man among you? If I were a man I would seize hold upon her."

MRS. BLESSING'S LAMENT.

One, one alone, stood by my side,
With pleading hands and voice she cried,
"Is there no help? Can no one here
Aid now our suffering sister dear?
Breathes there not here one mother's son
Who dares to aid this injured one?
Must she from her own sons be torn,
Her darling children left to mourn?
Crying in vain for mother dear
To wipe away the scalding tear.
Are love and honor both, all dead?
Oh neighbors! has your reason fled?
Can you look and see her go
To the dark maniac's house of woe?
Yet raise no voice, no hand, no eye,
To stay that dread calamity!
Throbs here no heart of sympathy?
Can no one say she shall be free?
Oh! in the sacred name of love,

Of liberty, of God above,
By all the tender ties of life,
Spare! spare! that deeply suffering wife.
Recording Angel! can'st thou see
A blacker shade of cruelty."—Mrs. S. N. B. O.

As soon as I was landed in the cars, the car door was quickly locked, to guard against any possible reaction of the public, manly pulse, in my defence. Mr. Packard, Deacon Dole, and Sheriff Burgess seated themselves near me, and the cars quietly moved on towards my prison tomb, leaving behind me, children, home, liberty and an untarnished reputation. In short, all, *all*, which had rendered life desirable, or tolerable.

Up to this point, I had not shed a tear. All my nervous energy was needed to enable me to maintain that dignified self-possession, which was indispensably necessary for a sensitive womanly nature like my own, to carry me becomingly through scenes, such as I have described. But now that these scenes were past, my hitherto pent up maternal feelings burst their confines, and with a deep gush of emotion, I exclaimed, "O! what will become of my dear children!" I rested my head upon the back of the seat in front of me, and deliberately yielded myself up to a shower of tears. O! thought I, "what will my dear little ones do, when they return to their desolate home, to find no mother there! O their tender, loving hearts, will die of grief, at the story of their mother's wrongs!"

Yes, it did well nigh rend each heart in twain, when the fact was announced to them, that they were motherless! My sons, I. W., and George were just about this time returning from their prairie errand, and this fact was now being communicated to them, by some one returning from the depot, whom they met near the same. When within speaking distance, the first salutation they heard was, "Well, your mother is gone."

"What?" said I. W., thinking he had misunderstood.

"Your mother is gone!"

Supposing this was only an old rumor revived, he carelessly replied, "No she isn't, she is at home, where I just left her, and I am now on the way there to take her to ride with me."

"But she *has* gone—I just came from the depot, and saw her start."

Now, for the first time, the terrible truth flashed upon his mind, that this is the reason George and I have been sent off on this errand, and this accounts also, for the attentions so lavishly bestowed upon us this morning by my groom, by my father, and by Mr. Comstock. Yes, this awful fact at last found a lodgment in his sensitive heart, when he, amid his choking and tears could just articulate, "George! we have no mother."

Now George, too, knew why he had been so generously treated to sugar-plums that morning, and he too burst into loud crying, exclaiming, " they shall not carry off my mother."

"But they have carried her off! We have no mother!" said I. W. Here they both lifted up their voices and wept aloud, and as the team entered the village, all eyes were upon them, and others wept to see them weep, and to listen to their plaintive exclamations, "We have no mother! We have no mother!" As they drew near the front of Mr. Comstock's store, seeing the crowd settling there, I. W. felt his indignation welling up within him, as he espied among this crowd some of his volunteer soldiers in his mother's defence, and having learned from his informant that no one had taken his dear mother's part, he reproachfully exclaimed, as he leaped from his wagon, "And this is the protection you promised my mother! What is your gas worth to me!"

They felt the reproaches of a guilty conscience, and dared not attempt to console them. Mr. Comstock was the only one who ventured a response in words. He said, "You must excuse me, I. W., for I did what I thought would be the best for you. I knew your father was determined, and he would put her in at any rate; and I knew too, that your opposition would do no good, and would only torment you to witness the scene. So I had you go for your good!" "For my good!" thought he, " I think I should like to be my own

C

judge in that matter!" He spoke not one reproachful word in reply, but quickly sought his mother's room, where he might weep alone.

But George, knowing the direction the cars went with his mother, ran on the track after them, determined he never would return until he could return with his mother rescued from prison! He was not missed until he was far out of hearing, and almost out of sight—he only looked like a small speck on the distant track. They followed after him; but he most persistently refused to return, saying, "I will get my dear mamma out of prison! My mamma shan't be locked up in a prison! I will not go home without my mother!"

He was of course forced back, but not to stay—only until he could make another escape. They finally had to imprison him—my little manly boy of seven years, to keep him from running two hundred miles on the track to Jacksonville, to liberate his imprisoned mother!

But O, my daughter! no pen can delineate thy sorrow, to find thy mother gone! perhaps forever gone! from thy companionship, counsel, care and sympathy! She wept both night and day, almost unceasingly; and her plaintive moans could be heard at quite a distance from her home. "O! mother! mother! mother!" was her almost constant, unceasing call. Her sorrow almost cost her her reason and her life. And so it was with I. W. He grieved himself into a settled fever, which he did but just survive; and during its height, he moaned incessantly for his mother, not knowing what he said! His reason for a time was lost in delirium.

But my babe, thank God! was too young to realize his loss. *For* him, I suffered enough for two human beings.

Here we leave these scenes of human anguish, to speak one word of comfort for the wives and mothers of Illinois. Conscious that there had already been innocent victims enough offered in sacrifice on the altar of injustice, in consequence of these cruel laws of Illinois against my own sex, I determined to appeal, single handed and alone, if neces sary, to their Legislature, to have them repealed, and thereby have the personal liberty of married women protected by law, as well as by the marital power. Consequently, in the winter of 1867, I came alone, and at my own expense, from Massachusetts to Illinois, and paid my board all winter in Springfield, Illinois, trying to induce the Legislature to repeal the barbarous law under which I was imprisoned, and pass in its stead a "Bill for the Protection of Personal Liberty," which demands a fair jury trial of every citizen of the State, before imprisonment in any Insane Asylum in the State. The Legislature granted my request. They repealed the barbarous law, and passed the Personal Liberty Bill, by an unanimous vote of both houses. So that now, no wife or mother in Illinois need fear the re-enacting of my sad drama in her own case; for, thank God! your personal liberty is now protected by just laws.

V.

My Journey.

Sheriff Burgess left our company at Kankakee City, twelve miles distant from Manteno, where he then resided. Not knowing at that time, but that he had the legal papers Deacon Dole claimed for him, in taking leave of him I thanked him for the kind and gentlemanly manner he had discharged his duties, as a Sheriff, in this transaction, adding, "you have only discharged your duty, as a Sheriff; therefore, as a man, I shall claim you as my friend." And, six months from this date, when he called upon me in my Asylum prison, and inquired so kindly and tenderly after my comfort and surroundings, I felt confirmed in my opinion that I had not misjudged him. Not long after he died, but not until after he had frankly confessed his breach of trust, as a public officer, in this transaction.

As my wounded heart still sought the relief of tears, I continued to weep on, and at length I ventured to express my sincere, deep anxiety, lest my children would not be able to survive their bereavement. Mr. Packard and Mr. Dole then both tried to console me, by assuring me they were left with kind friends who would take good care of them, and Mr. Packard said he had left a written document for each of them, which he thought would satisfy them, so that they would "soon get over it!" O thought I " soon get over it!" what consolation! to be told that your children would soon forget you! Nay, verily, I am too indelibly united to their heart's tenderest, deepest affections, to suffer an easy or rapid alienation. And so it proved—for three years this cruel wound in their sensitive hearts remained unhealed—they instinctively and persistently spurned the mollient he offered to heal it, viz ; " their mother was insane, and therefore must be locked up for her good."

I have been told they would give expression to their feelings in language like the following, and it being so characteristic of their natures, I have no doubt of its truth.

" No," Georgie would say, " mother is good enough now ! and haven't I a *right* to my mother?"

" No," Elizabeth would say, " mother is not crazy, and you know she is not—I do think Pa is possessed with a devil, to treat our good, dear, kind mother as he does. We know our dear mother is good, for she never has done anything wrong—she is kind to you, and she is kind to everybody."

The natural, unsophisticated natures of my children, rendered it very difficult for them to see the *necessity* of locking up a person, while they were doing good, and had never done any thing wrong !

The philosophy of that kind of insanity, which required this to be done, was beyond their comprehension. And even the maturer minds of my oldest sons, Theophilus, then eighteen, and I. W., sixteen, were equally slow in discovering this necessity. In short, three years was too short a time for their father to convince these children of this painful necessity. At length, wearied with these fruitless efforts to get my children to sanction his cause, he finally resorted to the authority of the father to silence them into acquiescence to his views. He therefore forbade their talking upon the subject, and made it an act of disobedience on their part, to talk about their mother. This taught them to use hypocrisy and deceit, for I. W., and Elizabeth would watch their opportunity, in the absence of their father, to talk upon their favorite theme, and when Elizabeth and Georgie could not evade this order by day, they would take the hours of sleep and talk in a whisper about me, after they had retired to their bed.

Another agency he employed to wean them from me, was, he would not allow me to be spoken of in their presence, except as an insane person, and in terms of derision, ridicule, or contempt. But notwithstanding all these combined agencies, he could not wean them from me, or lessen their confidence in me, according to his own statement, which he made to Mrs. Page on one of his yearly visits to the Asylum.

Some years after this date he said, " I never saw children so attached to a mother, as Mrs. Packard's are to her—I cannot by any means wean them from her, nor lead them to disregard her authority in the least thing, even now. I cannot even induce them to eat anything which they think she would disapprove of. She seems by some means, to hold them to obedience to her wishes, just as much in her absence, as in her presence. This influence or power is more than I can understand."

Yes, I knew full well that Mr. Packard did not understand the nature and disposition of my children, and therefore I felt unwilling to trust them with him. But how could I avert this fate? In no way. I had not chosen this separation—God's providence had permitted it against my wishes, and regardless of my prayer to the contrary. Now, what shall I do? Shall I murmur and complain at what I can not help, and when I know it will do no good? or, must I silently submit to this inevitable fate, and trust to the future developments of providence to unravel this great mystery? Yes, I must submit. I must not complain, while at the same time, I have a right to use all suitable means for a restoration to my family and duties; therefore as the result of this soliloquy,

I concluded to avail myself of the advice given me by my Manteno friends at the depot, viz: "Be sure, Mrs. Packard, and tell every one you see that you are on your way to the Insane Asylum, and for what, for possibly by this means, you may come in contact with some influence that may rescue you." Knowing that duties were mine; and events God's, I determined to dry up my tears and address myself to this duty.

I announced this determination to Deacon Dole in these words: "Mr. Dole I am not going to cry any more. Crying is not going to help me. I am going to put on a cheerful countenance, and cultivate the acquaintance of my fellow travelers, and enjoy my ride the best I can. I may as well laugh as cry, for I have as good a right to be happy as any other person."

"That is right, Sister Packard; you have as good a right to be happy as any one, and I am glad to see you smile again."

After exchanging a few remarks respecting the beauty of the country through which we were passing, and the delightfully calm and clear atmosphere, so tranquilizing in its influence over one's disturbed feelings, I looked about to see who were my companions, when I met the eye of a young lady, a stranger to me, whose eyes seemed to fasten upon me with such a penetrating look, that I could hardly withdraw my own without bestowing upon her a smile of recognition. Upon this she bent forward and spoke to me, and extended to me her hand, saying, "I am very sorry for you. I see they are carrying you to the Insane Asylum, and you do not wish to go."

"Yes, that is so, and I thank you for your sympathy; but I have concluded not to weep any more about it, as I shall need all my nervous energies to meet my fate with dignity and self-possession."

"But you are not insane, why do they put you there?"

"No, I am not insane, but my husband is trying to put this brand upon me, to destroy my moral influence."

"But why does he wish to destroy your influence?"

"Because I have defended some opinions in a bible class, where he is the minister, which he can not overthrow by argument, and now he tells me he is going to make the world believe that I am insane, so that my opinions need not be believed, for he says he must 'protect the cause of Christ.'"

"Don't he think it his duty to protect his wife?"

"He thinks it is his duty to protect her from injuring the cause of Christ, by locking her up in a prison!"

"I heard you speak of your children; how many have you?"

"Six—five boys and one girl."

"Six children! and he, their father, taking from them their mother, simply because you differ from him in opinion! O, 'tis too bad! how I pity you!"

At this point, she burst into tears, and resting her head upon the back of my seat, she cried and sobbed until she had completely drenched her pocket-handkerchief, when I handed her one of my own and she drenched that also—"O," she said, "you must not go! you are too good a woman to be locked up in an Insane Asylum."

I tried to console her, by telling her I felt it would all come out right at last—that all I had to do was, to be patient and do right.

She then put her arm around my neck and kissed me, saying, "how I wish I could help you! I will do all I can for you."

She then left her seat and brought back another lady, whom she introduced as one who wished to talk with me. From her I learned that the sympathy of the passengers was with me—that some had thought of volunteering in my defence, and this feeling was now gaining strength by the influence of my first friend's conversation amongst them. I saw groups of gentlemen evidently talking together about me—some conversed with me, and I had my hopes somewhat raised that something would be done to restore me to my children, and by the time the cars reached Tolono, I felt I was amongst friends, instead of strangers.

Mr. Packard could not but see that the tide was against him, for he sat by my side and listened most attentively to every word, and when opportunity presented, he aimed by self-vindication to counteract every hopeful influence from taking possession of my mind, by such remarks as these, "You say, wife, that the Lord prospers those whose ways please him; now, judging by this test, who is prospered in their plans, you or I? you see I succeed in all I undertake, while all your efforts are defeated. Now isn't the Lord on my side?"

"The time hasn't come to decide that question by this test, this is only the beginning, not the end of this sad drama. You may be prospered by having your way for a time, only to make your defeat all the more signal. I do not think it is certain the Lord is not on my side, simply because I am not now delivered out of your power. God has a plan to be accomplished, which requires all this to take place in order to its ultimate success. But I can't see what that plan is, nor why my sufferings are necessary to its accomplishment. But God does, and that faith or trust in the rectitude of his plans, keeps my mind in peace even now. Neither do I think it is certain the Lord is on your side, because you have been permitted to have your own way in getting me imprisoned. The end will settle this question."

Another attempt at self-vindication appeared in the following conversation—said he, "You think a great deal of your father, and that what he does is right; now I want to show you that he upholds me in doing as I now am, and approves of the course I am now pursuing, and here is a letter from your own dear father confirming all I have said."

As he said this, he handed me an open letter in my father's own hand-writing, saying, "Here, read for yourself and see what your father says about it."

"No," said I, shaking my head, "I do not wish to read *such* a letter from my father, for it would be a libel upon his revered memory. I know too, that if he has written such a letter as you represent, he has had a false view of the case presented to him. My father would never approve of the course you are pursuing, if he knew what the truth is respecting it. You have told him lies about me, or you never would have had his approval in putting me into an Asylum."

Still he persistently urged me to read the letter, so I could judge for myself. But I would not. This was the only kind of consolation he attempted to offer me.

We dined at Tolono, where I had the good fortune to be seated by the side of a very intelligent gentleman, at the head of the table, whom I afterwards found to be the general freight agent, who boarded there at that time. He sat at the end of the table, I sat next him on the side, and Mr. Packard next to me. This gentleman, in a polite, gentlemanly manner, drew me into a free and easy conversation with himself, wherein I freely avowed some of my obnoxious views, and my progressive reform principles, respecting the laws of health, physical development, etc.

He expressed his high appreciation of my views and principles, and remarked, "These have been exactly my views for a long time, and now I am happy to find one woman who is willing to endorse and defend them, and who can do so with so much ability." The entire attention of our table guests seemed centered upon our conversation, for all appeared to be silent listeners, and none seemed to be in any haste to withdraw—the cars giving us ample time for a full and leisurely taken meal. I noticed one of the female waiters, a very intelligent looking lady, seemed almost to forget her duties, so eager was she to listen to every word of our conversation.

After retiring with my husband to the sitting room, I recollected the instructions given me to tell all where I was going, had been disregarded at the table, where I ought to have replied to the gentleman's compliment, by saying, "I am happy to have your approval, sir, for it is for avowing these views and principles that I am called insane, and am now on my way to Jacksonville, to be entered as an inmate, to suffer the penalty of indefinite imprisonment for this daring act; and this, sir, is my husband, Rev. Theophilus Packard, of Manteno, who is now attending me there." This thought did flit across my mind at the table, but the habitual practice I had acquired of shielding, instead of exposing my husband, led me to resist this suggestion of self-defence and wise counsel. I saw now my error in yielding, thus foolishly, to this feminine weakness, and I, like Peter, went out, not "to weep bitterly," but to seek to make the best atonement I could for this sin. I sought and found that listening female waiter, and asked her who that gentleman was with whom I held my conversation at the table. She told me. "Will you please deliver this message to him? Tell him the lady with whom he conversed at the table is Mrs. Packard, and that the gentleman by her side was her husband, a minister, who is taking her to Jacksonville, to imprison her for advancing such ideas as he had so publicly endorsed and approved at the table."

The woman looked at me in amazement, and exclaimed, "You are not going into the Asylum!"

"Yes, I am. This very night I shall be a prisoner there."

"But you must not go! You shall not go! Come and consult the landlady—she may hide you."

As she said this, she took me by the hand, and led me to an open door, where, from the threshold, she introduced me to a very kind looking lady, in these words: "This is the lady I told you about, and her husband is taking her to the Insane Asylum; can't you help her?" Looking at me for a moment in amazement, she said: "Yes, I will. Come with me and I will hide you."

"No, my kind friend, it will be of no avail. My husband has the law on his side, and you can not protect me."

"But I will try. You must not go into an Insane Asylum. Come! and I will shield you."

As she said this she extended to me her hand, while the tears of real sympathy were coursing down her cheek. I replied, "O! sister, I thank you for your kindness and sympathy. But don't distress yourself for me. I shall be sustained. I feel that God's providence overrules all, and I know God will take care of me and my children." Just as I finished this sentence, Mr. Packard stood by my side, and he with a most respectful bow said, "Wife, will you go with me to the parlor?" I quietly took his arm, and bowing to my would be protector, walked with him to the parlor, where I remained seated by his side until the cars arrived, when I took his arm and went into them, and we were again on our way to Jacksonville. Here I met again my valiant female defender, who informed me that her advisers had decided that there was no way to rescue me from my husband's hands; but that it was certain that a lady like myself would be retained at the Asylum but a very short time, and would soon be restored to my children and liberty again. After thanking her most cordially, for her help and sympathy, we kissed and parted, never to meet again, unless in the unknown future. Now my last hope died within me, and as the gloomy walls of my prison could be but indistinctly defined by the gray twilight of a summer evening, I held on to my husband's arm, as he guided my footsteps up the massive stone steps, into my dreary prison, where by lamplight he introduced me to Dr. Tenny, the Assistant Superintendent, to be conducted by him to my lonely, solitary cell.

VI.

My Reception.

Yes, here within these prison walls, my husband and I parted, as companions, forever—he was escorted to the "guest chamber," while I, his constant companion of twenty-one years, was entrusted to the hands of my prison keeper to be led by him to find my bed and lodging, he knew not where, and to be subject to insults, he knew not what.

While he was resting on his wide, capacious, soft, luxurious bed, in the stately airy apartment of the Asylum guests, he did not know that the only place of repose provided for his weary wife was a hard narrow settee, with no soft pillows to rest her weary head upon. But he did know I had no darling babe at my side, but, solitary and alone I must compose myself to sleep, not knowing at what hour of the night my room might be entered, nor by whom, or for what purpose—for the key of my room was no longer in my own, nor my husband's hands, but in the hands of stranger men, and his wife entirely at their mercy.

Yes, this is all the protection I got from the one, for whom I left all to love, cherish and make happy, in return for his promised protection, with all the trusting confidence of woman. I never doubted but he would protect my virtue and my innocence. Yes, I trusted too, he would be the protector of my right of maternity also, for the dear children I had borne him. O, could I sleep amid these turbid waters, whose surging billows so mercilessly swept over my soul thoughts such as these; but one thought there was, more dreadful to my sensitive feelings than all others—now these dear children, these dear fragments of myself, must even bear the dismal, dreadful taint, of hereditary insanity, for their mother now lodges amid the hated walls of an Insane Asylum, as an inmate, and Oh! to whom can their mother now look for protection? To whom shall I make complaint if insulted? Oh, to whom? I can not write a letter unless it is inspected by my men keepers. Why is this? Is it because they intend to insult me, and deprive me of my post-office rights to shield and hide their own guilt? But can I not hand a letter clandestinely to the Trustees, as they pass through? If I could do such a thing, and entered a charge against their Superintendent, would this be heeded? Would not this Superintendent deny the truth, and defend his lie by the plea, that his accuser is insane, and this is only one of the fancies of her diseased brain?

Yes, yes, there is no man, woman, or child or law, who now can care for my soul, or protect my virtue. And yet, while I am an American citizen, I am excluded, without trial from society, and then denied any protection by law of one of my inalienable rights. I am not only outlawed, but I am absolutely denied all and every means of self-defence, no matter how criminal, nor how aggravated the offence may be.

My womanly nature does call for, and need some refuge to flee to, either to the law, or to man. But here, I have neither. Should my keeper chance to be a bad man, I have no refuge but my God to flee too—therefore, into Thy hands do I commit my body for safe keeping this night. My spirit, and the future of my earthly destiny, I have long since committed to Thy care, and now protect my body from harm, and give me the sleep my tired nature needs, and thus prepare me to bear the trials of to-morrow, as well as I have those of to-day, and Thou shalt have the honor of delivering me from the power of my adversaries. May no sin be ever suffered to have dominion over me.

With these thoughts, I fell into a quiet sleep, from which I awoke not until the morning of my first day in the Asylum dawned upon me.

VII.

My First Day of Prison Life.

At an early hour, I arose from my settee-bed, first kneeled before it, and thanked my kind Father in Heaven for the refreshing sleep I had enjoyed, and asked for sustaining grace for the duties of the day. To prepare myself for these duties I took my sponge bath, as usual, since Mrs. De La Hay, my attendant, had, at my request, furnished me a bowl from her own room, towels, etc., so that I could take my bath in my room, as this had long been a habit. I very much wished to retain while there. I soon found that she had especially favored me in granting this request, since it is the general custom there, to have all the ladies perform their morning ablutions in the bath room, and I could not learn that any, except my attendant, approved of washing all over, daily in cold water, as I did. And, as a general thing, their toilet had to be prepared before the same common mirror in the bath room. Therefore I requested Mr. Packard to furnish my room with a bowl, and pitcher, and a mirror, which he accordingly did, and before another night, I had a bed prepared like the other prisoners, which was a comfortable, narrow mattress bed, on a narrow bedstead. Mrs. De La Hay had done the best she could the night before, to accommodate me, since the beds in the Seventh ward were all occupied when I arrived.

After finishing my toilet in my room, with the aid of my own brushes and combs and small mirror, which my traveling basket contained, I was invited out to my breakfast with the other prisoners. At my request my attendants introduced me to my companions, most of whom returned my salutation with lady like civility. Our fare was very plain and coarse, consisting almost entirely of bolted bread and meat, and tea and coffee. But as I drank neither tea nor coffee, I found it rather dry without any kind of vegetables, not even potatoes, and sauce or fruits of any kind. As my diet had consisted of Graham bread, fruits and vegetables, to a great extent, I felt quite apprehensive lest my health would materially suffer from so great a change. Mr. Packard did not, however, now seem to care any more what his wife had to eat, than where she had to sleep, for so long as he stayed at the Asylum he was the table guest of Dr. McFarland, whose table was always spread with the most tempting viands and luxuries the season or the markets could afford. Mr. Packard did not even allow me the honor of an invitation to sit with him at this table; although the night before, a special meal had to be ordered for us both, he took his at the Doctor's table, while I had to be sent to the ward, to eat my warm biscuits and butter there alone.

I felt these indignities, these neglects, these inattentions, just as any other affectionate, sensitive wife would naturally feel under such circumstances. But, for twenty-one years I had been schooling myself to keep under subjection to my reason and conscience, the manifestation of those indignant emotions which are the natural, spontaneous feelings which such actions must inevitably germinate in a true, confiding wife. Therefore I made no manifestation of them under these provocations. At a very early period in my married life, had I learned the sad truth that it was impossible for Mr. Packard to appreciate or understand my womanly nature; therefore I had habituated myself to the exercise of charitable feelings towards him in my interpretation of such manifestations. I had tried to school myself to believe that his heart was not so much at fault as his education, and therefore, I could sincerely pray the Lord to forgive him, for he knows not what he does—he does not know how to treat a woman. I knew that the least manifestation of these indignant emotions would be misconstrued by him into feelings of anger, instead of a natural, praiseworthy resentment of wrong doing. And the laudable manifestation of these feelings under *such* circumstances, would tend to lessen, instead of increasing my self-respect. He held me in such relation towards himself as my father did towards himself, so that any resistance of his authority was attended with the same feeling of guilt which I would have felt in resisting my father's authority. And I, like a natural child, had always felt an almost reverential respect for my father's authority, and nothing to me seemed a greater sin than an act of disobedience to his commands; my conscience even demanded that I yield unquestioning submission to even the denial of my most fondly cherished hopes and anticipations.

Mr. Packard had been introduced into our family when I was but ten years old, and he had been my father's ministerial companion for eleven years, and when I married him he had been my lover or suitor for only a few months. Previous to this time I had only looked upon him as my father's companion and guest, but never as even a social companion of his daughter, who had always been taught to be a silent listener to her father's social guests.

This parental training of reverential feeling towards father's ministerial guests, had capacitated me to become an unresisting victim to Mr. Packard's marital power or authority. And as Mr. Packard's education had led him to feel that this marital authority was the foundation stone of the marriage union, he, of course, conscientiously claimed, what I was too willing to grant, viz: *subjection* to his will and wishes.

But undeveloped as I then was, my true nature instinctively revolted at this principle as wrong; but wherein, it was then difficult for me to demonstrate, even to my own satisfaction. But I can now see that my nature was only claiming its just rights, by this instinctive resistance to this marital authority. It was the *protection* of my identity or individuality which I was thus claiming from my husband, instead of its subjection, as *he* claimed. The parental authority, I admit, has a subjective claim, to a degree; but the marital has only the authority of protection. I believe that the moment a husband begins to subject his wife, that moment the fundamental law of the marriage union is violated. Both parties are injured by this act—the husband has taken the first step towards tyranny, and the injured wife has inevitably taken her first step towards losing her natural feeling of reverence towards her husband. **Slavish fear** is conjugal love's antagonistic foe—the purest and most devoted woman's love vanishes before it, as surely as the gentle dew vanishes before the sun's burning rays. Fortify this love ever so strongly, this principle of slavish subjection will undermine and overthrow the most impenetrable fortresses, and take the victim captive at its will. So had my conjugal love been led into a most unwilling captivity by my husband's tyranny, and all the charitable framework which woman's forgiving nature could throw around it, could not prevent this captivity, nor redeem the precious captive, so long as the tyranny of subjection claimed its victim! But to the triumph of God's grace I can say it, that during these twenty-one years of spiritual captivity, I do not know that I ever spoke a disrespectful word to my husband. I endured the soul agonies of this blighting, love strangling process silently, and for the most part uncomplainingly. I could, and cheerfully did do my duty to this usurper, as I would have done to a husband. But these duties had to be done from the dictates of settled principle, rather than from the impulse of true conjugal love.

I hope my impulsive readers will now be prepared to understand that it is not because I did not feel these insults that I did not resent them; but I had not then reached that stage of womanly development where I had the moral courage to defend myself by asserting my own rights. This stage of growth was indeed just dawning upon me; but O! the dense clouds attending this dawning of my individual existence! I had indeed practically asserted one of these inalienable rights, by not yielding my conscience and opinion to the dictates of creeds or church tyranny. Yes, I had maintained my rights of conscience in defiance of the marital power also. And this, too, had been the very hinge on which my reputation for sanity had been suspended. As Mr. Packard expressed himself, "Never before had Elizabeth persistently resisted his will or wishes—a few kind words and a little coaxing would always before set her right; but now she seems strangely determined to have her own way, and it must be she is insane."

Thus in my first struggle after my independence, I lost my personal liberty. Sad beginning! Had it not been better for me to submit to oppression and spiritual bondage, rather than have attempted to break the fetters of marital and religious despotism! No, I cannot feel that I have done either myself, or others, the least wrong, in the course I have thus far taken; therefore I have no recantations to make, and can give no pledges of future subjection to either of these powers, where their claims demand the surrender of my conscience to their dictation. And this is what they call my insanity, and for which I was sent to the Asylum to be cured. I think it will be a long time before this cure will be effected. God grant me the quietude of patient endurance, come what will, in the stand I have taken.

While these, and similar reflections were passing through my mind, the door of my cell was opened by a fine looking gentleman in company with Mr. Packard, to whom he introduced me, as Dr. McFarland, the Superintendent. He had but just returned from a journey East, so that Dr. Tenny, the Assistant, received me. Dr. McFarland politely invited me to accompany them to the "reception room." I gladly accepted this invitation to be restored to the civilities of civilization, even temporarily. I seated myself upon the sofa by Mr. Packard's side, and the Doctor took the big rocking chair, directly in front of us, and opened an interesting and pleasant conversation, by narrating incidents of his eastern journey. In a very easy and polite manner he led on the conversation to other points and topics of interest at the present day, and finally to the progressive ideas of the age, even to religion and politics. He very gallantly allowed me a full share of the time to express my own thoughts, while Mr. Packard sat entirely speechless.

As the tone and spirit of the conversation rendered it proper, I recollect I made a remark something like this: "I don't know why it is, Doctor, it may be merely a foolish pride which prompts the feeling, but I can't help feeling an instinctive aversion to being called insane. There seems to be a kind of disparagement of intellect attending this idea, which seems to stain the purity and darken the lustre of the reputation forever after."

"No, Mrs. Packard, this is not necessarily so; even some of the most renowned and gifted minds in the world have been insane, and their reputations and characters are still revered and respected, such as Cowper and Tasso, the greatest poets in the world, and many others."

I made no plea of defence in favor of my sanity, and particularly avoided any disparaging or criminating remarks respecting Mr. Packard, but simply let the conversation take the direction the Doctor dictated. But, as I then thought fortunately for me, he introduced no topic where I felt at any loss what to say, to keep up an intelligent interchange of thought and expression. In short, this interview of an hour or more, was to me a feast of reason and a flow of soul, and it seemed to be equally so to the Doctor, unless my womanly instincts very much deceived me. When I was returned to my ward, and behind the fatal dead lock, dining with the insane, I must confess I did feel more out of my proper place, than I did while in the reception room of refined society.

After noticing the manner in which the institution was conducted for the three succeeding years, I found that the interview I had had with the Doctor was a most uncommon occurrence. Indeed, I never knew of a single instance where any other patient ever had so fair an opportunity of self-representation, by a personal interview upon their reception into the Asylum, as he had thus allowed me. They are usually taken, forthwith, from their friends in the reception room, and led directly into the ward, as Dr. Tenny had done by me the night before. But unlike my case afterwards, there they were left to remain indefinitely, so far as an interview with the Doctor was concerned. Many patients were received and discharged, while I was there, who never had five minutes conversation with the Doctors while in the Asylum. Often the new arrival would come to me and inquire, " When am I to have an examination?" I would reply, " You never have an examination after you get here, for the Doctor receives you on the representation of those who want you should stay here."

" But I never had any examination before I came, and even did not know where I was being brought, until I got here, and then my friends told me I should have an examination after I arrived."

" I believe you are speaking the truth; for public sentiment seems to allow, that one whom any one wishes to regard as insane, may be deceived and lied to to any extent with impunity; and besides, the blinded public generally suppose that the inmates do all have to pass an examination here before they are received, which is not the fact. They take it for granted that all are of course insane, or they would not be brought here, as Dr. Tenny said of me to Mrs. Waldo, in reply to her inquiry, 'Dr. Tenny, do you call Mrs. Packard an insane person?' 'Of course I do, or she would not be brought here,' was his reply. And then the outsiders say, 'Of course they are insane, or they would not have been received.' Thus our insanity is demonstrated beyond a question!"

After dinner I saw from the grated window of my cell, the Asylum carriage drive up in front of the steps, when Mr. Packard was politely handed in, and the carriage drove off. Upon inquiry, I found he had gone to ride, to see the beauties of the scenery about Jacksonville, and the public buildings and handsome residences. "Oh," thought I, "why could he not have invited me to ride with him? And how could he seek comfort for himself, while he left his wife amid scenes of such wretchedness?"

Not long after, my attendant came to my room and invited me to take a walk. I most gladly accepted the invitation, struggling and panting as my spirit was, for freedom; and I found that the pure air alone exerted an exhilerating influence over my feelings, and I with another prisoner, proposed to walk about the buildings, to see the grounds, etc.

But we soon found ourselves followed by our watchful attendant, to see if we were not trying to run off! "Oh," said I, "is this the vigilance that I am subjected to? Is there no more freedom outside of our bolts and bars, than within them? Are we not allowed to be paroled like prisoners? No, no. No parole of honor is allowed these prisoners, for not one moment are we allowed to be out of sight and hearing of our vigilant attendant. And these are the walks and circumscribed limits Mr. Packard has assigned his wife, while he can roam where he pleases, with none to molest or make him afraid."

It is my opinion that this institution receives and retains many sane persons, of whose sanity Dr. McFarland is as well assured as he was of my own. I do believe that he became fully convinced in his heart that I was not insane, before our interview terminated; but since I had been already received by his assistant, he did not like to revoke his decision so abruptly as to return me directly into my husband's hands; neither did he wish to disappoint the wishes nor thwart the plans of a very respectable and popular minister of high standing in the Presbyterian church, for by this act he might possibly alienate some popular influences from his support; and one other thought may have had some influence over this decision (and will not my reader pardon my vanity if I mention it?) namely, I think the intelligent Doctor thought he would like to become better acquainted with me. By thus retaining me for a few days, he felt that I could then be returned to the satisfaction of all parties. His subsequent polite attentions, and the remark he made to me at one of these interviews, viz: "Mrs. Packard, you will not remain here many days," in connection with a remark he made Mrs. Judge Thomas, of Jacksonville, respecting me, has led me to feel that I did not then misjudge him. The remark was this, "Mrs. Thomas, we have a very remarkable patient now in our Asylum. It is a Mrs. Packard, a clergyman's wife, from Massachusetts. She has a high order of talent, has a very superior education, is polished and refined in her manners, having ever moved in the best society, and is the most intelligent lady I ever saw. I think you would like to make her acquaintance."

VIII.
The Parting Scene.

The next day I had a brief interview with the Doctor alone in my room, which was very pleasant and satisfactory to me—that is, I thought he could not think I was an insane person, therefore I had a little ray of hope to cling to, as Mr. Packard had not yet left. Dr. McFarland did not exchange a word with me upon this subject. But this dying hope was destined very soon to go out in utter darkness.

About three o'clock in the afternoon Mr. Packard came the second time to my room, and as he had allowed me to be in his company only during the interview I had with the Doctor, during the two days and nights he had been in the Asylum, I felt it to be a privilege to accept of his invitation to go to the reception room and have a talk with him there. I accordingly took his arm, without its being offered, and walked out of the hall. As we passed on I heard some one remark, "See! that lady is not alienated from her husband. See how kindly she takes her husband's arm."

I seated myself by his side on the sofa, when he said, "I am going to leave for Manteno in about one hour, and I did not know but that you would like to have a talk with me before I left."

"Then you are determined to leave your wife in an Insane Asylum. O, husband! how can you do so?" I then burst into tears.

"I hoped we should have a pleasant interview before we parted."

"Pleasant! how could it be pleasant to leave me in such a place? and do you think it will be pleasant for me to be left? Only think of those dear little motherless children!"

"I shall see that they are well taken care of."

"But you can not give them a mother's care. O, how can my children live without their mother; and how can I live without my children?"

As this strong maternal feeling of my nature came welling up into such a high pitch of intensity, it seemed as if my heart would burst with anguish, at this hitherto unaccepted thought. I arose, and with my handkerchief to my face, I walked the room back and forth, at the same time, begging and pleading in the most plaintive, expressive terms, that he would commute my sentence of banishment, so far as not to separate me from my children. O, do be entreated in some way, to allow me this one favor, and my grateful, thankful heart will bless you forever. O, it will kill me to be separated from those dear ones. My babe! O, what will become of him; and what will become of me, without my babe? O, husband, do! do! let me return with you to my children! You know I have always been a kind and faithful mother, and wife too, and now how can you treat me so?"

For sometime I walked the room, giving utterance to such, and similar expressions, without raising my eyes, or noticing the effect my plea was having upon him; but after a long pause, and vainly watching for his reply for some time, I looked up to see why he did not speak to me, when lo! what did I see? My husband, sound asleep on the sofa, nodding his head.

In astonishment, I indignantly exclaimed, "O husband! are you asleep? Can you sleep, when your wife is in such agony?" The emphatic tones of my voice brought him back to consciousness, when he raised his head, and opening his eyes, replied, "I can't keep awake; I have been broke of my rest!"

"I see it is of no use to say any thing more—it will avail nothing. We may as well part now as ever." Saying this, I walked up to him and extended to him my hand, and as I did so, I said, "Farewell, husband, forever! may our next meeting be in the spirit land; and if there you find yourself in need of help to rise to a higher plane, remember there is one spirit in the universe, who is willing to descend to any depth of misery, to help you on to a higher plane, if this can be done—and this spirit is your Elizabeth. Farewell, husband, forever!"

"I am sorry to hear you talk so; I hoped we should have a pleasant parting."

This was our parting scene.

Now let me introduce to my reader, a scene in the Doctor's office, which succeeded this. Leaving me in the reception room, he repaired to the office, to take his leave of the Doctor. Now it was his turn to cry. Availing himself of this right, he now burst into a flood of tears, which so choked his utterance, it was some minutes before he could articulate at all, when he at length exclaimed, "How I pity my wife! How hard it is to leave her here! O, if I only were not obliged to do so, how gladly would I take her home. She is such a good wife, how can I part with her? But I must do so, hard as it is, for her good." Thus he went on, acting this part of the drama to perfection. Indeed, so well, and adroitly did he act the husband, that the intelligent Doctor McFarland himself, was deluded into the belief that he was sincere, and that these were the tears of true sorrow and affection. Alluding to this scene months afterwards, he remarked, "I never saw a man so deeply afflicted, and even heart-broken, as Mr. Packard was, at parting with you. He was the most heart-broken man I ever saw. If ever a man manifested true affection for his wife, it was Mr. Packard."

Yes, he so completely psychologised the Doctor into the feeling that he loved me most devotedly, and was compelled in spite of himself, to incarcerate me, that the Doctor felt certain there had been a justifiable cause for my having been brought there.

Satisfied that his work was now well done, he took his leave of the Doctor, and his tears at the same time, and with a light heart and quick step, passed out on to the porch, where he stopped to give me one look of satisfied delight, that he had finally completely triumphed, in getting me imprisond beyond all hope of deliverance. Never had I seen his face more radiant with joy, than when he looked up to me, as I stood before the open window of the reception room, and threw me his kisses from the ends of his fingers, and bowed me his happy adieu. Yes, happy, that his conspiracy against my personal liberty had so completely triumphed over all opposition. Having secured the entombment of the mother, he had now naught to do but to teach her children to despise their mother, and treat her name and memory, with contempt and derision.

IX.

Disappointed Hopes.

Mr. Packard has gone! My last hope of deliverance through him, has now sunk into a rayless night of despair. Yes, utter despair of ever being liberated and reinstated in my family again. He has not so much as even uttered one syllable on which I could build such a hope. I never have heard him even say, he hoped I should ever get better, so as to be with him once more. What can this mean? Has he buried me for life? Yes, so his conduct speaks, and no word, or act contradicts it. Hopeless imprisonment! O, may my reader never know what these terms signify. I know what it is to endure endless torment, and hopeless bondage! and it is a terrible doom.

I did try to build a faint hope, upon the fact that he had brought only a small satchel of things with me, and these could not last me long, but before he left, he dashed this hope to the ground by telling me, he should send me my trunk, after he got home. In about three weeks, there did arrive a monstrous sized trunk directed to Mrs. Packard, which led the patients to exclaim, "Is Mr. Packard going to keep his wife here for life?" And how did my sad heart echo this fearful question.

But even amid this gloom, one ray of comfort gleamed forth at the thought, now I shall hear from my dear children. They surely will send some token of love and affection to their imprisoned mother. And to enjoy this comfort to its fullest extent, I asked the Doctor to allow me to unpack it in my own room, with my door locked. He kindly locked me in himself, seemingly rejoicing in my anticipated joy. My first surprise on opening it, was to see so few articles of clothing, and these of the very poorest kind, and in a state of the most tangled confusion, with rotten lemons and cans of fruit scattered amongst them to their detriment, poor as they were. The whole contents would not fill one-third of the trunk, and this caused the confusion in the transportation of the trunk. And why he should send so large a trunk to carry so few articles, has always been an unsolved mystery to me. But this feeling was soon lost in the bright thought of soon finding my childrens' love tokens. Each and every article was most carefully searched, to find what would be next to finding my child, for his own fingers must have held it and kissed it for his mother.

But ah! must I utter the sad truth, that no token, no letter could be found, on which my fond heart could rest its loving impulses? Yes, so it was; and being alone, I wept in deepest anguish at this disappointed hope. My sons afterwards told me that they all expressed a wish to send me a letter and many tokens, but their father had refused to let them do so unless he should dictate the letters. I. W. said he knew that to get such a letter as his father would dictate, would pain me more than it would to get none at all. And so it would have been, for on a narrow strip of paper, four inches long and two wide, I found pencilled, "We are glad to hear you are getting better; hope you will soon get well. Your daughter Elizabeth." This her father made her write to make me feel that she believed me insane; and he knew nothing would torment me so much as this thought from her. Indeed, I found that what I. W. had said was too true. I was more pained to get this line from my daughter, than I would have been to get none at all; for not knowing the truth, I did fear she was coming under the influence of this delusion.

I think the Doctor pitied me under this trial, for the next day, when in reply to his questions, I told him I found no letters, or love tokens, or messages from my children, he seemed astonished, and said, "I thought you would find many letters. I wonder they did not write their mother."

Another disappointment. I had especially requested Mr. Packard that my nice black silk dress and white crape shawl be sent, so that I could go to church decently dressed. But not only these, but all my other good articles of clothing were kept from me, not only while I was in the Asylum, but long after I was liberated; and then he was forced to give them up upon my father's authority.

Now my only hope of deliverance lay in the Mantenoites fulfilling their promise to get me out in a few days. Every carriage and man was watched, hoping to find in him my deliverer. But none came, until several weeks, when I was called from Mrs. McFarland's parlor into the reception room, to see Mr. and Mrs. Blessing, from Manteno, and a stranger, to whom they introduced me as Dr. Shirley, of Jacksonville. Dr. Shirley took the lead in the conversation, and I was delighted at the compliment he paid me in introducing subjects such as required intelligence and scientific knowledge to converse upon. Our pleasure in sustaining such an interchange of thoughts seemed to be mutually reciprocated, and I think we both parted feeling that we were wiser than when we met. I am sure this was the case with me, and from what Dr. Shirley said of me to those who had employed him to test my sanity, I think I did not misjudge him. In reply to their inquiry, "Is she insane?" he said, "She is the sanest person I ever saw. I wish the world was full of such women."

Now that my sanity was established beyond question, the Mantenoites resolved to liberate me, and therefore appointed a public indignation meeting for this purpose, to see what could be done to effect it. Mr. Packard hearing of this proposed meeting to liberate his imprisoned wife, sent to Chicago and obtained Rev. A. D. Eddy, D. D., and Mr. Cooley, of the firm of Cooley & Farwell, to come to Manteno and help him to withstand and defeat this philanthropic plan. They both came and did their work up thoroughly and successfully, in that they browbeat the Mantenoites, and silenced them into submission to the dictates of this ministerial and church influence. Thus this plan was defeated, and I was destined to another disappointment. Mr. Blessing told me clandestinely, he had come to effect my liberation if possible.

But these Mantenoites determined that their defeat should

not be a failure, and therefore they determined to try the *habeus corpus* act, and thus secure me a fair trial at least. But to their surprise, they found it exceedingly difficult, if not impossible, to extend this act to a legal "nonentity," unless by the consent of Mr. Packard, who stood for me in law, and of course he would not consent to any step which would allow me any chance at self-defence. Therefore, with the encouragement and assistance of his brother ministers, and the church, he learned how to ward off this attempt successfully.

Again the Mantenoites assembled, and by their generous contributions raised a liberal purse of money, to be used in my defence. They sent a delegation to the Asylum, to inform me of this fact, which they did, by carefully noting the time the Doctor's back was turned, to inform me as they walked through the prison halls. Said they, "Any amount of money you can have, if money can help you. Send to Theophilus, your son to take you out."

I simply had time to reply, "I can't send letters out." This was all we could say clandestinely. Although I could see no hope of deliverance through this source, yet the thought that I was being cared for by any one outside my prison, was a great consolation to me.

Through the influence of friends, my oldest son Theophilus visited the Asylum, and obtained an interview with me, a detailed account of which visit is given in my "Three Years Imprisonment," on page 127, therefore I shall not repeat this affecting scene. But the result I mention, to show how our hopes are germinated, only to be blighted by Asylum life. At this interview, Dr. McFarland fairly promised to co-operate with my son, in doing all in his power to get me out, and afterwards refused to do the least thing towards it, not even to send my letters to my son, nor would he deliver his to me. I know he received letters from him, for shortly after, I saw one on his office table from him, directed to me, and I took it up to read it, and he took it from me, refusing to let me know its contents. Now I found I was destined to another disappointment, for the Doctor had not only refused to co-operate, but was evidently defeating my son's filial attempts to rescue his mother. The agony of this disappointment was increased by the fact that the Doctor had deceived us both, in this transaction, therefore his word could no longer be trusted. I was very sorry to be obliged to come to this conclusion, for until this development I had regarded him as a man of honor, whose word could be trusted.

Another effort my friends made, was to go to the Govenor on my behalf, but he replied he could not repeal laws, nor enact laws—he could only execute laws, and if there was no law by which I could have a trial, or be liberated, he did not know of any thing that he could do for me. It was my husband's business to take me out, and if he refused, there was no law to force him, so long as Dr. McFarland claimed I was insane.

After all these sore disappointments, I found that my personal liberty, and personal identity, were entirely at the mercy of Mr. Packard and Dr. McFarland; that no law of the Institution or of the State, recognised my identity while a married woman; therefore, no protection, not even the criminal's right of self-defence, could be extended to me; and therefore I must intelligently yield up all hopes of my personal liberty, so long as Mr. Packard and Dr. McFarland lived and agreed in keeping me imprisoned.

X.

The Sunny Side of my Prison Life.

For the first four months of my prison life, Dr. McFarland treated me himself, and caused me to be treated, with all the respect of a hotel boarder, so far as lay in his power to do so.

As to medical treatment, I received none at all, either from himself, or his subordinates. And the same may be said with equal truth, of all the inmates. This is the general rule ; those few cases where they receive any kind of medical treatment, are the exceptions. A little ale occasionally, is the principal part of the medical treatment which these exceptions receive, unless his medical treatment consists in the "laying on of hands," for this treatment is almost universally bestowed. But the manner in which this was practised, varied very much in different cases.

For the first four months the Doctor "laid his hands" very gently upon me, except that the pressure of my hand in his was sometimes quite perceptible, and sometimes, as I thought, longer continued than this healing process demanded ! Still as I was then quite a novice in this mode of cure, I might not have been a proper judge ! But after these four months he laid his hands upon me in a different manner, and as I then thought and still do think, far too violently. There was no mistaking the character of these grips—no duplicity after this period rendered this modern mode of treatment, of doubtful interpretation to me. To Dr. McFarland's credit I must say it, that if shaking hands with his patients is his mode of medical treatment, I must give him the credit of paying no respect of persons in administering it. For indeed there was seldom an occupant of the Seventh ward who did not daily feel the grip of the Superintendent's hand. And I have no doubt but that this mode of imparting magnetism was in many instances beneficial to the patient. So far as its influence upon me was concerned, I cheerfully admit that I considered myself benefitted by it. My nervous system had been severely taxed, my sympathies had been stifled, and these heavy draughts on the vital forces of my nature had left me in a condition to be easily strengthened and benefitted by the magnetic influence of a strong and sympathising man. The affectionate pressure of his great hand seemed to impart a kind of vitality to my nervous system, which did help me bear my spiritual tortures with greater fortitude and composure. I felt that he did pity me, and really wished to be a true friend to me and my interests. Many thanks are due Dr. McFarland for the courteous, manly treatment I received from him during this favored period. I did not then think, neither do I now cherish the thought, that Dr. McFarland intended to manifest himself towards me in any manner inconsistent with the principles of a high toned, manly gentleman. Only one impulsive act did he allow himself to commit during this period, which I think his reason would not approve, so far as his personal treatment of me was concerned.

One day I was entrusted with the care of some of the Seventh ward prisoners, to recreate ourselves in the court-yard. Availing myself of the sources of amusement there furnished, I seated myself upon a swing, and also politely accepted the offer of a gentleman, who was reclining upon the grass under the shady tree, to swing me. After allowing him to do so for a while, I asked him to allow me to get off and let another take my place. But instead of receiving their thanks for this offer, Mrs. Gassaway, one of the prisoners, a wife, and mother of several children, bestowed upon me a most severe reprimand, not only for swinging myself, but also for allowing a "male patient," as she called my gallant, to swing me. Instead, therefore, of accepting this offer herself, or allowing any other one to accept it, she started with a quick step towards the ward, to report my misdemeanors to Miss Eagle, our attendant, as she threatened to do. I, of course, followed with my paroled prisoners after her, as I had been instructed to keep an eye upon them all; but instead of following them into the ward, I went alone into the Doctor's office, to report my misdemeanors at head quarters. I found Dr. McFarland standing at his writing desk, alone in his office. I rushed up in front of him, and in a very enthusiastic, amusing manner, made a frank and full confession of what Mrs. Gassaway termed my "great improprieties!" With his eyes upon me, the Doctor listened with the most profound attention to my confessions and plea for pardon, and as I finished by inquiring, "What shall I say to Miss Eagle in extenuation of Mrs. Gassaway's charges against me; he replied, "Say nothing; I will see that you are protected;" and as he made this remark, he stooped and bestowed a kiss upon my forehead.

Although I regarded this as a mere impulsive act, dictated by no corrupt motives, yet as I afterwards told him, I considered it an indiscreet act for a man in his position, "For," said I, "Dr. McFarland, men do not send their wives, nor fathers their daughters here, expecting that you will manifest your regard for them in *this manner*, and by doing so, you render yourself liable to just censure from the patrons of this Institution." The Doctor listened with silent attention to this reproof, and only remarked "It was only a kiss of charity!"

And here I will venture the remark, that had I been discharged at any time during those four months, I should doubtless have identified myself with that class of discharged prisoners who represent Dr. McFarland as no other than an honorable gentleman. And I am prepared to believe there are many whose experience would lead them to thus represent him, for, from their standpoint, he had been only the gentlemanly Superintendent. The greatest fault I could see in the Doctor's conduct during this period, was his receiving so many who were not insane, and in retaining those who had recovered their sanity so long after they were able to be at home. I saw several such sink back into a state of hopeless imbecility from this cause alone. Hope too long deferred made them so sick of life that they yielded themselves up to desperation as a natural, inevitable result. It was a matter of great surprise to me to find so many in the Seventh ward, who, like myself, had never shown any insanity while there, and these were almost uniformly married women, who were put there either by strategy or by force. None of these unfortunate sane prisoners had had any trial or any chance of self-defence. And I could not force myself to believe that so sensible a man as the Doctor, could really believe they were insane, without a shadow of evidence in their own conduct. But sadly foolish and weak as it was, he professed to believe they were, on simple hearsay testimony, in defiance of positive, tangible proof to the contrary. I once asked the Doctor how long he had to keep a person imprisoned, to determine whether they were insane or not. His reply was, "Sometimes six months, and sometimes a year!"

Another fact I noticed, that he invariably kept these sane wives until they begged to be sent home. This led me to suspect that there was a secret understanding between the husband and the Doctor; that the subjection of the wife was the cure the husband was seeking to effect under the specious plea of insanity; and when they began to express a wish to go home, the Doctor would encourage these tyrannical husbands that they were "improving." Time after time have I seen these defenceless women sent home only to be sent back again and again, for the sole purpose of making them the unresisting, willing slaves of their cruel husbands.

I do not blame Dr. McFarland for the sins of these unnatural husbands, but I do blame him for letting the Institution be used by them as a place of punishment to married women, as a prison, where they could appeal to none for help or deliverance, but to themselves. These husbands, like Mr. Packard, knew that no law could protect the wife from their despotic power, and they knew too, that the simple word of Dr. McFarland that they were insane, would legally entitle them to the use of this State's Prison as a calaboose, where their wives could be subjected to their husbands will. I think that Dr. McFarland, even while he treated these subjected women with decent, gentlemanly respect, was at the same time, inflicting upon them a most cruel wrong, in keeping them imprisoned, when he knew they were not insane. This is the only wrong I complain of from him, during those four months. He ought to have had the moral courage to say to Mr. Packard, "Your wife is not insane, and I see no reason why her personal liberty should be taken from her, therefore I shall discharge her upon my own responsibility, to take care of herself, unless you choose to do so. I am sure she is capable of assuming a self reliant position, and therefore ought not to be imprisoned." But he dare not do right and justice by me, or my associates, in this particular, but chose the cowardly course of compromising with this mean man; and thus he trampled the highest, noblest, instincts of his manly nature in the dust. By thus oppressing the weak, instead of protecting them, he ruined himself—his manliness suffered strangulation under this process, as the sequel will demonstrate.

But with this exception, no Superintendent could have treated a prisoner with more consideration than he did me. I was allowed to go into the parlor and visit with his wife or her guests, when I pleased. I was occasionally invited to eat at the Doctor's table. He instructed my attendants to let me go out whenever I pleased. He allowed my room to be furnished with the toilet comforts of any good boarding house. He allowed me to have a trunk in my room, and all the articles of my wardrobe that I needed. I was allowed my gold watch and gold spectacles, my three bladed pocket knife and scissors; in fact, everything a hotel boarder could desire. He furnished me books and papers to read. I could read, knit and sew, ride or walk, when I pleased, and to add to the feeling of trust and confidence he reposed in me, he gave me the entire charge of a carriage load of patients, and gave also, the reins of the horse into my hands, to ride as far as I pleased, and return when I pleased. This he did fourteen times, with no one to care for the horse or the patients, but myself.

He gave me money to go to the city and trade for myself, and his wife has sent me to trade for her, and for the house. His wife has employed me for weeks in succession, to cut and make dresses for herself and daughters, and the matron employed me to cut and plan work for the house. I cut and made twelve comforts for the house, and tied them myself, in my room. I made pants and vests for the house. I cut twelve dresses, for the patients. Indeed, there was always something I could find to do, for the comfort of others, and my own amusement. I was allowed to visit with most of the guests of the house. In short, but for the grated windows, and bolted doors of prison life, I should hardly have known but I was a boarder, whose identity and capacities were recognised, in common with other intelligent agents.

My companions in the Seventh ward, were a very pleasant source of social enjoyment. Among them, I found some of the most original thinkers I ever saw; and among this class, I found some of the best teachers I had ever had. Some of them were Spiritualists, and they taught me many new ideas, and set me on to a new track of exploration. They told me their visions, and trances and prophecies, many of which have been already fulfilled, in the events of the war. One lady had a prevision of the war, and was sent to the Asylum because she told of it! Another had a vision of the same, under different imagery, and she had to lose her personal liberty for telling of it. Both of these prophetesses, Mrs. Neff and Mrs. Clarke, have lived to see the exact fulfillment of their visions, and like Jeremiah, they both had to be imprisoned for foretelling future events. And sad as is the fact, these inspired women were compelled, even under the folds of the American flag, of religious toleration, to either be false to these true inspirations, or "Hide their light under a bushel," in order to obtain their personal liberty. Both of them told me, they were obliged to stop talking about it, before any one would admit they were getting over their insanity. But they had to endure the horrors of a Lunatic Asylum for months, and even years, before they could be induced to love the defence of the truth, less than their personal liberty. But neither of these prophetesses ever did, to my knowledge, deny the truth of these visions, nor would they own it to be insanity. They merely yielded to be gagged, on condition that they could be liberated, by so doing. Such manifestations as these, are what the Asylum calls *very* insane cases, so they had to be subjected to very severe punishments, and tortures, to bring them into this condition.

They both said to me clandestinely, the night before they left, "My views are not changed at all, in regard to these prophetic truths, yet I dare not own it aloud, lest Dr. McFarland hear of it, and I be thereby doomed to endless torment within these prison walls. If my attendants should know that I have uttered these views to you, they will report me to the Doctor, and he will order my friends to leave to-morrow without me, as he will tell them I am not fit to go, for my insanity has returned. Therefore be entreated, Mrs. Packard, not to betray me by reporting this conversation, until I am safely away from this horrid Inquisition."

Of course I did not report them to their tormentors, but I consider it to be my duty, to report this Inquisition to the American people, and thus appeal to their intelligence, to destroy these Inquisitions, which they are now blindly sustaining, under the popular name of charitable, humanitarian institutions. If the truth were known, I believe that much that is called insanity at the present day, is only a higher development of christianity than the perverted theology of the pulpit is, willing to recognise. It is my opinion, that much that is called insanity in these days of spiritual corruption, will be looked upon by future ages, with a feeling similar to what we feel towards those who suffered as witches, in Salem, Massachusetts. That persecution went so far, that the government was obliged to make a law, that all who accused others of witchcraft, must themselves suffer the punishment they had designed to secure to the witch. This law and its execution, put a speedy stop to these false accusations. Possibly, our government will be obliged to put a stop to these false accusations of insanity, in the same manner. If all those who *falsely* accused another of insanity, were compelled to be treated as insane themselves, I think the number of those brought before a jury, for trial on the charge of insanity, would be greatly lessened.

XI.

My Transition.

During the sunny days of my prison life I was allowed to have the free and unrestricted use of my pen, with all the paper and stationery I wished. My right to my letters, journals and private papers, was as freely acceded to me as any other inalienable right of an American citizen. And Dr. McFarland even respected my post office right so much as not to read my letters to my husband, nor do I think he read his to me. This, I found, was an almost unexampled practical acknowledgment of this sacred right of an American citizen, while under the locks and keys of one of its humanitarian institutions. Before I entered an Insane Asylum and learned its hidden life from the standpoint of a patient, I had not supposed that the inmates were outlaws, in the sense that the law did not protect them in any of their inalienable rights. I had ignorantly supposed that their right to "life, liberty, and the pursuit of happiness," was recognized and respected as human beings. But now I have learned it is not the case; but on the contrary, the law and society have so regulated this principle, that the insane are permitted to be treated and regarded as having *no rights* that any one is bound to respect—no, not even so much as the slaves are, for they have the rights of their masters' selfish interests to shield their own rights. But the rights of the insane are not even shielded by the principle of selfishness. What does the keeper of this class care for the rights of the menials beneath him? Nothing. His salary is secured by law, whether there be few or many under the roof which shelters him. Unlike the slaveholder, he can torment and abuse unto death, and his interests are not impaired by this wreck of human faculties and human life. Indeed this wreck is oftentimes made a necessity to the Superintendent, to prevent the exposure of his criminal acts. And since there is no law to shield the insane person, he is, by law, subject to an absolute despotism. Thus the despot is protected in his despotism, no matter how severe and rigorous he may become.

Now since the object of government should be to protect the rights of its citizens, it seems to me that the insane have rights which the government ought to respect, acknowledge and protect. And one of these human rights is to write letters to whom and when he pleases, as this would serve to restrain, in some degree, the absolute despotism which rules supreme behind the curtain. So long as the Superintendent was upright, and acted according to his highest sense of right, he would not care what his patients said or wrote about him. But when selfishness and wicked policy controlled his actions, he would fear his wickedness would be exposed if the patients were allowed to write what they pleased. I think it is because the deeds of darkness and cruelty are so common, instead of the deeds of kindness, forbearance and justice, which render the Superintendents so harmonious in the opinion that it is best to deprive their patients of their post office rights, when they are deprived of their personal liberty.

In my own experience I find this principle demonstrated, as the sequel will show. While I was treated with propriety, there were no strictures put upon my correspondence; but as soon as he began to pass on to the plane of injustice, he became jealous at once of the use I made of this right. I do not think any letters I wrote during these sunny days, would have excited his jealousy if he did read them all; but there was one document I wrote which did arouse all the evil influences of his nature into energetic action against me, and this was a written reproof I gave him.

It may be a matter of surprise to my readers that I should deem it my duty to reprove one who was acting so gentlemanly a part towards me. It was a surprise to myself, almost, that I should dare to risk myself in such an encounter, knowing as I did, that all my favors, rights and privileges, were suspended entirely upon the will of the Superintendent, and therefore, entirely subject to his dictation. But motives higher than those of self-interest actuated me, or I could not have done it. I know that I was a rare exception in the respectful treatment he was bestowing upon me; no other prisoner had been so much favored before me, if the testimony of his employees could be relied upon, and my eligible position had become the great topic of discussion among the prisoners and employees.

But by the omnipotent power of God's grace I was inspired with moral courage sufficient to espouse the cause of the oppressed and the defenceless, even at the risk of becoming one of their number by so doing. I plainly saw and felt that on the part of their oppressors there was power, but that they had no comforter. I felt conscious that I held an influence and power over Dr. McFarland, and I deliberately determined this influence should be felt in their behalf. And, like Queen Esther, I felt willing to cast in my lot with these despised captives, if necessary, to be their deliverer. I therefore depicted their wrongs, oppression and received cruelties, in the most expressive terms I could command, and on this statement of awful facts I based an appeal to his intelligence, his humanity, and his conscience, to become their protector and deliverer. I furthermore added, that unless he did treat them with more justice, I should expose his criminal conduct publicly, when I got out; but if he would repent of these sins against humanity, he would have nothing to fear, for we would all forgive the past if he would repent now, and do us justice in the future.

This document cast the die for my future destiny. The transition time had fully come, when comfort, attention, respect, privilege, all, all, were in the dead past, and discomfort, inattention, disrespect, contempt, wrong and deprivation are to mark the future of my prison life. It was for others' interests I plead—it was of others' wrongs and woes I complained. It was for them and their sakes I deliberately laid down my position as the Asylum favorite, and became henceforth the Asylum prisoner. From this time, for two years and eight months, I was not allowed to step my foot on the ground, and I fully believe it was the Doctor's purpose to make a maniac of me, by the skillful use of the Asylum tortures.

But, thank God! the mouths of the Asylum Lions were kept shut, so that they could not hurt me, and like Shadrach, Meshach and Abednego, the Lord brought me out of this fiery furnace without the taint of insanity upon me. I did not fear to trust the Lord in the line of my duty—he did not forsake me in my captivity. Although henceforth I became one with my fellow captives in suffering, yet never for one moment have I regretted the step I then took in their defence, nor the transition it assigned me.

XII.

My Removal from the Best Ward to the Worst.

One Saturday evening, after chapel prayers, Dr. McFarland took me by the arm and led me from the chapel into the Eighth ward, and as he left me behind the dead lock, said, "You may occupy this ward, Mrs. Packard." This was the first manifestation of the change in the Doctor's feelings towards me.

As he left, I said to my attendant, "Miss Tenny, what does this mean?"

"I don't know; all he said to me was, 'I wish you not to allow Mrs. Packard to leave the ward, and give her a dormitory bed.'"

"I don't know what it means either" said I; "he has never reproved me for anything, neither have I broken any rules that I know of. I wonder if my reproof has not offended him?"

"I presume it has; I have heard there was quite a stir about it."

I found it was generally known that I was preparing a document in defence of the prisoners' rights, and several had heard me read it; and although they insisted upon its truth in every particular, yet they all seemed to think I had no idea of the Doctor's power over us, or I should not dare to utter the truth so plainly to him. Some said, "We have often told him the same thing, but he takes no notice of it whatever, unless he gets mad about it, then he will send us to some bad ward to be punished for it." Others would say, "Mrs. Packard, you had better not give the Doctor that document, unless you wish to be sent to a dungeon, where you could never see daylight again." Another would say, "I will stand by you, Mrs. Packard, if you will give him that document, if he kills me for doing so; for it is the truth."

Fearing some of these predictions might prove true, I took the precaution to take an exact copy of the document, and sewed it up in a cloth, and hid it between the glass and the board back of my mirror, where it remained, undisturbed and unknown, to any one occupant of the Asylum, except myself, until I took it out myself, after I was liberated. I did this, thinking that if I should be killed there, it might some time be found, and tell the cause of my sudden or mysterious death; or if ever I should be liberated, it might be a vindication of my sanity, and explain the reason for my being retained so long.

Besides hiding this duplicate, I put every article of my wardrobe in perfect order, before going to chapel prayers that night, feeling a kind of presentiment of coming evil. I also told my friends in this Seventh ward, that I hoped they would save my things from destruction, if they could not help me, in case of an encounter with the Doctor. As it proved, I went to the chapel as well prepared for the event as I could have been, had I known what was to happen. My attendant, Miss Eagle, of the Seventh ward, told me that the Doctor came directly to my room after he had disposed of me, and shut himself in there alone, a long time, while he searched my things all over to find every manuscript I had in my possession, which he took from me. Knowing that I had a duplicate of his reproof, he determined to find it and destroy it. But in this attempted robbery he failed.

He then ordered Miss Eagle to send all my things to the trunk room, and not allow me to take my bowl and pitcher and mirror, although they both were my own. He ordered my new attendant, Miss Tenny, to treat me just as she did the maniacs, who were now my sole companions—to let me have nothing to amuse myself with, by way of sewing, reading, or writing. My associates in this ward occupied themselves in screaming, fighting, running, hallooing, sitting on the floor when they sat at all in their own rooms, as chairs were not allowed in this ward. There was scarcely a patient in the whole ward who could answer a rational question in a rational manner.

This ward was then considered the worst ward in the house, inasmuch as it then contained some of the most dangerous class of patients, even worse than the Fifth in this respect, and in respect to filth and pollution, it surpassed the Fifth at that time. It is not possible for me to conceive of a more fetid smell, than the atmosphere of this hall exhaled. An occupant of this hall, would inevitably become so completely saturated with this most offensive effluvia, that the odor of the Eighth ward patients could be distinctly recognised at a great distance, even in the open air. I could, in a few moments after the Doctor put me in among them, even taste this most fetid scent at the pit of my stomach. Even our food and drink was so contaminated with it, we could taste nothing else, sometimes. It at first seemed to me, I must soon become nothing less than a heap of putrefaction. But I have found out that I can live, move, breathe, and have a being, where I once thought I could not.

This awful scent was owing to neglect in the management of the Institution. This was not the visitor's ward. Seldom any, but the Asylum occupants, found their entrance into this sink of human pollution. The patients were never washed all over, although they were the lowest, filthiest class of prisoners. They could not wait upon themselves any more than an infant, in many instances, and none took the trouble to wait upon them. The accumulation of this defilement

REMOVAL TO THE WORST WARD. 91

about their persons, their beds, their rooms, and the unfragrant puddles of water through which they would delight to wade and wallow in, rendered the exhalations in every part of the hall, almost intolerable.

To endure this contamination, I felt certain my daily cold water bath must be continued; but how could it be done, with only one tin wash basin for eighteen persons? I found that we all could hardly find time to wash even our hands and face, before breakfast, in this single dish, much less could it be spared long enough for one to take a full bath. My attendant tried to get my bowl and pitcher from the Seventh ward, to accomodate me, but the Doctor forbid it. I asked him for it. He refused me. I then claimed the right to take a new chamber vessel, that was brought into the ward for another purpose, and tied a scarlet string around the handle to distinguish it, and kept it under my bed for my washbowl. By this means, I was able to continue my daily bath, although I found my feelings of delicacy revolted from the gaze of from four to six room-mates, who occupied the same dormitory with myself.

The Doctor expressly forbid my having a room by myself, but compelled me to sleep in this dormitory for one year, where, each night, my life was exposed, by the violent hands of these maniacs. I have been obliged to call up my attendant, some nights, to save being killed by them. Still, the Doctor would not let her give me a room by myself. I have sometimes thought the Doctor put me there for the very purpose of getting me killed by these maniacs. I have been nearly killed several times, and I have appealed most earnestly to Dr. McFarland to save my life, but he would simply turn speechless away from me! I have also asked him to remove some of the most dangerous ones for my safety, and the only response would be, to bring in a more dangerous one.

I made no complaints, never expostulated with him, nor spoke a disrespectful or reproachful word to him, in vindication of my own rights. I never made any confession to him of wrong doing on my part, nor presented any plea for pardon or forgiveness. Neither did he ever utter one word of explanation to me, why he was pursuing this course of treatment towards me. Neither could any one about the building ever get him to give them any reason for this change towards me, except, "It is all for her good."

But to the credit of my attendants, the two sisters, Misses Tenny, and Mrs. Waldo, the matron, I am happy to add, they did not feel bound to co-operate in all the Doctor's plans to abuse and torment me. Indeed, the oldest Miss Tenny, openly and boldly refused to treat me as she did the maniacs. In her own language I can vindicate her, for her conduct corresponded with her words. One day, after sympathizing with me in my privations, she said, "Mrs. Packard, I shall not treat you as I do the other patients, notwithstanding the Doctor has ordered me to. I shall use my own judgment, and treat you as I think you deserve to be treated." And indeed, she did treat me like a sister. I do not now see how she could have done better by me than she did; and to her kindness, and tender sympathy, do I owe much, under God, for being able to escape the many dangers and trials, which enveloped me, and come out from among them, unharmed. The two Miss Tennys deserve much credit, also, for the reasonable and judicious treatment they bestowed upon the other patients in this ward. In fact, they were the first truly kind attendants I had then seen in the Asylum. They were the first I had found, who seemed to fear God, more than they did Dr. McFarland. Even the day following the Doctor's order to not let me leave the ward on any account, she took me to the trunk room herself, and asked me to select any articles from my wardrobe I wished, and let me take my sewing box, containing my knife, scissors, and spectacles, etc., and gave me a drawer in the dormitory table to keep them in, and put the key of it into my own pocket. This was a marked act of confidence on her part, for there were strict rules in this ward, that no knife or scissors be allowed in the ward, even in the hands of the attendants.

Mrs. Waldo, our matron, extended to me her practical

sympathy, by doing many things for my comfort, which the
Doctor forbid. She allowed me to use a covered box with a
cushioned seat upon it, as a substitute for my trunk, and she
bought me a metalic wash bowl after a while, which I used for
nearly two years. for myself alone ;-and by a little strategy,
she and Miss Tenny secured my mirror for our dormitory, as
there was no mirror of any kind, in the ward. But this
dauntless act well nigh cost me my document, for we had
hardly got it hung on to its nail, when one of the wild patients
seemed to be seized with a furious spite against it, and rushing up to the table beneath it, took article after article upon
the table, and threw against it with almost incredible rapid-
ity; but just before she had time to hurl the tumbler and
pitcher against it, one of my room-mates seized the mirror
from the nail, and rushed with it into another room, while the
fragments of the tumbler and pitcher were flying in all directions, and the table being upset with terrible violence. After
this, I kept my mirror hid between my beds, except when I
wished to use it, or let others use it. But I occasionally
found some of the maniacs had taken it from its hiding place,
and were using it as they pleased; but by the most gentle and
adroit coaxing, I got it back again, safely. I once recollect
of getting one to give it to me in exchange for an apple.
But this mirror, like myself, seemed destined to elude all
attacks upon its destruction. The document within it, and
the spirit within me, seemed alike invulnerable.

XIII.

My Occupation.

As my readers now find me located in my new position,
they may, perhaps, like to know how I occupied myself. As
it was in consequence of my defence of others' rights and
privileges that I had lost my own, I now felt impelled by the
same spirit, to make other's wants my care, rather than care

for myself, by neglecting them. Indeed, I have found that the exercise of this spirit, is, in reality, the best antidote I can find for an oppressed spirit. Paradoxical as it may seem, I think the best way to train ourselves to bear heavy burdens, is to bear the burdens of others. It now seems to me, that unless I had known how to practically apply this principle, I must have inevitably sunk under my burdens; but the elasticity of spirit which benevolent acts alone inspire, capacitates the spirit to rebound, where it would otherwise be crushed by the pressure put upon it. And moreover, I summoned the will-power also to my rescue. I determined I would not be crushed, neither would I submit to see others crushed. In other language, I determined to be a living reprover of the evils I saw consummated in this Asylum. I did not intend to defend one line of conduct with my tongue and pen, and endorse a different line by my actions. I knew that preaching godliness had far less potency for good, than practical godliness. I had already preached my sermon; now, all that I had to do, was to put its principles into practice. I had asked Dr. McFarland to ameliorate the condition of his patients; I now determined to aid him in this good work, to the fullest extent of my ability. Therefore, for months and years from this date, I worked for this object almost exclusively.

I found that the attendants were very negligent in their duties; still, I did not feel disposed to blame or reprove them for these neglects. I felt that this duty fell on the Superintendent, and as I had already given him the reproof which was his due, I felt that I had no right to teach his attendants, only by the silent influence of example. In short, I tried to fill up on my part the defects I saw on theirs.

I commenced this line of conduct on the Sabbath morning succeeding my removal. As I have said, the patients were in an exceedingly filthy condition, and therefore their personal cleanliness was plainly my first most obvious duty. This morning I commenced by coaxing as many of the patients as I could, to allow me to wash their face, neck and hands in a bowl of warm, clean, soft suds; and then I shampooed as many of their filthy "live" heads as I could find time to do before chapel service. When the Doctor visited the ward that morning, I can not forget the look of surprise he cast upon the row of clean faces and combed hair he witnessed on the side seats of the hall. Simply this process alone so changed their personal appearance, that it is no wonder he had to gaze upon them to recognize them. Their rough, tangled, flying and streaming hair looked, when I began, as if a comb had never touched them. He simply bowed to me and said, "Good morning, Mrs. Packard!" and then seated himself upon one of these seats, and silently watched my movements, while I pursued this my own chosen calling. Without even alluding to the losses he had subjected me to, I simply remarked, "Doctor, I find I can always find something to do for the benefit of others, and you have now assigned me quite a missionary field to cultivate!" "Yes," was his only response. He did not so much as ask me how I liked my new room, or my new associates! but after seeing me shampoo one or two of his patients, he arose and left the hall, speechless.

The next day, Monday morning, I commenced the slow work of reconstruction and recuperation of the human faculties in sober earnest. I first obtained from my accommodating attendant, a bowl of warm saleratus water and a quantity of castile soap, a soft cloth and two towels, and a bowl of clear soft water. I then took one patient at a time into her room alone, and there gently stripped her and gave her a thorough sponge bath of this saleratus and water and soap, and then rinsed them well off with the pure water. I then laid aside all her wet, filthy, saturated and offensive garments, and put clean ones on in their place. After combing her hair, I would introduce her into the ward as a neat, clean, tidy lady, who was going to be an example in these virtues to all others! being careful, however, to prove the truth of these compliments by tending upon her as I would my cleanly dressed infant. By vigilance on my part, her clothes might be kept comparatively clean and dry for two or three days, before another change would be necessary.

Having thus cleaned the occupant of a room, I then cleaned the room in the same manner, with the aid of a pail of strong saleratus and water and scrubbing brush, I would at length succeed in finding the coat of paint I was seeking for, which had to be done by dint of patient perseverance equal to that required to find the skin of its occupant. It is no exaggeration to say that I never before saw human beings whose skin was so deeply embedded beneath so many layers of dirt as those were. The part cleaned would contrast so strikingly with the part not cleaned, that it would be difficult to believe they belonged to the same race, if on different individuals.

But the scrubbing of the walls and the floor is not the only portion of the room to be cleaned, by any means. It was no insignificant task to put the bedstead and the bed into a suitable condition for a human being to occupy. In many instances, the husk mattress I found completely rotted through with constantly repeated showers upon it, and this rot had in most instances become as black as soot, and retained an effluvia most difficult to tolerate. With the aid of the Misses Tenny I had all these rotten beds removed and emptied, and the ticks washed; then I cut out the mouldied part, and supplied its place with new cloth, and had it filled again with fresh straw or husks, which completed this part of the business. The sheets and blankets then passed through the cleaning process; but the white counterpanes which covered up these filthy nests did not need cleaning. They were kept white and clean, by being folded up every night and laid upon the seats in the hall, and in the day time they were displayed upon the beds to advertise the neatness and comfort of the house and beds! But if a sick patient should chance to lie down upon one of these advertisers of neatness, the white spreads, she was liable to receive some of the severest punishments of this inquisitorial prison, for this great offence against the "display of the house."

The cleaning of one patient and one room, **together with** the waiting upon those I had cleaned, took one day's labor. And this I continued, day after day, for about three weeks, before I got these eighteen patients and their rooms all cleaned; and by this time the process needed to be repeated. This I continued to do for nearly one year, until others began to wake up to the necessity of doing likewise in other wards, as our ward was by this time reported to be the neatest and best kept ward in the whole house. And even the odor of it could not be surpassed in purity.

This contagion for amelioration extended even to the Trustees, and as the result, at Dr. McFarland's suggestion, each ward was subsequently furnished with a nice bathing tub, which the Trustees designed only for the comfort of the patients, as the Doctor urged the need now of the weekly bathing of all of the patients. But I am sorry to add, this great luxury, like the institution itself, has degenerated into the greatest torment to the patient. The bath room is regarded by the prisoners there as the "calaboose" used to be by the slave at the South.

The Doctor visited this ward almost every day, but never to ameliorate my condition, or that of any other prisoner, so far as I could see. He would see the great drops of sweat rolling off from my face, from the excessive exercise this scrubbing and mopping afforded me, but I do not recollect that he ever advised me to desist. But Miss Tenny has told me that he had said to her, "You must not let Mrs. Packard work too hard, for I am afraid her husband won't like it." I do not think the Doctor cared for this ameliorated condition of his prisoners; but he dared not oppose it directly, since the filthiness of the Eighth ward had become so proverbial, it became a source of apprehension lest these mephitic exhalations might breed a pestilence in the Hospital. The typhoid fever had raged there during the summer months preceding this expurgating process. During this sickness, the Doctor had assigned to my care some of these typhoid patients, whom I nursed and tended night and day. I made the shroud of Mrs. Hart, from Chicago, who died of this epidemic there.

Mrs. Hart had been a most unwilling prisoner for seven long years, and from all I can learn, I believe she has been a victim of marital cruelty, but never was insane. Her husband put her in without trial, and the Doctor took her on his testimony, and kept her to please him, all the while knowing, as I believe, that she was not insane. This is only one of many of those innocent victims, who have been falsely imprisoned for life, under that most barbarous law of Illinois, which suspends the personal liberty of married women, entirely upon the capricious will of the husband. I saw Mr. Hart, her husband, who came simply for appearances, as it seemed to me, to see her during her last sickness, but who became so very impatient for her death, that he could not stay to see her die, although it was almost certain she could not live two days longer, when he left. Thus, his wife, whom his will alone had deprived of her children, home, and liberty for seven years, could not have granted her dying request, that he stay by her to close her eyes, but left, and coolly ordered her body to be sent home to Chicago, by express, in a decent coffin, when she did die. I helped dress the corpse of the unfortunate victim. I saw her passed into the hands of four stranger men in the dead of night, and carried mournerless, and alone, to the depot, to be sent to her children and husband, at Chicago.

Oh! what reckless sundering of human ties are caused by this Insane Asylum system! These children are taught to regard their mother as a worthless being, because she had the cruel brand of insanity placed upon her by her husband, signed and sealed by a corrupt public servant, whom a blinded public were regarding as an almost infallible man. Thus have the holiest ties of nature, been most ruthlessly sundered by the perfidy of this corrupt Institution.

As I witnessed the sum of all our social evils culminating in this most corrupt Institution, I resolved, that here, henceforth, and forever, my occupation should be, to eradicate, expose, and destroy this sum of all human abominations—the Insane Asylum *system*, on its present basis.

XIV.

How I Obtained my Papers.

Before entering upon my Prison scenes, as delineated in my journal, it may gratify my readers to know how I obtained my Asylum papers, containing portions of my journal, and my bible class papers, to which I have already referred, although by so doing, I must go back a little in my narrative.

The greatest part of my Asylum journal I secured, by hiding it behind a false lining in my band box. One day I found a piece of wall paper, and I clandestinely sewed this into my band box for a lining, behind which and around the box I hid my papers. Some of them I hid between the black cloth and the board on the bottom of my satchel. I cut open the edge and scaled it off with a case knife, and after filling the pocket thus made, I sewed it up, where they were kept undiscovered. Some I hid between the millinet crown and the outside covering of my traveling bonnet. I encircled this crown with so many thicknesses of paper, that it sometimes caused the exclamation, "How heavy this bonnet is!" I never told, until I got out of the Asylum, in what the weight consisted.

These bible class papers I regarded as my only available means of self-defence from the charge of insanity, therefore I clung to them with great tenacity. I intended to make them the basis of my plea in self-defence before the jury which Mr. Comstock had told me I must have before committment. But if this trial should be evaded in any way, I intended to retain them, as my only armor of defence. During the three weeks that Mr. Packard left my room, I kept them hid under the head of my bed; but the Saturday previous to my abduction, I concluded to keep them henceforth about my person, I therefore made arrangements to put a pocket into my under skirt; but before I had completed it I was called off to attend to other duties. But Sabbath night, when I espied Mr. Packard so carefully and clandestinely searching into all my private apartments, I felt alarmed for the safety of my papers, thinking they might possibly be the object of his search. Therefore, until my pocket was completed, I put them into a small box, and hid them in the wardrobe of my own room, and Monday morning, when I. W. got up, I called him to my room, to tell him where I had hid them, that he might, if necessary, save them for me. Said I, "My son, these papers may be your mother's only means of self-defence, and unless we can evade Mr. Packard's search, he will deprive your mother of this last and only means of vindicating her sanity. Now, my son, if I am ever kidnapped and you can not defend me, be sure that you protect these papers, for they are next to defending me, so far as my reputation for sanity is concerned. I intend to-day to finish my pocket and carry them about my person."

"I will certainly regard your request, and protect your papers." Saying this, he kissed me and left, assuring me he should soon be back and take me to ride to Mr. Rumsey's. But before he returned, my kidnappers came and claimed my person, but allowed me no chance to take my papers with me. It seems Mr. Packard feared I should take them, therefore to prevent my having any opportunity to do so, he ordered Miss Rumsey not to leave me alone in my room one minute after the physicians left it. Notwithstanding I had only half bathed myself when he forced an entrance into my room with an ax through the window, I was compelled to flee into my bed, to prevent my introduction to my guests in a state of nudity, he would not allow me to be alone long enough to complete my ablution. I not only asked this privilege, but I reasoned with him on the impropriety of compelling me to appear in this condition before Miss Rumsey. But all to no purpose. My reasons and requests were all answered by his saying, "I don't think it is best for you to take your bath alone. I think it is best for Miss Rumsey to be in your room."

I felt conscious that his real reason was to prevent my getting my papers; and I dared not make the attempt to get them, feeling certain she would either force them from me, or report me to Mr. Packard for him to do it, and then they would be discovered, so that I. W. could never get them. But unwilling to go without them, I decided upon the use of a little strategy to obtain them. I concluded to make a practical prayer for the preservation of my sane reputation, by obtaining the privilege of secret prayer in my room before I was taken away, and thus get them. Therefore I requested to be left alone, for a short season, for my morning devotion, adding, "You know, Mr. Packard, it is my invariable practice to pray alone in my room before entering upon the duties of the day, and I can not be denied this privilege to-day when I am in so much need of God's help for the trials of to-day."

But no, this favor could not be allowed me, and the only reason he gave for refusing my request was, "I do not think it is best."

My next appeal was to Sheriff Burgess, but he only echoed Mr. Packard's denial in his own words, "We do not think it is best for you to be alone in your room."

Mr. Packard then said, "You may pray in your room, but your door must be open."

Of course this defeated the practical prayer I intended to have offered in secret, and I was obliged to leave without my papers. And when on board the cars, the reflection that I had not even one line with me in vindication of my sanity, greatly increased the mental burdens laid upon me.

My son I. W., true to his promise to protect my papers, if he could not protect me, hastened to my room to get the box, but lo, it was gone! and never was he allowed to know who took them, nor where they were hidden. Among these papers was my will and a note of $600, which Mr. Packard had given me for that amount of my patrimony money which my father had sent me a few years before. This note I have never seen, nor have I ever had one cent of the money it secured to me.

Mr. Packard's pile of stolen papers was increased by several additions Dr. McFarland made to it by robbing me of my private papers while in my prison, and sending them to Mr. Packard. After my liberation from prison, I tried various methods to obtain them, but all in vain, until I made him the following proposal: Mr. Packard had for some time been trying to induce me to sign a deed, so that he could sell some real estate, and I had objected, unless he should give me some equivalent for what he had already unjustly taken from me. This he would not do. He therefore went to Esquire La Brie, and took an oath that his wife was insane, so that he could sell the property without my signature. Finding my refusal was not going to save my right of dower, or prevent his selling the property, I proposed to him that I would sign the deed on condition that he would restore to me my papers. He accordingly called in Esquire La Brie to witness my signature, and in his presence he gave me my papers, as I had proposed. This signature was acknowledged as valid, although two days before Mr. Packard had taken an oath on the Bible, that I was insane, and thereby incompetent to sign a deed! By means of this perjury on his part, my papers were restored to me.

XV.

Evidences of My Insanity.

When a person is once accused of being insane, the reflective mind naturally inquires, how is their insanity manifested? This question was often put to Mr. Packard, and knowing all would not be satisfied by his simple assertion, he was obliged to manufacture his proof or evidence to satisfy this class.

One evidence on which he placed great reliance was, "that his wife invited Universalist ministers to his house for entertainment during a Convention." Yes, I do plead guilty to this charge. I did offer the hospitalities of our house to ministers of this class under these circumstances: It was at Mount Pleasant, Iowa, that this Convention met and dedicated a new church, located a few rods from our house. To my great surprise Mr. Packard proposed to attend this dedication, which he did, and I accompanied him, and listened to a sermon of high literary merit, and to me, a morally sound and logical argument was for the first time presented to my mind, that God's infinite love and wisdom were sure guarantees of the world's redemption. The argument was this—"Where there is both will and power to cure, no evil can endure."

The church was crowded to overflowing, and the Convention being larger in numbers than their own people could conveniently accommodate, the Chairman of the Committee of Arrangements presented this fact to the congregation, and very kindly solicited their neighbors and friends, who could do so, to take them into their families, and all such were asked to leave their names at the stand as they passed out.

Since but a short time previous, the Congregationalist society had so large an Association they had been obliged to solicit the hospitalities of other denominations, and as I had called upon our Universalist neighbors to accommodate us, I instinctively felt that it was only paying a debt of honor and justice to offer now to accommodate their ministers. Therefore, as I passed down the aisle by my husband's side, I whispered to him that I could accommodate two. "Shall I give in our names for two?" said I. He paid no attention to me or my inquiry, but passed on by the stand without speaking to any one. Seeing it devolved upon me to make the offer, if made at all, I stepped up and gave in my name for two and passed on and overtook Mr. Packard a few steps from the door, and taking his arm said, "I have offered to take two, and I must now hasten home and prepare for them." He made no reply whatever, but his silence said, "I don't approve of it." Therefore I reasoned in defence of the act as an act of justice, etc.; and besides as all the labor of serving the tables, as well as the services of the maid of all work devolved upon me, I felt that if I was willing to do all this extra work, no one could reasonably object, as I thought. But fortunately for me, I had hardly commenced my preparations when the Chairman called and informed me that their friends were all provided for, so that my service was not needed; and after kindly thanking me for my hospitable offer he left me, with the feeling on my part of having done my duty, and here the subject was dropped.

But years after, to my surprise and horror, he brought this act up as evidence of my insanity! and his argument against me was, that if they had come, he might, in courtesy, have been obliged to have asked a Universalist minister to ask a blessing at his table, or even to lead in family prayers! and, only think! this too, in the presence of his children!

Another evidence of insanity he alleged against me, was that I gave a dollar towards building a Catholic church in Manteno. I plead guilty to this charge also. We had a very kind christian neighbor in Mr. La Brie, who was a Catholic from principle, in the same sense that Mr. Packard was Presbyterian from principle; that is, both had been educated to feel that their own was the true church, and therefore both were conscientious in sustaining them. Mr. Packard was trying to build up Presbyterianism by his efforts, and he, of course, expected to be paid for doing this work; but the society was new and feeble, and therefore in their struggles to raise his salary, the collector, Deacon Smith, called on Mr. La Brie to help them, and he with true christian charity, contributed yearly to Mr. Packard's support.

One evening I called on Mr. La Brie, to ask his opinion respecting my article on "Spiritual Gifts," which our bible class had refused to hear, and he very patiently listened and commented upon it. He expressed his opinion that it was a sound, logical, and invincible argument in favor of what the

Catholics had always considered the true view. This assertion very much surprised me, as I had always been taught to believe that the Catholics were a deluded people, believing nothing but absurdities; but now, when I found out that I had alone studied out a view of truth which they had always endorsed, and one to which our church would not so much as listen, lest it might be found to be heretical, I began to ask where religious toleration is to be found, in the Presbyterian or the Catholic church? I had here found the christian spirit of charity and religious toleration manifested to a far higher degree in Mr. La Brie, the Catholic, than in Deacon Smith, the Presbyterian.

I therefore came to the conclusion that there were not only truths in the Catholic church, but also good christians in it. As the scales of bigotry thus fell from my own eyes, I could see that the Catholics were just as conscientious in sustaining their church, as we were in sustaining ours; and finding what struggles they were making to pay their debts, I felt moved to manifest my new feeling of toleration, by giving him one dollar towards helping them liquidate their debt. And now for this act of toleration, I am called insane; for Mr. Packard argues that I should not thus be building up this "mother of all abominations," this "seat of bigotry and intolerance," unless I had lost my reason. The reason which remains in exercise in my organization teaches me that there are truths in all denominations and parties, and there are errors in all, and our reason is only normally exercised, in my opinion, when we use it in separating the good and true, from the evil and false.

Again, he says I call him the "son of perdition." I shall not plead guilty to this charge, for it is not strictly true. I have oftentimes tried to convince Mr. Packard that he was not a "totally depraved" man. But all in vain. He seems strangely determined to cling to this crowning virtue of his christian character, with a death-like grapple! It seems that all his hopes of heaven are built upon this foundation stone! In his creed, there can be no real virtue without it. So tenaciously does he cling to this position as the only redeeming trait of his character, that I have sometimes been tempted to say, " Well, Mr. Packard, I do not know but what you are what you claim to be, a totally depraved man, or the 'son of perdition,' for whom there is not found a ransom." When I come to admit his own position, and express an agreement of opinion with him, on this point, then he uses this concession as a weapon against me, as though I had accused him of being the "son of perdition."

Again, he accuses me of punishing the children for obeying their father. This is not true. I never did punish a child for obeying their father, but I have sometimes been compelled to enforce obedience to their father's authority, by interposing my own. Indeed, I think my children could never have reverenced their father's authority, without the maternal influence to inspire it, by requiring subjection to it; **for the fitful, unstable, and arbitrary government he exercised over them, was only fitted, naturally, to inspire contempt, rather than reverence.** But Mr. Packard has tried to undermine my authority, by telling the children they need not obey their mother, and I have been obliged to counteract this influence, by enforcing obedience, sometimes, where he has interposed and forbid their obeying me. This is what he calls punishing the children, for obeying their father, whereas, it is only requiring them to obey their mother.

Another evidence, and one which his sister, Mrs. Dole, presented to the jury on my trial, was that I once made biscuit for dinner, when I had unexpected company call, and had not bread enough for the table. The reason why this was mentioned, was because the counsel insisted on evidence being produced from my own actions, independent of opinions that I was insane, and she having been more intimate in our family than any other person, was compelled, under oath, to state what she saw. Being unwilling to own she had seen nothing insane in my conduct, and being bound to speak only the truth, she told this circumstance as the **greatest act of insanity she had noticed.**

But I trust my readers will be satisfied with this array of evidence which my persecutors bought against me, if I only add the sum total of proof as brought by Dr. Brown, an M. D. of Kankakee City, whom Mr. Packard bought to say I was insane, for the purpose of getting me incarcerated again for life in Northampton, Mass. This Doctor had left the wheelwright business and studied just long enough to experience the sophomorical feeling that his opinion would be entitled to infallibility, especially if given in the high-flown language of an expert; therefore, the last of fifteen reasons why he considered me insane, was in these words, as taken down by the reporter at the time, viz: "The fifteenth reason which I have written down, on which I have founded my opinion that she is insane is, her viewing the subject of religion from the osteric standpoint of christian exegetical analysis, and agglutinating the polysymthetical ectoblasts of homogeneous asceticism!"

XVI.

The Attendant who Abused Me.

Mrs. De La Hay, wife of Dr. De La Hay, of Jacksonville, was the only one of all the employees at the Asylum whom the Doctor could influence to treat me personally like an insane person. She has threatened me with the screen room, and this threat has been accompanied with the flourish of a butcher knife over my head, for simply passing a piece of Johnny cake through a crack under my door, to a hungry patient who was locked in her room to suffer starvation, as her discipline for her insanity. Besides threatening me with the screen room, she threatened to jacket me for speaking at the table.

One day, after she had been treating her patients with great injustice and cruelty, I addressed Mrs. McKonkey, who sat next to me at the table, and in an undertone remarked,

"I am thankful there is a recording angel present, noting what is going on in these wards," when Mrs. De La Hay, overhearing my remark, exclaimed, in a very angry tone, "Mrs. Packard, stop your voice! if you speak another word at the table I shall put a straight jacket on you!"

Mrs. Lovel, one of the prisoners replied, "Mrs. De La Hay, did you ever have a straight-jacket on yourself?"

"No, my position protects me! but I would as soon put one on Mrs. Packard as any other patient, 'recording angel' or no 'recording angel!' and Dr. McFarland will protect me in doing so, too."

On another occasion, hearing the sound of conflict in our ward, I opened my door, and saw Mrs. De La Hay seize Miss Mary Rollins, a prisoner, by her throat, and Mary pulled the hair of Mrs. De La Hay with as firm a grip, as she held on to her victim's throat. I, fearing the result, rallied help and parted them, when I found poor Mary's throat bleeding from an opening Mrs. De La Hay had made in it with her finger nails. I took a piece of my own linen, and bound it up, wet in cold water; and this cloth I still retain, red with the blood of this innocent girl, as proof of this kind of abuse in Jacksonville Insane Asylum.

It was my defence of the prisoners from Mrs. De La Hay's unreasonable abuse which led her to treat me as she did. It was not long after this defence of Mary Rollins, that I heard loud screams and groans issuing from a dormitory, when I and my associates rushed into the room to see what was the matter. There we found one of the prisoners lying upon her back, with Mrs. De La Hay over her, trying to put on a straight-jacket. This lady was screaming from physical agony, on account of an injury Mrs. De La Hay had inflicted upon her a few days before, when she burst a blood vessel on her lungs, by strangling her under the water. This plunging she had inflicted as her punishment for not obeying her when she told her to stop talking. And now this wounded spot on her lungs had become so inflamed, that the pressure of Mrs. De La Hay's hands upon it, together with the stricture

of the straight-jacket, caused her to scream from agony.
I inquired, "What is the matter? Why are you putting
the straight-jacket on that woman?"

Without answering my question, she exclaimed in a loud
voice, "Mrs. Packard, leave this room!" I backed out over
the threshold, still looking towards her victim, and repeated
my question, "Why are you putting her into the straight-
jacket? What has she done?" This time, she left her victim,
and came at me in a great rage, and seizing my arm, she said
"Go to your room." As she was leading me unresistingly
along, one of the prisoners took hold of her arm, and exclaimed, "Mrs. DeLaHay, do you know what you are about?
Do you know that is Mrs. Packard you are locking up?"

"Yes, I do, and I am obeying Dr. McFarland in what I am
doing. He tells me not to let Mrs. Packard interfere with
the management of the patients."

She led me to my room, where I was locked up until the
next morning. While there, I heard the Doctor's footsteps
in the hall, and I heard Mrs. DeLaHay tell him why she had
locked me up, and he sanctioned the act by leaving me locked
up, without coming to my room at all.

The next day I ascertained, that she was disciplining this
dormitory prisoner with the straight-jacket, because she had
found her upon her bed, trying to rest herself from the pains
this rupture on her lungs was causing her.

So far as Mrs. DeLaHay's treatment of me was concerned,
I do not consider her so much to blame, as Dr. McFarland
was. Unlike my other attendants, she was too weak to resist
the Doctor's influence over her, and therefore carried out his
wishes, while the others would not. Had my other attendants carried out his wishes, my Asylum discipline would have
been as severe as the other prisoners' were.

It was a very noticeable fact, that the very means Mrs.
DeLaHay used to secure and retain the Doctor's favor, by
abusing me, was the very excuse the Doctor made for discharging her; and the boast that her *position* protected her
from the straight-jacket, did not prove a very defensive armor,

for in a few months from the time she uttered it, she became insane and a tenant of Jacksonville Poor House!

XVII.

"Let Dr. McFarland Bear his own Sins!"

One day while in my room, I heard an uncommon noise in our ward, when, on suddenly opening my door, I saw nearly opposite, Dr. McFarland just as he had released his grasp of Bridget's throat, who had been struggling for her life, to avoid strangulation from his grasp. I did not see the Doctor's hand upon her throat, but I did see what she said was the marks of his thumb on one side of her throat, and of his fingers upon the other, and Bridget had a sore neck for some days afterwards, in consequence of it. Bridget, the prisoner's account of the matter is this; the Doctor entered the ward just after a prisoner had broken a chair, and the pieces were still lying upon the floor. Bridget stood by while Mrs. DeLaHay explained the case to the Doctor, simply as a listener. She had had nothing to do with breaking the chair. Mrs. DeLaHay also stood by, waiting the Doctor's orders. The Doctor turned to Bridget and said, " Pick up those pieces!"

"I shan't do it! I didn't come here to work! It is your attendants' business to do the work. He then, without saying a word, seized me by the throat, and the noise you heard was my struggle for deliverance."

"Why, Bridget!" said I, "How dare you speak so to the Doctor, and why didn't you obey him?"

"I wouldn't have done it if he had killed me! I didn't come here to do his work, and I wont do it!"

This was Bridget's account, and it was confirmed, not only by all the witnessing patients, but also by Mrs. DeLaHay herself. Bridget was a quiet, inoffensive prisoner. I never saw her evince anything but reasonable conduct, when she was reasonably dealt by, and she was one of my dormitory companions for many months. She was always obedient to reasonable commands, but like human beings generally, she felt that she had rights of her own, which ought to be respected.

Bridget has immortalized herself in my memory, by the lesson in theology she taught me the first night I occupied the room with her. It was under these circumstances. As was my uniform practice, I kneeled in front of my bed that night, before I got into it, to offer my silent prayer for protection and help, when Bridget, from the opposite bed, exclaimed, "Pray aloud!" I obeyed.

This being the first night of my consignment to this loathsome place, I had to struggle mentally, against the indulgence of revengeful feelings towards the Doctor, for the injustice of the act; therefore, to crush them out, I tried to pray for his forgiveness, and in doing so I made use of the expression, "Lord, I am willing to even bear his punishment for him, if, by this means he can be forgiven for this act of injustice towards me." Just at this point, Bridget interrupted me by exclaiming with great vehemence, "Let Dr. McFarland bear his own sins."

I am now of Bridget's mind entirely. Her sermon converted me from the theological error of vicarious suffering. I have never since asked my Father to let me bear the punishment of any other brother or sister, due them for their own sins; neither have I asked any other intelligence to bear the punishment due me for my own sins.

XVIII.

Attempted Reconciliation with Mr. Packard.

The last letter I wrote Mr. Packard, I told him plainly on what conditions I would return to him. But it seems Dr. McFarland was not willing we should be reconciled on such a basis, for he would not send the letter, although Mr. Packard was calling most persistently for letters from me. But he called in vain, as I said in this letter. I should never answer any more of his letters, nor write him again until this letter was answered. He begged of the Superintendent to get me to write, and he would show me these letters, when I would tell him, "When I get a reply to my last letter I will write, but not before, and if you, Doctor, ever wish me to write him again, send that letter, first." But like the deaf adder, he heard as though he heard not, and the ever repeated question would come, "*why* don't you write to Mr. Packard?" I finally told him "If you cannot understand my reason, and will not report it to Mr. Packard, he must ever remain in ignorance of the reason I do not write him."

But it seems he never communicated these messages, nor would he send the letter, but simply told him, "I cannot persuade her to write you." Finally, Dr. Sturtevant informed me, that Mr. Packard had wished him to try to persuade me to write him, and he asked me why I could not grant his request. I told him I had written, and the Doctor had the letter but he would not send it, and just as soon as that letter was satisfactorily answered, I would open a free correspondence with him. Whether the Doctor allowed him to report my only true reason I know not, but after that, the Doctor told me he had burned my letter, because he considered it "worthless." I know not whether this was the letter he thus disposed of, or some of my many others I had given him to send to other friends. This fact I do know, that so long as my letters were sent through *this* post-office, my friends never received them, with one or two exceptions. My journal contains copies of all these letters, which I have shown to those family friends to whom they were written, and they tell me they never received them.

Now here is a branch of the United States mail established within this public Institution, and the mail carrier transports it regularly, protected by lock and key, and yet I could not get a letter into it, nor get one from it, although directed directly to me. Indeed, I felt most keenly the truth of the remark the mail carrier made me, when I once met him and enquired if he had any letters for me. Said he, "Mrs. Packard, you have just as good a right to your mail as any other citizen of the United States." Why then is not this right granted me? Because one man chooses to say, " I will superintend this inalienable right, and usurp it when I please, and no one can harm me in so doing." I ask this Republican Government, is this protecting the post office rights of *all* its citizens? Who has a right to say, while I am not a criminal, " You shall be restricted in this right. You shall have this right usurped and ignored to any extent, as a *punishment* for being numbered among the most afflicted class of American citizens!" These terrible despotisms would be a far less dangerous institution, were the boarders allowed their post office rights.

If this right had not been usurped, in my case, it might have saved one family from the wreck of disunion. But Dr. McFarland would not allow a reasonable basis of reconciliation to be even presented for his consideration. Why was this? Was he unwilling there should be a reconciliation? Why should he wish to stand between me and my husband? These questions I leave my readers to answer. He *talked* as though he wished I would go to my husband, but he *acted* as though he had determined to make an impassable gulf between us. Well, if my husband will voluntarily resign his right to be the protector of his own wife, exclusively into the hands of a stranger man, can he blame this man for misusing this irresponsible trust? This voluntary resignation of the marital right into the absolute, irresponsible control of another, is an unnatural act, and therefore must be deleterious in its consequences. Dr. McFarland had become an adept in this nefarious work, and therefore he found ways and means of disbanding this happy minister's family, forever. Although Mr. Packard is not responsible for Dr. McFarland's sins, yet, like the drunkard, he is responsible for allowing this exposure to exist. He should have exercised some sort of supervision over his own wife's destiny, so far, at least, as to retain his own rights unmolested. So should the State exercise such a supervision over their own Institution, as not to allow their own State rights to be trampled under foot by it, as it now does, in suffering the dearest of all human rights to be utterly ignored by it.

The following are the terms I tried to send to my husband as the basis of a just union—the only kind of union that would ever receive my sanction again.

"1st. Mr. Packard must make the confession as public as he has made the offence, that his wife has never given him any cause for regarding, or treating her as an insane person.

2nd. He must allow me the unmolested exercise of my own rights of opinion, and conscience, and post office rights.

3rd. He must allow me to hold my own property in **my** own name, and subject to my own control.

4th. He must allow me to control my own children with a mother's authority, so far as the mother's province extends.

5th. He must allow me to be the head of my own household duties, and the mistress of my own hired girl.

6th. The attempted usurpation of either of these inalienable rights of a married woman, shall be considered as a dissolution of the Union."

I know such stipulations serve rather to ignore a husband's protection, as indeed they do; but where neither love nor reason will hold a man to be the protector of these, his wife's rights, what can the wife of such a man do, without some such stipulation, or laws, by which her identity, as a woman, can be maintained? The first is only virtually acknowledging my identity or accountability; that is, I am not a chattel, or an insane person, but a being, after I am married, as well as before; and unless a man can hold me upon a higher plane than the principle of common law places me upon, I am not willing to enter the marriage union. The law says I am a non-existent being after marriage, but God says I am an existent and accountable one still; therefore I claim the recognition of this higher law principle, or I compromise with this injustice by this act of disloyalty to myself.

The comclusion of my last letter to Mr. Packard, dated

April 28, 1861, ends thus: "And ere we finally part, allow me to call to your recollection that most important period of your life, when, at the altar of your God, in the presence of your fellow witnesses, you solemnly vowed to love your wife, to comfort her, to honor her, and keep her in sickness and in health, for better and for worse, in poverty and riches, and forsaking all others, to keep thou only unto her, so long as both should live. Let me ask you, have you kept this solemn vow? Your lost Elizabeth."

About this time I had a letter from Mr. Packard, wherein he lays his plans before me, and asks my advice! His plans were to break up the family and put out the children, and asks me to whom he shall give my babe, and to whom he shall give my daughter to bring up, and such like questions! But not a single intimation is expressed that the mother would ever be allowed the right to rear her own offspring. No, not even a wish was expressed that he hoped I might ever be able or capable of doing so; yet he could ask the counsel and advice of this *non compos* on these most important matters of vital interest!!

He then portrays the present condition of my family in facts like these. He says, Elizabeth has had a fall and hurt her side, so that it pains her most of the time, and yet does all the work for the family, except when her aunt Dole comes and helps a day occasionally." Poor child! how her mother longs to embrace her, and sympathize with her as she used to in my sorrows. How can a father put upon this child of eleven years, the cares of a woman—the care of a babe, in addition to the care of a family, while she needs to attend school! O how much inconvenience some men will willingly endure, to crush a married woman into that position of nonentity, which the common law of marriage assigns her.

I. W. too is feeling almost discouraged. He is so gentle in his disposition, he can not live without his mother's sympathy. O, my darling boy, be patient. God's time to help us is not yet come. I know it is hard for thy tender heart to wait so long. I can hardly bear it myself. Patient waiting is the hardest virtue for me to exercise. I had much rather work and toil than wait. But I will surmount all obstacles, and conquer all my impulsive feelings, by schooling them into entire submission to all God's appointments. If we could see all Gods plans as God sees them, we should be satisfied.

While these reflections were passing through my mind, Dr. McFarland called at my room and remarked, " Well, Mrs. Packard, what of the Manteno letter?" I replied, " the family are all going to destruction ; and his plan is to present such a view to my mind, as will induce me, for my children's sake, to plead to go home. He is trying to make me say " O, husband do take me home ! if you only will, I will think, speak and act just as you please to have me, and will never venture to think for myself again !' But his plan fails entirely." I shall never give him a chance to put me off a second time.

Then came his usual inquiry, " Have you a letter to send ?" I then told him, " Sir, do you think I shall submit to be thus trifled with? you know you will not send the letter I want you to send."

XIX.

Letter to my Children sent to the Wash-tub.

Among my Asylum papers I find a copy of a letter I wrote my children on some cotton underwaists, which I tried to send by Miss Wilson, of Kankakee city. As all communication with my children was cut off by the authority of Dr. McFarland, I was led to resort to strategy to secure this end. Therefore I procured some nicely dressed bleached cotton, and embroidered my daughter some double underwaists, on which I could easily and legibly pencil a long communication, such as my feelings prompted, hoping thus to bring myself to their recollection, so that I might not become an object of indifference to them. The Doctor knew that I was making these waists for her, and it seems he suspected the plan which might thus open some kind of communication between us, therefore as Miss Wilson was leaving, as a discharged patient, for her home in Kankakee, he, knowing that my Manteno home was only twelve miles from there, took her aside and asked her if she had any letter from me with her. She replied that she had no letter. "Have you anything from Mrs. Packard to her children?" "Yes, I have some waists for her daughter, which I promised to take to her." "Let me see them," responded the Doctor.

She then took them from her bosom, where she had placed them for concealment, and handed them to the Doctor. He unfolded them and saw the penciling on the inside, and after reading it, ordered them to the laundry to be washed and ironed before they could be sent! thus thinking he had swept the letter into oblivion. But his sagacity was outwitted by his prisoner this time, for if the exultant Doctor felt that all traces of my intelligence and sanity had been obliterated by the destruction of my letters, he will now see he was mistaken, when he sees this printed copy was preserved to be my passport to the world, of the state of his prisoner's mind while behind his dead-locks, and numbered among his "hopelessly insane maniacs."

INSANE ASYLUM, June 20, 1861.

MY BELOVED CHILDREN: So long as we are sure we have conscience and God on our side we have nothing to fear, although we are maligned by those who deny that conscience is designed as our guide. Let those who dare to disregard this silent monitor do so; but you, my children, will with me, dare to "serve the Lord," won't you? For it is only fidelity to its dictates which the Lord requires as his service. You are in danger of losing your souls by contact with those who encourage you to set aside conscience as your guide to heavenly happiness. In this net of false doctrines, Satan is ensnaring guileless souls, and leading them unawares into captivity to himself. Do, children, be warned, and escape this snare before it is too late.

But, children, since we can not secure the safety of **any** soul in opposition to their freedom, I rejoice that God does not hold us absolutely responsible for any soul but our own. To save ourselves depends upon ourselves; and he who is fully determined to "work out his own salvation with fear and trembling," is the only one who will experience this salvation. Children, do right in everything, whether you are praised or blamed, and you will certainly secure a crown of righteousness, and so long as you continue to do right, no one can take it from you. But one sin, one wrong act, may forfeit it forever; as only a small stream may drown one if he lies prostrate in it. O, beware of little sins, little deviations from rectitude, truth, honesty, uprightness, from kindness, from forbearance, from patience, from forgiveness, from charity. Encourage the very incipient beginnings of repentance on the part of offenders, by showing that your heart yearns and longs to meet it with forgiveness, with God-like forgiveness, bestowed on the gospel ground of repentance.

But, children, I fear you will think mother is preaching you a sermon, instead of writing a letter. Pardon me, if I have burdened you thus, for you know this is not your mother's way to teach you Christ's religion. Her way has been to practice godliness, and thus endeavor to be a "living epistle known and read of all men." But being absent, I am under the necessity of taking this method of instructing you.

Your mother is doing here as she did at home, trying to secure her happiness in doing right; although by so doing, I often offend others by becoming thus a "terror to the evil doer, as well as a praise of them that do well."

I can not express how much I regret the course your father has taken in separating me from your society and sympathy. But he is alone answerable for a great wrong by so doing. O, how I do rejoice now that I never wronged that man. I beg of you to do the same. Keep clear of guilt, however much he may tempt you. Remember, that to be angry, is but to punish yourself for another's fault. Love yourselves too well to do it, for you can not be really happy if you sin in the least thing. I do feel deeply sorry you have so desolate a home. But be patient, and all will be right some time. Never do the least thing but what you would be willing the whole world should know of it, for even your motives will all be revealed and exposed, either to your shame or your glory.

This fact rejoices my heart; for could the world see my heart as it is, as God sees it, naught but love and good will to all mankind, to every individual, could be found there. Time will develop that even my persecutors can not find a truer friend to them than I am—none more ready and impatient to forgive them, if they will but repent.

Don't be discouraged or disheartened, although the darkness which envelops us is so dense as to be felt, for these clouds are about to break in blessings on our heads. "Behind a frowning Providence he hides a smiling face." Do your routine of duties faithfully, as you used to do when I was your guardian, and God will take care of our destiny. I do fully believe he is now working for us, in the best possible manner. When we do meet, shan't we have enough to talk about? Won't we have "good talking times," as you used to say, when you sat in a circle about me, to hear me tell you true stories about my childhood? But good by, for the present. Your loving mother,

E. P. W. P.

XX.

How I obtained my first Writing Paper.

On March 9th, 1861, I was allowed to pack the trunk of one of my most intimate associates in my ward, Mrs. Betsey Clarke, who was to leave the next morning with her son, who had come for her. While packing it I had the good fortune to find four sheets of letter paper which had escaped the supervisor's notice. My good friend readily consented to let me have it in exchange for some articles of my wardrobe which she needed, and thus I, an Asylum prisoner, became the honest owner of four sheets of paper! a prize almost invaluable to me.

Hitherto all my efforts to obtain a sheet of paper had been futile, since the Doctor had given a general order to all the employees not to let me have paper or stationery of any kind after he had consigned me to this maniac's hall. I had written before this time on tissue paper, margin of newspapers, cotton cloth, or brown paper and such like, and had handed clandestinely letters written on these materials to the trustees and Dr. Sturtevant, our chaplain, and retained copies of the same on the same materials where I now find them With these helps I had kept a private journal, too, from which the facts of this book are compiled. Now, with these three sheets, I felt, under the circumstances, richer than any fortune could have made me. I wrote with a pencil very fine, so that I wrote two or three times the number of written lines as were ruled, so that I put a wonderful amount of matter on a very small surface.

Mrs. Hosmer, the sewing room directress, knowing how eagerly I watched her sewing-room to get such writing materials, ventured to try an experiment to gratify this wish on my part. Being a strict observer of all the rules of the house, she could not aid me in this desire without the Doctor's consent. She therefore bought a pocket diary, and asked Dr. McFarland's permission to make me a present of it on "New Year's." He consented, and I thus became the honest owner of another treasure of inestimable value. I used this most faithfully for one entire year, and had just written my final entry for the last day of December, and was just returning it into my bosom, its safe hiding place for one whole year, when lo! my door was suddenly and unexpectedly pushed open by the Doctor in his velvet slippers; he thus caught me, before my treasure was out of sight. He sprang towards me and seized it forcibly from my hand, before I could get it into my bosom, and sitting down began to read aloud from it, in spite of my protests against his seeing my private meditations. He made fun of some portions; others he tore spitefully, from the book, saying as he did so *"that is a lie!"* I begged that he would return it without tearing it. But he heeded nothing I said, either in defence of its truth, or of my claim to it, as by his consent I had obtained it. But instead, put it into his vest pocket, and walked off with it. This is the last I ever saw of this part of my Asylum diary. My journal covering this period is complete.

XXI.
An Honorable act in Dr. McFarland.

Mrs. Sullivan, a sane woman, was put in here by her drunken husband, on the plea of insanity. She was brought handcuffed, and half of the hair pulled out of her head. Of course the husband's testimony must be credited, for who could desire more to protect a woman than he? Yes, Mr. Sullivan, the warm-hearted Irishman, showed his regard for his wife in the same manner that Mr. Packard, and many other husbands do, by legally committing her to Dr. McFarland's protection, who, so far as my knowledge extends, has never yet been true to this sacred trust.

This quick tempered Irishman had a quarrel with his wife, because she asserted her inalienable right to a pair of new shoes, and he being the stronger of the two in physical force, got her handcuffed, and pulled out the hair from half her head with his own hand, and forced her in here as soon as the "forms of law" could be gone through with. And what could Mrs. Sullivan do in self-defence? All her representations would be listened to as the ravings of a maniac! What is her testimony worth after the "forms of law" have been gone through with, proving her insanity? Mrs. Sullivan is legally entered as an insane person, on legal testimony; and now the Doctor is shielded in doing what he pleases with her, for what is an insane person's testimony worth? Nothing. Thus shielded, he applies his instruments of torture to this oppressed bleeding heart, for the benevolent purpose of making her willing to return to her husband, and yield unanswering obedience to this martial subjection! Yes, his benevolent plan is at length achieved, and he soon succeeds in making her so much more wretched and forlorn then before, that her former woes and wrongs sink into oblivion in comparison, and she begins to cry and beg to go home. "O, take me back to my children and husband, and I will bless you forever." Now his patient is recovering! O, what an astonishing cure! "How much that great Dr. McFarland knows more than any other man the secret of curing the insane wife!"

But the cure must be sure and permanent, before her case is represented as fit for removal. She has not yet performed her share of unrequited labor for the State of Illinois, as its slave; and if she is a good and efficient workman, there may be weeks, months, years of imprisonment yet before her, ere her cure is complete! Now the doctor is the only competent one to report her case to her friends or husband. No attendant's report can be relied upon, much less the prisoner herself. All communication is cut off, and the slave has naught to do but to work and suffer in silent, mute submission to her prison keepers. She dare not utter a complaint, lest the tortures be again resumed. Her children may sicken and die, but she must know nothing about them. Indeed, she must be dead as to earth life, until her share of slave toil is completed. And if very useful as a slave, she may possibly get the diploma of "hopelessly insane" attached to her name as an offset for these many years of slavery! And then the friends solace themselves, that the very best means of cure have been used, since none so skillful as the learned Dr. McFarland can be found any where; and although they deplore the fate of an all wise Providence, yet, to Dr. McFarland their heartfelt gratitude will be most signally due, for the kind, humane treatment he bestowed upon her, by having done all that human ingenuity could devise, to cure her! A true and faithful picture of many a real case in this Asylum.

But how did Mrs. Sullivan's case come out? After a time, the thought of her poor, defenceless, unprotected children, with none but a drunken father to care for them, pressed so fearfully upon her maternal sympathies, that she ventured to plead to go back to them again. But in vain! No plea can compassionate the heart of her present protector. Her tears, her sighs, her entreaties, her arguments, fall unheeded and apparently unheard upon his ear, for he will not stop to hear a patient's story, however rational or consistent—yea, the more rational the more unheeded, apparently. She is then sent to the wash room or ironing room, and sewing room, and compelled to work to drown her sorrow or stifle its utterance. But what if her children do need her services more than the State? What does Dr. McFarland care for her children, or for the fate of a mother who has been cast off by her husband? Nothing. He cares for his own selfish interests, and nothing else. If to his view his advantage is gained, he will send her home; if not, he will keep her at work for the State; for the laws of his own suggesting protect him from all harm, no matter how much he harms the prisoners.

After months of faithful labor, he found the tide of the house was setting against him, by keeping this sane woman so long from her family, and when he dared not resist this influence longer, he sent to her husband to take her home; but he would not come for her. And now comes the honorable act on the part of the Doctor. *He lent her money and sent her home alone.* A few days after I ventured to congratulate the Doctor on doing so noble a deed, adding, "If what I have been told was true, you have represented her in the discharge as one who has been falsely represented as insane." This creditable part of the representation he indignantly denied, saying, "No, she came here insane, was cured, and sent home."

"No, Dr. McFarland, she did not come here insane; she came here an abused woman—shamefully abused by a drunken husband. She needed protection, but not punishment, such as you have bestowed upon her. But no, the 'lords of creation' must be protected! or oppressed woman will rise and assert her rights, and man then will fail to keep her down." What will men do, when this Government protects the married women in their right to themselves? O, when this great Woman Subjector, Dr. McFarland, is exposed, where will these men send their wives to get them "broke in?" O! where?

XXII.

Married Women Unprotected.

I came here in defence of the same principle that Mrs. Sullivan did, with this difference; she used her right of self-defence in a different manner from what I did. She used physical force in resisting usurpation; I did not. I never did, nor never will quarrel with any one. I have followed Christ's direction, "If thy brother smite thee on the one cheek, turn to him the other also." Yes, when my husband, only once however, has ventured in his insane anger to lay violent hands upon me, I have just quietly yielded, saying, while his clenched fist was threatening me, "Yes, kill me if you desire to, I shall make no resistance—my natural life is of too little value to me, to defend it at the risk of injuring you." By thus yielding, his reason was restored to him, and he would not harm me.

Mrs. Sullivan pursued a different mode of self-defence, but the issue is just the same in both cases. Our husbands, both succeeded in getting us entered here on the plea of insanity, and I, although so perfectly harmless in my mode of self-defence, am required to stay three or four times her term of imprisonment! But, O, for woman's sake I suffer it. I will try to continue to suffer on, patiently and uncomplainingly, confidently hoping that my case will lead community to investigate for themselves, and see *why* it is, that so many sane women are thus persecuted at this period of the christian era. The sad truth that man has fallen from his noble position of woman's protector, and become her subjector, when apprehended, may lead our Government to give protection to the identity of the married woman, so that she can be as sure of legal protection, where she does not receive the marital, as if she were single. When, therefore, she needs legal protection from marital usurpation, she can obtain it directly from her Government, as other citizens now can.

This period of subjection through which woman is passing, is developing her self-reliant character, by compelling her to defend herself, in order to secure the safety of her own soul. That class of men who wish to rule woman, seem intent on destroying her reason, to secure her subjection. If they can not really put out this light in her, which so much annoys them, they will credit this work as done, by falsely accusing her of insanity, and when once branded by Dr. McFarland's diploma of "hopelessly insane," they fondly think they can keep her under their feet. And this has actually been done in many instances, by the help of the Illinois Insane Asylum.

Instead, therefore, of going to the wash-room to serve the State of my adoption by my labor, I am trying to serve it by writing facts and impressions respecting this Institution, hoping thus to promote the interests of the State more directly, than in any other manner. The evils of this Institution are so momentous and aggravating, that my own private wrongs seem lost, almost, in the aggregate. And besides, the working of this Institution is so carefully covered up, and so artfully concealed from the public eye, that the external world knows nothing of the "hidden life of the prisoner," within. Therefore the journal of an eye witness taken on the spot, is now presented to the public, as the mirror in which to behold its actual operations. It shall be one of the highest aspirations of my earth-life, to expose these evils for the purpose of remedying them. It shall be said of me, "She hath done what she could."

Since the emancipation of the slave, the most unprotected class of American citizens are the wives of such men as claim subjection to be the law of marriage. The subduing husband has it in his power to make his partner the most abject slave in the universe, since the laws protect him in so doing. Since the common law of marriage deprives the married woman of her individual identity, she has therefore no chance, while her husband lives, to defend her inalienable rights from his usurpation. Even her right of self-defence on the plane of argument is denied her, for when she *reasons*, then she is insane! and if her reasons are wielded potently, and with irresistible logic, she is then exposed to hopeless imprisonment, as the response of her opponent. This is now her legalized penalty for using her own reason in defence of her identity!

My husband has not only accepted of my identity as the law gives it to him, but he has also usurped all the minor gifts included in it. The gift from God, which I prize next to that of my personal identity, is my right of maternity, to my right to my own offspring, which he claims is his exclusively, by separating me entirely from them, with no ray of hope from him or the law, that I shall ever see them more. This is to me a living death of hopeless bereavement. Bereft of six lovely children by the will of my husband, and no one dare defend this right for me, for the *law* extends protection to such kidnappers. Yes, any husband can kidnap all of his own children, by forcibly separating them from the mother who bore them, and the laws defend the act!! The mother of the illegitimate child is protected by the law, in the right to her own offspring, while the lawfully married wife is not. Thus the only shield maternity has under the laws, is in prostitution.

Again, my property is all shipwrecked, and legally claimed by this usurper. And as I did not hold it in my own name, as the statute laws now allow, I am, on the principle of common law, legally robbed of every property right. The husband does not expose all his rights to usurpation when he marries; why should he make laws to demand this exposure to his wife and daughter? Are women in less need of protection than men, simply because they are weaker, and therefore more liable to usurpation? Nay, verily, the weakest demand the strongest protection, instead of none at all. O, when will man look upon woman as his partner, instead of dependent? O, I do need the protection of *law* to shield my rights from my usurper; but I have none at all, so long as I am a married woman.

And Dr. McFarland assures me, too, that so long as I claim my right of opinion and conscience, no church will extend fellowship to me. Therefore, my attempt to follow Christ, in holding myself as a responsible moral agent, rather than an echo or a parasite, has cast me out of the protection of the law, and also out of the pale of the Christian church, if what the Doctor tells me is true. Well, be it so; I am determined to ever *deserve* the love, respect, confidence, and protection of my husband; and I am equally determined to secure a rightful claim to the fellowship of *all* Christian churches, by living a life of practical godliness.

XXIII.

My Life Imperilled.

My life is almost daily and hourly endangered. For example: I was one morning sitting in a side room by myself, for the purpose of enjoying my secret devotions undisturbed, which privilege the matron had kindly granted, as my own dormitory had too many occupants to allow me any opportunity of praying in secret, and being compelled, however, by Dr. McFarland's special order, to have the door of this closet wide open, while I occupied it for this purpose, I was compelled to submit to any such intruders as might chance to walk in. Miss Jenny Haslett was one of the two maniacs who came in this morning, and seated herself on a low stool at my feet. I was always obliged to carry my chair and foot stool with me wherever I sat down, and by this arrangement I had my Asylum writing table, my lap, always with me, and at these times I made my entries into my journal and diary. The other maniac sat on the floor under the window. I quietly read my chapter, while Jenny amused herself playing with the trimming on the front of my dress. I closed my bible, and resting my eyes upon her, reflected upon the sad condition of this human wreck of existence before me. She was a handsome delicate girl of eighteen years, who was made insane by disappointed affection, and although generally harmless, yet at times, liable to sudden frenzies, from causes unknown. I could often hear her crying in the dead of night for "Willie, O, my dear Willie! do, do, come back to me—O Willie! Willie! I do love you!"

It may be that I aroused some antagonistic feeling, and disturbed some pleasant reverie of hers, when I bent forward and with my hands parted the short hair which fell over her fine forehead, and then bestowed upon it a gentle kiss of tender pity. In an instant the response came, in a blow from her clenched fist upon my left temple, of such stunning force, that for a moment I was lost to consciousness; for the blow seemed more like the kick of of a horse, than the hand of a human which inflicted it. My spectacles were thrown across the room by the blow, but I was not thrown from my seat. As soon as I realized what had happened, I returned her fiendish gaze with a look of pity, and exclaimed. "Why Jenny, you have struck me!"

"Yes, and I am going to knock your brains out!" said she, with furious emphasis, and clenched fists.

Without speaking again, I quietly and calmly withdrew into the hall, where I found my kind attendant, Miss Minerva Tenny, whose quick perception read the tale, and without my speaking a word, she exclaimed, "O, Mrs Packard, what a wound you have got upon your temple! What has happened?" "Jenny has struck me; please get me some cold water to bathe it in." "You will need something more than water, it is a terrible blow ! I will go for Dr. Tenny." After bringing me the water, she went for him, and he, like a tender brother, came and pitied me, and while I rested my throbbing head against his strong manly arm, I wept for joy at the comfort his words of pity brought with them to my forsaken heart. "Dr. Tenny, can you protect my life?"

"Mrs Packard, I would protect you if I could, but, like you, I am a subordinate; my power is limited."

"Will not the state be held responsible for these exposures of my life, to which Dr. McFarland subjects me? I think this appeal ought to be made."

Without answering this question he insisted that he would do all he could to help and protect me. And he did do so. I think Dr. McFarland was restrained by his manly interference. Still, the citadel of his heart was not reached either by Dr. Tenny's or my son's appeals, to remove me to some safer ward; and never shall I forget the heartless response he made, as he, the next day when, for the first time, he beheld my swollen face and throbbing temples, as I lay in agony upon my bed, from the effects of this injury, after I had told him all the circumstances, how I simply bestowed upon her forehead a loving kiss as the only provocation, he simply remarked, as he turned away—" It is no uncommon thing to receive a blow for a kiss!" These were the only words either of sympathy or regret I got from the Doctor, although the wound was then in such a state of great inflammation that Mrs. McFarland expressed herself, "you may consider yourself fortunate, Mrs. Packard, if you do not now lose your eye as the result." For weeks I carried the marks of this blow, by a deep black temple and eyes, so that a stranger would hardly have recognized me during this period.

But instead of shielding me better after this, he not only let Jenny remain in the ward, but he afterwards brought up Mrs. Triplet, from the Fifth ward, and from this time she, the most dangerous patient in the whole female wards, was seated by my side at the table. I seldom seated myself at the table after this, without hearing the threat from Mrs. Triplet, "I shall kill you!" And I considered myself very fortunate if I left the table without being spit upon by her, or by having her tea, or coffee, or gravy, or sauce thrown upon my dress.

At one time my right hand companion was suddenly aroused to the attitude of self-defence, by having a knife hurled at her temples or eyes, by one of our insane companions opposite. This aroused others to seize their knives and forks and chairs, in self-defence, and there is no knowing what a scene might have ensued, had not our attendants been on hand to confine the infuriated ones. There is no knowing at what instant these scenes may occur, for I have often seen them, without the least apparent provocation, suddenly seize the tumblers, salt-cellars, plates, bowls, and pitchers, and hurl them about in demoniac frenzy, so that the broken glass and china would fly about our face and eyes like hail stones.

The defence which maniacs resort to is, rendering evil for evil, abuse for abuse, so that the beginning of a scene among twenty-five or thirty of them is no telling what the end may be. And yet this institution receives such, and puts them all into one room, while the family plead that *one* is too dangerous to trust in a family! What would they think to have twenty-five in one family? For more than two years has Dr. McFarland imperilled my life, by compelling me to occupy a ward among this class, not knowing at what moment my life might be taken away, or I receive some distressing injury. Many times have I made the most touching appeals to him to save my life; but even before I could finish my sentence, he would turn and walk indifferently away, without uttering one syllable. Once alone do I find recorded, that he deigned a reply, which was under these circumstances. Lena, a stage actress, who had become insane from a fall through the stage platform, had been dragging me around the ward by the hair of my head, and unless the attendant had been near to aid me, I might not have been able to extricate myself from her grasp at all. Lena had, like Jenny, always seemed pleased to have me notice and caress her, as was my habit with them all who would allow it, until this time, when she turned upon me and treated me as I have described. After stating these facts, I added, "Now, Doctor, I think a sane person is more in danger than the maniacs, for they will fight back, while I will not."

"Supposing," said he, "a person should enter your room with a loaded pistol and aim it at you, and you had one by you which, by your using first, could save your own life, would you not shoot to save yourself?"

"No, Doctor, I would not; because my nature does not prompt me to defend myself in this manner. I have such an instinctive dread of taking the life of another, that I would rather die myself than kill another."

"I should, and I think every one would do the same in self-defence."

"I presume you would, and so would most *men*, for they were made to be the protectors and defenders of the weaker sex, and the man who would not do it in defence of a defenceless woman, is less than a man."

However, I could not convince the Superintendent that he was under any obligation to defend my life, and unless I had strength and courage enough to defend it myself, I must die; for so far as convincing him that he had any responsibility about the case, it was impossible to make him comprehend it.

In view of such facts as these I should not be at all surprised, if, when the thoughts of the heart are revealed, it will then be manifest that he placed my life thus in jeopardy among maniacs, hoping they might kill me!! There is no fathoming the vast depths of his wickedness. I do not believe there is anything he could not be induced to do, if he felt that his self-promotion demanded it. His conscience would interpose no barrier to the perpetration of any act of inhumanity which he thought his popularity demanded.

XXIV.

Hope of Dr. McFarland's Repentance.

(FROM MY JOURNAL.)

My only hope of Dr. McFarland lies in his repentance. Mrs. Hosmer says, "The Doctor is a villain." I have been free to admit, from what I know of him, that he is a very cruel, unfeeling man. Still, unlike Mrs. Hosmer, I believe in repentance, and my only hope of him lies in this principle. Saul was once a very cruel man, but repentance saved him. And hope is not utterly extinct, that Dr. McFarland may yet, like him, repent.

Mrs. Hosmer says she can tell facts of his treatment of patients here, to her knowledge, which would make my flesh creep to hear the recital of. She thinks "as he has been, he still is, and will continue to be." When I bring up proofs of his being different in some respects from what he was before I reproved him, she insists upon it that these are only false appearances, assumed as a disguise to delude me and others into the belief that he has repented. She says the attendants who are humane, are not so owing to the Doctor's influence, but to a principle of humanity within themselves. She says that the Doctor has practiced this strategic policy so long, that he can easily delude and deceive one of as charitable an organization as my own. I admit that this may be the case; still, I think there is more hope in making my appeals to his honor, as a handle by which to lead him to repentance, than to make him feel that I expect no good of him. In order to lead him by his honor, I must feel a degree of confidence in the efficiency of this principle, or I shall be acting a double part myself. I can not make him feel that I have hopes of him, while I have none, without being a hypocrite. I feel that the secret of true love lies in winning rather than in driving the soul to Christ. By patient continuance in well doing, I wait for the bright fruition of the sustaining hope that he will yet repent sincerely; that he will turn from his wickedness and live a different life. I do long to see him brought to an acknowledgment of the truth, before I leave this Asylum.

I have reason to think his wife is already able to see the fallacy he is trying to sustain in calling me an insane person. She said to me, "you never would have been permitted to enter this institution had we known what we now do." This to my mind is saying, "we do not consider you a fit subject for this institution, on the ground of your being insane, nor have we reason to believe you have been so at home." She told me that Dr. Sturtevant's course towards their minister, Mr. Marshall, had done much to open her eyes to the truth. As much as to say, "if human creeds can so influence one man to trespass upon the rights of another, may they not have influenced Mr. Packard to trespass on the inalienable rights of his wife."

I intend Dr. McFarland shall never hereafter have occasion to reproach me for not having warned him, and used all available mean to bring him to repentance. He shall have occasion to say of me as Belshazzar said of Daniel, when the destruction came upon him, of which the faithful prophet warned him "O, Daniel, Daniel, would that I had heeded thy warning before it was too late!" In short, I intend to do my duty to Dr. McFarland and leave results with God.

XXV.

"You should Return to your Husband."

One day in my extreme distress I presented the following note to Dr. McFarland. "My Brother in Christ, I am suffering a temptation from the powers of darkness to swerve from my purpose of holy obedience to God's revealed will. As a sister in Christ, in deep affliction, I beg an interest in your prayers that my faith fail not. Your sister, in Christ, E. P. W. P."

After glancing at it, and reading so far as " to swerve from my purpose of holy obedience," &c, he feelingly inquired, "What do you mean by your temptation?"

"I feel only tempted to complain of my lot, and to impatiently wish to be delivered out of the power of my persecutors. Doctor, I do so want my freedom! But I am not tempted to desire it at the expense of my conscience, that is, I am not tempted in the least by a desire to return to my husband, nor could any influence tempt me to do this deed, since for me it would be a sin against God to do so."

"Well, to pray for you—I want to do for you! what can I do?"

"Do right; by letting me have my liberty to support myself, as other wives do who cannot live with their husbands."

"The only right course for you is to return to your husband, and do as a true woman should do; be to him a true and loving wife, as you promised to be by your marriage vow, unto death, and until you do consent to do so, there is no prospect of your getting out of this place! for until you will give up this insane unreasonable notion of your duty forbidding it, I consider this institution the proper place for you to spend your days in, for you must be maintained somewhere, by *charity*, if it is not true as you pretend that you have helpers outside who promise you pecuniary aid, but give neither you nor me any guarantee to that effect."

"I do not feel that I am an object of charity so long as I have health and abilities to render me self-reliant; although I know my situation is a very unpleasant one for a woman, reported to be lost to reason, to contend with. For who will desire or employ an insane person as housekeeper, cook, nurse or teacher; still I could try, and if I did not succeed I could drop into a poor-house, such as the laws of the state provide for the indigent to die in."

"What poor-house?"

"Jacksonville, if I could get no further."

"No, you have no claim there."

"Manteno, then."

"No, you are not a woman who can be trusted, for your own conduct here has proved you to be entirely unworthy of trust or confidence. You have abused the trust I have reposed in you, and betrayed me in every possible way, by misrepresentation and abuse. You have proved to me, that you are all that your husband represents you to be, that he is an injured and abused man, and you are a worthless woman, for it is impossible for your husband to be such a man as you represent him to be and sustain the spotless character, as a minister, which he does, and always has."

"Don't I know, Doctor, a little more of his private character, as a husband, than any other one? and is it not possible for one to assume a false character abroad? Have not the fall of many good men, reported above censure, proved that it is sometimes the case?"

"No, I think it is impossible for your account of him to be a true one, and I regard this institution as the only fit place for you, so long as you are not willing to return to him."

"Is it right, here in America to coerce a woman's conscience, compelling her to do what she believes to be wrong? My views of my personal duty is my rule for me, as your views are for you. I regard it as persecuting Christianity thus to treat me, and that the cloak of insanity is the only legalized popular mode of doing it at the present day."

"No, Mrs. Packard, you are talking unreasonably, in an insane manner, and all reasonable people will call it so, for you to so represent duty; and so long as you hold on to these views, there is no hope for a change that I can see."

"Now I understand you. Now I am satisfied, for the reality, however painful, is far less unbearable than suspense. I now know what Mrs. Hosmer told me is true, although I was loth to believe you were so entirely lost to justice and honor. She said there was no hope of my getting out of this institution so long as you superintended it."

"Did Mrs. Hosmer say so?"

"She did." He then tried to qualify what he had said. He did not seem to like to have me cherish that view exactly, but how he meant to qualify it I could not understand. I know that the utterance of simple unqualified truth is the hardest language which can be employed.

But on this simple weapon of naked truth I intend to rely for my own defence and protection. The world may credit or discredit my statements, just as they please; my responsibility is done with the utterance of it. The superintendence of another's conscience is not my work. God forbid that I ever put forth my hand, Uzza like, to steady the conscience of another, since I know that God alone claims the right to protect his own sacred ark. I intend no man or woman shall ever steady my own. This is God's exclsuive work.

XXVI.

Uncared For.

(FROM MY JOURNAL.)

I have been in bed for a few days to rest my brain by sleep and sitz-baths. The means have been blessed and I am better. For about two weeks I have been afflicted with a headache most of the time. This is something new for me. I scarcely ever had a headache in all my life. Indeed I hardly know what pain of body is, I am so blessed with such sound and vigorous health. But when the doctor told me I must return to my husband or die here, it cost me a mental struggle which has prostrated me upon this sick bed. It is these spiritual wrongs which cause woman so much feeble health, and break down the strongest constitution. Knowing this, I must try to fortify nature in every possible manner within my reach, so that the citadel of my health need not suffer detriment; for if that should fail, I fear my courage would fail with it. The degree of faith, trust and confidence I am able to summon into this field of action depends much upon the healthful vigor and nervous energy I can command. Therefore to keep my faith strong, I **must** keep my health good.

But O, the spiritual pangs Dr. McFarland causes me to endure! it does seem that soul and body must be severed by them. Were it not for the "balm of Gilead and the physician" there, I must have laid down my life ere this, if agony of soul could extinguish it. It does seem to me that I am experiencing what my Savior felt when he cried, "If it be possible let this cup pass from me; nevertheless, not as I will, but as Thou wilt." I feel that I am alone in the garden of Gethsemane, watching, praying and longing for human sympathy in vain to come to my help. But ah! they sleep! Could none, not even one friend come to rescue me out of the hands of my enemies? No, none. "No man careth for my soul." I must, single-handed and alone, contend for the truth in defending the rights of suffering humanity. But I can do it. God has not sent me into this field to fight alone; no, God and angels are my body-guard and helpers. I will fear no evil, for with such helpers, I am invincible to attacks. Although my physical strength does suffer, yet the means are being blessed, so that the congestion of the brain which I feared would cause my death, is now warded off, and I can hope that my strength will be equal to sustain the ponderous burdens my soul has to bear from the injustice of others. I am carried in triumph safely through such perils, and I now feel quite confident that my life will not be given as a prey to my enemies. I expect to achieve a complete victory over my sagacious foes. And although Dr. McFarland has kept me nine weary months already, to gratify the wishes of a wicked conspiracy; and although my heart is suffering, and I see no prospect of ever getting out of this prison, yet I fear not to act the true woman, and simply, quietly wait in patience, future developments.

But O, my Savior, I must tell thee all. I do so long to be with my dear children, that I do want to hasten the day of my deliverance, by working hard, and so getting my work done the sooner. I do not wish to shirk any duty; but on the contrary, I want to do all my appointed work here well, and then go to rest with my children, taking thy blessing with me. For even my children will be to me no blessing if secured at the sacrifice of thy favor and smiles. I only want God-given blessings, bestowed in God's own way and time; and to secure these I am only required to do right and suffer right.

While encountering Pharaoh's hardness of heart in Dr. McFarland, I must, like Moses, meekly suffer, until God delivers me out of his cruel influence. I believe the time has come when this hard hearted man must be punished for his iniquities. For a long time he has sustained the responsibilities of his position with honors not deserved. He has for a long time been trying to cover up the barbarities of his treatment of the prisoners, and has succeeded in making it appear otherwise. He has so deluded the minds of the Trustees and Legislature, by his sophistry and deep, cunning artifice, as to secure such laws as protect him in doing his nefarious work thus long undetected and unmolested.

But the "searcher of hearts" can not be deceived or deluded. He can not be controlled by misrepresentations and a covert of lies. Lo! God, himself, by his providence, is to bring him to justice; for after his long forbearance towards him, by giving him opportunities and space for repentance, he persists in clinging to his sins, instead of repenting of them. And now, Pharaoh like, he has sinned away his day of grace, so that repentance can not now be accepted and pardon secured; but on the contrary, he must suffer the punishment due for his transgressions. The curse which his own conduct has secured, must come upon him, and no human power can prevent it. I do believe Dr. McFarland is now, like Pharaoh, undergoing that hardening of heart process which God calls his work; that is, God will not let him repent until he has been punished. In other words, justice, stern justice, has taken the place which mercy before occupied. And when God hardens the heart, no man can soften it. Inevitable destruction invariably follows God's hardening process.

I do not now expect to get out of this prison by Dr.

McFarland's free agency, but only in opposition to it. A stronger than he must first take this Insane palace, and then the choice goods of his own manufacture will be in peace and safety. O, my God, hasten that day, for thine Israel, thy chosen ones, languish and mourn, deeply mourn their present unholy, wretched condition! I told Dr. Sturtevant the truth yesterday, when I said, "Some of the choicest spirits in the universe are here, suffering persecution, under the mask of hypocrisy, and the Superintendent here is cruelly unjust to us."

"Then be comforted," said he, "by the fact that 'there is nothing covered that shall not be revealed, or hid, that shall not be known,' and justice will, in God's own time, be sure to come to each, and every one." Dr. Sturtevant, our chaplain, does bring to us many heavenly messages, which have been to me a great source of comfort and consolation; my fainting spirit has often been revived, and my faith and hope strengthened by his ministrations.

This hardening process of the heart, such as God claims as his work, is only the developing of the real character, which character we had previously acquired by our own voluntary acts, while we had the liberty to choose for ourselves either the good or evil. But when we have reached a certain point, the ability to choose the good is supplanted, or, for a time, entirely taken from us, so that we can then only choose evil. God is then in his way hardening the heart.

XXVII.

Self-defence. Clandestine Letters.

The oppressor's guilt renders him peculiarly sensitive to any action on the part of the injured one, by way of self-defence. Therefore, in order to practice this duty, we are always compelled to use what some would regard as unjustifiable means. And yet, in exchange of circumstances, these complainers would feel no scruples in doing the same thing of which they complain.

Here I am literally entombed alive by fraudulent means, for a wicked purpose. The walls of my sepulcher are the walls of this Asylum. I am allowed no communication with the outside world. No one inside these walls can aid me in doing so, without proving recreant to his trust as an employee. And no visitor is allowed to take out a letter from a patient in a public institution, without the Superintendent's knowledge or consent.

Now what shall I do? Shall I quietly submit to these unjust laws, framed for the very purpose of perpetuating an absolute despotism? I am a law defender; I do not like to be a law breaker, and God is never compelled to violate law to bring about His purposes, neither does he allow us to transgress any moral or natural law, to accomplish our purposes, however desirable. When we see no way of getting out of a sad dilemma, except that of wrong doing, we are directed to "Wait, wait on the Lord," that is, wait until Providence opens a way for us. Like the traveller, in pursuing his onward course, coming in contact with the moving train, has nothing to do but to stop and wait until it passes by; thus Providence clears his track, without any law being broken. Therefore, however desirable it may seem to me, to be free to care for, and communicate with my precious children, yet, although this vision tarries long, I must wait until the train, however long, passes by, before I can possibly behold this prospect.

Again, I must not murmur nor complain, although I am most keenly sensitive to the humiliation of my circumstances. But I will not bow down to wickedness. I do, and act, as well as I know how, and will continue to do so, knowing that impossibilities are not required of me by my righteous Judge, for I know that every good act is an investment in the bank of faith, and its dividends never fall short. I believe too, that God requires me not only to pray that wrong doing be stopped, but also to act in concert with this prayer, and the wrong doing, which it is my duty to stop, are the sins against myself. I must begin at home, for I can never defend others until I can defend myself; for how can a mother defend her children, unless she can defend herself? I must defend myself not only for their sake, but also for the sake of society where I belong. I have already tried the force of argument, reason, and entreaty, to induce Dr. McFarland to allow me some chance at self-defence, but all in vain. I can not get his consent in this matter, therefore, the act being right in itself, and a duty also, I must act not only without his consent, but without his knowledge. Therefore, under the circumstances, a clandestine act of self-defence is not a sinful act because of its secresy.

But who shall I apply to, and how? are the next questions to be settled. I will first appeal to the Trustees, as they are the power to whom my earthly destiny is now committed, and they have the first right to superintend Dr. McFarland's actions, in regard to the prisoners under his charge; and I feel morally bound to try to get the Trustees to compel their Superintendent to act justly towards me.

Under the influence of such feelings I wrote the following letter to the Trustees, on a piece of tissue paper, which when folded compactly, occupied a space no larger than a silver quarter.. I knew they were to hold a session at the Asylum in March next, 1861, and it was to be my business to get this letter to them at this meeting. But here was the difficulty. Since hiding me amongst the maniacs the Doctor had evinced a peculiar sensitiveness at my being seen there, which was never manifested while I was an occupant of the Seventh ward. And he had even led the Trustees past this ward, without even allowing them to enter it, since he had consigned me to it. Now how could I give them my letter, either openly or secretly? No employee would do it for me, lest Dr. McFarland's displeasure be incurred, and then, of course, a "discharge" awaited them. Still watching and praying constantly, while they were in the house, I carried my little note in my pocket, hoping by some good fortune, I might yet get it into their hands.

At length my name was announced as wanted in the dining room. I gladly responded to the call, where I found Mrs. McFarland and Mrs. Miner waiting to receive me to hold an interview with me. Finding it too dangerous to take my callers into the hall which I now occupied, I was then allowed the exposure of my own life to be suspended long enough to entertain them in the dining-room. Happy beyond measure to find myself in the presence of a trustee's wife, my whole mental powers were centered upon knowing how to employ her as the confidential medium of my letter to the Trustees. But the fact was self-evident to me, that Mrs. McFarland had come as a spy upon me, lest I should, in some manner, either by word or look or letter, communicate to her some intimation of the injustice I was experiencing at her husband's hands. And so complete was the espionage she exercised, that I began to fear that this hope must expire in its bud. When they arose to leave, and as Mrs. McFarland's back was towards us as she opened the diningroom door, I watched my chance and buried this little note in the palm of Mrs Miner's hand, and closing her hand upon it, I gave it a significant pressure, as much as to say, "don't betray me, but do your duty;" and at the same time kissing her, so that the transfer seemed a perfect and satisfactory success; that is, I felt sure she understood my meaning, and was willing to aid me in doing anything right and consistent. Of course, she could and would read the open note before assuming any farther responsibility. And from the impression I received of her feelings, I was satisfied that she would do right about it. But whether I then misjudged her, I can not tell, or whether her husband kept the letter himself, or communicated it to the Trustees, I know not But this I do know, I never heard from the note, or from its influence.

That seed, though thus buried for seven long years, now rises to a tangible influence, and by its mute appeal to the law-makers who read this letter, it may lead them to see the necessity of demanding fidelity in their public officers, to whom they have entrusted the sacred right of their personal liberty.

To the Trustees of Jacksonville Insane Asylum, in session at their March meeting, 1861.

Gentlemen: Can I hope to get any help from you? Are you ministers of justice? Can the cry of the needy and afflicted find in you any response? Why, O, why is it that oppressed woman can not find in man a natural protector? O, the model man could not turn speechless away when oppressed innocence cried for help. O, will you, like Dr. McFarland, turn a deaf ear to my prayer? Can you hope to be heard when you call in your time of need, if you will? Gentlemen, here under your inspection, a faithful, kind, christian mother, and an Illinois citizen, has been imprisoned nearly nine months for simply exercising her God-given rights of opinion and conscience; and this, too, in only a ladylike and christian manner. Nothing else!

Now, can you be guiltless and let this persecution go on under your jurisdiction? Do remember, and be warned by God's unchangeable law, viz: "With what measure ye mete withal, it shall be measured to you again." Do be merciful to me that God may be merciful to you. Do allow me to live a natural life in America, so long as my own actions allow me a claim to my own freedom. Do deliver me out of the hands of Dr. McFarland, for he has claimed to be better than God to me, in that he says to me that his judgment is a safer guide for me than my own conscience!! O, horrible! And yet I am in the absolute power of such a man. Do, I beg of you, deliver me from this fear of evil! Do but give me the opportunity, and I will give you my pledge, if necessary, that America need no longer be burdened with me, as a citizen, than until I can get under the protection of the English crown, where I can hope to enjoy my rights of opinion and conscience unmolested.

O, America! My country, when will you erase the stigma you now carry, of having imprisoned an innocent, unprotected minister's wife, for simply obeying God, by trying to live a life of practical godliness? Shall a woman of America, when she consents to become a wife, and to her sorrow finds that the man whom she chose to be her protector, has instead, become the subjector of her womanly rights, be compelled to leave her offspring motherless, and be entombed alive, in an Insane Asylum, simply because there is no power in the laws of the land to protect her against the despotic will of her husband? O, when will my countrymen fear God, more than they do the oppressor?

Gentlemen, action, investigation, is demanded of *you*, by this appeal, in order that your souls be found guiltless in this matter. Dare to do your duty, and God will bless you.

Your suffering sister, E. P. W. PACKARD.

After receiving the above letter, I think a failure to investigate into the merits of the case was in itself a criminal act. Ignorance of the state of my mental faculties could no longer shield them, for the letter contains a sufficient degree of intelligence to arouse an investigation to see if what I claimed was true or false. But merely "doing *not*," did not extenuate their guilt, for the perpetuating of a wrong. It enhanced it; for the postponement of a difficult crisis only renders a settlement more difficult, and the evil consequences more inevitable and unavoidably certain. Guilt was daily accumulating by each added day of most wearisome imprisonment, and that tender babe was being thus deprived of its *right* to its mother's care, and that little flock of tender lambs were daily and hourly in suffering need of a mother's care and sympathy. Yes, the quicker the settlement, the easier and the better, both for them and the injured victims of this most cruel conspiracy. Now, they can not clear themselves of guilt, if, Pilate like, they do try to throw the responsibility off themselves upon Dr. McFarland. For they know that for his act they will be held justly responsible, in the same sense that the Superintendent is held responsible for the acts of his employees. For my aggravated and enhanced sufferings from this time, I hold the Trustees responsible; for it seemed that the Doctor's story was heeded and mine rejected, thus delegating an increased power to the Doctor to abuse me, just as his upholding Lizzy Bonner in her barbarities, only enhanced her power to harm still more.

Indeed I suffered so much from his tyranny, for nine months

from this time, that even the sight of the man, or the sound or sight of his name, was instinctively and inseparably associated with horror in my mind. But the details of this period of purgatorial mental anguish, as I find it delineated in my journal, it will be impossible for me to give within the limits of this volume. I did propose when I projected the plan of this book, to give the history of these wrongs in detail to the world; but I shrink from the task. The record of the adamantine pen God himself will give in his own way and time in complete detail. This record can never be obliterated, except by repentance on Dr. McFarland's part for the wrongs I have suffered at his hands. I am determined, by God's help, now to write my own history in chapters indelible and indestructable in my own honest deeds.

The following letter to Dr. Shirley, of Jacksonville, written during these days of anguish, on some cloth, or tissue tea-paper which I obtained from the sewing-room, I handed to Dr. Sturtevant after chapel service in a manner similiar to what I did with my note to Mrs. Miner, except that I confined my salutation to a shake of his hand as I slipped the note into it. But I am sorry to say I have more reason to think he betrayed me to the Doctor, than I have that Mrs. Miner did, for the Doctor told me himself that he had destroyed a "worthless letter" Dr. Sturtevant had given him from me, I doubt not but he spoke a truth in making that confession to me, and I think it was uttered under the influence of an exultant feeling which said, "So you see, Mrs. Packard, I can head you anywhere! you are my helpless victim."

"Never mind, Dr. McFarland, you did *then* hold me, and the letter too, in your power, but now I hold that letter in *my* power, to publish to the world, that my readers may see in what its "worthlessness" consisted; and I hold now myself and you too, where the verdict of public sentiment will compel us both to stand just where our own actions will place us." And Dr. Shirley can also see in what estimation I then held him. This opinion I based upon an interview I held with him in the Doctor's parlor, in company with Mr. and Mrs. Blessing, and as I was personally acquainted with no other man in Jacksonville, I of course made application to him as a dernier resort.

INSANE ASYLUM, March 20, 1861.

DR. SHIRLEY—*Kind Sir:* Constrained by the law of self-preservation, I feel compelled to make an appeal to your humanity for help. Yes, help for me, a helpless victim of severe persecution. I am sick, and need some human helper, for on the side of my oppressors there is power; yes, power to harm, too, yet I have no protection save Omnipotence. My heart turns instinctively to you, kind Sir, hoping and trusting that the God-like principle of manhood has not become extinct in you, and therefore, I have a foundation on which to make my appeal.

Dr. Shirley, I am indeed an injured woman, and my case ought to arouse and command an investigation; at least, so far as to grant me some kind of trial, before perpetuating my imprisonment any longer. Can you not do something to secure me one? I do beg and entreat, with all the power of woman's eloquence, that you do deliver me out of Dr. McFarland's hands. He is my oppressor, my unjust and cruel persecutor. He claims that "his judgment is a safer guide for me than my conscience." These are his own words; and I am in the absolute power of *such* a man. What protection have I under a man who ignores the conscience of his victim? Do deliver me from this fear of evil, and my soul shall bless you forever.

And I have given this usurper my written pledge, that I shall expose him to the world whenever I get out, unless he repents of his inhumanities to the patients. And he knows, too, that I am a truthful woman, and can never break this pledge.

Ask wisdom—do your duty—and do not yield to the temptation to fear to cope with the great Dr. McFarland in defence of the injured. Omnipotence will shield you in doing your duty. My heart is full, but my means of communication are entirely cut off, so far as the Doctor can prevent it. If possible, come to me, and I will tell you what I can not, and dare not write. O, do let a God-fearing humanity, not a man-fearing despotism, control your actions, and I trust heaven will protect you.

In the name of justice, humanity, and of the State, I have requested a meeting of the Trustees on my account; but Dr. McFarland's reply leaves me nothing to hope for in that direction. Still, duties are mine, and events God's. I know my life is worth preserving, for the sake of my six children, if for no other purpose, and "For me to live is Christ, and to die, gain." Still all lawful means I feel bound to use, to preserve life, and *then* I can say, God's will be done.

Your humble, earnest petitioner,

E. P. W. Packard.

XXVIII.

Miss Mary Tomlin.—A Model Attendant.

I never saw Miss Mary Tomlin abuse a patient, and she was my attendant for nearly one year. She, unlike most attendants, did not seem to become calous and indifferent towards them, because she would not allow herself to do the *first* unkind act. It is very noticeable here that the beginning of wrong doing is like the letting out of water, over the edge of a fountain. When the first few drops have trickled over, there is apt to be a few more, and a few more, until a deep and broad channel is soon formed through which the waters of human kindness are allowed to pass into a state of exhaustless annihilation. When this groove was once made, it was never closed up under the Asylum influence. The only security an employee or boarder could have of maintaining their integrity, lay in their not doing the first wrong act. This was the secret of her triumph over the contagion of that most corrupt house. She was entered in my ward, and although initiated under our most unexemplary attendant, Mrs. De LaHay, she seemed to have moral courage enough to allow her own principles instead of Mrs. DeLaHay's to control her.

Miss Tomlin exercised the utmost forbearance and kind endurance of the patient's weakness and frailties, such as I think was never surpassed by any attendant. She may justly be called a model attendant, so far as the treatment of the patients was concerned. Should Asylums secure such, and only such attendants, they might justly be called Asylums. I never feared for the fate of a patient when Miss Tomlin was in sight; even Miss Bonner's fierce spirit seemed subdued into temperate rage by her silent, gentle, but unresistable magnetism of kindness and tenderness. I recollect once how I pitied her when she called me to see the condition of Miss Sallie Low, a filthy patient, occupying a screen-room at the time, while passing through one of her "spells" of excessive fury, where she had divested herself of all her clothing, and was standing naked when I saw her, with her hands both raised, with all her fingers spread, with her mouth wide open in laughter, and her large black eyes showing the white on the upper side in wildness, her short, heavy, curly black hair standing all about her head in bristles, from the salve with which she had anointed both it and herself completely over, so that her flesh was about the color of a monkey. Besides, she had written, her marks upon the wall, as high as her fingers could reach. My kind attendant instead of being angry at her exulting patient, in view of the labor she had caused in cleaning her and her room, only laughed in return, as she exclaimed, "did you ever see a human being so much resemble a monkey!" With the help of another attendant she took her to the bath-room, and after patiently soaking her for a while in the bath-tub of warm water, she finally cleaned and dressed her, and introduced her into our dormitory as a woman who deserved our pity, instead of our censure, for "she is not to blame for causing me this trouble, and this is what I came here to do, to take care of those who cannot take care of themselves." Even her bath was administered in such a gentle manner that Miss Low, instead of offering resistance, enjoyed the fun first-rate, and came from it refreshed and invigorated, instead of being exhausted from death struggles such as Miss Bonner and such like attendants administered.

It does seem as if the State ought to attach a penalty to this perversion of the bath tub in this prison house. Only let the law-makers take but one bath here, under the hands of these furies, and I think they would vote for some penalty to their tormentors.

But were all the attendants as God-fearing as Miss Tomlin and Miss Minerva Tenny, this abuse would never be practiced. Such attendants would not misuse a patient if they were required to do it, for they fear God more than they do man. Miss Tomlin told me of an act of her's this morning, which reflects much credit upon her moral courage and integrity. The Doctor ordered Miss Goodrich from off her bed, Sunday morning, as he passed through, and Miss Tomlin ordered her back again, when he had passed out of hearing; for she felt that she knew better than he did what her health demanded. She said she had concluded to pursue this independent course, without talking much about it, hoping thus to evade the rule without opposition; when she was complained of, she said, she would then give her reasons, and she thought any intelligent person would be satisfied with intelligent reasons. I assured her this was the right course; still, I was sure it would awaken decided opposition, for the more reasonable, the more virulent the opposition it would arouse. And so it proved. Instead of promoting her, as she deserved to be, they willingly allowed her to resign her trusts to others far less fitted to honor them. And in defence of this course, I heard one of the authorities say, "Miss Tomlin is insane, in some respects, like Mrs. Packard!" Her insanity, like my own, consisted in her immovable defence of the principles of uniform kindness to the unfortunate.

Another most kind and faithful employee, Mrs. Hosmer, was accused of this same charge of insanity, for the same reason. Indeed, one of these authorities remarked, "If we could but get Mrs. Hosmer into the wards as a patient, we would treat her as we do the maniacs!" This is doubtless true, for her persistent regard for the patients' interests, was a constant reproof to their own indifference, and aroused the same antagonistic feelings towards her, which my course has elicited towards me; and the position of a patient here affords a noble opportunity for seeking their revenge in full measure.

I will close this chapter by inserting here a beautiful paraphrase on a passage in Psalms, which Miss Tomlin wrote herself, and handed me for my solace.

"I shall be satisfied when I awake in thy likeness."

In this dreary vale of sorrow,
    Oft my heart is sick and sore,
Waiting for a brighter morrow,
    Waiting, waiting evermore.

Hope deferred my heart is breaking,
    And I long to be at rest—
Aye! the sleep that knows no waking,
    Would be welcome to this breast.

Did I say "that knows *no* waking?".
    Nay, I would not have it so,
Better far to bear this aching,
    Than to sleep forevermore.

But I would awake like *Jesus*—
    Like unto the crucified—
When I'm fashioned in *His* image.
    Then shall I be satisfied.

Affectionately your friend,   M. TOMLIN.

XXIX.

Mrs. McFarland—The Matron.

It is due Mrs. McFarland that I say, that after I gave my written reproof to her husband, she seemed to be induced by its influence, to see the debased condition the prisoners were in, and expressed this feeling in these words: "Mrs. Packard, I never realized, until I read your Reproof, what a condition we were in. It has led me to determine to do what I can to reform some of the many evils which I can now see do exist here. We had so insensibly sunk into this condition, that we did not realize it until you showed it to us in your Reproof." To Mrs. McFarland's credit it should be stated, that she did try to alleviate the dreadful condition of the patients as much as it was possible for her to do.

After Mrs. Waldo left, she became matron, and she filled this office as well as she was capacitated to do. Her kind and generous sympathies rendered her a general favorite amongst the patients, and atoned greatly for the undeveloped woman in some other respects.

She sympathized with me in many ways, and tried to favor me, even in defiance of her husband's known wishes to the contrary. One day the Doctor found a carpet upon my floor, and as he stood upon the threshold of my room, looking at it for the first time, he exclaimed, "Who has been putting a carpet on Mrs. Packard's room?" My attendant, Miss Tomlin, standing by, replied in her very mild tone, "I believe it is your wife's work." He said nothing more, but the carpet remained on the floor until I left. And it was her influence among others, which let me have a room by myself, after one year's confinement to the dormitory. I sent a written request to the Doctor to let me have a wash bowl and pitcher, but he did not notice it so much as to refuse it. But Mrs. McFarland contrived to get me one, and gave me, also, a nice curtain to my window, and gave me a chair, too, for my room, a great, but rare privilege in the Eighth ward.

There was one time that the Doctor tried to so torment my feelings, that I felt that self-defence required me to withdraw all communication of thought with him, to save my feelings. Therefore, for months, I would not speak to him, not even so much as answer the most common question. Mrs. McFarland approved of this course, by saying to me, "Well, Mrs. Packard, I would not speak to him if I were in your place. If a man treated me as he has you, I would let him alone." And she told my attendants not to treat me as they did the other patients.

I will here give an extract from a letter I wrote her about April 30, 1862; "Mrs. McFarland, I have almost unbounded confidence in your womanly nature ; I believe its instincts are a safe guide in dictating your duty so far as it goes ; yet, I do not regard your judgment as so mature, that experience may not improve it. Will you therefore allow me to make a suggestion, when I assure you it is made with the purest motives, and the kindest feelings of my nature. I am prompted to do this, from the assurance I feel that you will allow the suggestion all the influence which truth, reason and common sense, urge in support of it." etc.

With regard to the suggestion I then made, together with many others, I will only say that, Mrs. McFarland almost always regarded them, and did often consult me, as her counsellor, in her family matters, as well as the interest of the institution.

The reform thus inaugurated, through her agency, led to the expression often made during these better days of prison life, "this house is a paradise compared with what it has been."

Dr. McFarland seemed to be the last and the hardest one to move in this direction ; but satisfied he could not stop the wheel of revolution by opposing it, he after a while, allowed himself to simply hang as a dead weight upon it, until the aristocratic ladies from Jacksonville insulted and ridiculed me in my room, when all at once a new spirit seemed to hold him, for a time, to be our co-worker, instead of an antagonist. This incident will appear in its proper place. There seemed to be something in his wife's increasing popularity which convinced him that it would not be policy to oppose her openly, for if he did, she told me she should do as I had done, "appeal to the Trustees" to sustain her ! Finally, from the influence of the outside pressure in favor of reform, the Doctor himself *thanked* me for giving him the reproof, and freely acknowledged that I intended it for his good.

Through Mrs. McFarland, as the focalizing agent of this reform, the tide of popular influence seemed to undergo an entire change. Instead of its being popular to abuse the prisoners, it became more popular to treat them with respect and even kindness. And finally, by a change of some bad attendants for good ones, I began to feel that the evils were becoming greatly lessened. And so it did appear for awhile. But I was everywhere told, "there will be a relapse if *you* ever leave this house, for the Doctor is afraid of you, as the only reason why he is making this spasmodic attempt to co-operate with his wife." From the Committe's report, and that of my personal friends I left in the Asylum, I have too much reason to fear that so it proved. My friends have assured me me that the "reign of terror" commenced anew when I left, so that abuse and cruelty again became the rule of the house, to a greater degree even than ever before.

Now I am fully convinced that this temporary reform, so far as Dr. McFarland was concerned, was merely the effect of policy, rather than principle—that he assumed this appearance merely to satisfy me he had repented, so that I might be induced to represent him to the public as worthy of confidence, on that ground; for he knew full well, that my conscience would not allow me to expose a *penitent* man's sins, however great the magnitude of his previous guilt. I find therefore, in my journal, from the time I began to hope he was treating the patients on the principles of justice, I have been exceedingly careful not to "Break the bruised reed, or quench the smoking flax;" that is, I encouraged every hopeful manifestation to the highest, and fullest extent consistency and truth would permit. Many blamed me on this ground, that I was too charitable to the poor sinner; but dictated as I was by the promptings of my own forgiving nature, I was thus inclined to cover more sins with this mantle of charity, than some would have thought proper or allowable. I never can find it in my heart to blame, where there is the least possible chance for encouragement. I aim to "Overcome evil with good," instead of attacking evil with evil, where there is any possible opportunity of doing so.

But there are cases where it is a mercy to be just to the sinner. Nothing but ruin will save them from ruin: that is, they never will repent until they are first punished; and the just punishment, which I tried so long and effectually to have him ward off, was the public exposure of his hidden iniquities. But persistency in his sins, has forced me to do, what for a time, I hoped I could be excused from doing.

XXX.

Guilty Husbands.

It was sometime in March, 1862, that I entered a kind of protest, against this house being used to shield guilty husbands, in the following letter to Dr. Tenny.

Dr. Tenny—*Sir:* Do bear with me while I give you my thoughts upon a subject you may prudishly feel I have no right to think, much less to speak or write about; but where woman is suffering injustice, I claim a right to speak in her defence.

I see Mrs. McKellum is returned. I can assure you, Dr. Tenny, that as true as Phrenology and Physiology can not lie, here is another case of abuse, where the innocent is punished, instead of the guilty. It is her husband who ought to be imprisoned instead of her, in a penitentiary, and there kept until he will subject his passions to the control of his reason. He never ought to see a woman, until his reason is restored to him, so that he can treat her as a woman, not as a brute.

Dr. Tenny, these men, calling themselves husbands, degrade the very name itself. Science and revelation, both foretell their doom. Judge Wood has caused the ruination of his lovely wife. Had justice been done him as it should have been, he would have been consigned to a penitentiary for having brought her here the first time, when she was not in the least insane. Had justice, instead of wickedness triumphed, Mrs. Wood's little flock would not now have been motherless. Because sentence against the wrong doer was not speedily executed, this innocent, defenceless wife and mother was returned to this Asylum, insane, to die a maniac, because her husband would not protect her, but tortured her into insanity, and that too, when she was in a condition to need the tenderest indulgence! As soon as the husband attempts to subject his wife as he would a child, that moment nature, in woman, revolts, and feels that her obligations to that man, are henceforth, forever sundered. He has perjured his vow of protection, and her devotion to him is annihilated with the subjection.

Dr. Tenny, the day is not far distant when these unnatural men will meet their recompense. In the mean time, "Offences will come, but woe be to him by whom they come," and woe too, to those who compromise with these vile deeds, as this Institution is doing in shielding these women captors. That I may wash my hands in innocency, I shall lift up my voice, and protest openly against these guilty husbands.

Yours as ever, E. P. W. P.

There is great occasion for alluding to the evil designated in the above letter to Dr. Tenny. For the public should know the fact, that selfish men who hold money and position in society, do use this house for a protection of their own guilt; and their public servant, Dr. McFarland, knowingly allows it to be thus perverted from the charitable design of its founders. Even the law of 1865, which was humanely designed to hedge up the door against this unjust incarceration of married women, has been most arrogantly and wantonly disregarded by this public servant; and his acts seem to say, "This house *shall* be used as a place where vile men can subject their wives to the dictates of their base passions!" And woman, oppressed and degraded as she was, found no refuge even under this law, until the gallantry of the Legislature of 1867 attached a *penalty* to it, thus demanding its enforcement.

This statement is corroborated, as my others are, by the Investigating Committee's Report. This Committee appointed by the Legislature, were instructed to see that this law was strictly enforced, hoping in this way to liberate these unhappy victims of marital cruelty, and to effectually guard, henceforth, against these unjust, false and cruel imprisonments.

This Committee, composed of Hon. Allen C. Fuller, Hon. E. Baldwin, Hon. T. B. Wakeman, Hon. A. J. Hunter, Hon. John B. Ricks, after a most thorough investigation of the records of the Institution, reported that they found one hundred and forty-eight had been admitted by Dr. McFarland, since the law of 1865 was passed, including a period of about two years, "without the proper *legal evidence* of their insanity, and the security required by law." Just consider, for a moment, the terrible inferential fact herein involved! If one hundred and forty-eight are found entered during about two years' time, without *legal evidence* of insanity, in defiance of an existing law which requires such evidence, what number may we conclude were admitted during the fourteen previous years, *without any evidence of insanity*, with a law expressly allowing this to be done? Has not Illinois a terrible account to settle with her married women, who have sufferered so much from her unjust law for the sixteen years of its enforcement? The honor of the State of Illinois demands restitution for the enforcement of this, not only most ungallant and unmanly, but even barbarous law against the married women of her State. Now if Illinois should dare to become the pioneer State in the emancipation of her married women from their slavish position of nonentity, she might, by so doing, not only erase this dishonorable stain upon her history, but also immortalize herself in thus securing her right to *then* be, what she now professes to be, a *freedom* loving State.

Again, in view of such facts, it well becomes every voter of the State to inquire, *whose* personal liberty, personal rights are safe in Illinois, while such an unmanly and unprincipled man as Dr. McFarland holds the key of this great prison house? This public officer has so long been in the habit of overriding and disregarding all law, both human and divine, in the treatment of his prisoners, that he has schooled himself to feel that he is the Institution over which "my policy" is the supreme and only law; in the same sense that some allege that President Johnson seems to act as though he was the United States, and "my policy" is the Constitution!

Thus it is evident that *false* imprisonment in Jacksonville Insane Asylum, was the dreadful doom which overhung every citizen of Illinois, until their Legislature of 1867 attached a *penalty* of fine or imprisonment, or both, to the Superintendent who should hereafter receive any inmate without *legal evidence* of insanity. Indeed, confident as I was, that this public servant was constantly admitting inmates, regardless of even the "forms of law," I could not find it in my heart to suffer this awful doom thus to overhang the wives and daughters of Illinois, without doing what I could to avert it. And I thank God, the effort has proved a complete success; so that now, no guilty husband of Illinois can longer hide his sins against the wife of his bosom behind the "dead locks" of Jacksonville Insane Asylum.

XXXI.

The Sane kept for the Doctor's Benefit.

The remark Miss C. L. English, a good attendant, from Chandlerville, Cass Co., Ill., made, conveys an important truth which the tax payers ought to know—viz. "It is plainly to be seen, the Doctor keeps sane people here from choice, to serve his private interests, knowing that the unrequited labor he gets out of them he can turn to his aggrandizement in his report of the finances of the institution." Yes, all this slave labor turns to his advantage as he reports it, thus buying their patronage, as it were, to secure his salary. This salary is thus earned for him by his slaves. His own action, or rather his inaction, shows that he is almost totally indifferent to the interests of his prisoners, only so far as his interests can be promoted by an assumed regard for their interests. He does not seem to care how many hearts he breaks with anguish, nor how many choice spirits he crushes into annihilation, if so be he can rise on their downfall.

But, O, Dr. McFarland, you can not kill a spirit; it lives after all you have done to destroy its existence, and in a body too, which God gave it to inhabit. All this terrible array of broken crushed hearts, which you vainly think you have destroyed forever, are all alive, and are now marshalling in dread array to work out your long merited doom.

The faithful hard working Kate has well earned her $2.30 a week, if any female attendant earns that amount by her work. She has been as sane a worker as any attendant in the house ever since I knew her, and I am told she had been just as competent and useful for many months before. And Kate is only one of scores of others of like type. And if they are ever discharged after these years of unrequited labor either their friends or the county will be required to pay the institution, in addition to all this unrequited toil, all that their clothing has cost them, besides the bill charged for making it, even if the patient has cut and made every stitch of it herself! How much more profitable to the pecuniary interests of the State is this robbing of its citizens, than it would be to pay their just debts! If it were not for this *slave* labor, the State would be compelled to have double the number of attendants to do all this work, which it now gets as a gratuity out of its prisoners.

Dr. McFarland is a good financier for the State in this particular, but a miserable one for the interests of the state's-prisoners under his care. If the State wish the interests of its unfortunates cared for, they must get some other person than Dr. McFarland to do this deed for them, or it never will be done. He knows that the pecuniary interests of the state demand such large pecuniary resources also, to meet the immense destruction of state property which is constantly going on, through his stolid indifference. Could the state but be allowed to know the management as it really is, not as the Doctor reports it to be, they would be horror struck at the extravagant, unnecessary and unreasonable amount of property destroyed here, merely as the legitimate result of this insane management. The rules as they are practically carried out are unreasonable and unjust in the extreme. The property is wantonly destroyed oftentime as the legitimate result of of this cruel injustice. There is no other manner in which they can express their just indignation of the power which is thus oppressing them. Therefore the amount of property unnecessarily destroyed, which is daily going on here, might relieve the wants of thousands who stand in perishing need of the comforts it might furnish for them.

O, Illinois! State of my adoption, when, when will you look intelligently, with your own eyes, into the practical operation of your Insane Asylum system, as it is now being practiced in your State Institution at Jacksonville? Never, never, will you see it as it is, until you can look at it through some other medium than Dr. McFarland or his Reports.

Just consider how unjustly I am treated here. Here my good, firm health is suffering from my close confinement; and in duty to myself I reported my state to Dr. McFarland, and asked if I could not be allowed fifteen minutes exercise in the open air daily, without an attendant, and he denied my request. I then concluded I would avail myself of the laws of the house, and go to the wash house or ironing rooms, and there work for the State, that I might thus secure the exercise and fresh air my health demanded. But lo! here I am met with Dr. McFarland's strict command not to let me out for this purpose, while other prisoners can go at their option. I have not done any thing to forfeit my right to this privilege, guaranteed by law to the prisoners, to my knowledge, or to the knowledge of any other one. And yet Dr. McFarland has just as good a reason for denying me this right, as he had for removing me from the best ward to the worst. Neither I nor any other one in the house have ever known his reasons for thus treating me; but on the contrary, we know that he had no right or excuse for doing so. Nothing but sovereign, arbitrary rule dictates his course of treatment towards me. Yes, he is ruling me with a rod of iron, and I, in my deeply sensitive nature, am suffering protracted martyrdom at his hands.

O! this lingering, terrible death of crucifixion! Could not the wrath of man have been appeased by something less excruciating? O, no. Despotic man must not only trample helpless woman under foot, but he must heighten her anguish by the stings of injustice. Oh, how many of these torturing stings my bleeding heart has felt, within the last seven months! Were it not for the "balm of Gilead, and the physician there," these stings must have proved fatal to my soul, to whose death alone were these darts directed. O, Jesus, if these fires rage so furiously in the green tree, what must be expected from the dry? "For the fire shall try every man's work, of what sort it is."

At the request of Mrs. McFarland, the Doctor finally consented to my going into the sewing room for one-half day each day, while other prisoners can go all day, if they choose. Thus, by sewing for the State, as its imprisoned slave, I can buy the privilege of exchanging the putrid, loathsome air of the ward, for the more wholesome, purer atmosphere of the sewing room for half a day. But instead of this being a relief, it seems to be only an aggravation of the evil, for the air of the hall seems doubly grievous and unendurable by contrast, and the incessant noise and uproar of the maniacs, seems heightened every time I return to the roar of the tempest after a short calm.

I think I can well pay my way, by making a vest or a pair of pants daily, to swell the aggregate of Dr. McFarland's report of the pecuniary profits arising solely from this slave labor. This is my only alternative to get better air for my health! If I were a male prisoner, I might perhaps be allowed, under a watchful keeper, to go on to the Doctor's great farm, and hoe his corn and potatoes, with his sixty other day laborers, which this house furnishes for his exclusive benefit. And thus, by Dr. McFarland's granting me the right to breathe the fresh air of heaven, I might help fill his coffers, by my unpaid labor. I might thus help Dr. McFarland to publish his benevolent deeds to the world, that he gives to the poor around him yearly, a bushel of potatoes from his own farm! Or it might help to buy some of the costly wines, and cigars, and confectioneries with which the Asylum feast tables are loaded, at the State's expense, to the credit of Dr. McFarland's great hospitality! Yes, it may pay for the intoxicating drinks the company of soldiers to which his oldest son belonged, used on that memorable occasion, when they, after this drunken debauch, stalked through our halls, headed by their drunken leader, to see us, the boarders of the house, put off with nothing but bread and molasses to eat, and nothing but a single saucer left to eat it from; for we were deprived of every cup, spoon, knife and fork, and chair, to supply the table of Dr. McFarland's guests. If we could have had one raisin, or cake, or candy, or apple, or any thing, left in the shape of fragments from that groaning table of luxuries, in exchange for the vegetables, strawberries, butter, sugar, and tea, they took from our table, we should have felt better satisfied.

I could not help sympathizing with the remark made by our kind attendant, Miss Tomlin, on the well remembered occasion—as we *stood* around our table, dipping our bread into our black molasses, the Doctor seemed inclined to shut this scene from the soldiers' view who followed after; but Miss Tomlin, instead of granting this wish, said, as she opened the door—"No, let them see us *as we are;* let them see how our table comforts compare with their own!" It may help too, to pay for the costly wine which Mrs. Coe told me she had seen carried, by the pail full, into the chamber of this elder son, to treat his companions with, taken from the Asylum storehouse of luxuries, charged for the "good of the patients." Seldom, very seldom, did a drop of these wines ever pass the lips of a patient, for his "good" or evil either.

Dr. McFarland's mode of "impressing" free citizens of these United States into *his* service is truly profitable, if not novel, in that it pays *him* well, as a public financier.

XXXII.

An Unpleasant Response.

The response I got to the congratulation I gave Dr. McFarland to-day, on his return from his Chicago trip, pains me a little. His wife standing by, I said "we welcome your return ; still, we congratulate you on being able to leave the superintendence of the house in so good hands as your wife's, in your absence. We feel that kindness rules her actions towards the patients."

"Your words are always so sweet and honied !"

"No more so than my feelings. They are correct reporters of my heart."

"Would that some of these sweet and honied words could be bestowed upon the husband you promised to love and honor !"

"He has had them in more abundance than any other man, but he shall never have another, until he repents."

O, how determined these men are to break down the conscience of woman, and thus annihilate her identity. Only let her be *their echo* or parasite and she is all right?

I am treating the Doctor as I have always tried to my husband, with the most patient forbearance, hoping thus to overcome the evil in him with kindness. Instead therefore, of reproaching the Doctor for turning with such heartless indifference from my appeals to him for protection, I just commit the business of punishing for these offences to an avenging God, and betake myself anew to the exercise of kindness and patient forbearance, still hoping that it may in this case prove a success, instead of a failure, as it did in Mr. Packard's case.

There should be no state rights in opposition to the central government. So there should be no individual sovereignty in opposition to God's government. Therefore no husband should require the subjection of his wife's conscience to his will, when it opposes what *she regards* as God's will. God grant, that the time may never wear away in me this spirit of resistance to such oppression.

XXXIII.

Is Man the Lord of Creation?

Dr. McFarland accused me yesterday of defending a principle which he claims would be subversive of all family government. He maintains that the government of the family is vested entirely in the husband, that the wife has no right to her identity; she must live, move and have her being in him alone. I admit that the recognition of her identity will endanger the overthrow of a family despotism, because the marital power will then be so limited as to compel a respectful regard to the inalienable rights of the wife; but on his principle, as the Doctor wants it, the husband must have the power to ignore all her rights, or he can not be "lord over all" in his family!

I claim that every family established on such a basis ought to be overthrown, as well as all other despotisms; and it is this principle which is at the present day sending devastation throughout the whole social fabric of society. Despotism can not live on freedom's soil. Divorce and disunion are demonstrating this fact, and they will continue to demonstrate and remonstrate too, against family despotisms, until this government will extend the right of "life, liberty and the pursuit of happiness" to the wives of her government as well as the husbands. Married woman has as good a right to her moral accountability as a married man; and God is her sovereign as well as he is man's sovereign. Man has no more right to interfere with her allegiance to Christ's government, than she has to interfere with his. Both must be judged independently before this highest tribunal, therefore each should be morally free to live up to their highest convictions of right.

On the Doctor's visit to-day he asked, "Mrs. Packard, what is meant by 'Wives, obey your husbands?'"

"It means to obey them in what is right, and not in what is wrong."

"What is meant by the husband being the head of the wife?"

"It means that he is the head, or the senior partner of the firm, and the wife the junior partner, or companion. He has this headship assigned to him instead of the wife, because he is the best fitted in nature to defend and protect the wife and children. He is the head, to protect, but not to subject the rights of the other members of the household. This headship gives him no more right to become the despot, than the junior position of the wife allows her to become his slave. Being associated as partners, does not confer on either, the right of usurpation."

"But what shall be done, when, on a point of common interest, they can not agree?"

"The junior must yield her views to the senior's."

"But supposing the wife feels that the husband's plans will bring disaster upon the family interests?"

"It is her duty to yield notwithstanding, after she has urged all her strong reasons against it, for unless she does, she trespasses on his right as 'head' of the firm. The risk must be assumed by some one, and as the head is compelled to bear this responsibility, he ought to be allowed to act in accordance with his own judgment, after the opinions of his junior partner have been candidly weighed. Then, if disaster follows, she has no right to complain, for this is one of the indispensable and inseparable liabilities of a co-partnership relation. Understanding this principle when she entered the firm, she would be domineering over an inalienable right of her partner to do otherwise. Unless this principle of justice can be peaceably conceded, there is no alternative **except a peaceable dissolution, or a civil war.**"

XXXIV.

Petition to the Trustees, Presented September, 1861.

To the Trustees of Illinois Insane Asylum.

Messrs: I, Mrs. E. P. W. Packard, wife of Rev. Theophilus Packard of Manteno, Kankakee County, Illinois, do most respectfully pray your honorable body to discharge me from this Asylum, and place me on a self-reliant position forthwith, for the following reasons.

1st. Because I am illegally imprisoned on a false charge. This I assume, on the ground that a person is supposed to be innocent, until he has been proved to be guilty. The charge of insanity has never been established, or proved against me, and I claim, that a charge which exposes an individual to a life long imprisonment, ought to be *proved*, before it is assumed that they are guilty and treated accordingly.

2nd. This, my imprisonment being a false one, eminently imperils the vital interests of this Institution, whose interests you are sacredly bound to protect. The mere "forms of law," regardless of the spirit, or intent of the law, will be found to be a bogus protection to the Institution.

3rd. I am entirely capable of assuming a self-reliant position, being in the full posession of all my mental and physical faculties, and having ever been an eminently practical woman, I already know how to use these faculties for my own pecuniary support, without aid from others.

4th. My long and dreary imprisonment among maniacs, is peculiarly trying to my sensibilities and my intelligence, and for you, Gentlemen, to protract it without investigation, seems unmanly, and unjust.

5th. It was only for the lawful exercise of my rights of opinion and conscience, that the charge of insanity was alleged against me by my husband, and I, therefore, am not willing to be returned to him until the question is settled at the bar of my country, whether a wife and mother in America can be protected under our Constitution, in the independent exercise of her rights of religious opinion.

6th. I think it would hasten this crisis, by allowing me my personal liberty, and thereby, a mother's guardianship over her infant children be sooner restored to them. It is a great wrong, thus to deprive six children, and one an infant, of a mother's tender care.

Gentlemen, as guardians of this Institution, allow me to inform you that this house has in some instances, been perverted from its original object, and is now being used as a penitentiary—a house of correction—a poor-house for the indigent and idle—a hospital for the sick—and for an inquisition. For my persecutors, it is being employed as an inquisition, where they hope to torture me into an acknowledgement of the Presbyterian church creed, and it is indeed true that all that human ingenuity can devise, has been most skillfully employed to make a maniac of me, since they find I will not recant. But, by God's help, I have hitherto sustained unharmed, these horrors and tortures, and reason still maintains its throne, and demands justice at your hands, or at the bar of my country.

Trustees of this Institution, on *you* now rests the responsibility of purging this house of these evils, and thus ward off the just indignation of an enlightened people, and the curse of an insulted God, which now overhangs it, threatening its destruction.

May divine wisdom guide you in the disposal of this petition of a persecuted woman. E. P. W. PACKARD.

P. S. A PROTEST. Dr. McFarland informs me that I am soon to be liberated and returned to my husband! Christian Gentlemen, I do hereby enter my most solemn protest against being returned to my husband. This shall never be done with my consent, and if done at all, it must be done as a mere act of brute force on your part. I shall never surrender my conscience to this traitor of Christ's government. His law says, "Judge ye not of your own selves what is right?" I shall obey this law of my Sovereign, and shall judge for myself what is right for me to do. I shall always yield to intelligence, and to argument based on truth, but to despotism *never.* I shall hold no fellowship with my husband, so long as he regards me as an unaccountable moral agent, "so help me God!"   A follower of Jesus.   E. P. W. P.

The above protest was added to my petition, and presented in person, to the Trustees, as they passed through my hall. As I handed it to Mr. Brown, the chairman, I said in presence of Dr. McFarland, "Will you gentlemen please have the kindness to consider this petition before deciding upon my case?" Mr. Brown took the document and gave it into the hands of the Secretary, saying "you take charge of it."

But, for the Trustees' sake, I am sorry to add that they took no notice of it, and so far as their action was concerned, my case was indefinitely postponed! I was left to continue on unnoticed, and uncared for just the same as before. They seemed to be just as indifferent to my interests as Dr. McFarland had been, and took no more notice of my petition to them, than the Doctor had of a similar one I had before sent him. What more could I do? If men to whom the public commit such important trusts will not discharge their duty, ought they not to be discharged themselves? Certainly. If the Superintendent is remiss in his duties, the Trustees ought to discharge him, and if the Trustees uphold an unworthy man, when they know he ought to be discharged, then they themselves, ought to be discharged, and so far as my case is concerned, I say, that from this time, if Dr. McFarland was guilty for keeping me there, then the Trustees are alike guilty.

The experience of my inner life, during this trial I find delineated in my journal of September 6th. If I am forced back to my husband, the act will be no more my act, than the fugitive's return is his own act. If God so permits, I know I shall be sustained in doing the best I can under the circumstances. I see not the way nor the plan of God in thus leading me in this self-denying course of obedience conflicting so much with my natural inclinations. But still I am satisfied. Let me but know my duty : 'tis all I ask. It is only thine own work and plan I am so blindly executing. Thine shall be the triumph or the defeat, not mine. Shall the instrument insist upon knowing the designer's plan, before consenting to be employed in executing the work? No, it is enough for me to know and keep my proper place, as an employee under the Master workman's control.

I believe I have a body-guard of invincible power to defend me in the discharge of every duty, and until my work is entirely done I am immortal. Although I am called to pursue a comet-like orbit, yet I have my path to revolve in, and no other planet can affect it, beyond its appointed limits. Velocity, momentum, onward force, is sometimes my only safety. I seem now to have reached that part of my orbit where accelerated motion is required to preserve its equilibrium. Great Sun of the Universe! keep me within thy influence and control, and never let me get beyond thy centripetal influence.

If I am sent back to Manteno as a fugitive, I intend to live entirely independent of human dictation, that does not coincide with my views of right and duty. I can not fellowship any church who regard me as an insane person, for such an influence will claim a right to control my conscience. If no church can allow me to be an independent, moral agent, I will belong to no church. Neither will I associate with the insane party. My associates shall be only those who respect my sanity.

If I am *forced* into the home of my husband, it will be no sin for me to be there, for the act will not be mine, therefore, I shall have grace to live a christian life with my children, since God's providence so appoints my destiny, for God requires no impossibilities.

The reason I can not voluntarily put myself unprotected again into the power of my husband, is because I see him without his mask. The people do not. I will not stain my soul with a falsehood to curry the favor of all the people. Wherever I am I will dare to do right, and then I know God will take care of me.

In a letter to my son Theophilus, I say, "The Trustees met yesterday, and have indefinitely postponed my liberation.

Ye, you my first born, and my other children, must still continue to suffer the cruel wrong of being deprived of a mother's gentle care. I did hope, that if the Trustees would not grant my petition, they would send me home *forcibly*, for then I should not do wrong by going. And then their responsibility of my imprisonment would have ceased. But no; they did nothing, and we must linger on, enduring this unnatural separation still longer. I am cast down, but not in despair.

"God will make the riddle plain,
So all our murmuring thoughts restrain."

XXXV.

The Rights of the Tax Payers.

LETTER TO THE TRUSTEES.

INSANE ASYLUM, May 10, 1862.

To THE TRUSTEES.—*Gentlemen:* Dr. McFarland has informed me that the State, not my husband, supports me here. I deem it my duty to protest against this act of injustice. Although I fully appreciate your intended kindness to me and mine, by placing me on the charity list; yet it is the injustice of the act that my nature instinctively revolts at. My children have no claim upon the charities of this State for their education. God has provided them with ways and means of being educated far superior to many children of the poor tax payers. If these indigent tax payers choose, voluntarily to deprive their own children of the means of education, for the benefit of my more favored ones, there would be no injustice in my receiving their gifts in this way. But to claim it of them, without their consent or knowledge, simply as a legal right, is unjust; for it plainly conflicts with the dictates of the moral law, which is, doing to others as I should wish them to do to me. I am not required to love my neighbor's interests better than my own. My own children

H

have a prior claim to my regard than my neighbor's Still, I have no right to seek their interests at my neighbor's expense, without his knowledge or consent.

Since my husband has broken his marriage covenant, and failed to protect me in my duties as a wife and mother, depriving me not only of my marriage rights, but also of all my rights as an American citizen, thereby depriving his children of their natural guardian and instructor, I feel that he has no right to seek to make pecuniary profits from the specious plea thus formed of educating his children.

You know not what you are doing, in supporting this man in his wicked plan of wronging the innocent without cause. God grant that your eyes may be opened to see your guilt in thus doing, so that you may repent in this life, where you can be forgiven, on the ground of making due restitution to me, for the multiplied wrongs you have inflicted upon me and mine.   Respectfully yours,

Mrs. E. P. W. PACKARD.

XXXVI.

The Imputation of Insanity a Barrier to Human Progress.

At one time I was made to feel exceedingly sad and sorrowful by a conversation I had with a lady who called upon me. I conversed freely and frankly with her, as usual, avowing my views and sentiments, and giving my reasons for the course I was pursuing. In her undeveloped condition she failed to comprehend them fully, and therefore, since the brand of insanity was upon me, she concluded these points which she could not readily comprehend, were products of my insanity! This, from her standpoint, being an inevitable conclusion, her mind would necessarily be barred against any convictions of truth which I might present to her reason or intelligence. These goggles of insanity through which she now looks, disturbs all her mental vision, so that she can no more apprehend a new truth through me, as its medium, than the scales of bigotry will admit any light through those who war with its dogmas.

Now supposing this position should be generally adopted, viz : that what we can not readily apprehend, is insanity ; what encouragement have we to make progress, or become the benefactors of our age, knowing that just as soon as we advance to any point of intelligence beyond another, we must be regarded and treated as insane, and thus expose ourselves to a life-long imprisonment unless we recant ? Is not the imputation of insanity the devil's barrier to human progress ? I feel that we ought to be very careful not to condemn what we do not understand, for in Christ's case, his persecutors were condemned as guilt of "blasphemy," for doing this very thing. The blinded Jews, who were wedded to their creed with as firm a tenacity as the Orthodox church of the present day is to their own, could not therefore apprehend the principles of the new dispensation, which Christ came to introduce, because it conflicted with their church creed ; therefore they accused this innovator with madness or insanity for promulgating such new, and strange doctrines. Like the same class at the present age, they did not wait to see evidence of his insanity in his evil actions, before they condemned him ; but merely for his expressions or utterances of opinions, he was condemned as a mad man. Now I think his accusers *acted* more like mad men than he did, when we come to take *actions* as evidence of insanity, instead of the expression of opinions. And even if we take their own basis of evidence, I think the Jewish dogmas which their church defended were as great an evidence of insanity in them, as the opinions which Christ taught in opposition to their standard of morals, were evidence of insanity in him. But I do not think that the utterance of opinions in either case, is any evidence of insanity. The Jews believed they had received their dispensation from God, and of course, they were tenacious in its defence, and could not readily see that the time had come for the old to give place to the new. So it is in all ages, some are slower than others to see that the time for the inauguration of any new truth has fully come, and therefore they oppose it with the same intolerant spirit which the Jewish ministers did.

But so far as the question of insanity goes, those show the greatest proof of being insane, who oppose this inauguration with vile slander, and ruinous scandal, and false imprisonment, and death, rather than those who calmly stand by the truth, and defend it with sound and invincible logic. It was this very inoffensiveness in Christ which so exasperated them against him, plainly showing that it was *they* who had the devil of bigotry in them, not him. It was they, the Jewish ministers, who were the blasphemers, instead of him whom they accused of blasphemy. The views and theories taught by Christ, were all humanitarian in their character; yet this did not shield him from the assaults of slander and the charge of insanity; neither will this armor prove a defence at the present age, even under the American flag of free religious toleration, so long as reformers are allowed to be publicly branded by these Insane Asylums. Whoever has the diploma of this institution forced upon him, must submit henceforth to fight his way through fire and blood to carry out his benevolent purposes to humanity; for at every inch of progress, he is compelled to face the barbed arrow of insanity, hurled at him by the intolerant and bigoted of his age. If by any possible means, the imputation of insanity can be removed from the track of the reformer, the wheel of human progress will be greatly accelerated.

Again my persecutors are guilty of the same act of uncharitableness in calling the natural developments of womanhood evil, or insanity, in me. This undeveloped sister insists that it is impossible for me to be what I profess to be, a true woman, and not have overcome the evil in my husband; since goodness is omnipotent. I acknowledge the potency of goodness, while I, at the same time add, that I do not believe that she or any other woman could have borne more patiently with a husband's faults, or have labored more kindly and indefatigably to overcome them than I have done. I regard such a man as a most subtle foe to conquer, and I do fully believe, that ultimately, through my instrumentality, if any, Christ will conquer him; but the time has not yet come. It is said of Christ, "Thou hast put all things in subjection under his feet," as I believe, for the purpose of raising them to a state of happiness and purity. Christ conquers, not to punish, but to bless his foes. I believe my twenty-one years of subjection to my husband's will, is not designed as a punishment to me, but as a blessed means of bringing me to lose all my natural loves in the love of God's will. Thus am I called to die to live again—to die naturally, to live spiritually. I hope this new life has begun in me. May it be developed into maturity!

Another point she could not understand in me is, that I call it a reproach to be called insane, when she says it is not a reproach to be insane. I do not regard an insane person as an object of reproach or contempt, by any means. They are objects of pity and compassion; for I regard insanity as the greatest misfortune which can befall a human being in this life. But to be regarded as an insane person, when I am not, is to me a reproach, which I find is a severe cross for me to bear; such as for example, to be reported to be a bankrupt, when I am not, is a reproach, because it is a cruel slander. But how much more malevolent and cruel is the slander, to be reported as lost to reason when we are not. I think the sensitive feelings of Christ led him to feel it to be a reproach to have his age say of him, "He hath a devil and is mad, why hear ye him?" As much as to say, "Why will you listen to what this 'babbler' says? he is not worth noticing, for he is merely an insane person, who don't know what he is about." Now, since he expressly says it is "blasphemy, in that they said he hath a devil;" and since blasphemy is the blackest sin which can be committed against Christ, have we not reason to fear it is of the same type of magnitude when committed against his followers?

But so far as I am concerned, I can forgive this injury which this sister has thus inflicted upon my sensitive feelings, although Christ says, blasphemy is a sin which can not be forgiven, "either in this life, or the life to come." I do pray that she may never know from her own sad experience, how deeply she has wounded my feelings; and never, until she is called to bear this same reproach, can she know how ponderous is the burden.

But while I am in this Institution, this thought does buoy up my burdened soul, viz; that all who know me personally, here, have entire confidence in my sanity, not even excepting Dr. McFarland! and I do believe that Miss M———* the Supervisoress expressed this heart feeling of them all, when she said to me, "Mrs. Packard, I believe you to be in the full exercise of all your mental faculties, with a sound mind, and no single act of yours have I ever known to contradict or invalidate this testimony?" Dear, kind Sister! how my heart thanks you for this defence of my spirit nature; your sympathy in this expression, is like balm to my wounded spirit.

Mrs. Hosmer, the sewing room directress, also has my sincere thanks for her testimony, given to Rev. A. D. Eddy, D. D., in reply to his question, "How is Mrs. Packard *at times?*"

"You have seen Mrs. Packard once: you have seen her always."

XXXVII.

Mr. James Lyon's Advice.

Mr. James Lyon, and his sister, Miss Jane Lyon, of Georgetown, Illinois, brought their sister here, and were allowed to remain in our ward for some time without the watch of an employee upon their lips. This was rarely allowed, especially where I was, lest some means of appeal be afforded me. I, of course, made the most of my opportunities, and conversed freely with them. They manifested sympathy for me, and a

---

*At her own special request, her name is omitted.

confidence in my word and statements, which was to me, at that time, a source of so much pleasure, that I feel impelled to record it as a kind of "oasis" in my prison life. Sad as they saw my surroundings to be, they advised me never to ask to return to my husband, but to wait; to stand firm and unmovable on this point. Mr. Lyon said he thought great good might result from my being sent here. He also said he should lay my case before the Judge of his county, and see if anything could be done for me.

Here I will state, that Mr. Lyon was then the first man who ever agreed with me, in my determination never to return to my husband. On this point I had stood alone except that Mary McFarland had one day uttered her assent in these emphatic words; "I would not go to him if I were in your place, for if I had a husband who put me into an Insane Asylum when I was not insane, I never would speak to him afterwards!" With these two exceptions, I stood alone, and battled friends and foes alike, in defence of the honor my nature demanded, to have no sort of fellowship with these deeds of darkness. And to this day I am satisfied with the stand I then took. It would seem to be as insane an act for me to consent to our reunion on his basis, as it would be for the North to consent to a union with the South on the basis of slavery.

XXXVIII.

Record of a Day.

The record of one day is a record of all, since I came to this ward. I rise with the breakfast bell, which rings about fifteen minutes before we are called to the table. I first drop upon my knees and offer a short prayer for protection and guidance, and then drink a tumbler of rain water, to keep my bowels free, which, in connection with my other health regimen, does prove effectual in producing this effect, which habit is so indispensably necessary to perfect health and mental vigor. I wet my head in soft water, and wash my hands and face and dress myself as quickly as possible.

I then throw off my bed clothes, article by article, giving each a shaking to air it, and stir up the husk of my mattress, and then leave them all airing while I eat my breakfast. I sleep with my window wide open, both summer and winter. After breakfast I finish making my bed, sweep and dust my room, and then invite the ladies of our hall to my room, to prayers, leaving each entirely free to come or not just as they choose. There is but one chapel service daily, and that is at at night. Sometimes one, sometimes three, and oftentimes no one responds to my invitation by coming to prayers. After reading and praying I commence my studies, by first writing in my diary and journal. I pursue a systematic course of studying the bible and writing out my conclusions, and then read some scientific book requiring thought and close attention, until eleven o'clock.

I then take a full bath of cold water, and then follow it with vigorous friction, accompanied with gymnastic exercises, adapted to te expansion of the chest and muscles of the system. I pursue this vigorous exercise before my open window until I find it a sweet relief to sit down and comb my hair thoroughly. I then complete my toilet for the day, all of which occupies nearly one hour's time. I am then in a condition to relish my dinner, after which, I read some light literature, or the daily paper, over which I often drop to sleep in my chair, and thus take a short nap. I then take my embroidery and do a certain amount, while I at the same time commit to memory certain passages which I have marked in my reading as worthy of particular note ; or, while doing my embroidery, I meet my attendants Miss Tomlin and Miss McKelva in the large dormitory, and there listen to readings from Shakespeare's plays which we mutually agree to do for our individual improvement. This occupies my mind completely until the horn blows for supper, when the farm hands are all summoned in from their work in the fields about five o'clock. I take no suppers at all, finding that two meals are all my present habits render necessary for the unimpeded and healthful operations of nature. I noticed that while I took my suppers my sleep was not so quiet and refreshing as it ought to be—that I awoke with a bad taste in my mouth, and had but little appetite for my breakfast. I felt rather averse to effort. I became aware that I was over feeding myself instead of refreshing nature with food. I therefore dispensed with my suppers entirely, and all these symptoms and indifferent feelngs subsided, and I felt well, that is, I had no special reason for considering that I had a body to care for, so quiet and unimpeded were its functions carried on. The body thus cared for instead of being an incumbrance to the mind, became only its faithful servant. My sleep is now really a luxury, even amid this den of howling maniacs, and my breakfast and dinners are peculiarly well relished, and I have not a pain or uneasy sensation in my physical system to call the mind's attention to, whatever.

How thankful am I for my practical knowledge of the laws of my physical nature; for I do believe that godliness, or living according to God's laws, is profitable in every respect; and ungodliness, or trespassing on nature's laws, can not be done with impunity.

After supper I lay aside my work, and devote myself to amusing the prisoners, by dancing and playing with them until after chapel service, when they are locked up for the night. I go through my gymnastics again at night in my room, and drink my tumbler of soft water, and pray, and go joyfully to bed to sleep, and pleasant dreams. I often feel when rising, as much relieved and rested from my troubles, as if I had really been absent from my prison, on a pleasant visit to loved friends. It sometimes takes me some minutes to realize where I am, on awaking from such pleasant dreams.

I often think this hell is not so unmitigated in its torments as the hell of lost spirits is represented to be, by their resting not, day nor night. Could not these prison torments be suspended by sleep, they must soon become too intolerable for physical nature to sustain. God grant me deliverance from endless, unmitigated torment!

The discipline of this hell has had one influence over my moral feelings which is certainly conducive to inward peace of mind, and that is, I am becoming comparatively indifferent to the "speech of people," which is really one of the greatest bugbears in the universe. I now think it is much better to do as we please, or as we think it right for us to do, promptly, and independently, than to square our conclusions by other people's estimates. Blessed be independence and moral courage! for by these traits alone can we secure the honor of God, and the approbation of a good conscience. Let me get above "folks," where I can breathe a pure atmosphere and live. The idea of suffocating and choking to death down in the vitiating atmosphere of a meddlesome and gossiping world, is very disagreeable. The record of every day's experience here of this doleful prison life, carries me farther and farther above this grovelling atmosphere, so that my mind finds peace amid tumult and noisy strife.

For the benefit of others who may be called to endure similar trials, I will add, that I find it an invaluable habit to be able to secure good sleep, and plenty of it, to fortify one invincibly against the attacks of "low spirits." To be a "good sleeper" is as indispensable to a happy, vigorous state of the intellect, as being a "good eater" is to a good physical condition. And my signal triumph over low, or depressed spirits, which never for one entire day disturbed my inward peace of mind, during all my imprisonment, is greatly owing to my constant practice of sleeping soundly from ten to eleven hours out of the twenty-four. The need of this habit was presented first to my mind by my scientific reading in the Asylum, where it was shown that whenever the brain had unusual burdens to carry, either in the form of trials or of deep study, a greater amount of sleep was indispensable to sustaining it unharmed.

XXXIX.

How I Bought and Retained some Paper.

Before narrating the incidents concerning the paper, I will here state a few facts incidentally bearing upon the subject. As I have before stated, orders were expressly given when I was removed to the Eighth ward, that I be not allowed to go out of it at all except to chapel service. These orders were strictly enforced for about five months, when orders were received that I might be allowed to ride and walk out with the patients. I have reason to think that I am indebted to Miss M——, for this privilege, as she was the first who bore to me the message in these words, "Mrs. Packard, the Doctor has given me permission to take you to ride to-day in company with his daughter Hattie."

Availing myself of this privilege I took with me the only capital I owned in the whole world, viz: a silver dime, which Dr. McFarland had given me, and which by an unaccountable combination of circumstances, he supposed was justly my due, determining if possible to invest this capital in paper, now the great want of my existence. At my request Miss M—— left me at Dr. Shirley's office, to get some unfinished work done on my teeth, while she and Hattie rode off. While they were gone I took occasion to step out to make my investment. But recollecting that five months before, in settling up my account at the "Philadelphia Store." I found myself indebted five cents above what I was able to pay, I accordingly asked Mr. Woodman to trust me for that, assuring him I should pay him the first money I got. He however gallantly replied, "it is of no consequence, you are welcome to it."

But as I felt bound in honor to fulfill my promise, I went directly to this store, and after stating the circumstances, offered my dime to meet my obligation, secretly praying however, that he would still insist upon it that it was of "no consequence" to him, for it was of great value to me—half my fortune! But in this, I am sorry to say, I was disappointed, for it was his clerk now that I was doing my business with instead of the kind Mr. Woodman, the owner. So after searching his money drawer over in vain to find the five cents my due, he left me alone in the store long enough to steal half his goods had I been so disposed, (but I did not steal anything, by the way!) and went to the bank to get my dime changed, and thus I got my five cents. But having no paper, as I had before offered to take it in paper, I hastened to the nearest bookstore, where I bought five cents worth of damaged foolscap, which amounted to eight sheets! Overjoyed at the success of my investment, being three extra sheets above the current price, I, with the lightest heart and the quickest step possible, returned to Dr. Shirley's office, lest Mary get there before me. But alas! the tardy bank was so long in changing my dime, that she drove up to the door just as I returned to be thus caught! But by carefully concealing my long roll of foolscap under my shawl as best I could, I thought I had satisfied her inquiry as to where I had been, by telling her I had been to the Philadelphia Store to pay a debt.

But alas! the long roll of foolscap would so protrude itself against my shawl as to lead her to suspect I had not told the whole truth in reporting myself. However she did not express these thoughts to me until that evening when just before chapel, she came to me with this question, "Mrs. Packard, did you get any paper when I took you to ride to-day?"

"Why do you ask me that question, Mary?"

"Because I thought I saw something under your shawl which you seemed to try to conceal from me."

"What if I did? havn't I a right to carry things without your knowledge?"

"You have no right to carry paper without my knowledge, for the Doctor has expressly forbidden me to let you have a scrap of writing paper, and if you have used the privilege I granted you by taking you to ride, by getting yourself paper, I must report you to the Doctor. Did you get paper, or did you not?"

"I did, Mary, get five cents' worth?"

"I must report you to the Doctor—it is my duty."

"I am sorry, Mary, your conscience dictates such a course, still if it does, obey your conscience, for I know you will favor me whenever you can conscientiously do so."

As she left the hall I, as quickly as possible, took the three extra sheets from my roll and hid them about my person, leaving the roll in the top of an old box which I was using as a trunk to keep my things in, with one dress simply covering the roll. After chapel, and when the ladies were nearly all locked up for the night in their rooms, the Doctor's steps were heard in our hall, and as he entered at one end, I left my room at the opposite end, and as we approached each other we met at about the middle of the hall, when standing directly in front of me, he remarked, with his eye fixed most intently upon me, "Mrs. Packard, did you get some paper when you you went to ride with Miss. M——, to-day?"

"Yes sir! said I looking him also full in the eye."

"Will you give me the paper if I ask you for it?"

"No sir!" with emphasis, said I.

"Will you give it to me if I *demand* it of you?"

"No sir!" with greater emphasis.

For a moment we stood looking at each other in silent amazement, then he said, "Where is the paper?"

"Amongst my things."

We then passed each other, he going to my room to attend to his business, and I to the opposite end of the hall to attend to mine.

When I returned, I found the Doctor searching the table drawer where I kept my choice things, the key to which I carried in my own pocket; but it seemed the Doctor had opened it with some other key. I wonder if there are any locks which Dr. McFarland's keys can not *lawfully* open!

After watching his movements, while he stood bent over my drawer, carefully opening every box, large and small, and pocketing such articles as he chose, such as bits of pencils, and old pens, and any articles of stationery he could find,

I left the room, while he was, ransacking the paraphernalia of woman's toilet, remarking to my dormitory companions as I left, "Ladies, bear witness to this robbery!"

Failing to find the paper he was in search of, he closed and locked the drawer, then asked the ladies if they knew of any other place where Mrs. Packard kept her things. Miss Goldsby replied, "She keeps some in this box, I believe," pointing to a cushioned covered seat near by. This box, the size of a common trunk, was full of my larger articles of wearing apparel, which he carefully searched throughout; but failing to find the roll of foolscap, because in such plain sight, near the top! he left, chagrined and mortified at his failure, and locking the door of my room as he passed out, he left me alone in the hall, while he, with a quick, anxious tread, passed speechlessly by me, out of the hall, closing the dead lock upon me.

As I alone paced the hall, silently ruminating upon my probable fate, I saw the hall door open, and the Doctor entered, followed by his porter. "Now," thought I, "I am to be transported off to some dungeon or secret cell, to suffer the penalty for telling the truth to him and my attendant," and stepping up deliberately, in front of the porter, I dauntlessly stood, with folded arms, ready to be unresistingly borne to my place of torture. The friendly porter, who had more than twenty times put the reins of the carriage horse into my hands, and received my "thank you," as often, just gave me a smile, and a respectful bow of recognition, and passing me, followed the Doctor into my room. He soon appeared again with what the Doctor supposed was my trunk, in his hands, and followed the Doctor with it up to the trunk room, where it was left beyond the reach of Mrs. Packard's accommodation. Thus the Doctor had the satisfaction of feeling that if Mrs. Packard has baffled him in finding the paper, he has been able to annoy her by taking her trunk! And, as the event proved, the Doctor, upon a second overhauling of my things in the trunk room, found the roll of foolscap; and being five sheets, he felt that this amount answered to the five cent's worth Miss M—— told him I had bought, so that, after unlocking my large trunk in the trunk room, and robbing it of all my letters, and papers, and manuscripts of every kind, he felt satisfied, feeling that at last his plan to defeat his prisoners of their rights had succeeded, even in my case.

But don't let the great Doctor feel too confident that he has gained the laurels of victory, after all, for he did not know that his wife furnished me with a better trunk, and more of my wardrobe than ever before, with a key to it also; and besides, the Doctor did not know that I still kept and faithfully used, the three large sheets of foolscap, from which I am now copying for the public advertising of himself, through this record of his own actions! No, neither did he know that this ungallant assault upon a defenceless woman's rights; aroused the just indignation of the house in sympathy with his victim; so that it came to be regarded as a part of the code of honor in that house afterwards, to evade the mandate to "keep all stationery from Mrs. Packard," so that the employees willingly followed the example which Mrs. McFarland set them, to furnish me with supplies, clandestinely, whenever they could safely do so. In this way, he, himself, furnished me with sufficient material to print a volume quadruple this size when it is all printed! Can not God cause the "wrath of man to praise him?"

XL.

The Aristocracy of Jacksonville Rebuked—Another Honorable Act.

One day, as Dr. McFarland was passing my door, I hailed him, exclaiming, "Doctor, I want to tell you of my trial. I believe you will pity me, for you did on my experiencing a similar trial when I first came here."

"O yes, I will pity you. What is it?"

"Doctor, I have been insulted by those proud ladies your wife took through here the other day."

"Why, or how, did they insult you?"

"I will tell you. They came to my room, where I politely invited them to be seated, and entered upon intelligent, ladylike conversation with them. But I quickly noticed they had come as spies—that they came to ridicule, instead of to comfort the sorrowing, and that all my effort to entertain them was to be at my own expense. That is, I saw by their manner that they regarded me as an insane person, and that all I said, no matter what, it was all looked upon as insane talk, such as they regarded as of no consequence, except as it afforded them subject for merriment and ridicule. Hurt as my feelings were by their sly winking and scornful smiles, which were freely exchanged whenever I spoke, I took no notice of it, so far as my manner was concerned, but continued politely and intelligently to entertain them; and when they abruptly withdrew, I politely invited them to call again, to which only one returned a response. By their significant looks and smiles as they passed out, they plainly said, 'We have seen enough of her insanity, let us go and find some other insane person to ridicule!' And they did ridicule many others in the same manner, leading them to exclaim as they left, 'They make us feel that we are a menagerie of wild beasts, to be gazed upon as show animals!'"

"It is too bad! They ought not to have treated you so. It was wrong, very wrong. I have discharged two attendants to-day for ridiculing a patient."

"You have done right, Dr. McFarland, and God will bless you for it. You have defended the rights of the oppressed by so doing. This is what God sent you here for, to protect the afflicted and care for them." I then added, "I feel very indignant at their insulting conduct, and I say it is a just indignation, such as the dictates of a right nature prompt. I do not, nor will I try, to restrain it by silence, for I feel called by God, 'to cast abroad my rage,' as he directs in Job xl: 11–15. Under this feeling of just indignation, I have written a reproof."

"I hope you have addressed it to them."

"Yes, here it is," handing him the following letter. After thoroughly reading it he handed it back saying, in a very firm decided manner, "put this letter into an envelope, direct it to Mrs. J. H. Bancroft, and put it into the post-office."

I did so, and the letter was sent too, and the next morning a delegation of these aristocratic ladies met the Doctor in the reception room. But for what purpose they made so early a call at the Asylum I have never yet learned. I only know that they had an interview there with the Doctor, for several attendants came rushing into my room assuring me the same ladies were there to whom I had sent my letter, and they thought they would soon call upon me to make their apology for their unchristian and uncivil treatment. But I am sorry to say, they never called upon me, neither did they ever send me an apology for this gross insult.

This fact has led me to conclude that the feeling often expressed by the sensible employees is true, viz : that this class of Jacksonville people despise the patients, and, more than any class of Asylum visitors, manifest this feeling in the most unmistakable manner towards the inmates, as occasion offers. These insolent visitors have long been a great source of annoyance to the prisoners there, therefore I feel called upon to expose them to the world. Had I any reason to suppose my private rebuke had benefited them, I should never have consented to thus treat the persistent transgressor by publishing this letter, to Mrs. Bancroft, Mrs. Lathrop and Mrs. Wells.

Insane Asylum, May 1, 1862.

Sisters : Have we not all one Father ? Are we not equally dependent upon our heavenly Father for life and all its blessings ? Is it therefore filial or becoming to claim more than he bestows, or abuse what he gives ?

You may perhaps be surprised at these questions, and wonder what can have prompted their utterance. I will tell you. Your call at my room was the occasion, and your treatment of me while there, was the cause. You treated me not as an afflicted sister, but as a brute. You did indeed visit me in my prison, but I was led to exclaim, ",would that you had not, for by this act you have inflicted a wound upon one of Christ's little ones. such as he will certainly be called upon to avenge. Yes sisters, you have harmed yourselves, and you have hurt me. The hurt on me will be healed, and by my patient endurance will only add to the luster of my crown of righteousness.

Sisters, what could be more cruel than to make light of and ridicule the afflicted members of God's household, as you did yesterday, when you visited our wards? Would you not have called the act an outrage on your feelings to find that your sick and agonized child was made an object of ridicule and contempt, by her more favored sisters? Would not your authority as a parent demand that these guilty ones be punished? Sisters, in behalf of injured humanity, I feel compelled to inform you that the weak, sickly and persecuted members of God's family are not brute beasts, but human beings, with human feelings, if not like yourselves, like your superiors on the plane of humanity and intelligence; and if you can find nothing human in your own proud hearts by which to judge of our feelings, I will inform you that we are a class of human beings so much superior to yourselves. that for our benefit, we wish to withdraw ourselves from the influence of your inferior natures, lest we be contaminated thereby. As for myself I feel bound to withdraw the invitation I extended to you yesterday to call upon me again, regarding you as I now do as beneath my notice.

When I find a human being in a female form who has so far perverted her nature, as to leave no traces of sympathy, or kind feelings towards others, but is only arrogant and proud, I feel it my duty to avoid such, and treat them only as fallen beings, still hoping and praying that the lost image of humanity may be restored, even if it must come at the expense of an Asylum retribution. Your sister in bonds.

E. P. W. PACKARD.

XLI.

"Love your Enemies."

Upon reviewing the scenes of yesterday I felt such an impulse of thanksgiving for this signal victory of right, that I felt like returning a thank-offering to the Lord for it. And I could find no better way of expressing it, than to try to cultivate a forgiving spirit towards Dr. McFarland, by trying to stimulate him in well doing, so that I might have a chance to forgive him on the gospel condition of repentance. Therefore for his encouragement in well doing I penned the following note and handed it to him, saying, as I did so. "Doctor, I feel that you deserve a certificate of good behavior, will you therefore accept of this from me?"

"A Love Message.'

Dr. McFarland, Respected Friend, I feel constrained to assure you that the noble stand you took yesterday is securing for you laurels from all true humanity about this house. Its involuntary utterance seems to be in all cases like what Mrs. Coe expressed when I told her of the affair. "good! for Dr. McFarland! This is an honorable act!" But this is not the best of it, "When a man's ways please the Lord, he maketh even his enemies to be at peace with him." "Be not weary in well doing, for in due season ye shall reap if ye faint not."   Your true friend,

E. P. W. Packard.

As the Doctor opened the note and his eye caught the heading, he uttered an exclamation of surprise, and after repeating the heading over twice aloud, he added. "Who would have thought of Dr. McFarland's receiving a "love message" from Mrs. Packard!"

I replied, "it is even so! I am no hypocrite—I am a true woman, and the love I bestow upon men does not hurt them."

"No, it does not," said he.

"The truth is, Doctor, I am resolved to risk the exercise

of a disinterested benevolence, however its legitimate development may seem to conflict with my selfish interests."

Without responding any further he pocketed his note and left me, perhaps to plot some way by which to turn this expression against me. I think I can fully appreciate too the danger which Mrs. Coe pointed out to me in treating the Doctor with "so much civility and kindness even after he has wronged you so much and egregiously." He may I know, by his policy, turn it very much against me, if he is so disposed to pervert it, or misrepresent me. Still, since God's directions are simple and plain on this point, " to love your enemies, do good to them that hate you, and pray for them who despitefully use you and persecute you," and my own forgiving nature does not conflict with these directions as appplied to the Doctor, I intend to be fearless in using every possible means that love can devise to save him; for it is to me a far more desirable object to save him than to destroy him; and so far as he is concerned I do not think my deliverance depends upon his decision or his action. God's purposes cannot be thwarted by my obeying his directions, although my doing so, may seem to conflict with the selfish policy which my reason may suggest.

God commands us to "do good to our enemies," and if I fully obey this direction, I must not only pray for him, but I must act and labor for his welfare. Judging from my own feelings, I do not see how I can really love an enemy and let him go unreproved and unwarned. But perhaps if I hated a human being I might answer the demands of my conscience by simply praying for him; but since I never knew what that feeling was by experience to hate any one, I may not be qualified to judge one who has. My nature prompts me to hate the sin and love the sinner, and my love for the sinner is so genuine and so real, that I can leave no means untried to bring him to see his sins and repent, since I know pardon from his Judge can be bestowed on no other condition. The greatest sin of my life as I now view it, lies in the fact that I have been too ready to forgive the wrong doer, and in my impatience to extend my pardon I have sometimes forgiven before I ought to have done so—that is, I have forgiven the impenitent instead of the penitent, and thus encouraged the transgressor in his sins. But through the discipline of my heavenly Father I now see my sin in this respect, so that henceforth I shall aim to extend to the impenitent the "love message" of warning and rebuke, and to the truly penitent, the "love message" of encouragement in well doing. To extend forgiveness to the impenitent, degrades ourselves also as guilty accomplices in their iniquities.

XLII.

How Mr. Packard gave me Paper, and how I lost it.

Mr. Packard visited the Institution twice during the three years his wife was imprisoned in it. But these visits were not designed to comfort and cheer her with the hope of deliverance from her prison life at some future time, but to perpetuate it, through his influence over the Superintendent and the Trustees. He visited me in my cell, and saw my companions, the howling, raving maniacs; and although he feared for his own life while among them, he expressed no fears for his wife's life. He tried to raise his voice so much above the roar of this tempest of human passions and seething hate, as to make his wife understand that she was under obligations of gratitude to him for replenishing her wardrobe for a longer campaign! But he failed to make her appreciate this obligation of gratitude due a benefactor, who was only restoring stolen property to its rightful owner. What obligation am I under to the robber who meets me in the street and robs me of all I have, my watch, and purse, and even my wearing apparel, and then comes and asks me to bestow on him my grateful thanks for presenting me my own wardrobe, *as his gift?*

Either the tumultuous elements surrounding me, or the lack of capacity within me, or both, prevented my seeing this obligation due him as my benefactor! My sense of justice will not allow me to thank robbers for gifts which are already my own property; therefore, this reverend divine was obliged to leave, feeling that he was a much injured man, because his benefactions were so little appreciated by his ungrateful beneficiary! Although the articles from my wardrobe which he brought to me in the prison, were the most inferior part of it, being in the main, my clothes which I had done wearing myself, and had laid aside for donations to my washerwoman and others more destitute than myself; yet, destitute as I then was, they were in themselves very acceptable, for I had ample time for making new things out of old, and thus I was able to appear in quite a respectable costume for that place.

But there was one article he brought me, for which I did really feel so grateful, I could hardly control this emotion by my principles or reason; that is, I felt so instinctively grateful for the large roll of writing paper, envelopes, and stationery he brought me, that I almost spoke my thanks, before reason had had time to give her verdict to the contrary. He saw that my joy was almost boundless, at this most unexpected possession. And as soon as he left, I commenced writing a letter to my children on it, feeling no need of secrecy now; and therefore, when Dr. McFarland caught me quietly using my stationery, he, in astonishment, inquired, "And where did you get your paper?"

"Mr. Packard gave it to me."

"How did Mr. Packard come to give you paper?"

"I don't know, sir. I suppose, however, he felt that it might be an innocent amusement for me to write here, knowing I loved to write when I was at home."

"How much did he give you?"

"Quite a number of sheets."

"Let me see it."

I then took the roll from under my pillow and handed it to

him, saying, "Here it is." Before this, I had taken out one-half of it, and hid it about my person. I did not tell him of this! He took the roll, examined it carefully and thoughtfully, for some minutes, then putting the whole under the breast of his coat, he remarked, "I will take charge of this." And he has been true to his word; for *I* have been relieved from this charge ever since.

But the matter did not stop here. The Superintendent arraigned the Minister as an intruder into his business, and authoritatively demanded of this husband why he had given paper to his wife. The husband replied, he did it for her comfort and amusement. The Superintendent then, after giving the Minister a severe reprimand, finished by the threat, that if he ever attempted to interfere again with his management or discipline of his wife, he should have the liberty of taking her away, forthwith! This terrible threat silenced the Minister into unanswering submission to the superior mandates of the Superintendent over the control of his wife's destiny.

XLIII.

Dialogues with Dr. McFarland on the Woman Question.

The Doctor has been talking with me to-day upon the feelings I manifested towards my husband. The Doctor asked," Mrs. Packard, do you think it would be considered as natural, for a true woman to meet one who had been a lover and a husband, after one year's separation, even if he had abused her, without one gush of affection?"

"Yes sir, I do say it is the dictates of the higher nature of a woman to do so in my case. He has by his own actions annihilated every particle of respect I have ever felt for his manhood, and thus my higher moral nature instinctively abhors him. To bestow upon such a man a gush of sensual affection, would be an insane act in me, inasmuch as it would demonstrate that my lower nature ruled my higher; whereas sanity requires that the higher rule the lower. I have obeyed the dictates of my conscience in doing so."

"Do you feel sure your's is a right conscience?"

"It is one I am willing to go to God's judgement bar with."

"Do you believe the bible?"

"Indeed I do, every word of it! it is our sure word of prophecy."

"Does not the bible require forgiveness?"

"It does, sir, on the ground of *repentance*, even seventy times seven. But without it, we are not allowed to forgive, lest it harden the offender in his sins. Mr. Packard has never by word or deed intimated that he has done one unjust or wrong deed in treating me as he has done, much less that he is sorry for it, and now for me to treat him as my husband, would be saying to him, "I think you are doing all right in treating me as you are." Thus I should be upholding him in his sins, by thus disregarding God's express directions."

Besides, Mr. Packard is not satisfied with branding me as insane, but is trying to defame my virtue also, and he bases this charge upon my benevolent regard for the happiness of others! O! most cruel man! Does he not know that my regard for God is superior to all others? Could the sovereign of my higher nature—conscience—be made the servant instead of the ruler of my lower nature? Nay, verily, my very nature renders it a moral impossibility! Oh! how my nature is blasphemed!

My husband has rebelled against the best government in the world, that of Jesus Christ; who has established the government of the individual conscience. He ignores that government, by insisting that his own conscience is a safer guide for me than my own. And because I cannot yield to this usurpation he is determined to ruin me. "Rule or ruin" is his motto. If I could only feel as some undeveloped women do, that it is right to give up the responsibility of their own actions to their husbands, I could then say "I will do and think as he pleases, since I am a nonentity after marriage!" If God regarded me as the law does, in this respect, I could willingly yield my conscience to get my children. But he does not. He holds me as an entity, subject to his own laws equally with my husband.

Therefore I cannot do wrong to get my children. While this sacred right of my nature is ignored by our government, I protest against this usurpation, and claim that my children are *mine*, by the first right of nature. Neither should my children be allowed to suffer this loss of a mother's care, for this is their God appointed heritage, and no man should dare to alienate their most precious boon of their existence. God has given them to me; and no law or man has any right to force me from them. I do believe that to have my body roasted at the stake, I should not have suffered a tithe of the anguish my spirit has already suffered by this unnatural separation. I have felt that I could echo the wailings of a mother here, who, with streaming eyes exclaimed, "Oh, I would willingly give this house full of gold if I had it, to be with my children!"

Whether a married woman can retain her personal identity or not, is the great practical question involved in my case. This great question should be discussed, examined, and placed in the focal light of the present age, so that an intelligent verdict may be rendered upon it. My painful experience furnishes convincing proof that the agitation of this question has become a practical necessity, for no woman can now develop her higher nature, under the subjective influence of this marital power, without the most fierce heart-rending struggles. O God! guide, direct, control, each and every influence bearing upon this momentous subject! For peace, regardless of justice, is a treacherous sleep, whose waking is death.

XLIV.

My Family Relatives.

Not far from this date I find a copy of a letter I sent to my own dear father in Sunderland, Mass., viz: My Dear Father, Dr. McFarland, the Superintendent, has given me permission to write you a letter. This is the first opportunity I have had to write you. Hitherto all communication with my friends has been denied me, except through my husband.

Father, I am entombed here without cause; but I am trying to bear my wrongs as patiently as I can. The suggestion has often been made, that I write you clandestinely, so that you might know how unjustly I am treated, and some have promised to write for me, but as yet I have thought it best to break no rule of the institution. My trust in the rectitude of a divine providence, is still unshaken, notwithstanding the clouds and darkness in which my destiny is inveloped. Yes, my dear Father, your Elizabeth is called to tread a very thorny path. Her road to heaven is through a vast howling wilderness, where no rills of earthly comfort are allowed her, to refresh her weary fainting spirits. Not only are all the comforts and blessings of a christian home denied me, but even my personal liberty already for nearly one whole year has been taken from me through marital usurpation.

O, my Father, how my heart has bled and my soul grieved in agony, at being thus separated from my own flesh and blood—my precious children. My own husband has forced me from my God-given charge, and imprisoned me, with no prospect but that it must be life-long, simply for daring to defend what I thought to be truth. He has made out a charge of insanity on this ground alone, while in all my conduct he can allege nothing against me. I have neglected no duties, have injured no one, have always tried to do unto others as I would wish to be done by; and yet, here in America, I am imprisoned because I could not say I believed what I did not believe.

O, Father, can't you help me? Can't you take me to your

own home for a short time, and try me, and see if I am insane? If you feel that you are too old to come yourself, do let brother Austin come and see me, at least. and then if he thinks this Asylum is the proper place for me, I will consent to stay. But with no trial, and no chance at self-defence, is it not unjust to leave your only daughter uncared for any longer? Do, Father, *do* something, to get justice done to me and my precious children.   Your affectionate daughter,

ELIZABETH.

Dr. McFarland received a reply to the letter to my Father. But not one word of sympathy or comfort for his persecuted daughter! O, can it be that my own dear father can turn a deaf ear to the appeal I made to him to "do something?" Yes, 'tis even so, for I have read the whole letter, with Dr. McFarland at my side. He brought it into the hall, and asked me to come and sit by him, when he took out the letter and handed it to me to read.

I read it with a throbbing heart; and when I came to the sentence, saying, "he hoped the charities of the Institution might be extended to his insane daughter, as he regarded the Asylum as the most suitable place for her at present," my heart almost sank within me. "O, Father," thought I, "will you believe the representations of Mr. Packard and the Doctor, and disbelieve your own daughter?" Yes, he does; he is determined to let me lie uncared for, believing I am insane, and therefore he is sustaining this conspiracy against me. And he, too, is rich, and asks the charities of this State!

For my father's defence, I will here add, that the Superintendent sent with my letter one of his own, which destroyed the influence of mine; and as the Superintendent and the husband both agreed in opinion respecting me, it is not so strange that a man nearly eighty years old, should heed their statements, rather than those of one whom he supposed was insane.   He had unbounded confidence in the integrity of his son-in-law, Mr. Packard, and he, of course, concluded that a man sustained by the State must be a reliable man, whose opinion demanded respect and confidence.   Therefore, instead of coming to my rescue, he sent on one hundred dollars to Mr. Packard, to help him in keeping my imprisonment perpetuated! Another fact. Mr Packard succeeded in influencing the Trustees to take me on to their charity list, and then carefully concealed this fact from my father, so that he could beg the more successfully from him, the patrimony which was my due. Thus he kept my patrimony, and got me supported by the State of Illinois.

I am sorry to say that my father sustained this cruel conspiracy for years, persistently resisting all light, except it came through the medium of the conspirators. But he did this ignorantly, not wilfully; for I rejoice to add, that when he did see me, in about eighteen months after my liberation, his fatherly feeling so gained the mastery of his bigotry, (he was a minister of the same creed as Mr. Packard,) that he soon saw his mistake, and then he tried to counteract the influence he had encouraged in believing me to be insane. He now fully believed I had never been insane at all, and from that time he has been a father indeed to me. As proof of this assertion, I here give his certificate:

"REV. SAMUEL WARE'S CERTIFICATE TO THE PUBLIC.

This is to certify that the certificates which have appeared in public, in relation to my daughter's sanity, were given upon the conviction that Mr. Packard's representations respecting her condition were true; and were given wholly upon the authority of Mr. Packard's own statements. I do, therefore, hereby certify, that it is now my opinion that Mr. Packard has had no cause for treating my daughter Elizabeth as an insane person. SAMUEL WARE.

Attest. { OLIVE WARE.*
{ AUSTIN WARE.

SOUTH DEERFIELD, August 2, 1866."

LETTER TO MY BROTHER, S. WARE, OF BATAVIA, ILLINOIS.

INSANE ASYLUM, June 15, 1862.

MY DEAR BROTHER: I received a letter from your wife, I think in September, kindly inviting me to come to your

*My step mother. My own mother has been dead twenty-four years.

house upon my leaving the Asylum. Thanks, many thanks, kind brother and sister, for this kind offer, for it is one I can fully appreciate. Yes, your sister Elizabeth has no place on earth she can now call her home, but a prison.

And I am not only homeless, but every means possible is used to impress upon my mind the feeling that I am friendless also. But I will not believe it. I know that adversity is the touchstone of friendship, and that sometimes, when we most need the sympathy and aid of friends, we find ourselves utterly forsaken. And I have too much reason to fear that my kindred have all concluded to leave me to the tender mercies of the cruel and disinterested.

Yes, a letter, received yesterday, from Father, clearly demonstrates the fact, that the cause of creeds requires that his daughter be branded with insanity! Indeed, there was not one word of sympathy, or one love message in it, although I had just sent him a kind letter. My persecution reminds me of father Chinique's experience, when his friends forsook him, because he had forsaken the errors of the Catholic church. So I, when, from the clearest convictions of conscience, forsook and exposed the errors of our church, and endorsed some truths found in the Methodist, the Baptist, the Unitarian, the Universalist, the Catholic, and other denominations; in short, when I endorsed the Truth, instead of Presbyterianism, for my creed, all my former friends almost, seemed to regard this extension of charity to other denominations, as an unpardonable offence, deserving eternal banishment from them and all civilized society! This is the penalty I am called to bear, for the crime of becoming a self-reliant thinker, and tolerant christian in the Presbyterian church. This Institution, my friends, and the church, may hold me on this rack of insanity as long as they choose; I shall hold myself in defiance of them all, an independent thinker, and a charitable christian. And too, I shall be all the more independent, on account of this opposition. I used to have an unbounded respect and reverence, almost, for Theologians and Doctors of Divinity; but I am happy to say, that now I have more respect for my own individuality, than for them all.

To you, my dear brother and sister, this may seem like an arrogant spirit; but it is not. I do not say, like these Theologians, that my opinion is the standard for any other individual; but, on the contrary, I say it is not. No other individual in the whole world is to be judged by this standard of belief but myself. Therefore, it would be arrogant in me to try to get you, or any other one, to adopt my standard as their own. God requires of you the same individuality that he is developing in me. God grant that you may be saved the fiery furnace I am compelled to go through to bring it out.

I do not know where these things are to end, but my trust in God is lifting my soul above all anxiety or fear of evil. If you can do anything for me, do it, and you shall have my most grateful thanks forever.

Your loving sister,   ELIZABETH.

I have no reason to think this letter was ever sent. Like my other letters generally, the Doctor otherwise disposed of it.

And here it may be due my two brothers to state, that they both, like my father, sustained this conspiracy for too long a time, through the misrepresentations of Mr. Packard. But like him, they did it ignorantly, not wilfully; for just as soon as they saw me, and had an opportunity to judge for themselves, they both became my valiant defenders, both publicly and privately, and have ever since seemed determined, by their extra kindness to me, to make all the restitution the gospel requires, as evidence of sincere repentance. Of course, I have long since, most freely forgiven them, for to me, they are like what Lazarus was to his sisters, "raised from the dead." This temporary death of their natural affections seems to have been quickened into a new, higher, deeper, and tenderer love for me than ever before.

But to sister Mary, my brother Samuel's wife, is due the highest compliment, for she is one of the precious few who escaped the psychological influence of this learned and popular minister, my husband, in that he could never, for one moment, convince her that I was an insane person. She, with my adopted sister, Mrs. Angeline Field, of Granville, Illinois, both stood erect before this minister, on their version of his statements, in maintaining their own individual opinions respecting my sanity. But sister Angeline, I am happy to say, had her husband, Mr. David Field, to encourage and sustain her in defending my sanity; while sister Mary had her husband to combat, in defending me.

XLV.

Old Mrs. Timmons Deserted by Her Children.

This lady was brought to the Asylum about one year and a half before I left. For several months she occupied the same ward with me, and from the day she was entered she was my daily companion. I took pleasure in her society as she seemed perfectly sane, and sorely afflicted at the fact that her friends would not let her remain with them at home. She was above sixty years of age, but showed no signs of premature old age or ill health. The longer I saw her, the greater was my astonishment that she should be called insane.

From her I learned the reason she was imprisoned was, that one night she got up in a sonambulic state and went to her son's bed, and inflicted two blows upon his cheek with an axe. This her friends regarded as evidence of insanity, although she had no recollection or knowledge of doing so.

This son brought her to the Asylum, and the dreadful scar on his cheek authenticated her statement. She always expressed the keenest sorrow and the most true penitence for having done this dreadful deed, for this was her favorite son. She was willing to do anything possible to atone for it, if she could but live at home with her dear children. She begged to be locked up nights by herself, lest she do an injury again to some one, but she could not bear to be put into this terrible place to spend her days as a criminal, when no one regretted the deed being done more than herself. The thought of having thus harmed her darling child was agony enough, as she thought, to make atonement for the deed, without suffering this awful penalty.

Mrs. Timmons had already endured one term of nine months imprisonment for this act, in an Asylum in Indianapolis, where she assured me the inmates were treated no better than they are at Jacksonsonville, and her friends knew that she had much rather be buried than to be put into another such institution. Yet, they could tell her she was not going into an Asylum, but only going to consult a physician about her health, and thus they decoyed her behind another "dead lock," to be free no more! As I listened to her expression of hopeless agony uttered when sure the Doctor could not hear, I could not but feel that the custom of professedly barbarous nations, which allows the aged and infirm to be left in the woods to be eaten by wild beasts, was not so barbarous a custom as this mode of disposing of unwelcome citizens, which the civilization of the nineteenth century has rendered popular; for the lingering protracted tortures of dying in this institution, are far more to be dreaded than the shorter quicker mode of being devoured by wild beasts. Indeed, I often heard this distressed woman express this preference in these words, "O, if I could only live under a fence, for my home, rather than here, I would rejoice in the exchange! anything or everything would I give for my liberty! any death would be sweet to such a life as this!" And yet this is a *christian* institution!

Her maternal feelings reached such a pitch of agony that it was to relieve her I consented to write the following letter for her, which I sent to her friends on my "underground express" April 26, 1862.

"INSANE ASYLUM, January 29, 1862.

My Dear Children: My heart is almost broken in consequence of the course you have taken towards me. Do write and explain yourselves, or what would be better, come and tell me, for as I now feel, it seems to me I shall soon grieve myself to death. Why could you not take care of your poor afflicted mother yourselves, and not again trust me with strangers where you know I have suffered so much. O, do tell me why you have treated me so. You know I told you I was willing to live in a room by myself, locked up both day and night if you were afraid of me, if you would only let me live at home and take care of me yourselves.

You know too I have always done just as you told me without objecting in the least, and now how can you put me off so again? Did not John tell me he had forgiven me for injuring him? and have I ever attempted to injure any one else? Is it not punishing me more than I deserve to imprison me twice for the same thing, when you say I was not to blame for doing it as I did?

You treat me worse than if I was a convict, for they do not deceive them, but tell them plainly, what they imprison them for, and for how long a time they must bear their punishment. But this time you did not even tell me why you imprisoned me, nor do I know that you ever intend to trust me with you again! O, I shall die of grief before long, unless you do something to alleviate my heart sorrows. I could not treat you as you have me, and O, how could you punish me so severely for doing a *sinless act?*

O, children, am I in danger of perpetuating my imprisonment by revealing to you the inmost feelings of my heart? If so, what shall I do? If my own children will not relieve their agonized mother, when it is so easy for them to do so, by simply taking me home, I do not know what I shall do.

The hope that you will do so as soon as you consistently can, after getting this letter, will sustain me, till then, and when that hope is gone it seems to me I shall die truly.

Do not delay one day, for you can not imagine how long time seems here; one day seems like a month elsewhere. It is not that I am abused physically, for I am not. It is not this which causes my suffering, but the thought of your treating your old mother as you are which is killing me. Yes killing me! For my sake do not let the Doctor know of my sending you this letter. Your Mother.

M. A. TIMMONS."

But I am sorry to say that her relatives, did let the Doctor know of it, and did nothing else to relieve her! The Doctor then removed her to another ward to cut off her communication with me, suspecting that I had helped, in some way, to get her letter out. I retained a copy of this letter in my journal, and give it to the public that my readers may see what feelings the Asylum discipline produces. Is it right to thus *punish* for a misfortune?

Her children came to visit her twice while I was there, and although they found her working like a slave for the Asylum and Dr. McFarland's family, and never having shown the least abberration of mind, they would leave her, with the promise that just as soon as they could get a room prepared for her in the new house, they were building with her own money, (they were rich) they would take her home. They told her the room would be ready in about three weeks, and although nearly six years have already elapsed, this promise remains unfulfilled! The mother who bore them and earned for them the comforts of their own homes, is still left to pine away, a prisoner's life of rayless comfort, doing the cooking in the Doctor's kitchen. When these children become old and gray headed, how will they like to have their children treat them as they are treating their mother? "With what measure ye mete, it shall be measured to you again."

XLVI.

Mrs. Cheneworth's Suicide—Medical abuse.

Mrs. Cheneworth hung herself in her own room, after retiring from the dancing party, last night. Her measure of grace was not sufficient to enable her to bear the accumulated burdens of her hard fate any longer, without driving her to desperation. I can not blame her for deliberately preferring death, to such a life as she has been experiencing in this Asylum. She has literally been driven to it by abuse.

She was entered in my ward, where she remained for several weeks, when she was removed to the lowest ward, where she has been murdered by slow tortures. If this Institution is not responsible for the life of Mrs. Cheneworth, then I don't know what murder is. She was evidently insane when she entered; she was not responsible, although her reason was not entirely dethroned. Her moral nature was keenly sensitive; her power of self-control was crushed by disease and medical maltreatment. She resisted until she evidently saw it was useless to expect justice, and was just crushed beneath this powerful despotism.

She was a lovely woman, fitted both by nature and education to be an ornament to society and her family. Gentle and confiding, with a high sense of honor and self-respect, she despised all degrading associations. From her own representations, I inferred she had been the pet and pride of her parents—a kind of household god in her father's family. Under these benign influences, her virtues were fostered, and she had the satisfaction of being loved and appreciated. She had been quite a belle, and finally from her many admirers, she married one of her own, but not of her parents' choice. In him she seemed to have found everything her heart could desire. He both loved and appreciated her, as well he might. She was small, delicately and gracefully formed, and peculiarly ladylike in her manners. She was a most accomplished dancer, having been trained in the school of the best French dancers in the country. Her complexion white and clear, with regular features, black, but mild and tender eyes, her hair was long, black, and beautiful. In short, she was a little, beautiful, fawn-like creature, when she came to this Institution. She had been here a short time once before, after the birth of her first child; and from her account I inferred that her restoration to reason was not then attended with the grim spectre of horrors which must have inevitably accompanied this.

She had left a young babe, this time, which her physician advised her to wean, since she was now in a delicate condition. Thus her overtasked physical nature, abused as it was by bad medical treatment, added to the double burden she was called to endure, could not sustain the balance of her mental faculties. Her nerves were unstrung, and lost their natural tone by the influence of opium, that most deadly foe of nature, which evidently caused her insanity. The opium was expected to operate as a quietus to her then excited nervous system; but instead of this, it only increased her nervous irritability. The amount was then increased, and this course persisted in, until her system became drunk, as it were, by its influence. The effect produced was like that of excessive drinking, when it causes delirium tremens. Thus she became a victim to that absurd practice of the medical profession, which depends upon poisons instead of nature to cure disease.

It is not natural to cure disease by creating disease. To poison nature, is not the natural way to eradicate poison from the system. To load nature with additional burdens, is not the way to lighten its burdens. But common sense dictates that the natural way to aid nature in throwing off her diseases, is to strengthen the powers of healing, and thereby directly assist her in curing disease. And nature's energies are strengthened, renewed and nourished by rest, quiet, sleep, food, air, cleanliness, freedom, exercise, etc.; and medical skill consists in adapting these agencies to their peculiar functions, so that the special want of nature may be met by its natural supply.

What Mrs. Cheneworth wanted was, the nourishment of her exhausted physical nature, by rest, food, air, and exercise. She did not need to have the powers of her system thrown into confusion by taxing them with poisons, which nature must either counteract and resist, or be overcome by them, and sink into death. Nature was importuning for help to bear her burdens, being already overtasked. But instead of listening to these demands, her blinded friends allowed her to be thus medically abused. After having suffered her to receive this treatment, and thus brought into a still worse condition—an insane state—when more than ever she needed help and the most tender, watchful care; then to be cast off in her helplessness upon strangers, who knew nothing of her character, her habits, her propensities, her cravings, her disposition, or her constitution; how could they reasonably expect her to thus receive the care necessary to her recovery? They probably did expect it, and on this false expectation placed her here for appropriate medical treatment.

What a delusion the world is laboring under, to expect such treatment here! Did they but know the truth, they would find that all the "medical treatment" they get here, is to lock them up! and thus having hidden them from observation, and cut them off from all communication with their friends, they then inflict upon them what they consider condign punishment for being insane! Why can not their friends bestow upon them this "medical treatment" at home, without the expense of sending them to this Asylum to get it? This is the sum and substance of all the "treatment" they get here, which they could not get at home—that is, they could not get *this treatment* from reasonable friends, any where, outside of these inquisitorial institutions. How doleful is this purgatory! thus legally upheld for the *punishment of the innocent!* Great God! Is this Institution located within the province of thy just government? or is this Satan's seat, that has not yet been subjected to thy omnipotent power?

Mrs. Cheneworth is only one among many, many others which her case represents. During the few weeks she was in my ward, after she first came, she was kindly treated. Perhaps her own parents could not have done better by her, than did Miss Tomlin and Miss McKelva, so far as their limited powers extended. They could not grant her that liberty and freedom she so panted for, nor could they gratify her longings to see her own offspring, and bestow upon them the love of her maternal heart; nor could they bring to her the sympathy of her fond mother, for which she so ardently longed; neither could they summon to her side her husband— her chosen protector—who had sworn before God never to forsake her in sickness or in health, although it was her most earnest wish that he might come and see for himself, her condition. No, neither of these influences could these attendants summon for her relief or benefit; but so far as the ward duties extended, they did as well by her as they could.

I never saw either of them get the least angry or impatient towards her, although she tried them exceedingly by her antics. They seemed to feel that instead of getting angry at an insane person, they were placed here to "bear the infirmities of the weak, and not to please themselves." Yes I feel that they have nothing to dread in the revelations of Mrs. Cheneworth's Asylum discipline. Of each of them I trust the Judge will say, "she hath done what she could" for her suffering sister. These attendants are highly cultivated, well developed women, who could enter into Mrs. Cheneworths feelings, and sympathise with her in her trials. They not only knew how to treat her nature, but their principles controlled their feelings, so that her trials might not be increased by any injudicious act on their part. Neither did they seem to despise her for being so sorely afflicted, but pitied and longed to help her.

Alas! for poor Mrs. Cheneworth! her days for reasonable treatment expired when she was removed to the lowest ward, and consigned to the care of Elizabeth Bonner. This attendant was a perfect contrast to her former attendants in character, disposition, and habits. She was a large, coarse, stout Irish woman, stronger than most men; of quick temper, very easily thrown off its balance, when, for the time being, she would be a perfect demon, lost to all traces of humanity. Her manners were very coarse and masculine, a loud and boisterous talker, and a great liar, with no education, and could neither read nor write.

To this vile ignorant woman was Mrs. Cheneworth entrusted, to treat her just as her own feelings dictated. Miss Bonner's first object was to "subdue her," that is, to break down her aspiring feelings, and bring her into a state of cringing submission to her dictation. Here was a contest between her naturally refined instincts, and Miss Bonner's unrefined and coarse nature. Any manifestation of the lady-like nature of Mrs. Cheneworth, was met by its opposite in Miss Bonner's servant-like nature and position, and she must lord it over this gentle lady. The position of the latter, as a boarder, must at her beck, be exchanged, by her being made to feel that she was nothing but a slave and menial. If she ventured to remonstrate against this wanton usurpation of authority over her, she could only expect to receive physical abuse, such as she was poorly able to bear. And O! the black tale of wrongs and cruel tortures this tender woman experienced at the hand of this giant like tyrant no tongue or pen can ever describe! She was choked, pounded, kicked, and plunged under water, until well nigh strangled to death. Mrs. Coe assured me this was only a specimen of the kind of treatment all were liable to receive at her hands, since she claimed that this was the way to cure them! and this she insisted upon, was what she was put here to do. Being strong, she was peculiarly adapted to her place, since no woman or man could grapple with her successfully.

This is the attendant who so often made it her boast that Dr. McFarland let her do with the patients just as she chose —that her judgement, her feelings, and her temper could be trusted in all cases! O, what is there of injury and physical abuse that this institution will not have to answer for, which has not been inflicted by brutal attendants; while Dr. McFarland has sustained them by knowingly approving of these things? I do not believe the Trustees would knowingly approve of these things. But Dr. McFarland's statements are regarded by them as infallibly correct, and as he represents the treatment here bestowed upon the patient, they doubtless feel confident that they are humanely treated. But did they know, what I know, I believe they would disapprove of it, and not like Dr. McFarland, try to cover it up, lest the interests of the institution be jeopardized by the investigation. The facts I have already placed before them in a written form, would of themselves arouse their interest and summon their immediate investigation, did they not so implicitly rely upon the Doctor's contradiction as proof of their fallacy! In this way they are believing lies, and under this delusion, they are not only winking at iniquities, but publicly sustaining them. It is in their power to ascertain the truth, did they feel determined to know for themselves. But this investigation would be attended with more trouble and inconvenience than it is to let it go on, and thereby these slothful servants of the public are justly held responsible for the wickedness of this house. O, what will the end be? O, sword! awake for our defense and deliver us out of the hands of our persecutors!

Poor Mrs. Cheneworth could not await this retribution, but was driven to seek the only defense within her reach, death, yes death. the most dreaded of all evils, was chosen rather than such a life as she was doomed to endure under the rule of this inquisition. I can not, no, I cannot blame her for killing herself. I do not think God will blame her. She was like one who deliberately rushed into the flames, to escape the barbed arrows of an invincible foe. She only chose the quicker, rather than the lingering, agonizing death, to which she seemed inevitably doomed to suffer, at the hands of Elizabeth Bonner.

The last time I saw Mrs. Cheneworth was at the dance, after which she hung herself, being found suspended from the upper part of her window by the facing of her dress. I never saw a person so changed. I did not know her when Miss Bonner introduced me to her that evening. O, such a haggard look! such despair and wretchedness as her countenance reflected, I have never witnessed. My feelings were touched. I asked her to go with me, and putting my arm around her waist, she walked with me across the ward to the window looking South. Here we conversed confidentially, freely. She said, "O, Mrs. Packard, I have suffered everything but death since we were parted!"

"But how has your face become so disfigured by sores, and what causes your eyes to be so inflamed?"

"I fainted, and fell down stairs, and they poured camphor so profusely over my face, and into my eyes and ears, that I have, in consequence, been blind and deaf for some time."

I do not know whether her chin, which was red and raw, was thus caused or not. She said the fall had caused her to miscarry, and thus, thought I, you have had to bear this burden in addition to the load of sorrows already heaped upon your tender, weak person. Said I, "Have you any hope of getting out of this place—of ever being taken to your friends?"

"No! none at all! Hopeless, endless torment is all that is before me! O, if I could only get out of this place, I would walk to my father's house. It is only fourteen miles south, here," pointing out of the window, "but O, these iron bars! I can not escape through them."

How I did pity her! But I could only say, as I do to others, "Do try to be patient as you can; for I do hope this house will not long stand, and that in its destruction, we may be delivered out of this place of torment." I had no other tangible hope to offer her drooping heart, already deadly sick from hope too long deferred. She said, "I wish I could get into the ward with you; I will ask Dr. McFarland, to-morrow, to remove me there."

"Alas!" thought I, "no request of yours will be heeded, as a source of relief to you; for it is not to relieve, but to torment you, that you are kept here. O, could I but inform your parents of their dear daughter's sad fate, surely they would come to your rescue." Then I thought of the letter I had sent to Mrs. Timmons' friends in her behalf, and how, like deaf adders, they would not hear, or would not believe my statements, unless endorsed by Dr. McFarland. I turned away, sick at heart, at sight of woes I could not mitigate or remove. O, when will the prisoner's bonds be loosed and the lawful captive be delivered? Notwithstanding, I think I offered to intercede for her, while, at the same time, I knew it would be utterly fruitless, as I have so often tried reason, argument and entreaty, only to find it useless.

"Yes, Sister, I can not but congratulate you on what I believe to be your happy exchange; for I do not think you can find, in all the universe, a worse place of torment than you found here. May'st thou find that rest in death that was denied thee on earth!"

Here we leave Mrs. Chenoworth, and turn with sorrowing hearts, to the group of bereaved ones at home—those fondly loved ones, who have thus been called to lay upon the altar of sacrifice, this precious victim. O, could you have forseen her sad fate, would you thus willingly have laid her upon such an altar? No, you would not. You could not, and lay claim to your humanity. You are not hard hearted and cruel towards this loved idol of your fondest affections. No, you would have cherished her with the tenderest care at home, had you thought it would have promoted her best good. Your hearts, I doubt not, wept the bitterest tears at the thought of being compelled to place her in an Insane Asylum. But these tears could not remove the necessity which you felt you had for so doing. Had you not reason in your own mind for believing that Insane Asylums were established for the benefit of the insane? Did you not suppose they had a competent medical faculty there, who knew better than yourselves, how to treat such cases? Yes, so you thought, as you ought to have had reason to think.

But alas! for a blinded public! Alas! for man who is placed under an irresponsible human power. Such power, man is not fitted to be trusted with. Despotism too soon usurps the rule of reason and kindness, and might takes the place of right. Authority supplants kindness, truth, and honesty. After this love of domineering has once taken possession of the human soul, it can only be held by sinister, artful policy. Helplessness, weakness, and dependence are the virgin soil where tyranny and despotism hold their most resistless sway. But under the influence of our free government, power would probably cope with it successfully; therefore its policy consists in cutting off these victims from access to any power by which they would be exposed and dethroned. Therefore, they not only prevent communications with their friends while here, but forestall their confidence in their statements after they get out, assuring them they were so insane while here that they can not report correctly, and therefore their representations must be listened to as mere phantoms of a diseased imagination. Therefore, their friends hear as though they heard not.

But the hitherto blinded public can no longer plead ignorance as an excuse for not grappling successfully with this legalized despostism. No; the Legislature of this State are already informed, through their own Committee, of the imperative need of such enactments, as shall hereafter forever prevent such *abuse of power*, by any future Superintendent, as their present incumbent is found to be notoriously guilty of.

XLVII.

Changes, and how brought about.

After occupying the old Eighth ward about a year, we were all summarily ordered to move into the new Eighth. During the summer of 1861, this new and airy part of the building was my home, although the patients were not materially changed in character. Again, in the last of the autumn, we were all moved into the old Seventh. Now the class of patients was changed to a more quiet class, and some of them, like Mrs. Timmons, sane and intelligent. Besides, we were now taking our meals in the dining room of the new Seventh—the class of prisoners I associated with, the first four months.

I felt that I was in the region of the intelligent world again, for part of the occupants of the new Seventh, were just as sane as most boarding school girls, or hotel boarders, generally. I seldom saw anything here, that would, outside of an Asylum, be considered insanity, or anything like it.

I can assure my reader that I was fully prepared to appreciate a return to civilized society, and this change was, therefore, to me a harbinger of good things. I could talk with my old associates at the other table, while at the table, and our fare and table arrangements were much alike now, which, of course, was a great improvement on our former style. I was allowed a good room by myself, and this being the first time for one year I had enjoyed this privilege, I felt that I had much to be thankful for.

Another change affecting my prison life, took place about two months after Miss M—— got permission to take me to ride, which occasioned the prison doors to be closed entirely upon me. I felt it my duty to enter a protest against my imprisonment, and in doing so, I asked Dr. Sturtevant, our Chaplain, to be my witness in the reception room. It was Sabbath, after chapel service that I went to him and asked him to meet me in the reception room. He consented, and we parted, he going down with Dr. McFarland and Dr. Tenny one flight of stairs, while I went down the opposite. When I was about two thirds of the way down, Dr. McFarland met me, and seizing my arm, ordered me back to my ward. I remained motionless. He then applied force, saying, "Have you no feet?"

"I have no feet to walk into prison with," said I.

He then tried to drag me back; but when he saw Dr. Sturtevant looking at us, he let go his hold of my arm, and I dropped from his grasp upon the floor below. He followed, and passed me without speaking, and joined Dr. Sturtevant and Dr. Tenny, where, after a short consultation, they passed down the stairs, while I still sat upon the floor. The fall had so stunned me, that for a few moments I hardly knew whether I could rise or not, but when I saw the three men who ought to be my protectors, and helpers, under such circumstances forsake me, I began to try my powers of self-dependence, and found I could not only rise myself, but could also stand alone too, without a man to lean upon! Strong in my own self-reliant strength, I hastened to meet my appointment with our chaplain in the reception room below, but found no one there. Nothing daunted by this failure on Dr. Sturtevant's part, I walked into the office and met the whole trio there. But for some unknown cause, Dr. McFarland seemed unwilling to face me, but, coward like, shall I say? fled out of my presence. The other two gentlemen did not run away, but looked me full in the face, while I entered my protest in the following language:

"I have a right to my liberty! No law in the United States holds me legally imprisoned! I assert this right—I shall never return a voluntary prisoner to my cell!" Turning to Dr. McFarland, who now stood in the door-way, I said, "You, Dr. McFarland, have *might* to put me there, but no *right*. I assert my rights from principle. I believe God requires me to take this stand. I am immovable in my purpose. You can carry me to the ward with the help of two of your men, and I have no one to defend me against this power. I shall offer no resistance to physical force. Use it if you dare! You do so at your peril." Then handing him a letter, I said, "I request you to stamp and mail this business letter, unread, to my son. This step is preparatory to a legal defence of my rights at the bar of my country."

Then turning to Dr. Sturtevant I said, "Will you, Sir, stand my witness that I now assert my rights, and therefore, am henceforth an involuntary prisoner here?"

He replied. "I am your witness."

"Now, Sir, my business with you is done, unless you wish to witness my forced return to my ward."

The carriage had been some time waiting for him at the door, therefore after asking me to excuse him, he left.

Dr. McFarland then said, "Are you going to compel us to put you back into the ward?"

"I shall never return a voluntary prisoner to my cell."

"Then I must get a porter to take you back;" and he went for his porter, and soon returned with a strong burly Irishman, Mr. Bonner, to whom he said, "I want you to take this lady up to the Eighth ward, she don't seem disposed to walk back."

He then took me up in his arms, but finding my weight too much for him, I suggested that they take me on a chair, and Dr. Tenny take hold with him. This plan worked well, and I was therefore transported up two flights of stairs in this manner, preceded by the Doctor, who unlocked the prison door to receive the prisoner—and no one could ever after say that I was a voluntary prisoner in Jacksonville Insane Asylum; for from that time I never returned a voluntary prisoner to my ward. The Doctor also forbid my attending chapel service after that, so that I never was allowed to step my foot on the ground until I was discharged. I never regretted taking this step, as now I had done all I could do to get my liberty, and having entered my protest, I was thus exonerated from all responsibility, as in any way a willing accomplice in the conspiracy.

There is one point in connection with this transaction, worthy of note—that is, that my falling down stairs as I did, is, in Dr. McFarland's estimation, evidence of insanity in me; and he also maintains that this is the only insane act he detected in me, during all my three years imprisonment! Now I think there was more evidence of insanity in Dr. McFarland's conduct in this transaction, than there was in mine. He ought not to have left one of his prisoners in my condition, until he had so much as inquired whether I could rise or not. He did not know but my bones were so broken that I could not. I think the Doctor's conduct was ungentlemanly to say the least, to treat a sane lady like myself, in this manner, and even if I had been insane, it would have been no excuse for this unmanly conduct towards one whom he claimed as his patient.

The final change I experienced, was in being removed from the old Seventh to the old Eighth again, after having enjoyed the privileges of civilized society for a few weeks. This, my second consignment to the maniac's ward, was in the following manner, as I find it recorded in my journal.

XLVIII.

My Battle with Despotism—No Surrender.

The Doctor has to-day assigned me again to the Eighth ward, against my wishes. Since entering my protest against prison life, no rule of the house is binding upon my conscience, still, hitherto I have thought it best to break none in open defiance of the powers that be, only in getting paper and pencils, when and where I could, and in sending letters on my "Underground Express." But this unreasonable sentence, or mandate I felt conscience bound to resist, and I have done so from settled principle. I claim the right of a reasonable being, in being influenced in, and through my reason, and henceforth, throughout my whole life, I am fully resolved to resist all dictation, coming in the form of despotic mandates in defiance of reason.

My first battle with despotism was now to be fought in resistance to this unreasonable command. Had the Doctor given me one reason why he wished me returned to the maniac's ward, I would have been satisfied to obey his command, even if I did not see the propriety of his reason. But he did not, even when I asked for one. The facts were these.

One day, after quietly enjoying my new surroundings for a few short weeks, the Doctor came to my room and in a very quiet pleasant tone remarked, "Mrs. Packard, I have given your letter to Mr. Russell, and the reply will depend upon him and his decision."

"Thank you, Dr. McFarland."

He then said, "Mrs. Packard, I have been making new arrangements—I have fitted up the ward above you clean and nice, and I am to occupy it with a quiet class of patients, with Miss Smith and Miss Bailey for attendants; I have thought it best to have you go and occupy the room above yours." That room was a screen-room!

I replied, "I did request to go to the new Eighth, to my airy, corner room, that I might have the benefit of purer air, since I am now so closely confined within doors, but I do not wish to go into the ward you assign me, because Miss Smith is a cruel attendant, and I am becoming so extremely sensitive to wrong and abuse, that I can not, nor shall not, witness it without interference, even if you put me into fetters for it."

Here he remarked, "Perhaps you might benefit her—do her good."

"Perhaps I might—I have thought of that; still, I feel that I owe a duty to myself, also."

Here he passed on, simply remarking, "I have decided to have you go."

"And I have decided not to go! It will be merely an act of brute force on your part that puts me there. It is a requirement of despotism, and I am conscience bound to resist it."

Mrs. Page, one of the sane prisoners, said to me when the Doctor was out of hearing, "It is your duty to yield to despotism, if it is Beelzebub himself who issues the command, if it comes in *man* form!" But Mrs. Page and I differ in opinion on that point. I agree to yield to reason everywhere—to despotism nowhere.

The attendants from the Eighth ward soon called for me. I declined going, and related the above conversation with the Doctor. Miss Smith replied, "I do not abuse the patients—the charge is a false one."

"I hope it is; Miss Clauson says she thinks you are trying to do as well as you know how, and I hope you have improved. Mrs. McFarland told me she disliked the way you treated the patients, and she wished you were away; but she added, 'she is good to the sick, and I wish to give her all the credit she deserves.' But should we be together," I added, "I can assure you, I shall be a true friend to you—I shall respect and honor your conscience—I shall defend the abused and the wronged everywhere, whether attendant or patient."

They replied, "We shall not, of course, force you to go with us," and went to report me to the Doctor.

Next, Dr. Tenny was sent, to try what influence he could

have over me. I told him that "I could not see why the Doctor could not treat me as gentlemanly as he had of late begun to treat the maniacs, in asking them civilly, whether they were willing to go to another ward; and he has, to my knowledge, left it to their own wishes to decide this question. I know this is a great progressive step for him to take in the right direction, but why should I be singled out just now as an exception to this new era of events? Despotism is making another attack for mastery over his better nature, and he ought to be restrained, for he has no moral right to rule a re-sponsible moral agent, except through their reason. For his good, as well as my own, I shall never submit to his rule over me in any other manner."

Dr. Tenny replied, "He can not be governed by the wishes of the patients. It is my opinion you had better go."

"It is my opinion I had better not go. So we differ in opinion here."

Mrs. McFarland next came, and tried to influence me to go voluntarily. I remained firm. Many of my friends about the house, and my companions in the new Seventh ward tried to induce me to give up to the Doctor, and as I gave my reasons to one Mrs. Farnside, she remarked, "Well, suffer it to be so now."

About eleven o'clock the next day, Dr. McFarland with two of his porters, entered my room while I was packing my trunk to be transported. The Doctor very politely asked me if I would not go up myself. I replied, "No Sir! I refuse from principle. I regard your order as an act of despotism, which I can not conscientiously countenance."

"Very well," and turning to the porters he said, "You take this lady up very gently, and carefully, don't hurt her, and carry her to her room."

"Thank you, Doctor, for your kind cautions to handle me gently, for I am not as well as usual to-day, although better than I was early this morning. Can I finish packing my trunk?"

"Yes. O yes. certainly. Your things shall all be taken care of."

K

At my suggestion, the porters then formed a "saddle-seat" with their hands, upon which I sat, with my hands upon their shoulders, and thus they transported me very gently and safely to the upper ward, followed by the Doctor, and preceded by Miss Gerta DeLaHay. When within the limits of the ward, I said to my guard, "I can walk now—I will not burden you any further." I then thanked them for carrying me so gently, and turning to Dr. McFarland, I inquired, "Can these men bring up my trunk?"

"Yes, certainly, you shall have all your things."

The Doctor was true to his word—I had all my things removed with me to this ward.

As the Doctor left with his porter I remarked to my attendants "the Doctor can do a mean thing in the most alert gentlemanly manner possible. But I am determined to be a match for him in playing 'the lady' as far as he did 'the gentleman.' His manner reminds me of Mrs. Waldo's remark, 'do the thing in a christian spirit, and all will be right!' But I think it is as impossible to do a wicked act in a christian spirit as it would be to murder or steal with a christian spirit. Now I am under your care, and I have not sinned in coming, for the act was not mine, but Dr. McFarland's, therefore, I hope to enjoy the smiles of an approving conscience, here as well as elsewhere. Will you now introduce me to my new associates?"

Miss Bailey replied, "Mrs. Packard, I do not think there is a patient in this hall who can answer a rational question in a rational manner."

"I will not trouble you then to introduce me. Where is my room?"

She then showed me the screen-room the Doctor had assigned me. My attendants were amazed at this appointment and insisted there must be a mistake. But I told them this was the room above mine, and I should obey his orders in taking it. But before my carpet was cleaned and brought, Miss Smith had inquired of the Doctor why he had given me a screen-room, when the astonished Doctor, said he did not know it was a screen-room, and directed her to let me have my choice of all the rooms in the hall.

I accordingly chose a pleasant front room, which I occupied until I was discharged. I was allowed one favor here which had before been scrupulously denied me, during my prison life, and that was to have the liberty of closing the door of my room in the day time.

I was never locked in my room nights, by any attendant after I had a room by myself. This too was a rare favor. As the Doctor has said, he had a quiet class of patients in this hall, so that with my closed door, I had a nice quiet place to write "The Great Drama," which was written in this room. The way in which this came to be written will appear in its proper place.

XLIX.

Good comes of Seeming Evil.

I am now quietly settled in my new quarters. My prospects for quiet, rest and study, were never brighter. So true it is, that good comes out of seeming evil. The darkest providences are often the stepping stone to prospective good. I have indeed been crucified again. The cross I have been hung upon, although by some, is regarded with contempt, yet like the scars the noble soldiers receive in battles, for the defense of their country, are yet, to be looked upon in their true light. I have had a battle against the rule of despotism here— I did not surrender, neither was I conquered. Though the thing aimed at was accomplished, yet the power of despotism here is weakened more by the triumph than it could have been by the defeat.

Miss Mattie Shelton, one of my attendants in the old Seventh said to me, "I can't blame you for doing as you do, we are all ruled with rigor here."

"It is true that all who will submit to be trod upon, will surely be thus subjected. I shall stand on my own self-defense, and so must all who stand here. I hope Dr. McFarland will never try to rule an intelligent woman with force again."

"Miss Johnston, attendant in the new Seventh says, 'Mrs. Packard, you are strong both in mind and body, so you can bear this crucifixion better than a weaker subject could.'"

"If I can help woman by suffering in her stead, I will rejoice in my sorrows."

Under this date I find a copy of a letter I handed to Dr. McFarland, the first time he called upon me after my removal, as follows:

Dr. McFarland: My heart is full, and I dare not attempt the verbal utterance of its deep emotions, lest I fail in this form, to give you a free and adequate expression of them. Therefore, pardon the intrusion of one more note upon your notice. Dr. McFarland, I love and respect your manly nature; and inasmuch, as my love is genuine, just in that proportion am I grieved to see it eclipsed. The brighter the orb, the more conspicuous are its spots. The sun darkened! Can there be a more fit emblem of earthly dreariness? What would an earth life be worth to woman with the manhood eclipsed? Let man, to whom woman clings so instinctively, become perverted, so as to persecute, instead of protect her, and she feels that the sun of her life is extinct. When man, made in God's form, loses this native dignity, I shrink as instinctively from such a nature, although in a man form, as my physical nature does from the touch of fire. And the pain which my moral nature experiences by such a contact, can be described by no emblem so fit as the effects of fire upon the live flesh.

You may think me extravagant in my figures; still, I trust not, for your nature has not become so entirely perverted as not to appreciate and understand what I mean. Doctor, you are a true man. Despotism has eclipsed and darkened your nature, temporarily; but I am sure the sun has not ceased to shine, but when the eclipse passes over, it will shine out again, in all its original splendor. Indeed, my faith assures me that it will pass over with you, sooner than with many inferior orbs. O, for humanity's sake, God grant to hasten the time. O, what a sight, to see one man dare to stand boldly upon his manliness, and defend injured woman, in defiance of human laws! The world waits for such a man.

Your sincere friend, E. P. W. P.

To the casual reader, these changes may seem to conflict with the statement I have elsewhere made, viz: "From this Eighth ward I was not removed until I was discharged, two years and eight months from the day I was consigned to it;" but they do not in reality, for, although, for the purposes of repairs on the building, we changed our locality, yet the class of occupants did not thus materially change. And I find, on looking over my journal, that during these two years and eight months, there were a few weeks during that time, that Dr. McFarland did allow me to ride and walk with the patients.

L.

Reading Books and Papers.

There is a library connected with this Institution, which the public designed for the use of the prisoners, and there are a large number of papers generously sent to the Institution as a free-will offering for the benefit of the prisoners.

But it is due to the public and the patrons who bestow these gifts so kindly, that it should be known that these books and papers very seldom find their way to the prisoners in the wards. Even while I was an occupant of the Seventh ward, it was with great difficulty I could get either; and while in the Eighth, it was almost impossible for me to get one, except clandestinely and by strategy. And were it not for the special kindness of Dr. Tenny, Mr. and Mrs. Coe, and Mrs. Hosmer, I should have been left to famish from mental starvation. It was war time, too, when daily events of the most thrilling kind were occurring, and I felt it to be a great privation to be deprived of the news of the war.

Among my Asylum papers I find a copy of a letter I handed to Dr. Sturtevant, one day, after chapel service, wherein my feelings upon this point are portrayed as follows:

APRIL 20, 1861.

DR. STURTEVANT: Dear Brother in Christ.—Entombed alive, as I am at present, I, as an intelligent being, suffer greatly from being deprived all communication with the world outside this Asylum, so far as Dr. McFarland can prevent it; and fully believing that you, kind Brother, "suffer as bound with me," I venture to ask of you an expression of this sympathy, by furnishing me with the reading of the *Independent*, weekly, by bringing it to me, one each Sabbath, when I will exchange the previous one.

Did you but know how I long to keep informed of what is transpiring now in my country, at this eventful crisis, I do know you would pity me; and not scruple to grant so reasonable a request, of an afflicted sister in bonds. Still, I will not murmur if you turn me off with an excuse, rather than grant my request; for I know that God rules in the hearts of men, and he turneth them whithersoever he will; and I have long schooled myself to submission to all God's appointments, as providence develops his wishes.

Since I am suffering for conscience sake alone, I see no prospect, on the natural plane, but that it will necessarily be life long, since I never can relinquish my right to "obey God rather than man," when I know these mandates conflict. So long as I will not take man's judgment instead of my conscience for my guide, I must remain imprisoned in this Asylum! And yet, this is free America!

Yes, Dr. Sturtevant, I fully believe that my country will not prosper, so long as woman is suffered to be thus treated. But so far as I am concerned, "all is well." Nothing can harm me. God is my only trust and shield. Fear not for your sister in bonds, although her persecutions increase almost daily in intensity. By the help of your prayers, and those of God's faithful ones in my behalf, I know I shall be ultimately delivered out of the hands of my sagacious enemies. By faith I stand. Through God I shall do valiantly. I shall trust God by *doing right*, and thus wait his deliverance.

Your sister in bonds,   E. P. W. PACKARD.

To the discredit of Dr. Sturtevant, the honored President of Illinois College, and the sacred profession of the ministry whom he represents, I am sorry to add that he took no notice of my request, not even so much as to give me any excuse for not lending me his *Independent* to read!

The letter shows what confidence I then had in his christian character, and in his manliness as being "woman's friend." And it was a true index of my feelings towards that class, who profess to be the ministers of our holy religion, and the practical followers of that Master whose cause they pledge to defend as their chosen profession. Therefore, as a sister in need, I, of course, expected a christian response to my appeal to one of this class especially. But lo! "ye did it not," must certainly be said of *this man*, among this revered profession.

This incident has taught me that it is not the profession which makes the man, but it is the manner in which its duties are performed and its high responsibilities are discharged, which is to determine the standard of merit among ministers, as well as men in other professions. In short, ministers must be judged by the same standard as other men—they must stand or fall upon their own individual actions, not upon their position or profession.

Another lesson taught me by this incident and its subsequent events, was, that if we do right, we shall feel right: if we do wrong, we shall feel wrong. So long as this, our chaplain, treated me as a man and a christian, he felt like a man and a christian towards me. But just as soon as he forsook this standard of action, his feelings forsook this standard. He began to treat me unsympathizingly—he began to feel cold towards me; and the more he manifested this coldness the more unsympathizing and unfeeling he became. Thus he closed up the avenues to his warm, manly heart, by his own heartless actions, or inaction, which, if continued sufficiently long, will inevitably ossify this noble heart, which was made to reflect Christ's own image.

But Mr. J. C. Coe, finding how I was situated, very magnanimously took a St. Louis daily paper for the express purpose of supplying me with the daily news, and Mrs. Coe, his wife, daily brought it to me under her apron; so that it was not known at headquarters how I got my knowledge of passing events, any more than how I passed out my letters.

Dr. Tenny also kindly brought me the *Independent* weekly, which he took at his own expense, and for the purpose, as he said, of accommodating some of his friends in the Asylum.

Mrs. Hosmer brought me some of her papers also, occasionally, and by a special permission from Dr. McFarland, she brought me, at times, a volume of her own books to read, on the subject of Swedenborgianism.

Why the Doctor wished to deprive his prisoners of this relief and amusement, is a mystery I could never fathom. I sometimes thought it was to increase the mental torment of his prisoners, that he thus heartlessly denied them this right the State had granted them. I have heard intelligent patients beg and plead with him to bring them a paper or a book to read, while he would pass speechlessly on, seeming not to hear a word they were addressing to him. This indifferent manner would sometimes arouse the indignation of the petitioners to such a pitch that they would heap curses upon him after he left, often affirming, "He comes to the wards for nothing else but to torment us!"

But I am happy to say, that during a favored period of my prison life, he not only allowed me to read Dr. Channing's works, but I think he has exchanged the volumes for me himself, and once he brought me one of his own volumes of Shakespeare's works.

I notice in a Chicago paper of January 14, 1868, Dr. McFarland advertises for books to be sent to the Institution for the benefit of the patients. I think if the public knew how indifferent he feels in relation to the wants and comforts of his patients, they would not be over anxious to stock their library with books while Dr. McFarland was the State's Librarian.

LI.

Abusing Mrs. Stanley.

My worst fears respecting the management of this ward, I am sorry to say, were fully realized. Miss Smith was naturally very quick tempered, and having had it aroused, by ward scenes, into a most unhealthy exercise for many r onths, she had now become extremely irritable and cross also, so that her atmosphere was anything but salutary and pleasant to the prisoners under her charge. Indeed, the contrast between her management, and the quiet, kind and gentle influence of Miss Tomlin, and her associate, Mrs McKelva, was truly painful, and, to me, a return to the old system of punishment and abuse, was rendered doubly painful, after so long a cessation of hostilities. Had I been removed from the Asylum instead of to this ward, I should have felt confident in the pleasing hope that a reform had really been inaugurated, when I now see that it was only local and spasmodic in its extent and nature.

My feelings were first hurt in witnessing Mrs. Stanley's abuse. She is a high spirited, quick tempered lady, about thirty-five years of age, the mother of several children. She had been delicately reared, of aristocratic feelings, and unused to labor, except so far as the superintending of her servants and nursery are concerned. Indulged and gratified herself, she had not learned how to have her wishes crossed, and maintain at the same time her equanimity. Miss Smith ordered her one day off from her bed, in terms so authoritative and stern, that it aroused the invalid's temper, and she remonstrated, and claimed the need she felt of lying upon her bed on account of sickness. This argument was considered by Miss Smith as a justifiable reason for laying violent hands upon her, and pulling her suddenly from her bed upon the floor, when, as usual, a fight was commenced, and Miss Bailey was summoned to assist Miss Smith in "subduing" Mrs. Stanley! After fighting awhile, Mrs. Stanley constantly ordering them to let her alone, they concluded to try the "cold bath" to "subdue" her. Fearing and dreading this punishment more than all others, she, in the most reasonable manner urged the soundest logic against it, in her present state of health, and then begged and prayed that, for her health's sake, if nothing else, they would spare her this exposure. She said, "Miss Smith, I am sorry! I ask your pardon! O, do forgive me! pray do, I won't do so again." Still they persisted, regardless of her entreaties, confessions and prayers. I went to the bath room, hoping my presence might restrain them, and I begged them to forgive her. But they would not. After pouring a pail of cold water on her head, Mrs. Stanley said "won't you now kiss me?"

"No!" said Miss Smith, "I won't kiss those who will talk as you do."

Here I said, "do forgive her! for you will sometime want forgiveness yourself." She then stopped with the threat, "if you speak another word you shall not have one mouthful of food all day!"

Miss Smith then turned to me saying, "I am not going to take abusive language from a patient."

In a low tone I replied, "you must remember she is insane, and you cannot expect her to do as a sane person would."

"She is not as insane as she pretends to be; she knows how to behave better, and I will not bear abuse from her!"

"We sane ones ought to bear more than we can expect them to bear," I replied.

Another incident connected with the fight. Mrs. Kinney, a very sympathetic patient, seeing how Mrs. Stanley was being misused, interfered, and pulled Miss Smith off. Here was another severe fight, which resulted in forcing Mrs. Kinney into a side room, and locking her up. After all the fighting was over, Miss Bailey looking at her finger remarked, "I don't know but my finger is broken." I thought "if you inquired if you had broken any of the patient's bones, it would be becoming." Thus this weak, delicate woman, who was placed here, to receive kind, humane treatment, as the laws direct, is thus allowed to be abused, her own health and nerves to suffer perhaps an irreparable injury, from those from whom it is impossible to escape; and wrongs from which too, there is no redress, since all the witnesses are out-awed by the brand of insanity!

The oppressed find in this ward no comforter, except it be in defiance of the reigning powers. I have, and do still, defy them, so far as to try to comfort the broken hearted, to sympathize with them in their sorrows, and these are the evidences of my insanity, which call for my protracted martyrdom!

There is no necessity for abusing a patient. I have seen both systems tried, abuse and kindness; and kindness is by far the the easiest safest course. And besides, these prisoners are the boarders of the house, and the attendants are the hired servants, and this distinction ought to be recognized as an inspiring feeling of respect attending the patient's welfare. Kind attendants, sometimes get abuse from maniacs, but feeling required to "bear the infirmities of the weak," they never feel justified in returning abuse for abuse, "but contrawise blessings." They soothe and calm, where the irritable attendant excites into the heat of passion. Under Mrs. DeLaHay's reign of injustice, I have seen the forbearance and magnanimity evinced, operate to inflame her malignity, and have heard her even twit them with imbecility and weakness, thus calling these heroic virtues "their insanity!" When she would move them into a manifestation of resentment, she would exult, as if she was now justified in abusing to any extent, *because they are insane!*

LII.

Subduing a New Prisoner.

One night I was aroused from my slumbers by the screams of a new patient, who was entered in my hall. The welcome she received from her keepers, Miss Smith and Miss Bailey, so frightened her, that she supposed they were going to kill her. Therefore, for screaming under these circumstances, they forced her into a screen room and locked her up. Still fearing the worst, she continued to call for help. Instead of attempting to soothe and quiet her fears, they simply commanded her to stop screaming. But failing to obey their order, they then seized her violently and dragged her to the bath room, where they plunged her into the bath tub of cold water. This shock so convulsed her in agony that she now screamed louder than before. They then drowned her voice by strangulation, by holding her under the water until nearly dead. When she could speak, she plead in the most piteous tones for "help! help!" But all in vain. The only response she got was "will you scream any more!" She promised she would not, but to make it a thorough "subduing," they plunged her several times after she had made them this promise! My room was directly opposite with open ventilators over both doors, I could distinctly hear all.

This is what they call giving the patient a "good bath!" But the bewildered, frightened stranger, finds it hard to see the "good" part of it. The patient was then led, wet and shivering, to her room, and ordered to bed, with the threat, "If you halloo again, we shall give you another bath." The night was very cold, and I lay under my winter's amount of bed clothes to keep me comfortable, while this shivering girl was allowed only a sheet and one thin blanket to cover her. She told me the next morning that she lay almost frozen all night, and complained of universal soreness for many days after. For a long time I could see black and blue spots all over her body, caused by this violent handling of her tender frame, in putting her through the process of initiation—"the subduing."

The next morning I was awakened by hearing Miss Smith reprimand her most sternly for wanting her shoes, which she could not find. Instead of trying to pacify her, she forced her shoeless patient to the bathroom, and held her head under the streaming faucet! The frightened one screamed for "help!" for she had not yet learned the sad truth, that she was out of the reach of all human help, now that she had passed the fatal "dead lock" of a *charitable* State institution.

She kept calling for her shoes. Miss Smith had promised them to her after she had washed. This being done, she called for her shoes. Now Miss Smith requires her hair to be first combed, and having obeyed this order also, she again calls for her shoes. At this point, my feelings drove me to the spot, to defend the rights of the stranger, where I found Miss Smith, with upraised hands over her victim, ordering her to "stop!" I whispered in Miss Smith's ear, "I would get her shoes for her."

She turned angrily upon me, and said, "I shall not be interfered with! I know what I am about—I havn't seen her shoes—I know nothing about them."

I left, and went to breakfast. Soon after, Miss Smith came in with her unhappy, shoeless patient, and ordered her to sit down and eat her breakfast. The patient wanted her shoes first, but no request of hers was noticed. "You may eat or not, just as you choose," said Miss Smith, as her only response to her inquiry for her shoes.

This was her first meal among this great crowd of strangers in this strange place. I could not help pitying this friendless one, and as I passed her on my return from the dining room, I put my arm around her waist, and kindly invited her to come to my room, telling her, at the same time, that I would be a friend to her, and treat her kindly. She replied, "That is all I want." I told her I would ask the attendants to find her shoes—that it was their duty to attend to her wants, and keep all her clothing safe for her. Her neck was cold, as her dress was very low, and she had lost her cape. I sought for it in her room, but not finding it, I asked the attendants for it, but they said that they knew nothing about it. I then lent this shivering girl a sacque of my own, and asked her to sit down in my room, upon my trunk, which I had covered with a cushioned top for a seat for my guests. She seemed rejoiced to have found a friend, and clung to me as to her last hope. She would not leave me without a promise that she might return. She said her father told her she should have all she wanted when she got here, and that I should see a great many nice things. "But all I want is to be treated kindly."

I told her I thought the attendants would soon look for her things—that they had many to look after—that we must try to be patient. She waited several hours; again her lost shoes began to trouble her, as she wished to go out, if I would accompany her; and if she might return again to my room. I offered to lend her a pair, and had just handed them to her, when Miss Bailey came in with the missing shoes and cape also. The other prisoners were now going to walk, and she wished to go too, but Miss Smith decidedly refused, giving her no reason, except, "I think it is best you should not go."

I tried to relieve her disappointment, by telling her, "I presume they choose to wait a few days, to see how you behave. They may fear you will try to run away now; and besides, you have not rested from your long journey in the cars, and they think it better that you keep quiet a few days."

She seemed easily satisfied, and remarked, "I presume the bath will do me good, but I hope I shall not need another. If ever I have to take another bath, won't you be with me?" She said she thought that was baptism; she had now been twice baptized—once in a creek, and now by these two women!

She often complained of being hungry. I went to Miss Bailey, and asked her if I might take her key and go to the dining room closet, and get her some bread and butter, as the law allows the patients a piece between meals, if they need it. Miss Bailey said, "I think she must be hungry, for she did not eat any breakfast," and went and got her some, herself. I devoted the day to her comfort and amusement, and she seemed, before night, to be quite cheerful and contented. She was uniformly quiet and peaceable, and disposed to do the best in her power. I am fully satisfied that the scene in the bath room was entirely owing to mismanagement on the part of the attendants. There is never any occasion for fighting a patient. The State has furnished a screen room for the restraint of the pugnacious ones, and the room should be used for only such, and at such times as they need restraint.

Another initiating process. Miss Smith said she thought she should be obliged to cut off her hair, since she had "creepers" in it. The patient did not wish to lose her fine hair, and I remonstrated against it, saying that I thought she had no right to do so without their own or their friends' consent, for they always felt bad to find it had been done, when they had recovered. Besides, the Institution furnishes ointment for the evil she deplored. I made a thorough investigation myself, and found no cause for the excuse she gave for cutting her hair. I found the reason she wished it shingled, was, to save her the trouble of combing it. She yielded to my appeal, and thus was the long black hair of this young lady saved to her, by my interposition. I had given my word to this lonely one, that she should find in me a friend, although I knew not what disaster to my own interests might be the result. But, since I have nothing to lose but my life, I am willing to risk it in defense of the oppressed and down-trodden. I will simply dare to do my duty, remembering Christ's word, that if "I am ashamed of him and his words, he will be ashamed of me." I never was in any place where Christ's principles were so ignored and contemned as in this doleful prison house. I have detailed this single case as a type of others of daily and almost hourly occurrence here, the bare mention of which would fill a volume.

LIII.

Treatment of the Sick.

I had for my dormitory companion for more than one year, Miss Emily Goldsby, who was sadly afflicted with epileptic fits. It was for this she was sent to this Asylum for treatment, and for this purpose she consented to come. But like all other similar expectations, this hope went out in utter darkness, under her Asylum experience. Her mental faculties had already become somewhat impaired, in consequence of these fits, and both she and her friends, fondly hoped that under the medical treatment of the far famed Dr. McFarland, the *cause* of this aberration might be mitigated, or removed. But she had scarcely anything done for her by way of medical treatment, although I often heard her intercede with the Doctor, to either do something to cure her, or send her home to her friends. But he could not be prevailed upon to do either, so that she lingered out a most wretched imprisonment of many years, uncared for and apparently forgotten. Her friends thus finding that it was easier for them to be relieved of the care of her, than it was to take care of her themselves, and when at last they were obliged to take her away, they cast her into a county house! She not only got no treatment for her disease, but no care even when she had her fits, except what I gave her. One night, before I could get to her bed, she fell on to the floor in one of her fits, and broke her collar bone. This accident caused her a great deal of suffering, and she daily appealed to the Doctor for relief; but he would turn silently away without seeming to hear her. I finally influenced Dr. Tenny to look at it, and see for himself that she had need of medical help. He was satisfied that the bone was fractured, and sent her some liniment which relieved her pain.

She had, at several different times, periods of unusual irregularity of conduct, so that she could not sleep for several nights in succession, nor could her room-mate sleep with her. I was her constant and only watcher, and nurse during the whole year, including these periods. One time, after several sleepless nights, I said to Dr. McFarland, "I am willing to do my share of hospital nursing, but I am not willing to sacrifice my health in this cause, and therefore, I wish you would make some change for a few nights, at least, so that I may get a little sleep." But he passed on without making any reply whatever, leaving me to quiet my patient as best I could, and get my own sleep where I could find it, or go without it if I could not.

There was another lady in our hall who needed medical treatment, for a weakness which caused her attendants some trouble about her bed; and although she was over sixty years of age, she was punished for it as if she were a child, instead of being medicated as she needed. She was lady-like, intelligent, perfectly submissive, and uniformly quiet. She was always neatly and genteelly dressed, and had I met her outside of an Insane Asylum, I should never have had a suspicion of her being an insane person; I never saw anything like insanity in her. This lady had to be punished daily, morning after morning, with the horrors of the plunge bath, because she caused her attendants trouble about her bed. She was not to blame for causing them this trouble, for she could not help it. She used to come to my room after these death-like strangulations by water, and say, "O, Mrs. Packard, I thought they would kill me this morning! I only wish I had died, for now I am only spared to go through it again to-morrow, for I can't help it. I lie awake all the time I possibly can for fear, but sleep will overcome me, and then I am guilty of an 'insane act,' as they call it, for which there is no escape from this terrible punishment." I reported her case to her married daughter who visited her. But she took no notice of this defense of her mother's rights, but left her defenseless as ever, at the tender mercy of the Superintendent, in whom she expressed the most unbounded confidence! This daughter's visit to her mother is described in the following chapter, showing the legitimate tendency of Insane Asylums to extinguish natural affection. I present it to my readers as I find it recorded in my journal.

LIV.

Mrs. Leonard's Visit to her Mother.

Yesterday I met Mrs. Leonard, who is here on a visit to her mother. I advised her to take her mother home, and bestow upon her a daughter's kind and dutiful care and attention, instead of leaving her to the care of strangers.

She replied, "Why, I think it looks pleasant here. Don't you enjoy staying here?"

"No, I do not; this is a very unnatural life, compelled to live as we do. Defenseless, exposed to abuse, separated from all our friends, and cut off from all intercourse with them, shut out from the world and all the privileges of society and citizenship, and worse than all, confined for an indefinite period."

"Why, I think I could be happy here."

"You may perhaps have an opportunity to test it; you may become insane, and then confined here; or you may, like many others, be confined here without being insane, and thus learn by your own experience, what it is to be cast off by your own children, as you have cast off your own mother; for 'with what measure ye mete, it shall be measured to you again.' Your mother is liable to abuse here, and I am her witness that she receives it, too."

"It seems pleasant here. I do not think they would make a false impression upon strangers."

"A stranger passing through here, knows nothing about the management of the house. When the friends visit, they are told by the employees, that their friends are well taken care of—that they are contented and happy; and if the injured one dares to contradict these statements, they are sure to be punished for it as soon as the friends get out of sight. Besides, these visitors are instructed not to heed anything the prisoners say, and an attendant is to keep her ear open to the conversation which her charge has with strangers, and is instructed to urge them on if they tarry to hear anything they wish them not to hear. The patients fearing to tell the truth, and denied an opportunity of doing so, the visitor leaves with a very false impression, and this dust which is thrown into his eyes, prevents his seeing anything for himself, just as is the case with you now."

"But the friends place them here, believing it is for their good," she replied.

Yes, under this sophistical plea they take the first wrong step. The neglected and injured relative, finds a class of emotions germinating in his heart, which inevitably culminates in alienation, and irreconcilable enmity frequently ensues.

The wrong doer makes the first infringement upon the law of love by not doing as they would be done by. Every advanced step in the wrong direction leads them into deeper and deeper darkness, until at length, they become so blinded and callous that they lose all traces of humanity, and thus become entirely perverted and fallen.

" I could clearly discern in Mrs. Leonard, that she had become sadly indifferent to her mother's welfare. She had got rid of a burden by putting her off upon the care of others; the laws approved of her course : it was even regarded by perverted humanity as her duty thus to treat her ; the tender yearnings of her true nature were stifled, and she was left to moral judicial blindness. I told her she would not like to be thus cast off, if incapable of taking care of herself; instead of this, she would claim that this was just the time she most needed her friends' care and assistance. When well, and able to care for herself, she had better be then abandoned, rather than in a defenseless condition. O! these insane institutions are one of Satan's well designed plans for the detriment, and ruin of humanity, under the specious plea of benevolence. We know it must be Satanic in its origin, for its first principle is a trangression of the divine command of love, to our friends and relations. How can it have become possible that these houses could have secured such a hold upon the conscience and intelligence of the nineteenth century in enlightened America? It certainly must be a perverted christianity which could countenance, and sustain institutions of such notoriously infamous character. It is the specious deceptive character of these professedly benevolent institutions, that render them so dangerous, and such a snare to the world.

If they would only show their real character openly, as Inquisitons and Penitentiaries, of the worst kind, the danger to humanity would be mitigated to the greatest extent; for few are so lost to a desire for the esteem of others, as to do such an outrageous act openly and professedly, for the purpose of torturing their afflicted friends by sending them to the Inquisition for that purpose. But as it is, thousands are doing that very deed knowingly to themselves, but ignorantly to the world, through the specious plea of sending them to a hospital for " their good." Does not the arch adversary exult in this successful achievement of his purpose to destroy humanity, through this perversion of his peculiar godlike faculty—benevolence? Has he not employed his strongly marked agent, Dr. McFarland's benevolent organization, through whom this strategic plan can be made practical! Is any plea more often urged in support of his despotism here, than " their good requires it!" What more popular argument could he use in support of his deceptive acts, than " their good" in the estimation of " the great, the good, the intellectual, Dr. McFarland's opinion requires it?" O, Dr. McFarland, " their good" is only one of your artful plans to promote your own self-aggrandizement!

This morning Mrs. Leonard came to the bars, and seemed desirous of speaking to me. I left my work, which was cleaning my bedstead, went to the bars and talked a little more with her. I told her the patients in this ward were treated like slaves and menials; that the attendants claimed to be their overseers, and ordered them to do the work which they were hired to do. This morning, Miss Smith has ordered them to wash their own bedsteads, and requires them to do it, whether they are willing or not. Some object, saying that they are not put here to work—that they have not been used to such work, and the laws do not require it of them. Still she says they shall obey her, in all she chooses to tell them to do, etc. There is Mrs. Stanley, for instance, who has not been used to such work, having had hired help all her days, and she objects, but Miss Smith told her she should have no breakfast until she had done all she had told her to do. She started for breakfast; Miss Smith ordered her back, repeating her threat. I did not tarry to see how the quarrel terminated. One fact is evident, she went without her breakfast, and seemed to feel like a much injured woman. I told Mrs. Leonard that Mrs. Stanley was right in saying to Miss Smith that she had no right to speak so to her, and order her about in that style, for the laws forbid it—Miss Smith being her servant, and the laws expressly forbid involuntary servitude. Still as it is, we are regarded and treated as their slaves, or as convicts in a Penitentiary, condemned to work or risk the penalty of disobedience. I added, "this is one of the greatest systems of oppression and cruelty to human beings, the world ever witnessed."

She listened with the indifference of a stoic, apparently, and left me abruptly without making any remark. I returned to my duties, feeling that I had done all my duty to her, to get her eyes open, to see what the rules of the house are. My hope was that the latent spark of filial feeling towards her afflicted mother might be revived, and she, under its natural promptings, be induced to take her mother home. But all my efforts to enlighten her, seemed like water spilled upon the ground. She evidently seemed to regard all my talk, as the representations of an insane person, whom she considered beneath her notice or attention, except to hold me up, to scorn and ridicule. She plainly made light of it. God grant that I may never be left to violate any of my obligations to any human being, so as to give my testimony in favor of relations thus deserting their own kindred in the time of their greatest need.

So far as my influence and example go, they shall find this testimony in favor of kindness, the most unremitted, to my afflicted kindred. I will do all I can to secure the same to afflicted humanity wherever found. Should my husband become a raving maniac even, I would not consent to his being put into a hospital so long as any kindred of his own could take care of him. A mother's authority, if necessary, should secure for him the personal attentions of his children in his behalf, so far as was necessary to aid my own personal efforts for his comfort and happiness.

I would think of the reward which Mr. and Mrs. John Hardy, of Shelburne, Mass., have received for themselves, in taking care of their insane son, eighteen long years, so kindly, invariably, and unremittingly; although they may, on entering upon their reward, exclaim, "we have only done our plain duty to our child." God, their Judge may reply, "I acknowledge it to be true, and on this ground you have proved your loyalty to my government, by obeying the parental laws of the nature I have given you, and not, like my disloyal subjects, rejected its teachings, and left the unfortunate one to stranger hands."

I should feel although weariness and painfulness, might attend the act, yet no selfish considerations should induce me to swerve from, or remit our attentions to his comfort and his wants. This sacred promise I now make, and record, that I and my children, will be true to this pledge—So help us God!

LV.

Mrs. Emeline Bridgman—or Nature's Laws Broken.

This Mrs. Bridgman has been an inmate of this Asylum, for the last ten years; has been one of the most unfortunate victims to the deteriorating, debasing influences of such institutions, to the true aspiring nature which God has given us.

Her nature is a specimen of a superior order of female organization, very tender sensitive feelings, exquisitely susceptible to emotions of a spiritual nature, feeling an insult to her self-respect and native dignity to the most highly sensitive degree, exhibited by a feeling of shame, mortification and self-distrust, which seemed so deeply stamped upon her soul as to render it impossible for her to rise above it. So long has she suffered the shame of being regarded insane, that she has become morbidly sensitive, and it seems now to have become morally impossible to overcome it. She has a superior intellect, conservative in its character, yet fully capable of apprehending clearly new ideas, new views of truth, although instinctively averse to progress or change in her opinions.

The orthodox system of theology, as the conservative divines of the last century taught, is her standard of truth, and all deviations from this standard, she is almost tempted to regard as a sacrilegious act. Her will is very persistent, almost inflexible; her temper forgiving, her spirit trustful; still, fearful and doubtful as to the future. All her hopes lie buried deep in the past. No ray of hope illumes her future in this life, and her hopes of the future rest upon a hope that she was made a subject of regeneration twenty or thirty years since. On her evidences then, that she had experienced a change of heart, she now rests her hope of final safety, believing that when this instantaneous change of heart has been once experienced, there is no probability of a failure in receiving a heavenly inheritance.

Her nervous system became deranged from a physical cause at the age of eighteen. She was then sent to the Worcester Hospital, Massachusetts, where she remained a short time under the treatment of Dr. Woodward, the Superintendent. She soon recovered, and entered upon the practical duties of life with interest and satisfaction. She was happily married, and lived eight years with her husband, when she became a childless widow. Her life has since been like "the troubled sea which can not rest." Her nerves have become so chronically diseased, that they constantly disturb her mental repose.

Her friends, at her own request, let her enter this Asylum, hoping the result might be as favorable as it formerly had been. But they were disappointed. Instead of receiving the kind, humane, Christian treatment here as she did at Worcester, she was treated most abusively and brutally. Her sensitive feelings thus received such a shock, followed by such a feeling of degradation and shame, that it has become impossible for her to rally and recover her lost self-respect. As one specimen of the manner of treatment to which she was subjected, she told me that in taking her baths, they forced her to disregard, and tried to crush out every refined, virtuous, and elevated feeling of her nature, telling her, in most unmistakable language, that they considered this eradication of modesty as the object and intent of their discipline and treatment. Of course, her godlike nature instinctively revolted at this heaven-defying sacrilege, this crushing of the divinity within her. This, added to the abuse which was inflicted upon her tender, sensitive frame, was too much for her powers of endurance. Her nervous system, her aspiring feelings, her noble nature, could never rally, so long as this abuse continued; and it has continued for ten long successive years. Rather than to live in this agony, she sought death; not that she made any attempts to commit suicide, but she often begged and prayed that they would kill her outright, rather than by this slow torturing process. No; so long as she exhibited any natural feelings under this torture, she was subjected to the cruel rack. Her sound logic, her entreaties, her prayers, her just and holy resentment, each and all, only seemed alike an occasion for inflicting some new form of degradation.

Mrs. Bridgman was scrupulously neat in her habits; but regardless of this, she was forced into the water tub where several others had bathed, who were peculiarly filthy in their personal habits, so that the water was not only highly colored, but covered over the top with a thick scum of filth. Into this she was plunged, head and ears, to their heart's content, and held under the water. Then, as her flesh was of an uncommonly fine texture, sensitive in the extreme, she must be scrubbed with a corn broom, which had been first dipped into a dish of soft soap, to lather her entirely over with from head to foot, and then washed off with the thick water already so soapy as to almost consume the skin. Here she was rubbed and scrubbed, as if her skin were a rhinoceros's, and then locked into her room, where the cold was so intense that her hair was often frozen to her pillow.

I inquired why she did not report the attendant's conduct to the Superintendent. She said she did try to, but he would not credit her statements, since the attendants contradicted them, assuring him that they had not abused her. He regarded her truthful representations as the ravings of a diseased mind, and the attendants' conduct was tacitly approved, as judicious and correct. Thus she found that all she had accomplished by reporting them truthfully, was an approval of their practice from the Superintendent, and a secret grudge against her, which she would be sure to know of in her future aggravated and increased sorrows.

And now, since she has been made to become a mere wreck of her former self, as to her personal habits, and her refined manners and fashionable appearance, having become necessarily almost indifferent to the opinion of others, as a result of her loss of self-esteem, her earthly prospects seem to be entirely blighted, even in the meridian of life; and all the natural result of the rule of this wicked Institution. That she did not become a maniac long ago, is one of the mysteries of God's providence. Since I have known her she has not been insane. She has been one of my most esteemed associates—as an intelligent and capable woman—as competent to attend to the practical duties of life as ever, could she only be induced to make the effort. But all her ambition and self-esteem being prostrated, by the abuse she has experienced, her case seems almost hopeless—her usefulness for this world destroyed, except so far as her case may be employed as a warning, a living memorial of the barbarous influences of the Insane Asylums upon humanity, as they have been and still are conducted. If it had not been for these institutions, she might have been, ere this, a useful and happy woman; and had she been cherished and cared for by her kindred, as their true hearts then prompted, instead of trusting her to the care of strangers, she might have recovered her health and spirits, and long have been a blessing to them and to the world. But alas! this willing victim has been offered a living sacrifice to the Lunatic Asylum! and under the specious pretence that her good might be secured!

Several of her friends have died since she has been here, but she was not allowed to know anything of the event, until she chanced to see the notice of their death in the papers!

O, can this entombing of kindred alive, be for their or our own good? Is it for our own good to cut off our afflicted friends, and so desert them, as to root out all traces of sympathy in them, or interest in their welfare? Is it for their good to put them where the affectionate yearings of their fond hearts have no object to cling to, and no means allowed through which to exercise their emotions? Can a natural development of the faculties be secured by this most *unnatural* process? No, no; those who have survived this machinery are the exceptions; those who are injured the almost universal rule. Mrs. Bridgman never was a fit subject, for the Asylum, since she never was an insane person, in that she has never been lost to reason. She is diseased in her nervous system, and instead of treating her as a criminal, she needs unusual forbearance and kindness, to inspire her with self-confidence and thus draw out her self-reliant feelings and efforts. All depressing, debasing influences, are deathlike in their influence over her already weakened powers of resistance. The only irregularity of conduct indicating a dethronement of reason, was a propensity to pick her clothes to pieces. This appearance of restless uneasiness, would seek vent from the ends of her fingers by nervous twitches upon something tangible, which effort seemed to be an almost instinctive act of self-defense from the overflowings of her pent up mental agonies. I could not blame her any more than I could blame a drowning man for catching at a straw as a reliance of self-defense. Although the drowning man's act is in itself an unreasonable act of self dependence, yet we do not call it an insane act under his surrounding. So, although in reality, Mrs. Bridgman's acts of self-relief are not reasonable in themselves, yet under the anguish of her mental throes, she should be excused as innocent of an act really insane. If her sufferings cannot be assuaged by judicious kind care, she should be allowed great latitude in seeking any way of relief her instincts might prompt. She has been most wantonly and thoughtlessly punished, being innocent, so that she is almost raving, under this insult and abuse of her moral nature addded to her physical sufferings. O, how I have heard her entreat Dr. McFarland to let her out of this place! his utter indifference to her cries only confirmed her in feeling, that this is a place of hopeless torment, from which she can never escape. Nor can it be right under any circumstances, to keep a human being in such a state of involuntary suffering, or to add to this suffering, state personal imprisonment. She has been allowed to visit her friends several times, within the ten years, and remains with them a few weeks or months, but the memory of the Asylum so haunts her, that its fear and dread are inseparable from her existence. This Institution should place an insuparable barrier to her entering it again; her friends ought to adopt her anew into the affections of their hearts, and make her feel sure that they will never again forsake, but cherish and love her as they would wish to be, in exchange of circumstances. But from Dr. Tenny's account I fear they cherish no such intention, but like other alienated perverted kindred, will feel justified in placing her here again; thus ridding themselves of a burden upon their care and attention. Rid of a burden! What can be more humiliating to a proud noble nature than to feel that they are looked upon as burdens by their friends such as they are willing to resign knowingly into a state of hopeless unmitigated sorrow. O earth! earth! is there any spot in this great universe where human anguish is equal to what is experienced in Lunatic Asylums!

Are we not experiencing the sum of human wretchedness? Can a woman's sufferings be greater than are Mrs. Bridgman's? To me she is the very personification of anguish. O, my heart has so ached for her that I sometimes feel that I would lay down my natural life to relieve her.

I did try to comfort her, by imparting genuine sympathy in deeds of kindness, and she would sometimes say that she found some comfort in my room, but none anywhere else. I have often assured her that if ever I got a home where I could do as I please, I would like to adopt her into it most cheerfully as my sister, and she should find in me an unfailing friend.

I have studied into the *cause* of her disease of the nervous system, and so far as I can judge, it was caused by her disregarding the laws of her nature, as a woman, in working extra hard at the time she was unwell. She said she suffered so much pain at such times, that she sought relief by hard work, and this exertion being unnatural, only increased the evil she designed to remedy. Her temporary relief was purchased at the price of future sufferings. A chronic disease was the result, which has since manifested itself in untold mental agonies. If women would have resolution enough to be quiet at such times as nature and reason both dictate, they would be relieved of a vast amount of suffering, which is inseparably connected with thus trifling with this law of our nature.

It is said that the Indian women who are so peculiarly exempt from female diseases, do invariably lie by one or two days at such times, and these are the only times that they lie in bed, by sickness—in consequence of which, they are almost as hardy as the men. To them, the curse of the fall seems almost annihilated. If civilized women would only learn this lesson from their uncivilized sisters, they might hope to enjoy the same immunity from suffering which they do.

Since I feel conscientiously bound to regard all the laws of my being as God's laws, and now regarding this in that light, I cannot feel exempt from its obligation. Eighteen years of obedience to this law has demonstrated the fact, in my case, that civilized women can by so doing be as exempted from suffering as their uncivilized sisters. O, that civilized women would dare to be as healthy as Indian women are, by daring to be as natural in obeying this law of woman's nature; then might we hope for progress, based on the plane of sound and vigorous constitutions in their offspring.

LVI.

The Guilt of Folly.

There are some crimes, the charging of which, falsely, is worse than the crimes themselves. So with my husband's false accusation of insanity in me, he commits a greater crime against me, than it would be in him to really become insane. The false accusation is a crime, whereas the thing charged is no crime. Neither is he guiltless in treating me as insane, when this delusion of his is only the result of misapprehension, for he is to blame for getting into this deluded state. He has resisted known light, and a persistence in his folly has so blinded him that now he can not see correctly. At the same time, he is to blame, because he ought not to have got into this state. Like the drunkard, who unconsciously harms another, is guilty, for he ought not to have got into this unconscious state. The good of society requires that folly, as well as rascality, should be responsible for their own actions.

Again, this state of folly can only be controlled by brute force or fear, since while in it, they are dead to all influences of a higher kind. And the just punishment of this folly is demanded as a warning to others to avoid such a state. These victims of folly must be held in check, by force, until consciousness so far returns as to lead them to see the wrong they have done; and this time has not come, until they feel sorry for their trespass upon others' rights. My husband must see that there is no hope of help for him, until he can see that he has done wrong; then he will be in a suitable state to receive his pardon from me. Until that time comes, he can not appreciate forgiveness if it should be offered. It is my duty to hold him there until he does.

Again, this accusation is a crime of great magnitude, because there is no chance of a termination of my imprisonment while on this basis. Real insanity may possibly be cured, and thus hope lies for the insane in the future; but the case of the falsely accused is hopeless—for if unchanged, he is treated as insane, and if he becomes insane, of course his case is hopeless. There are certainly some of the most reasonable persons in the world imprisoned here, apparently hopelessly, simply because some individual has chosen to represent them so, and they justify themselves in this accusation, on the plea that they have a right to their opinions. So they have the same right to their opinion that a traitor has to justify himself, on the ground that it is his opinion that the government ought to be overthrown! Traitors have a right to their opinions as traitors, and they also have a right to the penalty which the law attaches to such opinions when practically expressed.

The defamer pleads that he has a right to destroy the character of one whom he regards as an errorist, since he claims these errors injure society, and therefore a benevolent regard to community demands the slander. Now we never have a right to do wrong, and no evil can be justified on the ground that good requires it. Goodness is never dependent upon sin for its maintenance or support. Right and justice are sometimes demanded by goodness, but never does it demand wrong or wickedness for its defense. It is the highest treason to our Heavenly Father's government, to try to destroy the moral influence of a member of his family, in order to promote their own selfish purposes. It is an attempt to overthrow God's government, in the individual, to represent him as insane when he is not, for it is his accountability he is thus trying to destroy.

That it is a crime to call a sane person an insane one, appears too, in the mental torture this charge brings with it.

It is very embarrassing to a sensitive person to be looked upon in all they say or do, as an insane person. The least mistake, a slip of the tongue, a look, a gesture, are all liable to be interpreted as insanity, and the least difference of opinion, however reasonable or plausible, is liable to share the same reproach. So that an advocate for any new truth, or any progressive science which must necessarily dethrone human dogmas, while under this charge, is under a paralyzing influence. But let any other person who is not thus branded, advance the same ideas, they would be regarded as evidences of intelligence of a superior order. And although truth is not changed by the medium through which it passes, yet, as the world now is, in its undeveloped state, it more readily listens to a new truth coming through a medium of acknowledged sanity, than when it comes through one who has the diploma of insanity attached to his name. But still, the medium is not the truth, neither is the truth enhanced or diminished by the medium who utters it.

Again, it is a crime, because hundreds are kept here to whom an imprisonment is as much of an outrage as slavery is to the bondman. Because some insane persons are sometimes dangerous, it is thought right to keep all who are called insane, *prisoners!* Thus, the most sensible people on earth, are exposed to suffer a life-long imprisonment, from the folly of some undeveloped, misguided person. And the tendency of imprisonment itself, is sadly detrimental to a person who has intelligence enough to realize that he is held under lock and key. To persist in treating them as though they were unable to take care of themselves, is to undermine self-reliance and self-respect. In short, it tends to destroy all that which is noble and aspiring in humanity, more directly, and more surely, than any course the great enemy of the race has hitherto devised. To subject a human being to the legitimate influence of this Insane Asylum system, is like the Hindoos throwing their children into the Ganges, most of whom are drowned, of course, but the few who do escape are those who retain life with peculiar vigor and tenacity. Yes,

I am sure that any one who can go through here, and come out unharmed, may well be considered as insanity proof. God's grace must work in them, to will and to do right in all things or no security is granted them; and those few cases of successful resistance are like the pure gold, the hotter the fire, the purer it becomes. The christian graces which are here called into exercise, are thus strengthened, purified, concentrated, intensified, so that the minor temptations and onsets of the powers of darkness are now looked upon as mere skirmishes, compared with the fierce, deadly battles of this Asylum life.

Again, the guilt attending this folly is great when we contemplate how very difficult it is to get out of this prison at all. I find this idea illustrated in my journal in the following manner. "I have just been noticing the struggles of a fly, lying upon my window-sill. It vainly strives to regain its natural position, and every collateral influence only increases its fruitless struggles; but when I placed my finger directly over so its feet could clasp it, immediately it assumed its upright position, by a perfectly natural motion. All its previous efforts, unaided, were not only fruitless, but exhausting to its energies, so that when help came, it was weak from this exertion. So I have been long striving to deliver myself, unaided, but all in vain. But when my efforts have attracted the attention of some competent influence directed by a power from above, I shall experience all needed help to rise to the position God has designed me to fill. Now since my deliverance depends wholly upon the influence of a power above me, I must learn to trust it by faith, and like the fly, lie quietly prostrate, waiting patiently until help comes to my rescue."

Again, the guilt attending the folly of imprisoning sane people, or those who have never forfeited their right to their personal liberty by their own insane or criminal actions, is seen in the expense it incurs to keep them at Jacksonville Insane Asylum. It gives the tax payers a just cause to complain of enormously unjust taxes, while it cost the State of Illinois one thousand dollars a year to keep each of their prisoners at that Institution. If the statement made before the Senate in the winter of 1867, by Senator Ward of Chicago, who was appointed by that body to investigate the management of that Institution, is true—viz: that as the Institution is now conducted, it cost Cook County, one thousand dollars a year, for each occupant from that County; and he added "I will engage to take care of them at that price myself!"

Now if the people would but exercise their own good common sense in this matter, they would find that their own afflicted friends could be far better cared for in their own homes, than they are now cared for at this Institution, and that the expense attending it would be materially lessened, by a return to the simple principles, of natural humanity and common sense in the treatment of this unfortunate class. Until this is the case, the guilt attending the folly of our present system, must be needlessly enhanced by the enormous taxes demanded in support of these institutions on their present corrupt basis.

LVII.

Mrs. Watts Driven off from her Sick Bed.

Mrs. Watts was most peremptorily ordered off her bed while sick, by Miss Smith, and this distressed woman was compelled to stand leaning against her bed all day, suffering from severe pain. She had no chair or seat of any kind in her room, and was not allowed to sit upon her bed, so she must stand all day or lie upon the cold uncarpeted floor, so that her bed need not be tumbled, lest company might pass through and thus prevent as good a display of the house! After listening to the quarrel from my room, I went to comfort her, and found her as I have described. I expressed my tenderest sympathy, telling her that if it was in my power I would do anything in the world to relieve her, but that I was just as helpless as herself. I kissed and left her, saying "I will do all I can for you."

I then took Miss Bailey, the other attendant, into my room and with tears in my eyes, I plead her case and appealed to her compassion to take her part, and let her lie upon her bed, saying "it is your right to act independently when you see the patients are wronged." She assented to all I said, but did nothing. I then went to Mrs. Watts, and offered her my bed, assuring her I would protect her while there. She positively declined doing this, saying "I guess I can bear it as the rest have to." I left her leaning against her bed, hoping some one would come in to whom I could appeal for her. But no one came. After dinner I found her sitting upon the cold floor. I then brought her my chair, and insisted that she should use it. This she was willing and glad to do. At night I took it back and told Miss Smith what I had done. She seemed impressed with a feeling of guilt and apologized for having done so, and gave me encouragement to hope she would not repeat the offense.

The next day I made a most earnest appeal to Dr. Tenny in behalf of the sick in our ward, to which he responded by saying, "I do think they ought to be allowed to lie upon their beds when sick."

"Then do use your influence at headquarters, for we cannot get a chance to tell our grievances to the Superintendent; he will no more listen to a patient's complaint, than he would defend them from abuse!"

LVIII.

Dangerous to be a Married Woman in Illinois!

After seating himself in my room, Dr. McFarland, commenced a conversation by asking this question. "Mrs. Packard, would it not be natural for me, in order to ascertain what had been your conduct before coming here, to inquire, first of husband, then of parents, then of brothers and sisters, and on their testimony form some opinion of your state?"

"Yes, naturally you would; but in my case, these relatives have not seen me for seven years, except brother Samuel, of Batavia, who has visited me only once during that time; and besides, opinions will not convict a criminal. Facts are needed as proof. A murderer is not convicted on opinions, but on facts."

"But insanity is not a crime, but a misfortune, and different kind of evidence is required to prove it. It is a disease, and as physicians detect disease by the irregularities of the physical organization, so they must judge of insanity by the views they take of things."

"But, Doctor, is not the conduct the index of the mind, and if these views are not accompained with irregularities of conduct, ought these views alone to be treated as evidences of insanity?"

"Yes, a person may be insane without irregularities of conduct."

"But have we any right to restrain the personal liberty of any one whose conduct shows no irregularities. For instance, should you like to be imprisoned in one of these wards on the simple opinion of some one that you had an insane idea in your head, while at the same time all your duties were being faithfully performed?" He made no reply.

After a silence of a few moments, I added, "now if you, Doctor, or any other individual, will bring forward one act of my own, showing lack of reason in it, I will own you have a right to call me insane."

After waiting a long time, he said, "was it not an insane act for you to fall down stairs, and then to be carried back to your ward?"

"That was not *my act* in being carried back to my ward. It was your own act, and my falling down stairs, was an accident, caused too, by *your* ungentlemanly interference; and the object I had in view by asserting my rights, was a rational one, for I had good reasons for doing so."

"O, no, no, the *reasons* are nothing."

"Yes they are; for unless you know the reasons which influence the actions of others, many acts would appear insane, that would not, if we knew the reasons which prompted the act. I asserted my right to my liberty from principle, not from impulse, in compliance with the advice of Gerrit Smith, viz: "when you have done all that forbearance, kindness and intelligence can do to right your wrongs, all that is left for you to do is, to 'assert your rights,' kindly, but firmly, and then leave the issue to God."

After another pause he said, "what motive, Mrs. Packard, could I have for making you out insane, if I considered you were not? Would money prompt me to do it?"

"No, Doctor, I don't think money has influenced your mind in my case; but you have so long been in the habit of receiving women on the simple verdict of the opinion of the husband, without proof, that you seem to think there is no necessity of using your own judgment at all in the case. And you do not seem to apprehend the glaring truth of the present day, that woman's most subtle foe is a tyrant husband. It is might, not right, that decides the destiny of the married woman. You know I am not by any means, the only one you have thus taken in here, to please a cruel husband. You have received many since I have been here, such as Mrs. Wood, Mrs. Miller, Mrs. Kenny, and many others. Indeed Doctor, this fact has become so notorious here, that our attendants echo the remark made by Elizabeth Bonner, the other day, viz: 'I did once think I would get married; but since I have been here, and seen so many wives brought here by their husbands, when nothing ails them, that I am resolved never to venture to marry in Illinois! I can take better care of myself, alone."

"And Doctor, I agree with her in this conclusion. It is fatally dangerous to live in Illinois, under such laws, as thus expose the personal liberty of married women. This kind of married slavery is worse than negro slavery, and it must be abolished before the reign of righteousness prevails. Resolution is pacific, and I am resolved to secure peace on no principle but justice, freedom and right. With resolution, firm and determined, I am resolved to fight my way through all obstacles to victory—to the *emancipation of married woman!* I assume that my personal identity is my God given right, and I claim that this right shall be recognized in the settlement of this great woman question.

None to my knowledge sustain me in my path of self-denying obedience to the cause of married woman's emancipation. But when the victory is achieved, there will be no lack of voices to chant this triumph. If, while in the hottest of this battle, some of these plaudits could be heard, it would be a help far more needed and welcome than when we have laid off our armor. But he whom God guards is well guarded. It is the fate of many who seek to do good, to have to resist their friends, and face their foes. To be God's chosen instrument to raise woman to her proper position is a glorious office, and those who win this crown, must be willing to bear this cross. The public conscience is in motion, and the great moral force my enemies are struggling against is the gospel, enforced by conscience.

LIX.

Interview with Mr. Wells, of Chicago—A Victim of Homesickness.

At one of our dancing parties, I had the satisfaction of meeting Mr. Wells, of Chicago, whom I found upon acquaintance, to be a man of pleasing address, of fine talents, and possessing a good share of learning and intelligence. While others were engaged in dancing, we would oftentimes be conversing on subjects of common interest respecting the management of the Asylum. There seemed to be a perfect coincidence in our views in relation to this subject, and we secretly agreed upon a plan of exposing it when we got out. But he became a victim of homesickness to the highest degree, which caused his death. This long pent up indignation would sometimes vent itself in vehement language. For example, one night at our dance, I inquired if he had heard from his friends. He replied in a most vehement and impressive manner. "Friends! I have no friends! I will never have a friend again! They have been the curse of my life! Curse on all the friends I ever had!"

I told him I could respond to his sentiment, as could almost all others who have been put in here by their friends. It is indeed now true, that "a man's foes are they of his own household." And if any doubt it, I think if they were once put in here by their friends, they would then be compelled to believe it. I told him what a Miss Hall, a very smart young lady said, who had been here for a few weeks; "If my friends can put me into such a place as this, they can not care anything for me; I am knocked about as if I were nothing but a dog. I am Miss Smith's mere slave or brute. It is enough to drive one's senses and intellect all away from them, to be treated as we are. Those who have established such institutions must be criminals! What can they mean, to let that saucy, mean girl drive us about so? And there is no escape, no appeal from her impudence!"

"And, Mr. Wells," I added, "have you not ascertained that this is one of the most prominent features of the 'treatment' we are sent here to receive? They must make us feel that we are utterly deserted, with no sort of appeal, to inspire in us a reverence for the despotic will which rules supreme here."

"Despotic will! There never was a greater despot lived, than now lives in that man," pointing to Dr. McFarland, who was now approaching us. "But we must separate—the Doctor must not see us together." Saying this, he arose and walked to another part of the hall. After the Doctor left the hall, we resumed our conversation. "Mr. Wells, have you suffered from Dr. McFarland's tyranny, personally?"

"Indeed I have; I could now show the deep ridges upon my limbs here," placing his hands upon his lower limbs, just above his knees. "marks of the rope with which I have been bound to the bed rack in the lowest ward!"

"What! you bound with ropes! what did they bind you for?"

"Because I insisted upon having my little poodle dog in my room for my amusement, and his safety. I had just paid three dollars for it, intending to carry it as a present to my little son at Chicago. But being denied this solace, I contrived to evade the command to take it from me; and finding it in the coal-bin, when I was out one day, I managed to get it back, unnoticed, to my room. But alas! this happiness soon terminated; for orders soon came from head quarters, that 'Mr. Wells be put into the lowest ward, and confined to the bed rack, as his penalty for this act of disobedience.' I made every appeal possible to Dr. McFarland, to induce him to mitigate my sentence; but all in vain. Said I, 'Doctor, you are a father, can you not sympathize with me in my desire to receive a welcome from my darling boy, and in return bestow upon him a gift which I know will delight him?' He made no reply, whatever, but turned away as if he heard not a word I said!"

"That is just as he has treated me, although physical abuse I have not suffered; yet, what is worse, I feel his iron grip upon my every inalienable right—all, all are at his bidding, subject wholly to his will alone. Mr. Wells, this is a State Institution, can you tell me how such a despotism could have taken root on Illinois soil?"

"Mrs. Packard, the people of Illinois know nothing about this Institution, except through the Doctor's one-sided reports. He, himself, has run the Institution into a despotism, and now it is hard to convince a blinded public of it, as he has made them feel that he is almost infallible. He is of Scotch descent, and he has stamped the monarchical feeling of his nature upon this nominally republican Institution."

"But can it not be known? Can't we tell of it, when we get out?"

"Yes, Mrs. Packard, I am determined upon that. I command a printing press at Chicago, and I will print all you will write, and will write myself; and this shall be the first great work I shall do, after I get out of this place. I am *determined* in this matter. But don't let the Doctor know of this fact, for he never will let us out alive if we do."

"But I have already told him of my determination, and that is what he is keeping me for."

"O, Mrs. Packard, you will never get out then; but I will tell of your case when I get out, and help you, if I can."

Here the party broke up, and taking his offered arm, he escorted me to the door of my room, where we parted forever, with these words; while bending over me, he whispered in my ear: "Mrs. Packard, my press shall be used for your benefit; but, Keep dark! Keep dark!"

In one week from this time Mr. Wells was a corpse. His desire to see or hear from his wife and children in Chicago, reached such a pitch of intensity, that nature could bear no more. His large, capacious brain became convulsed under the mental agony of too long suspense—of hope of hearing from his wife too long deferred, and these fits continued, with but few very short lucid intervals, until he died. The day he died, Mary, the Doctor's youngest daughter, came to my room, and remarked, with tears in her eyes, "It is too bad! it is too bad! Father ought to have sent Mr. Wells' letter."

"What do you mean, Mary?"

"About one week ago Mr. Wells gave father a letter, to be mailed to his wife. In this letter he wrote how terribly homesick he was—how he could not stand it much longer without hearing from her—that if she disappointed him this time, it would kill him. He knew it would kill him. The hope of getting a reply to this letter would keep him up until there had been time to get a reply, and then 'if I don't get one, *I shall die*. I can't bear another disappointment and live through it.' He then asked his wife's forgiveness for all the hard things he had spoken or written about her putting him into such a place, saying, as his only excuse, 'You can not imagine how much I am suffering. But I can, and will, forgive all, if you will now take me out, or even write and tell me you will do so. But if you do not promptly respond to this letter, in some way, farewell forever! It will be my last! I shall die of anguish!" Now," she added, "Mr. Wells is dead, and father has got that letter yet!" The very day he expected a reply, and got nothing, he went into convulsions, which continued until he died.

LX.

An Asylum Sabbath.

It was my good fortune to find the Sabbath day here observed or kept in what I call a christian manner. It was observed as a day of rest, as God's command requires. There were more tumbled beds, this day, than any other. The rule of other days, "keep them off their beds," was, in a measure, suspended on this day for rest. It was very seldom that company entered the wards on this day, therefore this suspension of the rules for "display," was no detriment to the reputation of the house. I felt that, for myself, I could better meet the demands of my conscience under the influence of this house, than I ever could outside of its walls. As I had all my life been connected with a minister's family, I found, of course, little time for the rest the command enjoined upon me. Besides attending to the necessary labor attending eating and sleeping, as on other days, I was obliged not only to dress myself, but my children also, for church and Sunday school, and attend two or three public services, besides the Sunday school and teacher's meeting, perhaps, in addition; so that when my resting hour arrived, I would usually feel more the need of rest from weariness, than any other day of the week. Now, since I have allowed my common sense a little latitude in this direction, I am convinced I was then breaking the Sabbath, most egregiously, by pursuing this course. Instead of being rested as I ought to have been, in mind and body, by the Sabbath, I so used it as to unfit myself for the renewal of weekly toil with fresh vigor.

I now understand that God *rested* from his labor on the Sabbath, and so should we. He has so constituted us, that more than six days of continued, unbroken labor, without extra rest, is a detriment to our mental and physical faculties. To go to meeting too much, may be breaking the spirit of the command, as well as working too much. It is rest that we need, and it is rest we should feel bound to take on this day, as an act of obedience to a law of our nature. We should so spend the day as to find ourselves refreshed and invigorated for the active duties of our calling; otherwise we break the Sabbath.

LXI.

Letters to Dr. McFarland.

INSANE ASYLUM, April 28, 1862.

DR. MCFARLAND:—It is time for me to know whether you are indeed my friend or enemy. My stand must be immovably taken to treat you as a friend, or just as your own actions reveal to me your true position. You must allow me to be my own keeper, by giving me a key or a pass, or you compel me to regard myself as a most wronged and injured woman, whose self-respect requires her to regard you as her subtle foe. Yes, Doctor, if after all the love and kindness, light and reason, forbearance and trust I have so implicity reposed in you, as a truthful, honest man, you now resist these combined influences, and persist in your wrong doing, I must be true to you, and unvail your character to the world.

If you attempt to sustain your character, by defaming mine, and by that act compel me to defend my own, by exposing yours, you must see that by so doing, you will work out your own destruction.

Dr. McFarland, the simple story of my wrongs which I have received at your hands, since I entered this house, pub lished as they will be for the world's perusal, will arouse such indignation in community as will hurl you from your high position, to your proper place, and your family will be, through you, so stigmatized, that coming ages will hold your name in contempt.

O, Dr. McFarland, I have hoped even against hope, that the adamant of your proud heart, would be permeated by the force of truth, so that you could be saved from ruin, instead of being ruined to be saved. But if you will not do me the simple act of justice which it is in your power to do, I must do you the justice your neglect demands. Or as I told you in my Reproof if you will not be my deliverer, you must witness my deliverance in your destruction.

Your true Friend, E. P. W. P.

ANOTHER LETTER TO DR. MCFARLAND.

July 12, 1862.

My *Professed* Friend—I am exceedingly sorrowful, and it may be unto death, unless some of my many sorrows are by some means alleviated. And O, Dr. McFarland, strange as it may seem, my fond heart turns instinctively to you, as my helper! What a paradox of inconsistencies we are. Now my reason and judgment, and my most bitter experience assures me there is no hope for me in this quarter; still, my heart will turn to *man*, as my protector, and there is no man left but you to turn to.

You must *do something*, or the bow long strained to its utmost tension will break. I cannot bear these accumulated burdens of life much longer. And O, to save one who has been the truest friend you ever had, will you not grant me one request? O, dare I utter it only to be denied, or to receive only a silent, heartless, indifferent response?

Dr. McFarland, will you not remove me forthwith to the County poor-house, where I understand the law allows you to put those whom you regard as worthless members of society—hopelessly insane persons. O, do let me speedily take the position your decision assigns me on earth, with Mr. Stickney, as a hopelessly insane pauper of this State for life!

Do not longer compel me to be tortured by being eye and ear witness to abuses which my afflicted sisters here are constantly liable to receive at Miss Smith's hands. Miss Smith says herself that she is not fitted for her place—that she is conscious she is getting worse and worse every day—still she says that you say you do not wish to part with her. O, Doctor if it is to agonize me, that she is retained, your end is accomplished.

Another thing, my table fare cannot be more uncongenial to my feelings. To sit down to an oil cloth covered table, with nothing upon it to eat except what is distributed upon our plates, and if that is insufficient in quality or quantity, our only remedy lies in picking up what we can find of the leavings from off the plates of the filthy maniacs; since the food is all distributed before we sit down, except the bread, and to that we are not entitled until all fragments are disposed of. Since I eat no hog meat, I am often compelled to make my entire meal on bread and potatoes and salt, sometimes no butter.

O, you cannot imagine, until placed in our circumstances, how delightfully refreshing was a taste of a pine apple which your kind Mary brought me yesterday, from your table, after searching in vain to find anything to satisfy myself from the leavings of the maniacs. And Sir, to one who has uniformly moved in the choicest and best society, and with feelings refined and cultivated, it is humiliating in the extreme, to be thus situated. And for what, am I thus cast out as evil, to spend the remainder of my life among those who are regarded as the filth and offscouring of humanity?"

O, well may this country be draped in mourning, while by its heaven defying laws, it upholds such iniquity; such abuse of woman! Do please, speak to me upon this subject if nothing more, for total indifference to my sufferings and wrongs is more intolerable to my nature than frank denial.

Your friend in anguish of spirit.

E. P. W. P.

But this, like all other appeals, either spoken or written,

the Superintendent chose to take no notice of whatever, seemingly for the express purpose of torturing the feelings of his helpless prisoner, to the highest point of endurance. O, the anguish of spirit that man has the psychological power of inflicting upon woman, no language can describe, For her sake, Great God, break his power speedily!

LXII.

My Attempt to get an Attendant Discharged.

MY NOTE TO MY ATTENDANT.

Miss Smith: I advise you to resign your office as attendant, on the ground of your incompetency to fill the office as it should be filled, on account of your quick, overbearing temper. Your health is not good, and your nerves are in danger of becoming incurably diseased, by the strain upon them, which your present responsibilities demand.

For your own good, I ask you to resign immediately, and in this way supersede a discharge on the ground of abusive treatment of the patients.

Your true friend, E. P. W. P.

MY NOTE TO DR. TENNY.

Dr. Tenny: It is wicked for you to keep so incompetent an attendant here, as Miss Smith, on account of her quick, overbearing temper. If you do not discharge her forthwith, I shall expose you to the world, for sustaining an attendant who treats the patients worse than brute beasts.

Miss Hall came to my room yesterday, and said, "Can I not get away from the influence of that wicked, vile girl, who knocks us around as if we were dogs, and the men don't seem to be much better, for they don't care how we are treated when we are alone; it is enough to drive all my senses out of me." Dr. Tenny, 'tis true, the patients are actually afraid of their lives, from Miss Smith's violent, insane temper. She certainly shows more devilment than any person in the hall.

Miss Bailey is prepared to endorse me, for she says she will not bear the blame of Miss Smith's abuses. She says it is wrong, and she will not bear the responsibility any longer.

There is not one in this house, who knows Miss Smith, but what feels that she is wholly incompetent for her position, on account of her temper; and how dare you defy the public sentiment of this land, in countenancing such abusive treatment of the insane in this Institution? I assure you, you are running an awful risk in so doing.

An act of indiscretion on her part, the night of the last dance alone, entitles her to a discharge, independent of her abuse of the patients. She locked Mr. Jones and Miss Bailey in our dining room, where they had gone to extinguish the gas, and left them there alone, in total darkness, and went off, leaving her key in the door. Miss Bailey felt much hurt; and she had good reason to feel that she had been insulted mistreated. It is a wanton exposure of her reputation; and if the Doctor will discharge Miss M ——, and retain Miss Smith, he is certainly an unjust man, and is a respecter of persons in his judgment. Yours truly, E. P. W. P.

Miss Smith carried my note to her to Dr. McFarland, and he read it. She asked him if he wished her to leave, adding, "if you do, I will." She said he replied, that he did not wish her to leave. She added, she was tired of the wards, and would like to change her situation. He said she might have the first opening in the ironing room, in exchange for the wards. So this is all the good it does to try to influence Dr. McFarland, by reasons based in truth. Appeals in the name of humanity seem to have lost all power over him. I have reason to believe that Mrs. Coe told him of all the cases of abuse mentioned in the document for the *Independent*, for she assured me she should tell him, if he could be made to listen. She said he might turn away, and not hear it, as he often did; like the deaf adder, he would not hear.

But if he would not hear the truth from her, he has received it from me, and knows Miss Smith is an abusive attendant. Still he keeps her. Miss Smith told me, yesterday, that the

Doctor had never reproved her for misusing the patients, n or ever tried to restrain her. No principle controls the Doctor's actions, except that of policy.

I often think of what Mrs. Grere, one of the sufferers here, said: "If Dr. McFarland won't do right, can't he be made to do right by some power?" O, yes, Mrs. Grere, there is a power which can make him do right, and that is the power of a just law. Let justice but unsheathe its flaming sword, and like all tyrants when they discover a power above them, his proud heart, will be led to beg for that mercy which he now refuses to others.

Miss M ——, to whom reference is made in the last sentence of my note to Dr. Tenny, is a poor, dependent orphan, an outcast from her Catholic friends, on account of her having embraced Protestant views. She is about eighteen years old, and has been made self-reliant at a very early age, by her surroundings. Her strength and maturity of character are thereby far in advance of her years. She has a genuine Irish heart, loving and affectionate in the extreme; buoyant and happy in her disposition, firm and uncompromising with injustice and iniquity of every kind. She has filled, at different times, several offices here, as supervisor, attendant, and assistant matron. She was also Hattie McFarland's most intimate friend. She was invariably kind to the patients, from principle, as well as feeling. She was an attendant of my ward at the time she was discharged, and I regarded her as one of the kindest and most sympathizing friends the patients ever had among those employed here. She was frolicsome and sportive, the welcome companion of all. She seemed to feel neither above nor beneath any one. She claimed the respect of all, on the ground of deserving it. Such was her character—a perfect contrast to that of Miss Smith. The latter is independent, as to friends, property, and influence; and still, the good Dr. McFarland would discharge this kind, dependent orphan, and protect the wicked, independent Miss Smith, simply because he chose to do so, for reasons best known to himself. The indiscreet, thoughtless act which occasioned Miss M——'s discharge, was going with Hattie McFarland into the gentlemen's ward, and walking over their newly made beds in the dormitory, and thus enraging the feelings of the attendant, Mr. Po, who prided himself exceedingly on his skill in bed making. He went, under the influence of his excited feelings, to the Doctor, and procured her discharge.

She felt too indignant at this ungallant act, to make any apology to him for trampling his beds, therefore her discharge could not be repealed.

If Dr. McFarland felt that the interests of his Institution demanded this sacrifice of the orphan's situation and means of support, he had a right so to do. This favoritism of the Doctor in judgment, appears to have hardened his moral sensibilities, so that, added to his other perpetrated wrongs, he seems to be approaching that state in which it is easy to "believe lies," rather than the truth "whose damnation is just," the Bible says. But since damnation does not mean eternal torment, but simply a terrible process of painful discipline, for the good of the sufferer, I look beyond this awful gulf to their prospective future, and see them restored, redeemed, purified, lost to all that is evil, alive to good only. There I see the triumph of the Cross.

Can Christ, who gave his life to redeem the whole world, leave such a man as Dr. McFarland in endless torment, and still be true to his promises? If Judas, whom Christ himself called a "devil," is a member of the human family, and on this ground entitled to the benefits of redemption, why can not Dr. McFarland, or any other sinner, have as good a title? But since, as a man, he has sinned, and thus perverted, but not destroyed his nature, as such, he will be made to repent, and thus secure his lost image—lost, or obscured by sin, temporarily. But occultation is not annihilation. Being under the power of evil for a time, and the manhood being entirely eclipsed thereby, does not extinguish the orb of humanity, which is eventually to shine with the effulgence of the Deity, for it is a part of the Godhead itself. In every human soul God multiplies himself. If the perversion of our being is to be the endless law of our nature, in a single instance, then evil is omnipotent, and nature, or good, is its subject. But it is not so; nature, or the God-given tendencies of our being are the only ineradicable influences in the universe. These perversions or irregularities, 'are but the temporary effects of an antagonistic force, whose principle is destined to ultimate destruction.

LXIII.

A new Attendant Installed—Something New.

Miss Adelaide Tryon, a young school girl of eighteen years, was introduced into our ward, to take Miss Smith's place. To all appearances, she is a girl of weak mind, and small abilities; but time alone well test her, and develop whether she is fitted for the place or not.

My first impressions of her are not good. still I intend to suspend judgment till a fair trial. My mind may be a little prejudiced, from my first interview. I went into the dining room, after breakfast as usual, to get my ice, when I met her at her duties. Since the ice had not come up, I waited a few minutes, and entered into a conversation with her. She answered me rather short and abruptly, evidently trying to impress the idea upon my mind, that she regarded me as beneath her notice, except as her under servant.

She ordered me to hand her the knives and forks, for her to put around the table, which I did; after which she ordered me out of the dining room. I silently obeyed, and returned to my room to ponder over the peculiar trials to which an imprisonment among maniacs rendered our moral nature liable.

While upon my knees praying for grace and patience to bear them with a christian spirit, my devotions were suspended by the entrance of Miss Hall. She came with a full heart

M

of grief and sorrow to pour out her complaints to me. Here God had sent me a remedy for my own sorrows; I must bear her burdens, to lighten my own. Like many others here, Miss Hall is suffering for the sins of her friends towards her, and now in addition, she has to bear the sins of Dr. McFarland's injustice towards her.

After she left, Miss Tryon came to my room and attempted to bolt in, very unceremoniously. I arose and opened the door and introduced her in, when she, in a very abrupt manner, remarked, "I came in to see what you were doing; what have you in your hand? Are you fond of reading?" etc.

After answering her civilly, I tried to converse with her in an intelligent, ladylike manner; to which she seemed heedlessly indifferent, evidently seeming to regard what I said, as idle talk, beneath her notice. Here, this little school girl feels at liberty to lord it over me as much as she chooses, regarding me and my society with contempt!

Mean as she seems, I wish to do her good as a sister. But in order to do so, I think I must tell her that I am not her servant—that she is my servant, that I am a boarder here, and she a hired servant to wait upon the boarders. If she attempts to rule over me, I shall regard it as an insult, such as I shall feel morally bound to resent. But by forbearance and patience, she may be led to see her faults for herself, and avoid them in future. I have told her that I was the means of getting her here, for it was through my influence that Miss Smith was finally discharged from the ironing room, since I reported her to the Doctor for her abuse of the patients. She said, "you won't report me, will you?" "I don't expect to have occasion to do so, for I trust you will be kind to them.'

It is due Miss Tryon to add that she became a reasonable and kind attendant; and so far as her subsequent treatment of me was concerned, I had no occasion to complain of her, and as providence appointed, I was delegated by her father to be her guardian! This was a new thing in Asylum life, to have an attendant put under the care of a patient! The facts are these: Miss Tryon one day brought her father to my room, and after introducing us, as I responded to her ladylike knock, by opening the door, she left us, and I asked him into my room, when we soon found ourselves engaged in earnest and intelligent conversation. As he took his leave, he remarked, "Mrs. Packard, I see you are a sensible woman; now, may I not be allowed to place my daughter under your charge, since she is young and inexperienced, and needs the guardianship of some one like yourself."

"Certainly Mr. Tryon, I not only thank you for the compliment, but I should be happy to accept the charge, and will promise you I will be to her a true friend."

Apparently pleased and satisfied with my response, he took a respectful leave, and joined his daughter in her room, where he asked her about me, who I was, etc.

To her reply that I was a patient, he expressed his astonishment by exclaiming.

"Why, she is the most intelligent lady I ever saw! There is not the least particle of insanity about her! There must be some mistake about that."

"I think so too," she replied, "for she has been just as she is now, during the three weeks I have been here, and all in the house say she has been just the same, ever since she has been here."

"There must be some mistake—there is foul play somewhere —I shall speak to Dr. McFarland about this," replied her father. And he did speak; and the result was, Miss Tryon, had express orders from Dr. McFarland never to let her father into the ward again!

LXIV.
My Protest Deprives me of no Privileges.

Miss Tryon our new attendant has gone home on a visit of two days. I asked her to let me have her keys while she was absent, urging that Miss Tomlin did so when she went away, sometimes—that the Doctor knew of it, as I had told him, and he had simply bowed assent. Still I told her not to grant my request without asking the Doctor's permission; she, being a new attendant, it would not be best for her to take such a responsibility. She asked the Doctor and he refused his consent. Now the point is established in my mind that I sacrifice no privileges in keeping my promise to never return a voluntary prisoner to the ward. For he had before directed the attendants not to let me out of the wards, and he had himself forbidden my going to the chapel any more after I had protested. Now his *professing* to wish me to enjoy the privileges of the house, are shown to be entirely hypocritical and false. He only wishes to break down my conscience by thus trying to induce me to break my word and lie.

Did he feel willing I should enjoy the parole which his other prisoners do, he would give me a pass or a key as he does to Mrs. Page, a prisoner here, and some others. He only wishes to make the impression that my confinement is self-imposed, when in reality it is just as he wishes, and just as he would have it if I had not made my vow. I know, by his artifice and sophistry, he can use it in a way to vindicate himself; when in reality he would not have it otherwise, had I not entered my protest. He gravely tells me he wants I should enjoy the privileges of the house, and then when I desire it for two days only, he even denies me this limited day of grace. He knows I could not go out and return a *prisoner*, but by having a key I could and not break my vow, and now he won't grant this favor for even two days. If he denies me this privilege for two days, what reason have I to think I could have it all the time? None at all. He thinks his sagacity will take me captive on this point; but let us see if the sagacity of some other intelligence is not equal to his own here too. I have only to maintain a consistent, upright course, by simply doing right in all respects, and thus I shall in the end overcome his selfish policy in protecting himself in doing wrong.

How I do long to see the issue of this long sad drama! My

faith has long since assured me what to expect, but visions only, will not entirely satisfy me. Dr. Tenny does all he can to help my spirits, by his respectful attention to my wants. I can go to him with my requests, and they are not met with a repulse.

The moral barometer indicates a storm, but I fear it not, I am in no danger with my Pilot. Nor am I discouraged because so many tempests betide me. The last will sometime have passed away. Then with my dear little ones, I shall find a safe harbor, where we shall find rest from fear of evil. My entire trust is in the skill of my faithful Pilot to guide my foundering bark o're this life's tempestuous sea. If I am wrecked, it will be because my Pilot's skill has for the first time been inadequate to the great emergency. Then I must be the first one to proclaim, "There is no safety in trusting to the God within—human wisdom is superior to the divine!" The end of this vision will speak for God, and not against him.

I never will take the destiny of my own life, into my own hands by doing wrong, nor will I seek to escape present trouble by disregarding the monitions of my own conscience. I am fully determined to see where simple obedience to God's will, as indicated by my guide, will land me. The world shall know, by one faithful experiment, how trust in God is rewarded. If my course leads to ruin, it is because we have no safe guide, within, upon which to rely.

Dr. McFarland a Respecter of Persons.

LXV.

I showed Dr. McFarland the reply of Henry M. Parker, Esq., to the District Attorney of the United States Court, Boston, Mass., after he had relinquished the case against the Gordons, for treason. In this he had shown that it was dangerous business to arrest citizens for mere differences of opinions, and calling it treason, without proof from their own acts, that they were traitors. He said the people would not tolerate it, but would arraign and prosecute such for their acts; and not only so, but would make them liable to civil action for damages.

I told him the same principles were involved in this case, as in my own; that I had been charged with insanity without proof, and my persecutors were liable to be called to pay the damages due me for this unconstitutional act of abuse and outrage upon my constitutional rights as an American citizen.

He treated the whole subject with utter contempt, as beneath his notice, simply because the sentiments expressed were those of a lawyer, rather than those of a judge! I told him the principle was the same, whoever uttered it.

My nature compels me to hold all truth in respect, whoever is its medium. It is not the medium which gives character or importance to truth, but the evidence it carries within itself, that it is truth, whose author is God himself. I feel as much bound to respect the utterances of truth coming from an insane person, as from any other, even Dr. McFarland himself, or any other great man. What an index does this furnish of the Doctor's character! Is he not a man-pleaser rather than a God-pleaser? Does he not care more for the praise of men than for that of God? Is the approval of his own conscience of as great importance to him, as the favor of men? Of great men who can promote him to some post of honor? Would he not yield his conscientious scruples, if they impeded his temporal advancement? God only knows! But since "by their fruits we are to know them," I should infer from this expression of sentiment, that he was wanting in real integrity, in manly principle. Here I, who so much long to see some manhood on whom I can rely as an earthly protector, am left entirely to the tender mercies of such a false, perverted man. He seems to hold my temporal destiny entirely at his disposal.

Shut out, as I am, from the world, and all communication

with it, except through the medium of this unprincipled man, who would not scruple to misrepresent to any degree, to promote and accomplish his sinister purposes, how can I expect the real truth can ever be known?

Yesterday he gave additional instructions to guard our hall from the visits of strangers, doubtless fearing some secret communication through them to me, thus forming a link with the world. He evidently trusts to his sagacity in keeping me hidden, as his means of self-defense. Yes, Dr. McFarland, all your sagacity is demanded, to defend yourself from trouble on my account. You have already allowed this house to be employed as an Inquisition too long, to satisfy the tax payers that you are a proper man for your position. These tax payers have a right to demand of you how their money has been expended. When the truth is known, that you have employed it in perverting it from its appropriate use—benefitting the insane—and have employed it in persecuting some of the best of American citizens, they will indignantly demand satisfaction.

When I think of my present situation—how utterly helpless, hopeless, defenseless, and wretched it is, so far as natural appearances indicate, and then contrast it with your prospects for the future, I am led to feel it is not the worst possible after all. My hopes are all in the future; yours are buried in the past. My worst fears have been realized: yours are to come. I am suffering from falsehood and slander; you are to suffer from the truth. I have the promises for my support; you, the threatenings to dread!

LXVI.

Kidnapping the Soul.

Another remark Dr. McFarland made, which found no response in my nature, except a feeling of scorn and indignation—I told him what I had done here as evidence of my possessing practical talents, by which I was fully capacitated to take care of myself and others. His reply was, "There is a lady in the lowest ward who can do all these things!"

What is this argument? Is it not because one whom we consider unquestionably insane can do these things, that it is no proof of your rationality, to be able to do them?

I replied, "Perhaps there is; but can she show by her writing, which is a correct index of the state of the mind, that she is intellectually sound; and does her conversation and conduct show her to be morally sound, with no irregularities in any department of character?"

I believe I know several cases there, who are not insane at all; but, by calling them so, and keeping them there, leads them to regard themselves as hopeless cases, just as he is trying to do by me. I believe he has deprived hundreds of their earthly existence, as accountable beings; and he, as yet, has in no instance, been called to account for it. O, it is high time that this thing be looked into, and restitution be made. I could have replied, that "Hurd, a very crazy old man, could rake hay better than he could, and therefore *he* was an insane man on the same plane as Mr. Hurd."

Is not the slander of insanity the most cruel kind of defamation that can be instigated against another? From what right does it not exclude us, except that of eating and sleeping like animals? Nothing more or less. And can this highest of all wrongs and insults to a human being, be looked upon with any degree of allowance, by him who bestowed these moral natures upon man?—the very godhead thus crushed out of a human being, and he be made to believe that he is only a brute beast, with no claims upon his fellow creatures, higher than theirs—to put a high toned, sensitive, developed human soul upon this level, by base design, for base purposes, by the basest of malicious lies! Is it not a sin of the deepest die? Can there be any greater blasphemy against God, or against the Holy Ghost? I know, by tasting this cup to its bitterest dregs, what it is to feel this deepest wrong—this kidnapping of the soul—depriving a human being of his God bestowed accountability. To kidnap a human being, and treat him as a slave, is a terrible outrage upon human nature; but this is not to be compared with the still blacker crime of kidnapping their accountability, and making them nothing but brutes. Slaves are allowed to exert their abilities to work, and thus feel that somebody is benefitted by them; but the insane are considered below them. They are not allowed to feel that they are capable of being of any manner of service to the world, but degraded as useless burdens, which others must carry through life—as paupers, whose only satisfaction to themselves and others, is the fact that they can die, and thus rid the world of a useless animal!

A tender, sensitive girl, who feels this degradation very severely, came to my room this morning and said, "I had rather be taken out and shot, than to be looked upon as an insane person and treated as one.'

So had I, and so would hundreds of others here, could they have their choice. O death, death is sweet to such a life as this; and did not conscience interpose a barrier, suicides would be of daily occurrence! A feeling of relief comes over me, when I hear of such an occurrence, at the thought that one soul more is liberated from the Asylum. And O, when one has been thus degraded here, to come back again! Can anything be more dreadful! The return of a fugitive to slavery is sad; but sadder far, to sustain a second imprisonment as an insane person! An imprisonment as a criminal, does not begin to compare with it in cruelty—a criminal is regarded as a moral being. He is not locked up to be deprived of the godhead within him. His capacity to become a wicked, guilty person is allowed him; and this capacity, even with guilt attending it. is less to be dreaded, than a feeling of annihilation, an extinction of human capacities and being.

This is the "treatment" for which Dr. McFarland endeavors to awaken gratitude in me, for having been permitted to enjoy here freely so long! But I can not manifest my gratitude for this great privilege, by thanking him for thus making me the recipient of so much misery. Since he has recommended my case to the Trustees, he has regarded the responsibility as resting entirely upon them. Could I be guiltless in God's sight, and allow another to suffer what I have, for fear of any consequences attending myself? I could never meet my Judge, unless I had given a truthful representation of this Institution! A few may have left here without realizing the nature and tendency of the Asylum System. Either they were too insane to detect and judge correctly of it, or too unsympathizing to feel for others. Others there were, who saw and fully appreciated these things, but who were so overjoyed at their deliverance, that they seemed to forget their former impressions. Others, remembering them with most vivid distinctness, were heard to avow their resolution, never to speak of these things, outside the Institution, lest it revive these impressions. They looked upon them as a kind of horrid nightmare, which they wished to banish, as soon as possible, from their recollection.

LXVII.

Orthodox Heaven and Hell.

If this is not the Presbyterian heaven and hell combined, so long preached by Mr. Packard, I do not know what is! Endless torment, inflicted by a heartless despot, from whom it was impossible to escape, and whom it is as impossible to move to pity or compassionate his helpless victims, is but the symbol of this Pandemonium. If hope once reaches here, it is in despite of him and his power and influence.

This is also their heaven; since we here have hard "seats" to sit upon, and nothing to do or amuse, except to sit and sing, in presence of the writhing of lost spirits! Rest and sing! What *rest* can a benevolent sympathizing nature experience, while he knows another soul is in torment!

There is no rest for active benevolence. So long as one soul is unredeemed from Satan's power, I must work for *that* soul's deliverance, before I can sing "Worthy is the Lamb that was slain to redeem mankind." The confident assurance that it will be redeemed, is the only ground upon which I can rely for peace and quiet in the mean time. Attractive as are the hard seats of heaven for "rest" to the idler to me they have no attraction. All my godlike powers thirst for action, and use. Inert, stupid indifference to other, interests, is, to my social sympathetic nature, a moral impossibility; and I heartily pray God to deliver me from a mansion in *such* a heaven, in company with *such* spirits!

My experience of it here in this Asylum, has been enough for me. If this is the character of heaven, for which we have borne the discipline of our earth life, I say I wish my earth life never to terminate, for such a heaven of "rest" is hell to to me.

Again, can hell be a worse institution than this, while it punishes the best citizens for the offenses of the worst? There have been hundreds imprisoned in it whose only offense is being true to the promptings of the spirit of God within them. They are more natural, more godlike than their cotemporaries, and the laws are so insane in their application, that they punish the best citizens, for the offenses of the worst. The dictatorial dogmatist contrives with the sagacity which the "old serpent" imparts to him, to so misrepresent and vilify the honest self-sacrificing christian, who is striving to live out the dictates of an enlightened conscience, that he is either compelled to compromise with iniquity, or, if steadfast for the right, he is made to endure the false charge of insanity. Henceforth he must be regarded as an incompetent being, incapable of self-government, and thus subject to all the abuses and insults which can be heaped upon him. Like his Master, he is now called to pass through Gethsemane's garden alone, with none to listen to his sorrows, or alleviate his anguish, with wakeful, generous sympathy. Even his own familiar friend, in whom he trusted, his bosom companion, has lifted his heel against him, and now no one dares to comfort or defend him against this accuser.

Thus forsaken, deserted, desolate, he finds no refuge left him, except the tower of faith, whose dome of love shelters his lonely heart. If that tower is so strongly fortified as to prove invulnerable, he is safe. If not, he is left refugeless, with no home or shelter on earth or in heaven. He is now the ready prey for the roaring lion, who delights in his ruin. He then becomes insane, made so, by the indefatigable efforts of his friends, aided by the evil influences of this inquisition. His high and noble nature is driven to desperation by these combined forces, and his reason becomes lost in frenzied impulse! Why, O, why, is it that such institutions were permitted to get a foothold upon the free soil of our republicanism? Why cannot our natures, made in God's image here, be allowed free scope for a natural development? Why cannot the intellectual and spiritual nature of man here have free scope to run to perfection? Is it because the spiritual nature of man can only become perfected by opposition, by restraint, by overcoming obstacles? Can its strength and power of self reliance be only thus acquired? Oh if the blood of martyrs must be the seed of this Spiritual Church, as it has been of the Christian Church, cannot the long list of martyrs which this Institution has furnished, be sufficient for this age of spiritual development? or, must every stage of spiritual progress be thus marked by the sable robes of martyrdom? Is not the time at hand when man may be free to obey the impulses of his spiritual nature, without being called insane? These holy influences I cannot, will not, resist, defenceless as I am. The inner law of my own mind shall never yield to human dictation, encouraged by the conviction that the end of this American Inquisition cannot be far distant.

LXVIII.

A Scene in the Fifth Ward—A Good Omen.

One afternoon, Miss Tryon came to me in quite an exhausted condition, exclaiming, "I am actually weak and faint from witnessing a scene of abuse in the lowest ward. Bridget Welch, Elizabeth Bonner's assistant, has been treating one of her patients most barbarously. I never saw a human being so basely abused. Bridget, in her passion, seemed more like a fiend than a woman. If Dr. McFarland could have seen and known how she treated her patient, and approved of it, he must be a very different man from what I had supposed."

I told her "the Doctor does know and approve of things most horrible here. I could prove that Elizabeth Bonner had said the Doctor once caught her, in one of her passions, abusing her defenseless victim, and gave her a smile of approbation, leaving her to expend her fury to her heart's content."

She replied, that Bridget had told her that she and Elizabeth were fighting Miss Rollins, and the Doctor caught them at it, and simply passed on, exclaiming as he passed, "That is right; give it to her, unless she will give up." "But," she added, "it don't sound like Dr. McFarland."

"No, it don't sound like him in his ostensible character, but I fear it is like him in his real character; he is a very deceitful man. He looks well after his ostensible character, and plans very adroitly, to delude, deceive, and pervert the truth, so as to shield himself publicly from the imputation of inhumanity. When he finds he has gone too far in encouraging abuse, and is in danger of exposure, he is careful to give the tide of feeling a new turn, by discharging the attendant for abuse, and thus reserve to himself the credit of being humane to his patients. Thus he puts upon our merciful sex, the credit of the inhumanity of his acts, and claims to himself the humanity. In reality, he instigates them to do what their nature revolts at, but what they feel compelled to do, to retain his approval; then he will add abuse to abuse by discharging them for doing as he wished them to do!"

She said Bridget Conelly had refused to leave the dining room at the request of Bridget Welch, the attendant. Instead of dealing gently with her, to induce her to go, they used authority over her, which did not increase her readiness to obey. Then commenced a terrible scene of battle; the attendant seized Bridget by the hair, when Miss Tryon came to the rescue. She endeavored to pacify both parties, by trying to induce Bridget Conelly to leave the hall. But her endeavors were not successful in making peace. By the help of another attendant, they undertook to secure the obedience of Bridget by brute force. Thus they succeeded in what they called "subduing her." Having done this, and even after the patient had yielded, they inflicted upon her a terrible beating. Then throwing her upon the floor, they kicked, pounded, and stamped upon her with both feet. They repeatedly knocked her head upon the floor with great violence, pulled up her head by the hair, pounding it with vehemence. It seemed as if this process must have beaten all the sense out of her, which was indeed the case. She became almost insensible before they finished. Exhausted and overcome with suffering, her strength now entirely failed. In this condition they dragged her, as if she were a dead carcass, from the dining room, across the long hall, then locked her up, and left her alone to her fate. Miss Tryon said she seemed nearly dead. I said to Miss Tryon, "The Doctor ought to know it."

"I do not like to tell him, being a stranger here; and I may get the ill will of the attendants. Dr. McFarland often instructs us to observe the by-laws, which say we must take the attendants' part, when called upon to do so, and I did not continue to do it when I found how she was misusing her."

I felt that I could appreciate her feelings, and could not urge her to tell the Doctor; but I felt that a responsibility rested now upon me, and retired to my room to seek wisdom to know and do my duty with reference to it. While thus employed, Miss Tryon came to my door, and asked me to promise her that I would say nothing to the Doctor about it. I told her I would not make such a promise; that I had the demands of my own conscience to meet, and I should do what seemed my duty. I added, however, "You have nothing to fear, Miss Tryon, from what I do; it will not harm you, for you are deserving great praise for what you have done. The stand you have taken, has shown you to be true to your nature—to the dictates of humanity; such a position can not harm you. It will exalt you more than any course you can pursue. Don't fear to do right; to be true to your kind instincts, for this is the only true road to preferment."

I again asked for light to know my duty, and concluded to report to the Doctor myself. I accordingly did so, when Dr. Tenny came to my room. I have found by observation, that Dr. Tenny possesses a heart. He has not permitted the generous, tender sympathies of his heart to ossify as Dr. McFarland has done, by turning a deaf ear to the claims upon his sympathy, which his suffering patients demanded of him. We can go to Dr. Tenny, feeling that his ear is not deaf to the dictates of reason and humanity. We find he has a heart to pity, and feel that he will do what, in reason, he can for us. The prompt, vigorous response he made to my appeal, shows him to be still alive, and not "dead in trespasses and sins." After patiently listening, and giving me opportunity to unburden my heart to him, by telling the particulars of the case, as Miss Tryon related them to me, he sought the Doctor's office with a quick step, and there related the affair as I had told him, accompanying it with such enthusiasm and indignation, that it seemed to arouse the intellect of Dr. McFarland. He saw that unless he did something, others would! He accordingly summoned Bridget and Miss Tryon to his presence, and the latter was called on to relate the story herself. She did so, and Bridget did not deny it. The Doctor then summoned Bridget to his office, and gave her a discharge.

Well done, for Dr. McFarland! You shall have all the credit due you for doing right, whatever influence compels you.

LXIX.

Every Moral Act Influences the Moral Universe.

(FROM MY JOURNAL OF 1862.)

I congratulated Dr. McFarland upon his energy exhibited in grappling with evil here, in discharging Bridget so promptly. Said I " if you would but pursue this course with equal energy, a little longer, you could soon eradicate all the abuses which now exist here. Evil begins to hide its head in shame here now, and that is one step towards its extermination. If Lincoln would but grapple with the rebellion with equal energy, and put slavery into the grave it has dug for the Republic as he ought to, the government could be saved."

He replied, " he ought to do so, but he is too good a man to do it."

" Yes, I see he is afraid to do right, for fear of consequences, but this is not from an excess of goodness, but from a want of it. Goodness dares to do right, fearless of consequences. It is pusilanimity or weakness which fears the result of right doing."

I think the most effectual aid we can give Lincoln to bring him to do right, is by doing right ourselves. Every energetic act in us adds potency to the moral element by which he is to be moved to action. Every act of a moral agent influences the entire moral universe. Each upright act adds to the strength of goodness or righteousness, and every evil act, gives additional power to the principle of evil. It is like throwing a stone into a lake, the utmost bounds of which feels the influence of the ripple occasioned by its fall. As the ocean is made up of the drops, so the moral universe is composed of individual moral acts. Good and evil seem now to commingle in this great ocean life promiscuously, and the current of both seem now to alternate with almost equal force. What is needed is a condensation of the good influences of the universe into one vast gulf stream, sweeping irresistibly through the great ocean of moral life, bearing down all obstacles which evil interpose to its progress. When this gulf stream is once formed and set in motion, its progress will be irresistible throughout the moral universe. God is now at work separating these elements, and the good is to accumulate and condense into one great engine of power for the world's benefit.

LXX.

The Death Penalty to be Annihilated.

Some of the moral forces of the universe have already ripened into vigorous manhood, and through their combined influence, evil is becoming timid, and seeks concealment, which is one step towards its annihilation.

Like the concealing of the gallows from public onservation into the prison yard, within the prison walls, indicating that the death penalty is to be destroyed, and it is now on its way to destruction—this may be what is meant by death and hell being destroyed—that the death penalty and punishment both are to be annihilated in that community where moral power has acquired its manhood strength, and can stand alone self-reliant, independent of penalties for its existence, just as a child naturally outgrows his educational influences, and with them, the penalties of disobedience, which in his infancy and childhood are necessary helps to his virtues. But when these have acquired manly strength, he no longer needs restraint and penalties, but can be trusted to take care of himself independent of dictation or control from others. In his own heart he has the only monitor he needs for virtuous action, viz: the dictates of an enlightened conscience.

Dr. McFarland says he does not believe in annihilating the death penalty for murder—that he has not progressed so far as that—for he says, "Did not God command life to be taken for life? Did he not command Agag to be hewn in pieces as his punishment?"

I replied, "Yes, he did, but I do not therefore infer that we have a right so to do for He himself was the law-maker and the executive of the Jewish code. Of course every law was just and right, being wisely adapted to the infant state in which the race of men then existed."

He inquired, "do you think the race is in any better condition now than it was then?"

"I consider they are in a more developed state; good and evil are both stronger and more vigorous, because their capacities have increased. In consequence of this growth or development, a different kind of training is required to adapt itself to man's higher nature. For example, you would not feel justified in using the same kind of discipline over your developed son of twenty-one years, as with your son of three or five years. To attempt to compel him with penalties and restraints as you do your child, would be trifling with his manhood, insulting his manly feelings, and would justly bring you and your authority into derision. So God having himself controlled the race in its childhood, and as their father until they were of age, when they must require a different kind of training, he then abrogated the Jewish code, and instituted in its place, the Christian dispensation, of which Christ was the expounder. Now, instead of returning "an eye for an eye, and a tooth for a tooth," we must return good for evil, and leave judgment and vengeance for our wrongs, to Him who judgeth righteous judgment. For he says "vengeance is mine, I will repay." I do not think it is right for one sinner to punish another sinner. None but a righteous person is capable of inflicting a righteous punishment. God knowing this, instructs us to leave this matter entirely to himself. He may raise up and qualify a class of capacitated judges from the human race, to whom this power of judgment may be delegated.

"But I think this will never be the case, so long as God's image in man is so defaced. This lost image of the godhead must be restored in man, before he can be fitted to be God's representative on the earth as judge of his fellow men.

"I think the time is not far distant when righteousness shall be established on the earth; when Christ-like men will rule supreme over fallen perverted humanity. Then the demon, Penalty, will give place to the law of love and kindness, by means of which the trangressor will be reformed and restored to virtue, instead of being crushed down and debased by penalties as he now is. His god-like nature is now trampled in the dust, and no efforts to rise are encouraged, but rather smothered by attempts to degrade him to the level of a beast. Punishments of a corporeal kind, are only adapted to man as an animal, in the earlier stages of his existence; their influences can never be salutary after he has become a reasonable and accountable moral agent. He then sins through his reason and his intelligence, and he must be punished through his moral faculties as God has ordained. Shame and contrition, must be awakened through the influence of respectful kindness, to the wrong doer; not by trying to degrade the noble faculties of his nature, to a state of insensibility to moral influences by punishments.

"The more man becomes developed as a reasonable being, the more sensitive he becomes to those penal enactments whose legitimate tendencies are to obstruct, limit and destroy the natural aspirations of a moral agent. The age of penalties, seems now to have culminated in this horrible civil war, wherein the developed reason of man, is fiendishly employed in inventing means of destroying one another in the most barbarous manner. This crisis once passed, I believe the reign of peace will be inaugurated, wherein virtue will be protected, and cultivated by the influence of love and kindness, entirely independent of penalties and restraints."

Now I claim, that these principles of punishment are applicable to these Asylum Systems, and also of reforming Dr. McFarland, and other great sinners.

LXXI.

I was Punished for Telling the Truth.

The power of truth is irresistible, and disturbs this hidden nest of iniquity. I make no side thrusts through fear of the powers that be, knowing that they are wicked powers that cannot harm me, because held in check by the Highest. And so long as I do not prove traitor to this highest power, I can claim protection under it. But the first compromise with these hidden powers of evil cuts me off from all claims to the protection of the higher constitution.

They try to make themselves believe that it is slander which I utter when attacking the evils of this house; still they know them to be sad truths, which they would vainly deny, and reproach me, the medium, as insane, hoping thus to render my testimony nugatory. Did they see I attacked only fancied evils, they would not be thus disturbed by my testimony. But since they know it is real tangible truth, which I speak, therefore their consciences accuse them, and in despair they are driven to seek this means of quieting them. Could they only make me act as they have made Mrs. Farnside act, they would be relieved of an intolerate burden. Then they could tell of my own actions in support of their theory of my insanity, without telling in connection with them the great provocation which elicited such a mode of defensive action. Mrs. Farnside was subjected to an ordeal which she could not sustain. She fell into a passion before this temptation, and under the influence of this temper, she lost her dignified self possession. She descended from the plane of lady-like resentment, to their own low plane of brutality, and acted *then* like her tormentors.

Thus she put herself in their power, so that they can now say of her that "they were afraid of her," just as she had had reason to say of them, that "she was afraid of them;" and for this very reason she had to defend herself from them. Although there is precisely the same reason for fear, in both cases, yet, Mrs. Farnside bearing the brand of insanity, has to be represented as dangerous on account of her insanity, while their own insanity, although more marked, is entirely left out. So it is in this hidden den of iniquity, the innocent do suffer for the guilty actions of their keepers.

Seeing at a glance the artful workings of this hidden mode of treatment, I determined to face the enemy in open opposition to the powers that be, resisting all the consequences to myself or others; therefore I became a staunch advocate and defender of truth and justice, being extremely careful however to be just to myself, while I was trying to be just to others. That is, I was careful not to put myself in their power, by coming on to their plane at all. From this higher platform of principle, I could look down upon them on their lower plane of passion, policy, deception and brutality, and, from this standpoint, I could command the moral courage to be their reprover, and their reporter to the world. They envied my position and determined to take my fort by strategy, since open attacks had proved so unsuccessful. Their chagrin at their hitherto signal defeats had become exceedingly embarrassing, and as their machinery had hitherto proved successful in almost every other instance, they were very loth to abandon the siege. It was for this reason I was kept so long, and made to feel the force of all the combined powers of this dark house of darkest deeds, before they would abandon the siege against this impregnable, invincible fortress of calm self-composure. They feared me, not because I would fight them as Mrs. Farnside did, but they feared me because I would *not fight* at all. It was for this reason Dr McFarland wrote to my friends, in the heat of these battles, " Mrs. Packard has become a dangerous patient, it will not be safe to have her in any private family!" And Mr. David Field, of Granville, Illinois, wrote in reply to this information, and very respectfully inquired what evidence I had given in my own actions of being a "dangerous patient;" when he insolently replied, "I do not deem it my duty to answer impertintent questions!"

He knew that it would be "dangerous" to have me in any

private family long, for then they would find out what he had, that I was an uncompromising defender of truth and justice, and *such weapons* he feared, and might well call them "dangerous" to his interests in the hands of a *free* woman! He knew too well, that no bribes, no threats, no punishments could throw me off from the track I had chosen to pass my earth life upon. And since I had baffled his skill and gigantic powers in this attempt, he was sure the only safe place for *such* a woman, was behind the dead-locks of an Insane Asylum!

Mrs. Chapman told me one night at the dance, that she had inquired of Mrs. McFarland why they did treat me so abusively, so unreasonably, so persistently evil; to which she replied "it is because she slanders the house."

I replied, "there is nothing so cutting as the truth; they have become convinced that I am a fearless truth teller; therefore they fear me. She is at liberty to prove my representations slanderous and false, if she can, but she is not at liberty to defame my character to disprove them."

She then added, "I have also consulted Dr. Tenny about your case. I said to him, how can you treat Mrs. Packard as you do? it would drive me distracted and dethrone my reason entirely, to be put through such a process; and then to persist, so long, in so abusing an innocent and injured woman, is beyond all precedent; how can you do so?"

"I am only a subordinate, I cannot help it," was his reply.

I then told her, "Mrs. McFarland has been an angel of consolation to me; when I was so exceedingly sorrowful, before Miss Smith's discharge, she actually shed tears of pity for me, and did try to raise my dying hopes, by assuring me, I might hope her husband would send me home before long."

"Yes, she can *talk* sympathy, but why don't she *do* something for you? Talking sympathy is not what you want; you want to be treated as your character deserves to be treated."

"Mrs. McFarland did say she could not help my being placed

amongst the maniacs, to be subject to their injurious treatment, but she said she would send me something occasionally from their own table. And she has done so. Once she brought me herself under her apron or in her pocket, a tumbler of jelly and a teaspoon to eat it with. And another time I had a quantity of loaf-sugar and lemons and a pitcher of ice water sent into my room from their kitchen. She also consented to Mrs. Coe's (the cook) bringing me good things from their kitchen, or anything else she chose to bring, for my comfort. And Mrs. Coe has availed herself of this right, and brought me apples in abundance, and raisins, and oranges, and prunes some of which she bought with her own money. She brings me strawberries and sugar, and cherries and melons, which Mr. Jones the Superintendent of the Asylum farm sends me, by permission from Mrs. McFarland, so that through her influence, I have my sorrows lessened perhaps as much as it is possible for her to do, under the circumstances. Indeed, since Mrs. Coe has been our cook, and this license given her, I have hardly been a day without some extra luxury in my room for my health and comfort, such as fruits, cakes, and confectioneries. Now I think this is " doing something."

" Yes, it is a comfort to be thus cared for in your now forlorn condition, but that is not restoring you to your family and society, as you ought to be."

" No it is not, but the *hope* of being so, is next to the fruition, and Mrs. McFarland held this hope before me as a solace by saying, "I can assure you the Doctor will never consent to take you into this Institution again; you may settle your mind upon that point, and I think the Doctor did very wrong to listen to Mr. Packard so much; and he ought to have sent you home long ago!" and such like rays of hope. But I sometimes think, Mrs. Chapman, that I have felt more impatient since she inspired this hope than before. I have been like the soldier so long trying to keep down an inordinate desire to see my children once more, a free woman, that the least probability of the closing of the campaign almost fills me with ecstacy, and each blighting of a hope of this kind seems harder and harder to be borne. Another thing I have found, Mrs. Chapman, to be indispensible to my support, is to keep myself constantly employed, that my mind do not prey upon itself. My heart is so keenly alive to emotions and impressions, that a track is necessary for me to move upon, or it might become morbidly sensitive if left to itself. I therefore conscientiously employ each hour according to a set plan for systematic employment. And in this too, I am aided by Mrs. McFarland, for she lets me buy cotton knitting yarn, by the pound, and as much muslin as I want to embroider bands and trimmings of any style I choose. And I am accumulating an immense amount of embroidery for my own and my daughter's under-clothes, expecting, as you see, to live in the world a long time yet to need it!"

"Yes, the bow of hope is always to be seen in *your* horizon."

"Is it not well to have it so?"

"Yes if you can—but were I in your situation I think I should give up in despair."

"What would that accomplish?"

"Nothing, but to let them see the wreck they had caused!"

However her argument failed to dispirit me. Indeed I felt stronger for her sympathy, and determined to let matters take their natural course, believing that the dark riddle would be sometime made plain to my comprehension. I was now suffering what I was put in to receive—a "dressing down" for daring to speak the truth respecting the church dogmas; and now I must not turn back, but face this new enemy I have called into the field, by boldness of speech here—and must endure my punishment for telling the truth about the Insane Asylum dogmas. Yes, I am being punished for telling the truth! And God grant I may never escape from this calaboose of torture, by recanting the truth respecting creeds or Asylums!

LXXII.

Wrong Actions are Suicidal.

I asked the Doctor if he would answer one question, to determine whether I was a "discerner of spirits," or not, viz: "Has there not recently sprung up in your heart a desire that justice should be done me?"

"Yes, you are correct in discerning that spirit in me; but as to the time you are not."

"If I have been mistaken there, I should be glad to know it; for if you have hitherto exerted a protective power, I have failed to perceive it. It is a mystery I can not solve."

"It is no mystery; it is perfectly plain."

"I don't see how you can protect me, and yet deny me the right of self-defense."

"What you call a defense, is really an assault."

"No, Sir. I do not assault. I only try to defend myself against an assault upon my rights and character. Is the defense of the government an assault upon the South? No, it is defending itself against a villain who has assaulted to take its life. In defending my character, I am compelled to destroy Mr. Packard's, simply by exhibiting my own. And I have a right to my own character; and when it is assailed by slander, I have a right to live it down; and if his character can't stand before my sanity, he must fall—not because I assaulted him, but because he assaulted my sanity. I have done nothing to destroy his character. He has done the whole work himself.

Wrong actions are suicidal in themselves."

LXXIII.

Mrs. Sybil Dole—A Fallen Woman.

Fast day. I do believe in the efficacy of prayer. Praying breath is not spent in vain. God has broken for me my chains of married servitude, and now it is my chief business to get my prisoner's bonds severed. I struggle, labor, and pray for this daily. But delays are not denials. Is defeat an indication of God's disapproval? or is it a test of my fidelity and perseverance in surmounting obstacles in doing my duty? I believe I am sometimes tempted, by the suggestions of friends, as well as enemies. O, God, do let me know when Satan *sends* me a message, as well as when he brings me one.

I think the arch-deceiver oftentimes employs the husband as the bearer of his messages to his wife, by allowing him to destroy her identity. The wife yields to the husband the right of a despot, to rule her independently of her reason. Mr. Packard's sister, Sybil Dole, wife of Deacon Dole, of Manteno, is an example of this class of fallen women. She thinks it is her duty to do what her husband requires her to do, even if her own reason and conscience dictate to the contrary. This is wronging ourselves of the right to be ruled by the Christ within us. It is forging our own chains, to confine us in the pit of destruction. When we have once broken our allegiance to Christ, by obeying man in preference to him, we have seceded from God's government, and must henceforth be regarded as traitors, by all holy intelligences. Every subsequent act enhances our guilt, so we at length become conscientiously wrong. At this point, no force but omnipotence can turn us. "Blindness hath then happened unto Israel." Mrs. Dole is now employed as Mr. Packard's coadjutor, in carrying out this dreadful conspiracy.

Once at our house, I heard her give me this answer to my question, "How do you like the New Church doctrines?" viz: "I can't tell whether they are true or not, for I dare not trust my reason to decide; I want Brother to judge for me. Although it may appear clear to me, yet there may be sophistry which my mind can not detect."

Her brother, in whose presence this remark was made, feeling complimented by it, replied, "It is difficult for an undisciplined mind to detect the fallacy of the reasoning."

Here she trusts her brother's reason more than her own,

and thinks she is doing a praiseworthy act by so doing! when in reality, she is taking the direct steps towards extinguishing her own reason entirely. And she has already become so insane as to be used as her brother's tool, in carrying out his plot against me and my children. Whatever he dictates, she feels no scruples in doing. If she allowed her own nature to control her actions, she, being a mother, could not encourage her brother in taking me from my darling babe and other precious ones, claiming that she had a better right to train my own flesh and blood than I had myself! No, no. Were she the true woman of nature God made her to be, she would sooner cut off her right hand than put such heavy burdens upon a sister as she has placed upon me to bear. But she has become so hardened and obdurate, in her long disloyalty to God's government, that instead of bestowing one word of womanly pity upon me for being thus bereft of my darling children, she even boasts of the obligations she has placed me under to her for taking care of my own children *for me!*

No, Mrs. Dole, I do not thank you for taking care of my children; but I would rather thank you to let them alone, and let them receive the care of that mother whom God had placed over them for this very purpose. God, through our unperverted natures, requires us, to "weep with those who weep, and rejoice with those who rejoice;" but perverted nature, like Mrs. Dole's, rejoices in the sorrows of her sister, and weeps over her successes. It is my prayer that her eyes may be opened in this life to see the great wrong she has done, in using her influence to break up our once happy family, by listening to her brother's misrepresentations, instead of the dictates of her own reason and conscience. That she did yield, is evident, from the fact that she wrote to my son at Mt. Pleasant, Iowa, about the time of my abduction, that she had seen no evidence of insanity in his mother, but she must believe she was insane, because "Brother says she is!"

Would she feel that I should be doing right, if I should encourage her husband in taking her from her family as I was taken, simply on the representations of her angry husband, even when my own observations demonstrated them to be *false* representations? No, Mrs. Dole would feel that when such tender ties as bound her to her children, came to be thus sundered, she was under no obligation to me for first making her children motherless, and then bestowing upon them her care. For her, I can offer the prayer Christ did for his murderers, "Father, forgive her," believing Christ meant by this petition to ask his Father to bring his accusers to repentance, knowing that his Father himself could not forgive them unless they did repent first.

So, sister, repent! I can forgive you all, and so can our common Father, on this, his own condition.

LXXIV.

Can a Blind Person See?

The Doctor and I have had another talk upon the fallacious evidence which opinions afford, of insanity, just as the color of the eyes is a fallacious evidence of blindness. Said I, "Supposing an application be made to the Blind Institution here, to admit a seeing person, reported to be blind, by her husband, and his testimony corroborated by forty* witnesses and two physicians. Now, supposing this Institution, established for the blind alone, should have become so perverted, as to admit any person, who had any disease of the eyes, or even a weakness of the optic nerve; therefore this entirely sound person is admitted, on testimony, and the Superintendent confirms this testimony that she is blind. This accumulated amount of testimony does not satisfy the individual that she is blind, nor a party outside, who claim she is not blind. Now what is to be done? The lady contends she can prove, from her own acts, that she can see, and the Superintendent, after closely watching her for two years, fails to find in her one act indicating any loss of sight. Must not the individual

---

*Mr. Packard brought forty church members' names to support his testimony against me.

herself be tested, in order to settle this controverted question? Supposing an impartial tribunal decide that the lady herself, has given them every evidence that can be given, that her sight is not in the least degree impaired—what does this array of opinions that she is blind, now amount to, before the fact that she does see distinctly? Now let this case be published, demonstrating the fact that the Superintendent of the Blind Institution insists upon it, that a lady is hopelessly blind, when she really can see clearly—would the public feel confidence in their Superintendent's decisions afterwards? I think not; but on the contrary, they would decide that the Superintendent must be blind himself, and therefore unfit for his office. But supposing he should admit that the lady can see, but she don't see *right;* for instance, she contends that the moon looks to her as large as a cart wheel, while he says it should look only as large as a saucer. Now the common people, or the public tribunal, more than ever, see their Superintendent's folly; for the very fact that it looks to her as large as a cart wheel, demonstrates that she is not blind, and that her organ of vision, too, is not peculiar, for there is just this difference in the size of the same object, as seen through different organizations. Now, Dr. McFarland, tell me, is reason, which is the eye of the soul, extinct, while the individual gives every evidence that it is in full and healthy exercise?"

He replied, "There is a certain kind of disease of the eye which can not be detected by common people; it takes great learning and the highest kind of professional skill to detect it; and besides, this kind of optical disease is hopeless—there is no cure for this kind of blindness."

"You mean, Doctor, that when blindness is caused by this peculiar disease, it is regarded as a case of hopeless blindness?"

"Yes, it is so."

"You say it requires great skill to detect the *cause* of this kind of blindness. Does it require anything more than simple common sense to detect *blindness* itself?"

The Doctor here took an abrupt leave of both me and my argument, without even answering my question.

LXXV.

Human Instincts Above Human Enactments.

There is no liberty where there is no law. Liberty is complete only where every man is efficiently protected in the exercise of his rights. The press is not free where nothing is printed which has not been examined beforehand by authority. Freedom without responsibility is an impossible thing. Every human right is limited just by that one principle of common sense, that no man has a right to do wrong. The freedom of the press is limited, just as the freedom of lucifer matches is limited. The freedom of the press is not a freedom to commit any crime against the rights of individuals or against the commonwealth.

God's laws are above all other laws, and therefore human instincts are above all human enactments. No matter what the penalty—the more atrocious and cruel, the more certain are they to be disregarded. No human power can stand a law, in violation of our natural instincts. Every law made for peace, at the sacrifice of principle ought to be abrogated. Toleration is not freedom. The very word implies a power to restrain.

Our present Insane Asylum System ignores these principles. It says, "God's laws are subject to human enactments." It tramples upon the highest and noblest instincts of our nature, and enthrones an autocrat to rule over them, instead of the rule of reason. The law of sympathy, which God has established in our natures, as one of its noblest elements, suffers strangulation under this Asylum System.

Instead of developing this faculty in a normal manner, by caring for and administering to the unfortunate one, whom Providence has placed under our charge, for our own especial discipline and development, we admit the human law of charitable institutions to usurp this holy instinct of human sympathy, and its aspirations die out for want of their natural nutriment to perfect the vigorous growth it naturally seeks for in the human soul. Thus God's law, or our human instinct of sympathy, is supplanted by human enactments.

No matter how large the compensation offered in lieu of this usurpation, nothing can compensate for the blemish our divine natures receive by this soul strangulating process. The orphan, for instance, who, in order to receive the benefits of the Orphan Asylum, is compelled first to sever the purest and holiest affection of his nature—the love of his parent—as his necessary passport to the benefits of the Institution. The price is too dear—the equivalent received can not be commensurate to the loss sustained to secure it. But if, instead of depriving the orphan of a mother's love—its God given heritage—they should so disburse the charities of the Institution as to secure this influence to the child, as the first God given right of his nature; then these charities would act in concert and harmony with God's law, instead of conflicting with it, as the Orphan Asylums now are compelled to do by their present system.

So in the case of the insane—to sever them from the sympathy of their own kindred, is to deprive them of the first God given *right* of their nature; and no adequate equivalent can be rendered as a compensation for this usurpation. But if the charities of our present Insane Asylum System could be appropriated so as to act in concert with this influence, then would this system bless both the giver and the receiver of natural affection and human sympathy. They would then be *doing right* by their unfortunates, and as the result of a law of our nature, they would consequently *feel right* towards them. Whereas our present system compels them to *act wrong* towards them, by severing them from home influences; and they, of course, come to *feel wrong* towards them, as the inevitable result. First comes a feeling of indifference, as the result of casting off a responsibility which God had laid upon *them* to bear; then succeeds the feeling of alienation, as the heart gradually ossifies by this extinction of human sympathy, which a neglect of our practical duties to our natural responsibilities produces.

I never knew this legitimate tendency of our present system to lead to any different results, when practically applied. Therefore, in order to place the axe at the root of the evils of our Insane Asylum System, and other eleemosynary institutions, there must be a recognition of this great fundamental truth, that human instincts are above human enactments.

LXXVI.

The Prisoner Who Called Himself "Jesus Christ!"

One evening at our dancing parties I was introduced to a fine looking young man, with whom I held a very agreeable and intelligent conversation, wherein I failed to detect any indications of loss of reason, or mental unsoundness. Knowing that he was a new arrival, I, of course, looked for some mental aberration, as his passport to the privileges of our Institution. But having signally failed, after the most searching scrutiny, to detect the slightest title to this claim, I began to fear here was another smuggled victim of some evil plot. The longer I conversed, the more confirmed was this suspicion. Determined to pursue my investigations on this point, I sought and found his attendant, and inquired what was the character of the insanity of this young man.

He replied, "I am as ignorant as you are, Mrs. Packard, on that point. I have watched him with the closest scrutiny ever since he was entered, and have entirely failed to detect the first irregularity in any respect. Indeed he is the most kind, obliging and exemplary person I ever saw, and as for sympathy and tenderness towards the patient I never saw it surpassed in any one."

"I fear we have got another bogus candidate for the honors of this Institution;" replied I, "for I am sure that so far as intelligence and reason are concerned, he is a most unfit person to receive the brand of insanity."

"That is my opinion of his case thus far," replied his attendant, "and yet I may be able to detect some peculiarity upon a longer acquaintance; still from his appearance during the weeks he has been under my care, I should judge he was the last person who ought to be put under a lock and key."

"I very much fear he is another of the many victims of unjust persecution, sent here by those who employ this Institution to shield their own crimes, for there is evidently guilt somewhere, in entombing such a promising young man as he is. Won't you please ascertain if you can, what are the facts in the case, and tell me at our next party? for I am making observations and seeking facts for a book on this subject."

At our next party I accordingly pursued these inquiries, and found that, although he had been on the most vigilant search for facts on which his imprisonment was predicated, he had found nothing that could afford any solution to his mind of this dark mystery. He more than confirmed his previous defense of his entire sanity, by adding, "he is the most forgiving, kind, tender, sympathizing person I ever saw."

"Yes," though I, "here is doubtless another instance where there is too much christianity for this perverted age to recognize, and therefore he must be offered in sacrifice upon this altar of insanity. Can it be that men as well as women, are imprisoned here, because they exhibit too much of Christ's spirit? I will find out whether this brother in bonds is of this class." With these thoughts I met my new friend, and extending my hand, said, "good evening, Mr.——, I dont recollect your name."

"My name is Jesus Christ."

"Jesus Christ!" thought I, I was taken aback—I knew not what to say—O, this is your insanity, this is your criminal offense, doubtless—but how is this? *I* am determined never to call a person insane for the utterance of opinions, merely, no matter how absurd—but here is an opinion where, I fear my philosophy will be balked—my principles are not going to stand this test!

With these thoughts, I ventured to pursue my investigations, and recollecting how reasonable and sensible he had appeared, I asked him in reply to this introduction of himself, "but how is it, Sir, you can call yourself 'Jesus Christ,' when he is the son of God, and came to earth, and was here crucified for sinners?"

"O, I am not *that* Jesus Christ, but another Jesus Christ—he is my oldest brother, and I being of the same family bear the same name, but, of course, there can be but one oldest brother in the great human family, any more than in any other family. Hav'nt you more than one son in your family?"

"Yes, I have five sons, my oldest is named Theophilus, my others, Samuel, George, etc."

"Well, but are they not all Packards, the Samuel as well as the Theophilus, and is there any more impropriety in calling George the youngest, a Packard, than in calling Theophilus, the oldest, a Packard?"

"Why, no, not in that sense."

"Just so it is in God's family—all his sons are Jesus Christs as much as the first, just as soon as they become perfectly developed into his spirit. Such are Jesus Christs, whether on earth or in heaven, as much as Jesus of Nazareth, was; but they are all different persons. There is but one Jesus of Nazareth, but there are as many Christs as there are true perfected men. Such are all brothers bearing the same common name, after Christ is fully developed in them."

"Then you claim that the Christ is fully developed in you, do you, and that on this account you call yourself 'Jesus Christ?'"

"Yes, I do. I consider that I am now perfect in God's estimation, in the same sense that his oldest son was perfect. This is fulfilling the command to 'be ye perfect in Christ Jesus'—meaning, perfect in Christ Jesus' estimation. I am not perfect in the estimation of the church, or the world; but in God's estimation, I have obeyed his command, in this respect. Do you think God would have commanded his children to do impossibilities? and if they could not become perfect in his estimation, he is an unreasonable being in issuing such a command."

So here my "Mr. Jesus Christ" had explained himself to simply mean that he was a perfect man. He insists that he is not the Christ, the world's Savior, but simply a perfect person in Christ Jesus' estimation. Now, where is his insanity? even his "hobby," where has that gone? Just into the belief of the perfectionists, as it was defended by Dr. Finney and others of this class.

Now comes the question, shall this man be locked up in an "Asylum" because he says he is a perfect man—in a style of language peculiar to himself—in order to force him to abandon his originality of expression, and become an echo of other men's forms of expression? Yes, because he is insane on this point. Insane! because he chooses to utter an opinion respecting his own character in original language! What a dangerous person to be allowed his liberty! Won't he kill somebody; for somebody has chosen to call this peculiarity, *insanity*, instead of a singular mode of expression. Still he is dangerous, for we do not know what an insane person *might* do, although his opinions of himself seems to be true—that is—he seems to exhibit the Christ spirit to an uncommon degree, yet, he *may* kill somebody! therefore he must be locked up. It won't do to wait until he *has* killed somebody and then imprison him as we do criminals after they have committed a crime; we must imprison this man not only before he has committed any crime, but even before he has shown the first indication that he ever intended to commit a criminal offense. Yes, he claims that he is Jesus Christ, and so long as he acts like Jesus Christ, he must be locked up to make him like other people, lest he kill somebody!

Now I think if all those who call themselves "Jesus Christ," and act like Jesus Christ, ought to be locked up for fear they *may* kill somebody, all those who call themselves "totally depraved," and act as though they are totally depraved, ought to be locked up also, for fear *they* may kill somebody too!

LXXVII.

Letter to Judge Whitlock, of Jacksonville.

In July, 1867, while in Jacksonville, to meet the Illinois Investigating Committee, I met Judge Whitlock, before whom the cases at the Asylum were tried, after Dr. McFarland had sent off all those whom he thought would not be condemned by a Jury as insane. Of course, this number would be expected to include none except those whom he could hope to induce the Jury to believe were insane.

The Investigating Committee remark in their Report, that "it is a *noticeable* fact, however, that the number of discharged patients represented as *cured*, during the time between the appointment of the Committee and the time of their examination of the records, is *double* that of any given length of time previously." The reason for this double number of sudden and remarkable cures (?) during this period, is self-evident to any reflecting mind. Dr. McFarland knew that the coming crisis must inevitably expose and bring to light this large class of sane prisoners which he was holding without "*legal evidence*" of their insanity; and therefore, to prevent the exposure of this nefarious work, he sent off this class of prisoners as among the "cured" in their discharge!

Although, like Mrs. Sarah Minard, wife of Ira Minard, of St. Charles, Illinois, who was one of this class who had been unjustly retained there for nine years, there had been no change in them from the time they were entered until they were discharged, yet, being recorded as "cured," or as "hopelessly insane," as my diploma *from him* designates, he hoped "my policy" could thus conceal his guilt in the matter. And it did, for a time, suspend the verdict of public opinion from deciding against him. For, when the Report of Drs. Johnson and Patterson, and other Superintendents was published, that in their opinion, there were none "improperly retained" there, it led the public to suppose the report that there were sane people confined there, was false and without foundation, until the State's Investigating Committee, afterwards found the *reason* for their not being found there was the dischage of this double number of "cured" patients!

But notwithstanding, Judge Whitlock found among them one good old minister who had been a most unwilling prisoner there for many years, and whose intelligence was so marked and apparent, that he felt most keenly the degradation of the plane he was so unjustly placed upon. The Judge told me that, after the most searching examination of nearly three hours length, he could not detect the least indication of unsoundness of mind, or loss of reason—that he reasoned masterly upon all subjects, both scientific, legal, political, and religious, and he was just on the point of deciding that he was sane, when the Doctor came in, and his opinion was asked respecting his sanity, and his opposite opinion turned the scales against him. This minister, seeing that the Doctor was going to cause his terrible imprisonment to be perpetuated, felt "excited," as any other sane person would naturally feel under such circumstances, and in this state of mind became a little unguarded in his expressions, and gave utterance to some novel and original expressions of thought, such as the "machinery of God's government," and such like, when the Judge decided, without waiting to hear his own interpretation, which might have been as satisfactory as was the "Mr. Jesus Christ," that he was insane ; for on one point he had expressed an opinion he did not at once understand!

My sympathies were aroused for the old man, and I defended his sanity and his liberty, when the Judge decided, "No, he is insane on *that point*, and therefore he ought to be locked up for fear he may kill somebody!" And it was to convince the Judge, if possible, of the fallacy of this position, that I sent him the following letter the next day:

JACKSONVILLE, July 26, 1867.

JUDGE WHITLOCK. *Dear Sir:*—Supposing I should go to those Judges whom I have heard defend that it is inhuman to imprison a human being on the plea of insanity, simply for the utterance of absurd opinions, and should say to them,

"Judge Whitlock does not agree with you in opinion on that point; and I have heard him argue, that since these delusions and absurdities demonstrate that his reason is dethroned in a measure, fidelity to his interests and community both, justify us in taking from him that most blessed boon of his existence—his personal liberty—for he may kill some one if we do not! and we may possibly cure him by locking him up in a public hospital!"

Supposing, Sir, I should add, "Now I regard these views of Judge Whitlock as absurd and inhuman, and on these points I regard him as unsound, unreasonable, plainly indicating that his reason is in some measure dethroned; and on his own principles, he ought to be locked up, lest he may kill somebody! for it is not safe to have a person at large whose reason is in any measure dethroned, for we do not know what an insane person may do!"

Supposing these Judges should say, "We agree with you, that Judge Whitlock is insane on these points, although he is a man of acknowledged ability, and veracity, and integrity generally, yet, for his good, and the safety of community, we think he had better feel the application of his own principles to himself, and thus mete out to him the same measure he is meting out to others, hoping in this way to bring him to his reason, or set him right on this point. He may possibly come out the defender of human rights and personal liberty, and he may kill somebody if we do not!"

Judge Whitlock, I do not say I shall do this thing, but supposing I should, and the first you know, you are brought before a Jury, on the charge of insanity; and the Jury should decide that Judge Whitlock is not perfectly sound in his mind—"he reasons absurdly on the subject of human rights—he is insane." What would be your defense?"

I do not engage, Judge Whitlock, to publish your argument in my forthcoming book. I only say, I retain a copy of this letter and should like to have you give me your reply in writing. Very respectfully yours, E. P. W. PACKARD.

Judge Whitlock's reply has not yet been received.

LXXVIII.

Difference between Contentment and Patience.

In reply to my saying to Mrs. Page, a sane prisoner, "I find it impossible to be contented with my present lot, although it is my constant prayer that I may be patient and contented," she remarked, "I wish to inform you that patience and contentment are two very different virtues. You are not required to be contented to suffer unjust imprisonment. Your nature revolts at wrong and injustice, and you cannot be contented to have it continue; but you ought to be patient to wait God's time for its removal."

The question arose in my mind, does not patience in its fullest exercise include contentment? That is, must I, in order to practice the virtue of patience be content with prison life under present circumstances? Paul says, "I have learned in whatsoever state I am, therewith to be content." And he was unjustly imprisoned—did he learn to be contented with it? If so, I must, for there is no christian grace or virtue which is not obligatory upon me to possess. Now have I been like one "beating the air," in trying to school myself to contentment, or am I striving after unattainable virtue? Must a slave be content with his lot, as a slave? Can he be content with his lot while at the same time he is striving to escape it? Can we be contented while writhing in anguish from bodily disease, while at the same time we are striving to remove the disease?

Again, whatever is permitted, is God's appointment. Must we therefore be content with things as they are? We must be contented in the sense that we must not murmur at our lot, but patiently strive to remove all removable evils attending it; and what are at present beyond our control, we must bear with quiet resignation.

"With cheerful feet thy path of duty run,
God nothing does, nor suffers to be done,
But what thou would'st thyself, could'st thou but see
Through all events of things as well as He."

Now, have I not done all in my power to get justice done me, and as yet, all in vain? Must I therefore conclude that evil, is for the present, the best state possible, for the greatest good results? And is all that I have done like water spilled on the ground? No, I do not cherish such feelings. I believe all conscientiously used means for the removal of evils are like good seed, which, although long buried, will sometime spring up and bear fruit, corresponding to its character. But like good husbandmen, it becomes us to have patience, long waiting if need be, for the appearance of the tender blade. O, if I could but see the tender blade, how it would quicken my hope—how patient I could then be. But to be patient now without anything of sight to rest upon is a greater, because a more difficult virtue to cultivate. I may never in all my existence have another such opportunity for this highest exercise of faith. If I have disquietude of spirit, a lack of perfect peace, it must be because my mind is not fully "stayed on God." I find seeking the natural to support faith upon, is paralyzing the spiritual, on which alone it should rest and depend.

And now knowing as I do that I am suffering wrongfully, why can I not rest wholly upon God's promises, and his character for my support, and not be so eagerly watching for their fulfillment, before God's time come to vindicate himself? Should my faith fail in this, my greatest emergency, might I not have reason to fear that some other furnace would be prepared in which to try it, which might be more severe than the present? O, yes, there is no safety but in trusting God, by doing right, and thus feeling right. Therefore I trust I am doing right by trying to be contented with my present trials, unremoved, and having food and raiment—let me be content to be without children, without home, without society, without liberty! I have litterally given up all things for Christ's sake, and now all I have to do is to simply trust his word, that they shall be restored to me in tenfold measure. O, let me not forfeit this title by impatience or murmuring.

This disponsation seems to be characterized by the principle of overcoming evil with evil; human hearts have to be purified so as by fire. But when the Christ principle has permeated the human soul so as to be its abiding, living element, we may hope that evil will then be overcome with good. As an attempt to cure disease by inflicting another disease, may be better secured by invigorating the powers of nature, thus capacitating it to cure and throw off its own disease; so, instead of meeting a moral evil by a worse evil, just meet it with kindness, which draws into exercise the better emotions, only to be quickened into a deeper and stronger life by the exercise of them. Thus capaciated they can overcome the evils of nature, by surplanting them with good. Instead therefore of curing an evil by inflicting a worse, we eradicate it by the substitution of its counterpart, virtue.

LXXIX.

My Successful Attempt to Obtain my Freedom.

A few days prior to the September meeting of the Trustees, 1862, in a familiar conversation with Dr. McFarland in my room, I remarked, "Doctor, I don't like to spend my days here doing nothing; why can't I fire a few guns at Calvinism, before those Trustees, who are to meet in a few days?"

"Why, Mrs. Packard, they are Calvinists, and the chairman is a member of the Presbyterian Synod of the United States!"

"I don't care for that—I should not hesitate to give my views before the Synod, itself, if allowed. And besides, it is all the better for your cause that they are, for my views will be likely to be regarded by them as insane, because a difference of opinion is insanity you know on the minority side of the question, of course! Now one, alone, against so many—and that one a *woman*, too—what have you to fear?"

This was enough. He was converted into a free and full

consent that I might fire all the guns I pleased at Calvinism, and he would furnish me with all the paper I wished to write my views upon.

"Now," thought he, "Mrs. Packard will unmask herself, thus demonstrating to the Trustees that I represent her correctly in calling her insane. Yes, she'll hang herself!"

The Doctor was true to his promise, and brought me paper himself, the first sheet he had ever brought me, and I, true to my engagement, made out the most clear, concise, and comprehensive view I could of the whole system, of Calvinism, as I apprehended it, by contrasting each principle with the Christian principle, showing the system to be "doctrines of devils," instead of doctrines of Christ!

This document as I then prepared it, and laid before the Trustees, is in print, on the 19, 20, 21, 22 and 23d, pages of the first installment of "The Great Drama," six thousand copies of which are already in circulation, entitled, "Calvinism and Christianity Compared."

The Doctor examined my document, and finding it all right he engaged to call for me the next day, in the afternoon, and take me down to the parlor, where I should there meet the Trustees. Keeping my wardrobe in order for the dancing parties, I easily found a very suitable summer costume in readiness for the occasion, which, with a tasteful head-dress to relieve the sky-blue trimmings of my white lawn dress, I made quite as good an appearance as any one need desire. Therefore with more of a queenlike feeling, than that of an imprisoned slave, I took the proffered arm of the Doctor, and was escorted by him into the parlor of these grave, dignified gentlemen, and in the most gallant manner he introduced me, first to the chairman, and then to the other gentleman, separately, after which, he led me to a most conspicuous seat by the chairman, when I withdrew my arm from his own, and sat down.

Here I must notify my readers that there was one gentlemen present to whom he did not introduce me, and to whom I did not speak. But, as I afterwards learned, he did speak of me, and of the impression I made on his feelings, as he saw me so politely escorted into the room by the Doctor, in these words, "I never saw a lady look so sweet and attractive as she did!"

Now, I will introduce the gentleman to my readers as, Rev. Mr. Packard, the husband of this lady.

The chairman, Mr. Brown, then addressed me in these words, "Mrs. Packard, we have heard Mr. Packard's statement, and Dr. McFarland has informed us that you have something you would like to say to us. We will allow you ten minutes to say it in."

Taking out my gold watch and looking at it, I remarked, to the Doctor who sat opposite me, "please inform me when my time is up, will you? and I will stop at any moment you designate."

Nodding his consent to do so, I commenced reading my document with a clear, calm, distinct voice, to a silently attentive audience. So profound was the silence, I could almost hear the joyous pulsations of my own heart. On, on, I went, demolishing fortress after fortress of the Calvinistic creed, and notwithstanding the havoc and devastation, thus caused by the skillful use of the weapon of truth and common sense, still I was tolerated. Neither did my time keeper inform me that I was most egregriously trespassing upon the limits of the time assigned me, although my ten minutes was soon lost in the fifty minutes they allowed me, before our interview terminated.

Having finished my "exposure of Calvinism and defense of Christianity," I was emboldened by their toleration to ask another license, which was, permission to read another document which I had clandestinely prepared and taken with me, but which the Doctor had never seen. That this license was most cheerfully and readily granted, was indicated not only by an unanimous hand vote of the Trustees, but also by the accompanying exclamations, "Let her go on! Let us hear the whole!"

In view of this generous and cheerful response, I playfully

remarked, "I should think appearances betoken that I am in the element where freedom of opinion is tolerated."

"We don't know about *women* thinking as they please! We must look after *them*," responded Mr. Club.

He was promptly silenced, however, by the noble "woman's right's" Miner, remarking in a very decided tone, "Go on! Mrs. Packard, Go on!"

After thanking friend Miner for his generous defense, I proceeded to read my unknown document to equally attentive listeners. This document exposed "the conspiracy" of their Superintendent and Mr. Packard against my personal liberty, in as bold and uncompromising terms as my exposure of Calvinism had been given in. Still I was tolerated!

The Superintendent and the Minister listened in mute amazement to this dauntless revelation of the truth and their own guilt. Without denying one of my statements, or offering a single apology, Mr. Packard left the room at the request of the Trustees. The Superintendent soon followed. The Trustees now acted the part of cross-questioning attorneys, while I their witness, was secretly exulting in the opportunity thus afforded me, of making farther revelations of the depth and magnitude of this malign conspiracy.

The playful, easy style and manner in which I made my statements, seemed to dissipate the sanctimonious gravity of this august body—so that they came to seemingly regard me as one of their number, instead of a culprit under the grace of court! They manifested a willingness to do anything and everything I asked. Mr. Brown told me himself, that he saw it was of no use for me to think of returning to my husband, but gallantly offered to send me, independent of him, to my children at Manteno, if I thought best to go; or, they would pay my passage to go to my father in Massachusetts; or, they would pay my board in Jacksonville, if I chose. In short, I could have my liberty to do just as I pleased, as they were satisfied the Insane Asylum was no place for me.

I, of course, thanked them most sincerely for this offer of liberty, for it was to me the most blessed boon of my existence, but I added, "Gentlemen, it is of no use for me to accept the offer at your hands, for although you acknowledge by this act that I have a right to my liberty, yet, you have no power to protect this right to me; for since I am a married woman, I have no legal protection of my person, or any of my rights, only as this protection is guaranteed to me through the voluntary act of my husband. The law does not *compel* him to protect or support me outside of an Insane Asylum, if he only chooses to claim that I am insane. This charge from my husband, even before it is proved against me, annihilates all my rights as a human being, not even excepting the right of self-defense from this charge. But on this, his single allegation, confirmed by the signature of your Superintendent, he can lawfully imprison me for life in this, or some other Insane Asylum. No father, brother, son or friend, or even our Governor, himself, has the power to protect the personal liberty of any married woman in this State, while such a law exists on Illinois' statute book. There is no protection of my personal liberty under the American flag, so long as Mr. Packard lives, therefore I may as well spend my days in this prison as in any other."

The Trustees replied, "We pity you—it is a hard case—we never before realized how defenseless a married woman was under our laws; but what can we do for you? Is there anything?"

"Yes, gentlemen, there is one thing you can do, and only one that I can see, by which you can exonerate yourselves from complicity in this transaction, and at the same time confer a great favor upon me, which is, to furnish me with a key, or a pass, by which my personal liberty would be in my own hands, rather than in your hands as it now is. I might continue to stay for the present, as I have done, subject to the rules of the other prisoners, in all other respects, except that of being my own keeper. I have felt it my duty to protest against my false imprisonment, and have, thereby, shut myself up more closely than the others are, for in my protest I said I shall never return a voluntary prisoner into the wards; neither can

I do so, for I regard this vow as sacred. Indeed, I can not now even return to the wards voluntarily, without a key or a pass. And if you force me back, it is *you* who are imprisoning me, and on you must hereafter rest the responsibility of being accomplices in this conspiracy."

They did not give me a key, nor a pass, neither did they request Dr. McFarland to do so, but thus compelled the Superintendent to carry me back in his own arms, as was the case. But they did confer upon me the right to advise with the Doctor, assuring me I might do as he and myself could agree it was best to be done.

Accordingly, the following day the Superintendent called upon me in my room, and introduced the subject by saying, "Well, Mrs. Packard, the Trustees thought you hit the mark with your gun!"

"Did they? Was that what they were shouting at, after I left the room?"

"Yes, it was; for I told them that you wished to 'fire a few guns at Calvinism.'"

"I knew, Doctor, that I had put in a heavy charge, but I determined to risk it, and improve my chance lest I should not get another. I some feared it might burst the cannon! But it did not; for I see none of them believe me to be an insane person, after all."

"Mrs. Packard, won't you give me a copy of that document, for what is worth hearing once, is worth hearing twice."

"Yes, Doctor, I am perfectly willing to do so, for I should like you to have a copy, and the Trustees also, and I should like my father to have one, and my early friend, Rev. H. W. Beecher, and some others of my Orthodox friends. But it is very irksome for me to copy. How would it do to get a few printed in handbill form, and send them to my friends?"

"I think it would be well to do so, and I will pay the printer. You re-write it, and add to it what was said, and I will see that it is done, forthwith."

"Do you mean to have both documents printed; the exposure of the conspiracy, also?"

"Yes, the whole; and anything else you choose to add."

"Well done, for Dr. McFarland! If you are going to give me such liberty, I shall feel that I am a free woman; and this may possibly prepare the way for my liberation."

The paper was faithfully provided by the Doctor, and I, with the most elastic feelings which this hope of deliverance inspired, went to work to prepare my document for the printer. But before twenty-four hours had elapsed since this liberty license was granted to my hitherto prison bound intellect, the vision of a big book began to dawn upon my mind, accompanied with the most delightful feeling of satisfaction with my undertaking. The next time the Doctor called, I told him that "it seems to me I must write a book. The thoughts and their arrangement, are all new and original, until suggested to my mind by this sort of mental vision. What shall I do, Doctor?"

"Write it out just as you see it."

He then furnished me with paper, and gave directions to the attendants to let no one disturb me, and let me do just as I pleased. I commenced writing out this mental vision, and in six weeks time I penciled the substance of "The Great Drama," which, when written out for the press, covers two thousand five hundred pages of note paper. Can I not truly say my train of thought was engineered by the "Lightning Express?" I had no books to aid me but Webster's large Dictionary, and the Bible. It came wholly through my own reason and intellect, quickened into unusual activity by the perfect state of my health, from the most persistent conformity to the laws of health in eating, sleeping, and exercise, and by the inspiring hope of coming freedom. The production is a remarkable one, as well as the indicting of it, a very singular phenomenon. If, during my life-time, this "Great Drama" can be published and not imperil my personal liberty, I shall be happy to give it to the world. But until that time arrives, when an original thought can be spoken or written, without incurring the charge of insanity for such an act, my personal liberty is only safe, while this manuscript is hid from the age in which it was written.

LXXX.

The Dawning of a New Dispensation.

The reader will perceive by the preceding chapter that a new dispensation has dawned upon me—that the Superintendent is regarding his prisoner in the light of a citizen, rather than a slave. And if any of my readers feel disposed to censure me for seeming so readily to forgive this great sinner, let me remind them that they may perhaps be better prepared to judge correctly of my feelings if they could exchange situations with me.

Ever since the Doctor had taken my part in the insult of the Jacksonville aristocrats, I had an occasional cause to feel that my happiness was not an object of such stoical indifference to him as it formerly had been. And besides, I had noticed that just in proportion as I had Dr. McFarland's approval, just in that proportion was I regarded as a terror to the evil doer; neither was my influence over those who were doing well lessened by it. Therefore benevolence itself would prompt me to "impress" this influence into a good cause, if possible. And with me it has always been a settled purpose to train my own children and scholars to do right under the influence of encouragement, rather than censure. I am more watchful to find out some cause for just approbation, rather than for fault-finding.

This being my native or home element it is not strange that I should seize with avidity the first opening bud of promise on this barren stock of manliness, which daily passed under my observation. Yes, I did strive with all the charity and forgiveness I could command, to find every hopeful sign that could be possibly summoned into the exercise of encouragement to the well doer; for my principles led me to despise the flatterer as well as the slanderer—that is, I could no more praise without cause for praise, than I could blame without cause for blame. Both being falsehoods, I could practice neither, and it was not possible for me to determine which evil of the two was the greatest, therefore I strove to avoid both.

Again, my theology teaches me that in every human being there is a soul to be redeemed. That in every rock there is a well. Could I not therefore hope that the drill of long and patient perseverance might yet reach this spring in this Doctor's flinty heart? Yes, I had my hope quickened into a spasmodic life that the latent spark of manliness in this hardened sinner, might yet be developed into the strength of a vigorous life, corresponding to his intellectual strength. It was my aim and purpose thus to develop him, by the only power in the universe adequate to this work, and fitted for it, and that is, " woman's influence." Indeed I fully determined that in the same ratio that he had tried to crush the womanhood in me, in that same proportion would I raise the manhood in him. And although my first effort for his elevation cost me banishment from the scenes of civilization, to dwell among maniacs, yet this did not dispirit me, or cause me to regret the effort.

I know too, that God does not require one sinner to punish another sinner, for he has expressly claimed the right of punishment as being his own prerogative. The Great Father of the human family has not delegated the right to one child to punish the faults of another child, but on the contrary, he claims the right of punishment as exclusively his own right. Therefore as his child I am bound to refer to my Father, the settlement of the wrongs I receive from my brothers and sisters. All he allows me to do is, to do them good, that is, to defend myself by benefitting them, not by injuring them. Now the greatest good I could bestow upon Dr. McFarland was, to influence him to stop sinning, by doing justice towards me, forthwith. And now that he had taken the first decided step in that direction, I aimed to urge him onward by every possible influence.

Again, I do not feel called upon to judge of the motives of my fellow sinners. If they *act right*, it is none of my business what motive prompted the act. For example, if Dr. McFarland allows me the right of self-defense, and thereby secured my personal liberty, I have a right to acknowledge the act as a good one, even if he was compelled to do so through fear of exposure or punishment, or even if selfish policy, and nothing else, prompted him to do this good deed. His subsequent course has demonstrated that he had no good end in view, so far as I was concerned, in allowing me to write this book, but on the contrary he determined to use the book as the means of getting me again incarcerated. As he had allowed me to expose Calvinism before the Trustees, for the purpose of getting their sanction in calling me an insane person; so he now allowed me to write a book, hoping thus to secure the sanction of my readers in calling me insane. And notwithstanding the whole plot had been conceived and executed on the principles of the most conceited selfishness, yet, I have no right on that ground to call the act a wrong, or a bad act. These may have been the highest motives this hardened sinner could possibly exercise, on this low plane on which his persistent iniquities had placed him.

And since my Father in Heaven does not ignore *fear*, as a bad motive, why should I? He says, "the *fear* of the Lord is the beginning of wisdom," evidently representing this principle as the very lowest round of the ladder of human progression; yet being an agent employed by God for the sinner's arrest in his downward course, we should not despise it, lest we thus "quench the smoking flax, or break the bruised reed."

But the caviler may say, "what goodness can be attributed to the act of giving you what was already yours by the right of inheritance, as a human being? Your right of self-defense was not Dr. McFarland's to bestow, even if he did allow you to use this right, while others withdrew from you every opportunity for its exercise. It was yours already. You did not seem to feel under any special obligation to Mr. Packard for giving you your old clothes on this principle."

"No, I did not, for he was at this time beyond the limits

of Christian fellowship. I felt conscious that the law of love required me to withdraw from him all fellowship, believing he belonged to that class whom we are commanded to treat in this manner, for their good. I had borne with him until forbearance had ceased to be a virtue; for every act of fellowship bestowed, only encouraged him in his course of wrong doing. I had for twenty-one years pursued this uniform course of persistent kindness, only to be trampled under his feet, for so doing, and now circumstances compelled me to treat him on a plane lower even, than the fear of punishment. From that class who cannot be moved even by the lowest motive in human development, I feel bound to withdraw myself, knowing that stern justice alone can now move them in the line of repentance, and as he had denied me the least shadow of justice in the right of self-defense, it was now meet that he should experience the justice he had denied me.

This was not taking justice into my own hands, it was only leaving him to his own chosen way to work out his own destruction, unimpeded. All hope of deliverance from this incorrigible sinner, had long since gone out in utter darkness. He had deliberately put me off upon another man's protection, by withdrawing his own entirely.

And I must say that I felt a little exultant, under the thought that my entrance on the Doctor's arm might possibly make him feel that I had found in the protector he had chosen for me, one that suited me better than the one of my own choice! Here let me say to my husband, that as it is perfectly natural for me to love the opposite sex, it need not be a matter of surprise to him if I should come to love the only man he allowed me to associate with, for three years, especially if I can find in him anything worthy of my love. And failing to find the jewel I sought for in this personification of a man, I determined to develop it, if woman's influence could do it, and now my hopes so long buried, were just germinating, and that they might perfect the beautiful buds of promise was to me my soul inspiring business to hasten this consumation.

Under the influence of these new and most joyous emotions I pursued my delightful employment of writing my most novel book. The gallant and now gentlemanly Doctor's visits were most welcome seasons of rich and varied interchange of thoughts, so that my mind seemed stimulated into a new and healthful activity from this powerfully magnetic influence. The sound of his footsteps in the hall, and his gentle knock at my door now caused my heart to bound with joy, as before it had caused a throb of anguish, to know that he was on his way to my room, into which he would bolt the most unceremoniously, without caring whether he was welcome or not. Now to be treated as a lady, in this gallant manner, by this once boorish man, was to me the inauguration of a new and delightful era of my prison life.

But the brightest day has its clouds, and the finest gold has its dross, as will be demonstrated in the following chapter.

LXXXI.

The Moral Barometer Indicates a Storm—A Hurricane.

Woman's love for man is based on the principle of reverence. We can never truly love a man who has never inspired in us the feeling of fear, or reverence. A woman's nature calls for protection, as instinctively as the climbing rose calls for something stronger than itself to climb upon. She can not, naturally, cling to a nature weaker than her own, any more than the vine can naturally climb without a stronger support than its own to cling to. Fear, respect, and reverence, are emotions which superiority alone can inspire. I can not exercise the feeling of reverence towards a being whom I do not look up to, as to a superior. A child can not reverence his parent, unless that parent can command the feeling of authority over the child. Until this fear, or authority is established, the foundation stone of the edifice of filial love is wanting A servant can not reverence nor love his master, unless the principle of authority is established in the master. Let the servant, or the child feel that he can rule the master, or parent, and thus hold this authority in his own hands, then the foundation for contempt or irreverence is established.

God commands the love of all his creation on the principle of superiority, which inspires reverence for his authority, and from this root, the purest, tenderest, most confiding love, naturally germinates. Woman's nature is peculiarly fitted to love such a being, feeling him to be the embodiment of strength and power, such as she wants, to meet her instinctive aspirations. God tells us he has made man in his image, and therefore, on this basis, she turns to him as her natural protector. She finds in man, this tower of strength and wisdom, which she, like the vine is in search of, to live a natural life.

When she finds a man combining strength and wisdom superior to her own, she as naturally desires this power as her shield and defense, as she naturally desires food and sleep, to meet a demand of her nature. For example, my nature being endowed with the instincts of a natural woman, have ever sought for a personified deity in a man form, to reverence and love. This feeling was first exercised towards my father, whose authority and kindness quickened this latent spark into activity. His authority was the stepping stone to God's authority. He was, to my childish nature, God's representative, and just in proportion as I reverenced my father's authority, just in that proportion did I reverence God's authority.

As the child, in time, lost itself in the mature woman, so the filial love for my father became merged into a higher love of manhood, that of companionship, as well as protection. Unlike some children, I could not find in my father that kind of companionship my development demanded. He ruled me still, but not through my freedom, as my intelligence demanded. This, therefore, stilled this confiding spirit, because it could not act in conflict with reason.

And so it was with the feelings awakened by my husband's authority; he mingled with it so much of the awe of the ty-

rant, at the same time denying me the protection of t'
that my higher love, the conjugal, was never quickened into natural life under either influence. This great want of my nature, spiritual freedom, was never met or gratified, until this period, when, under the manly protection of Dr. McFarland, I was allowed to be spiritually free in writing an indeepdent book, free from all dictation.

The awe of the tyrant was now settling into a reverence for a mighty power, adequate to the great emergency. As he had had almost omnipotent power to crush, so he now had this same power to raise and defend me. The power of the husband, the power of the Trustees, the power of the State, had all been delegated to him. As to the power of protection, he was all in all to me now; and the spiritual freedom granted to me by this power was almost God-like.

Dr. McFarland knew that one great object in my writing my book, was to destroy the evils of Insane Asylums, and he knew too, that in order to expose these evils, I must necessarily expose *him* in his abuse of power. Still, like the Trustees, he tolerated the truth, sad though it was—for example; one day he came to my room after I had just completed a delineation of himself through his own actions, which presented him in a most unfavorable light, and as I allowed him to see all I wrote, if he wished it, I handed him these sheets, saying, "Doctor, what will you do when such facts come to be published? Can you stand before them?"

After reading them carefully through, he remarked with a deep sigh, "If I stand at all, I must stand before it, *for it is the truth!*"

Could I help reverencing a power who would thus submissively and coolly take this severe chastisement from one whom he regarded as his dependent? No, I could not. I felt that here was a eulogy, a compliment bestowed in a manly style, surpassing anything I had ever witnessed. It said to me, "Mrs. Packard, I can trust you—I will trust you, for you are such a truthful witness I dare not confront you." Yes, his fortitude, his patience, his tolerance under my castigation, severe as his own unvarnished actions made them, really moved my pity, and led me to exclaim, "O, Doctor, how could you compel me to write such a hateful record! How could you act so meanly! How I do wish I had no such sad truths to tell! Now Doctor, you must give me a chance to redeem your character as a penitent. Won't you do so?"

Yes, he did resolve to be my manly protector, by letting me write just such a book as I pleased, thus trusting his character, as it were, entirely in my hands. O, this trust! This sacred trust, second to nothing but the ark of truth! Under the influence of these feelings, the legitimate offspring of such exhibitions of manliness, I prepared the first installment of "The Great Drama," for publication.

I told him the manuscript was ready for the printer, and inquired if he held himself responsible to publish this, by the first offer he had made me. Of course there was ground for hesitation by the enhanced expense. I, therefore, offered to write to my son and get the extra amount, to meet this emergency. Still he hesitated—I thought too, I could detect the old "policy" principle coming into life again, aiming to supplant the self-sacrificing spirit of benevolence, which seemed to be just taking root in his heart. I trembled, knowing that my all, depended upon his *continuance* in well doing. I asked wisdom. It was impressed upon my mind to write him a letter—I did so, and as I took it to my attendant, Miss Mills, and asked her to carry it to the Doctor's office, and deliver it herself, I said, as the presentiment of the coming storm came over me, "This may bring a storm of indignation upon me; if it does, do the best you can for me, but don't tell a lie to help me."

In this note I had expressed my fears, that the fear of man was gaining the ascendancy over his better nature—that instead of daring to trust himself where the truth would place him, as his higher nature prompted. I feared he was settling down on to the plane of selfish policy, so beneath the noble dignity of his nature, and I gently warned him of the consequences of such a relapse, saying, "I shall be just as much bound to expose the truth, as before;" but with this relapse I could not save him with this cause of truth, as he would not then be the penitent, which was indispensable to my saving him with the ark of truth. In short, I added, "If you fail to keep your promise to publish my book, or help me to liberty, I shall feel bound to fulfill my promise to expose you."

In about one hour from the time Miss Mills delivered the note, I heard his footsteps in the hall, and I could also almost hear my own heart palpitate with emotion as the step approached my door. I responded to his rap as usual, by opening the door, and extending my hand, said, " Good morning, Doctor!" but my salutation was not returned, and instead of accepting my proffered hand, he sternly remarked, " Step out of your room!"

"Step out of my room! did you say?"

"Yes."

I obeyed, when no sooner was I past the threshold, than he pulled my door together, and locked it against me. Then holding his key in his hand, as much as to say, "I hold your destiny by the power of this key, and I hold too, that precious book now in your room under the power of this key; it therefore becomes you to be careful what you do!" and standing in front of me, he said, " Mrs. Packard, I consider that note you sent me as unladylike—as containing a threat."

Pausing a moment, I replied, " Dr. McFarland, that note contained the truth, and nothing but the truth. I promised you when I had been here only four months, that I should expose you when I got out, unless you repented—I don't take it back! I don't recant!"

Without saying another word, he took hold of my arm and led me gently into a screen-room, and locked me up! This was the first time I had ever been locked in a screen-room, and now his own hand had turned the bolt of this maniac's cell upon me! Unlike screen-rooms generally, this room had a chair in it, which the prisoners said the Doctor carried in himself before he came to my door.

Having of course here nothing to do, I took the chair and

placing it before the corner of the room, I seated myself and tipped it back, and resting my head against a pillow I took from the bed, I tried to compose myself to sleep, knowing that good sleep is as good an antidote to trouble, as I could then command. In this position I quietly rested with closed eyes, for two hours, thinking over the probable fate of my book. "There is one part of my book," thought I, "which will escape this destruction, for Miss Mills had yesterday taken the first volume down to Mrs. Chapman of the Seventh ward. The Doctor won't find this in my room, thank good fortune!"

But I am sorry to say this part of my soliloquy did not prove true, for the Doctor, after searching all the things in my room, even the bedding, both of the ticks, and both of the pillows, and not finding this book which he knew was ready for the press, he finally inquired of Miss Mills if she knew where one volume of Mrs. Packard's book could be found. My kind attendant, recollecting my instruction, "Don't tell a lie to help me," felt bound to tell the truth, which she did. The Doctor, therefore, went to Mrs. Chapman's room and demanded the book. She took the manuscript from between her ticks and handed it to him. "Now," thought I, "this paltry thief has got every scrap of my precious book into his own hands! besides all the other manuscripts and all the stationery of every kind, which I had in my possession that he could find." But thanks to a good Providence, my entire journal escaped this wreck.

Although the greater part of it passed through his fingers, yet he knew it not! It was all rolled up in small, separate portions, in the different articles of my wardrobe, and as the Doctor handled over each and every article of linen in my trunk, he little thought that the contents of this book then passed unobserved, through his fingers, by being wrapped up in these articles, and fastened by a pin. Had he removed one pin and thus found one roll, he would, doubtless, have removed all the pins, and thus found them all. But it seems the Doctor's curiosity was satisfied with the examination of a lady's wardrobe, without looking to see with his own eyes the style of embroidery upon her linen!

After this general overhauling of my things, it seems the Doctor was not satisfied, for he then went to every female employee, and in the most excited state they had ever seen their Superintendent, asked them the question he had asked Miss Mills, viz; "Do you know of any place where Mrs. Packard keeps her papers?"

None, except Miss Mills, were able to inform him on this point, for my prudence did not allow me to make a confidant in these matters, of any person in the house except myself, not even after the new dispensation had been opened upon me; for I knew that it is not all gold that glitters, and possibly this gold which I thought I had found in the Doctor, might not stand the smelting process to which I knew it must yet be subjected! I now saw the wisdom of granting to great sinners a "day of probation," before taking them into "full fellowship!"

When my "new convert" had got through his "backsliding" business, he came to my room, and unlocking my door found his prisoner as quietly sleeping, to all appearance, while this wrath cloud of indignation was expending itself about her, as if she had no responsibility of any other person's actions resting upon her except her own.

I opened my eyes, and said to the Doctor who stood in the open doorway looking at me, "Can I come out now?"

"Yes."

"Can I go to my room?"

"Yes, of course."

He then followed me to the door of my room, and as he unlocked it and disclosed to my view the empty box upon the floor, which two hours before contained my precious book, and my bed and toilet articles presenting the appearance that my room had had a crazy occupant in it since I left it, I turned my eyes from that sad scene to his face, and simply said, in a quiet, soft tone, as I laid my hand gently upon his arm. "Doctor, never fear! God reigns! This will all work right!"

LXXXII.

The Clouds Disperse.

This sudden tempest which had just passed over the moral horizon of earthly destiny, had in its violence left my earthly prospects a complete wreck. Nothing tangible was now to be found to rest my troubled soul upon. If it were not that my anchor had been cast within the veil, and found there a firm foundation to rest it upon, this foundering bark of my earthly destiny must have become a perfect wreck. But, thank God, this refuge of faith failed not, and thus I stood unharmed. Even my peace and composure of soul never forsook me for one hour, but on the contrary I and my friend Mrs. Olsen, seemed to be the only hopeful ones in the Asylum, as to the effect of this moral hurricane. From every part of this spacious house I could hear that the wail of pity for me was being expressed in language as various as the sources whence it came—I received many of the most tender messages of sympathy suited to the emergency. But in one particular all agreed that I should never see my book again.

"It is lost! forever lost—as to your ever seeing it again," was the great unquestioning fact on which their sympathy was predicated. Since I kept my own secrets in more than one particular, these sympathizers did not know on what ground I built my hope, when I assured them all, I should get my book again. "He will return it to me. He will not burn it," was my decided response, to their kind and generous sympathy. This was to them a mystery they could not fathom, and I must add in truth to myself, that it was almost as much so to myself; but, like Abraham, I felt that my darling book would in some way be saved, as was his darling Isaac. But, like him, I only knew by the assurance of faith in God's promises. I knew that whatever I lost for truth's sake would be restored to me fourfold. I had deliberately exposed my book to save Dr. McFarland's soul; that is, I was willing to probe deep into this sinner's corrupt heart, lest the "hurt be healed slightly," and therefore I told him plainly the consequences of backsliding, hoping thus to hedge up the way against it. But instead of this, the sunlight of truth caused these buds upon the house top to wither and decay—the resolution of holy obedience had not yet found the good soil of firmness and moral courage to take root in, so as to make it a principle of permanent growth.

But what must now be done? Must he be left as an incorrigible sinner, past all hope of redemption? My faith said—"No, try again." I did try again, and when the next morning he came his usual rounds, and found me sitting in my room quietly sewing with my door wide open, and my room full of prisoners, listening to my conversation for their entertainment, I arose to meet him at the door, and as I extended to him my hand, I said, with a smile, "Doctor, will you shake hands with me, this morning?"

Oh, yes—yes—most certainly," and at the same time took my hand and while he held it, I remarked in an undertone, with my eyes resting upon his hands, "Doctor, the Lord gave, and the Lord has taken away, blessed be the name of the Lord!"

After gazing at me in amazement for a few seconds, and saying by his manner, "what kind of material are you composed of?" at length he said, "Why, Mrs. Packard, your book is all safe."

"Of course it is safe, in *your* hands, Dr. McFarland!"

He then passed on, considering what ground his prisoner had for reposing so much confidence in her keeper, especially after he had proved so untrue and so unmanly to her. "Is she determined to make me worthy of trust by trusting me?" thought he.

Yes, so it was, and as I knew it to be a law of our nature that we are apt to become what we are taken to be, I knew the best way to make a man of this being, was to bestow upon him the trust and confidence of a woman, hoping thus to inspire again the latent spark of manhood, which was now passing under another eclipse.

The next time when he found me alone in my room, I asked him to sit down and let us talk over matters a little. He did so, and I asked him the question, "Doctor, which is the most lady-like or christian-like act; to ruin a person, by exposing them without warning, or to warn them first, and thus give them a chance to escape the exposure, by repentance?" Seeing the self-condemnation the answer involved, he chose silence, as the better part of valor this time.

I then tried another question—"Doctor, which would be the most chivalrous act, for a man to keep his promise to a lady whom he had promised to protect, or to take a defenseless woman, and by an act of might, lock her up in a room where she could not defend herself at all, and then rob her of all her valuables? Would it be a noble, and manly act, to treat a woman who had never harmed him, in this manner? Just make the case your own Doctor; supposing a man should take you from your office, and lead you into a room and lock you up, and then with secret keys should ransack your valuables, and all your private notes and papers of the greatest value to you, he should lay claims to as his own—what would you call such an act? Would you think there was much honor to boast of in that kind of use of the power *might* gave him over your rights?"

Getting no replies, and choosing not to harrass my condemned culprit too much, I next remarked, "Doctor, when I consider what a valuable soul there is to be redeemed in you, and then resolve to try one more effort to secure its safety, this passage is often presented to my mind, 'of some have compassion, making a difference: others save with fear; pulling them out of the fire.' But Doctor, I have to go so near the fire to get hold of you, that I get burnt myself, sometimes!"

At this point he threw back his head and laughed outright, seeming not to know what to say, but by his looks and manner he seemed to say "you are an anomaly I cannot comprehend."

By a series of lectures of a similar character, this poor sinner was at length brought to see and realize the meanness of the act, and with a feeling of self-abhorence and self-condemnation, in about three weeks he was moved to send back my papers, unasked, with an apology for not having done so before!

He also withdrew his order to my attendants, to not let me have any writing materials whatever, and now ordered them to aid me in every possible way in granting me facilities for doing so. It was thus, under the auspices of a cloudless sky, I again resumed the delightful work of preparing "The Great Drama" for the press, and under the benign influence of a cloudless manhood I henceforth pursued my onward way.

The moral victory thus achieved, increased rather than diminished my spiritual freedom. The anxious Superintendent became satisfied that it was useless to try to confront me in the line of my duty. He saw that no policy but that of moral rectitude could secure my sanction—that no fear, but the fear of sin, could conquer me into subjection to any human power, so that this final conquest over the principles of despotic power brought his principles of selfish policy to a final end, so far as his treatment of me was concerned. I never could ask any man to treat me with more deferential respect than Dr. McFarland uniformly did from this time.

And here let me credit to this man the compliment, I honestly think is his due, viz: that there are few men who are able to excel Dr. McFarland in his gentlemanly appearance when he feels disposed to assume the gentleman.

Now every noble manly act of protection extended to me in the very respectful manner in which he bestowed it restored to me with renewed strength, such entire trust and confidence in his manhood, that I could say, "my heart is fixed," trusting in Dr. McFarland as my *God* appointed deliverer and protector.

I had no reason to feel, after these three long years of absolute desertion, that another man lived on earth who cared for my happiness, but Dr. McFarland—Therefore in choosing him as my only earthly protector, I merely accepted of the destiny my friends and the State had assigned me, and in return for this boon thus forced upon me, I willingly offered him a woman's *heart* of grateful love in return, as the only prize left me to bestow.

LXXXIII.

My Oldest Son Obtains My Discharge.

Theophilus, my oldest son, had been anxiously waiting, now nearly three years, when he should be "of age," so he might liberate me from my confinement. He visited me four times during my incarceration, and had done all that lay in his power to do, to procure my discharge, although his father had forbid his visiting me at all, and had threatened to disinherit him in case he should break this command.

This same threat hung over my second son, I. W., also, but he, like his brother, chose rather to expose himself to be disinherited, rather than to suffer his mother to languish in her prison, without human sympathy.

Cheering as it was to my fond heart to receive their true sympathy, it was saddening, also, to know that all and every effort they were making for my deliverance was abortive—that no possible hope of relief could be expected through them until they were twenty-one.

Their father, knowing their determination to help me to liberty as soon as they attained this age, tried to guard this avenue of escape, by negotiating with an Asylum in Massachusetts, to take me under their lock and key, hoping thus to elude their action. But ere this plan was consummated, Mr. Packard was notified by the Trustees that he must remove me in June.

Theophilus not knowing of this arrangement, made application to his father to consent to his removing me from my prison, assuring him that if he would allow him this privilege, he would cheerfully support me himself, from his own hard earnings. Knowing he could not legally remove me without his father's consent, he made this proposal to induce him to do so, and his father knowing, too, that he must take me out soon at all events, consented to let him thus assume this responsibility.

Therefore, with a light heart, he sought his mother's cell for the fourth time, and was most politely introduced into my room by the Doctor as a "new man," just espousing the rights, privileges, and powers of an individual man, subject to no dictation but that of law and conscience. "Here," said he, "is a *man* who proposes to assume the responsibility of being your protector—he has had his father's consent to do so, and I have given him my own, and do hereby discharge you into the hands of this new man. Mrs. Packard, you are at liberty to go with your son where you please, and I do hereby discharge you into his hands."

Thanking him, as the Superintendent, for this discharge, I begged the privilege of consulting with him as our mutual friend, respecting the best course to be pursued. Said I, "You know, Doctor, that the law holds me still subject to my husband, and therefore my son has no legal power to protect my liberty only so far as his father's promise goes as its security. Now I have no confidence in that man's word or honor, and therefore I consider myself eminently exposed to be kidnapped again, and put into the Asylum, at Northampton; so that without some other guarantee of safety than his promise, I prefer to remain here until I can finish my book, which will take about six weeks, and then I can have a means of self-defense in my own hands, which I can use independent of any legal process. Now I must be boarded somewhere these six weeks; why can not my son pay my board here, as well as any other place, and thus let me complete my book, unmolested by any change until then?"

The Doctor replied, "I see no objection to your doing so if your son has none."

Theophilus replied, "I wish mother to do just as she thinks best, and I am satisfied."

Accordingly it was decided, by the consent of all parties,

that I should remain there until my book was finished, and that my son should pay my board during this time.

I then, as a boarder, not as a prisoner, accompanied my son on foot to Jacksonville, (the Asylum being about one mile distant,) where we consulted printers, respecting the terms on which they would print my first volume—bought some paper with my son's money, and returned to my boarding-house, but not to a prison, because I was not now an *in*voluntary prisoner, although the bolts still confined me, with no key or pass of my own to unbolt them.

In this sense, my prison life terminated four weeks before I was removed from the Asylum, and I really felt safer under the gallant protection of Dr. McFarland, than I could have then felt in any other situation.

LXXXIV.

The Trustees Force me into the hands of Mr. Packard.

In about four weeks from the time of my discharge into the hands of my son, the Trustees counter ordered this Superintendent's action, and claimed me as *their prisoner* still, by ordering me to be put into the custody of my husband on the 18th of June, which time completed my three years term of false imprisonment!

Although the Trustees had told me through their chairman, Mr. Brown, that I might do just as Dr. McFarland and I should think best, and although the Doctor had already discharged me, and he had agreed to the arrangements above mentioned, yet regardless of all these claims of honor and justice, they deliberately trampled my every right into the dust, and treated me as the law does, as a legal nonentity, whose rights no one is bound to respect.

Yes, this is the respect which the identity a woman in America gets, by assuming the bonds of the marriage union! When will the time arrive, when the marriage law will respect the identity of the *woman* as well as the *man*?

On the 17th of June, Doctor's orders were sent to my room, by Miss Sallie Summers, the Supervisoress, that "Mrs. Packard's trunk must be taken out of her room and packed."

Against this order I entered a protest in these words. "In the name of Illinois and as its citizen, I claim that my right to the disposal of my own wardrobe be respected—that no hands be laid upon it without my consent. I therefore forbid you or any other person disturbing me or my things, in my own hired room, until I consent to such interference."

My reply was reported to the office. The next order was "If Mrs. Packard makes resistance, lock her in a screen-room!"

To this order I replied, "I never offer physical resistance to the claims of might, over my inalienable rights—but I give you no license or consent to touch one article in this room belonging to myself."

The Doctor then with the help of Miss Summers, searched my room, bed, toilet and drawers and took from them every thing belonging to me, and laid them into my trunk—then the porter was ordered to take my trunk into the Matron's room to be packed. This trunk now contained my entire book, journal and private papers, indeed all my treasures, even the sacred looking-glass wherein my Reproof to Dr. McFarland, was concealed. What would be their fate, I knew not. But thanks to the Power which held my usurpers, no article of my manuscripts was taken.

The book was of course seen and examined, but my private journal was passed through their fingers unnoticed; for the Matron and Supervisoress were only required to number the articles, and each article, large and small, being pinned up separately, it was not necessary to examine the center of each roll where lay a portion of this journal, which the Doctor so much dreaded.

Nothing was taken except the inkstand Dr. Tenny had given me, and the package of note paper my son had bought for me. For this trespass, if not theft, I still hold the Institution responsible, in addition to what had been previously taken from me wrongfully.

MY REMOVAL.

Dr. McFarland showed the coward on this occasion, by delegating his orders to Dr. Tenny, and availing himself of a leave of absence just at this time. I think he had better have faced the battle! instead of fleeing before he was pursued! However his orders were faithfully executed, even to the book's all being carefully packed, no part was missing!

Does not the Lord shut the mouth of lions so that they cannot hurt others when he pleases? Did I not have a host fighting for me, although unseen to mortal eye? Yes, for so "the Lord encampeth about those who fear him and *he delivereth them.*"

The next morning, Miss Summers, came with the order, that "Mrs Packard must be suitably dressed by nine o'clock to go with her husband on board the cars."

To this order I replied, "Miss Summers, I have no objection to being dressed to-day so as to suit the requirements of this mandate, even to the extent of wearing my bonnet and shawl suited to my traveling dress, and will do so with your assistance in bringing me those articles, but as to accompanying the said gentleman to the cars, I shall never consent to do this."

She accordingly exchanged my morning wrapper, for my traveling dress, and packed my wrapper in my trunk. I then put on my hat and gloves and laying my sunshade across my lap, I sat down in my chair before the window and went to reading, as I had no other employment in consequence of the assault of the previous day.

While thus employed, my door was suddenly and violently opened by Dr. Tenny, who, without knocking, or even asking leave to enter, violently pushed the door against my bedstead, which I had placed before it, as was my habitual practice, to prevent intruders, having no other means of fastening my door on the inside. I could easily move the bedstead back four inches, and thus respond to a rap almost as quickly as I could have turned a button or a bolt if I had had one, and I had done so to give the Doctors entrance hundreds of times.

But now this hasty, uncivil entrance into a lady's private room—by which my bedstead was pushed almost upon my feet, as it was forced diagonally across my room by the great and sudden violence of the door against it, and as it was opened I saw three stout men standing at the door—almost frightened me, and having disobeyed no order, I was not a little surprised at Dr. Tenny's impetuosity on this occasion. I felt like saying to my captors as Christ did to his, "have ye come out against me as a thief, with swords and staves for to take me?"

Dr. Tenny then said, "Mrs. Packard, your husband is in the office waiting to take you to the cars in the 'bus which is now waiting at the door. We wish you to go with us for that purpose."

Looking at me for response, I said, "Dr. Tenny, I shall not go with you for that purpose. And here in the presence of these witnesses, I claim a right to my own identity, and in the name of the laws of my country, I claim protection against this assault upon my personal rights. I claim a right to myself—I claim a right to remain unmolested in my own hired room."

Turning to his porters he said, "take Mrs. Packard up in your arms and carry her to the 'bus."

After instructing my new bodyguard how to construct the famous "saddle-seat" once more (an indispensable appendage to the enforcement of the "nonentity" principle of the common law, in cases where intelligence claims the recognition of an identity!) I quietly seated myself upon it, and after the attendants had, at my request, properly adjusted my clothing, I held myself again in readiness to be offered a sacrifice on the altar of unjust legislation to married women.

My guard transported their "nonentity" safely down three long flights of stairs, preceded by Dr. Tenny, and followed by my female attendants, to the door of the 'bus, where the Rev. Mr. Packard stood holding the door back for the reception of this living burden of non-existence.

Living burden of non-existence! Married woman's *legal* position under a Christian government!

Think! Law-makers! Is this the way to raise woman to a companionship with yourselves? Do you think this Reverend husband, could look upon such a spectacle and feel the inspiration of reverence for a being whom the law thus placed in his absolute power? or, would not a man of his organization more naturally feel a contempt for the worm whom he could thus crush beneath his feet?

Yes, a worm! a thing! not a being—is married woman before the principles of common law. What wrongs cannot be inflicted upon woman on this principle?

And what power of self-protection can she use in case of any assault and battery upon her person or her rights?

O! my gallant Brothers of this Republic! just place yourselves in my exact position, and from this standpoint, frame such laws as would meet your own case. Then your doting daughters will never be liable to suffer a similiar experience.

I found other employees from the house had been appointed to accompany this Reverend gentleman to the depot, to assist him if necessary in the disposal of his "human chattel," and with these gentlemen I held a conversation on our way to the depot. But with this Reverend, I did not deign to speak.

I told these men I should not need their services any longer —that I should go as any other unattended person did, into the cars, as I did not recognize the claims of this legal protector at all, and should ignore them entirely, by holding no sort of fellowship whatever with him. Therefore I wished they would see that I was put on board and comfortably seated, and I would excuse them from further duty. I could buy no ticket for I had no money. I told them I knew not where I was bound to, whether into another Asylum, a Poor-house, or a Penitentiary. No one deemed it necessary to inform a "nonentity," or a "chattel" in these matters, for this act might be an acknowledgment of a right of choice in a "chattel," which would be absurd, you know!

But from what my son had told me, I supposed he was going to put me into an Insane Asylum at Northampton, Mass.

for life, as a case of hopeless insanity. Indeed I knew that was his ultimate purpose concerning me, therefore it was, I did not *willingly* pass into the hands of this man, for this purpose.

"GO WILLINGLY!"

Written on the occasion of Dr. McFarland's saying that Mrs. Packard must be removed by force from the Asylum, in case she did not *"go willingly."*

"*Go Willingly!*" to such a doom !
My God ! O lay me in the tomb,
Ere such a terrible decree
Bind me again by lock and key.

Where is the mother—where the wife,
Daughter or sister, who her life
Would " willingly" resign to thee,
Who thus would wield thy lock and key ?

" *Go Willingly !*" my future life
To battle in that stormy strife,
Torture my fluttering heartstring there
Amid the wailings of despair ?

" *Go Willingly !*" to waste life's hours,
Its aspirations, hopes and powers,
To bury my affections there,
In those dim haunts of black despair ?

" *Go Willingly!*" to read my doom
Thus graven on a living tomb,—
Where hope or joy can never come,
Till death shall call the prisoner home ?

I'd rather rove the world around,
Chained like a criminal on ground
Where God's own sun my light would be,
Without the aid of lock and key !

" *Go Willingly* " *Thyself!* and find,
Cure of thy *own* " disordered" mind!
The very willingness would be
Proof of a fixed insanity.

      Mrs. S. N. B. O.

I was put into the Asylum without my choice or consent, I was thus removed without my consent, and contrary to my choice. In either case my identity was ignored, in that my right of choice is not recognized in either case. By my protest, I alone recognize it, *and claim it,* illegal as this claim is. Like the fugitive, I claim protection under the higher law, regardless of the claims of the lower law.

My argument seemed to illuminate these gentlemen to see that my principles required me to resist the "nonentity" principle of the marriage law in this tangible manner, hoping thus to demonstrate its injustice to the comprehension of the law makers.

This having now been openly done, I had nothing farther to do but to be passed on as coming events should indicate.

I recollect one remark made by one of these attendants, was, "we shall miss you, Mrs. Packard, at the Asylum, for there never has been a person who has caused such a universal sensation there, as you have. You will be missed at our dances also, for you are regarded as one of our best dancers!" I thanked him for the compliment, ill-deserved though it was.

Before closing this chapter, I feel bound to say that the action of the Trustees in this case was far from being upright or gentlemanly. They had given me unqualified liberty to do as their Superintendent and I should agree to do. Their Superintendent had already discharged me. He had made a bona fide bargain, in presence of a witness, that I might use that room of the Institution as my hired room until I had finished my book. I was no longer subject to his, or the Institution's control, as a patient. Now to have these gentlemen ignore this business of their Superintendent in this summary manner, and at my expense, seemed ungallant at least, if not unjust and illegal.

Again, these gentlemen had in their hands, in my own handwriting, a protest against being put into the hands of my husband, assuring them it would never be done by my own consent. They had also heard from my own lips my reasons for taking this stand, and Mr. Brown, the chairman, had told me himself that he saw it was of no use for me to go to my husband ; and yet, after all, he could issue this order to a boarder in the Asylum, that she must be forced into the hands of this her persecutor, just when the way seemed prepared for my deliverance, by means of my printed book.

If my readers wish to know why the Superintendent was not on hand to defend the rights of his boarder, I must refer them to him for this answer, for he has never told me his reasons for doing so. Therefore, I can only offer you my own conjectures on this point. I suspect this "young convert," was seized with another temptation to "backslide," too powerful for his "weak faith" to withstand, and therefore he had tried to throw off the responsibility of my removal on to the Trustees, hoping by this means to secure Mr. Packard's co-operation in destroying my book, without doing so directly himself, and wishing at the same time to retain my good will, he hoped his absence might better subserve all these ends than his presence. Therefore he made Dr. Tenny his agent in doing this mean work, by proxy.

One reason for coming to this conclusion lies in the fact that after I got home I accidentally ascertained that the Doctor had advised Mr. Packard to burn my book and put me into another Asylum ; and he had volunteered his aid in doing so! I also accidentally found a letter from Dr. McFarland wherein he says to Mr. Packard, I have laid your request for Mrs. Packard's re-admission before the Trustees, and have used my influence to have them consent to take her. But they decidedly refuse to do so, on the ground that the Institution is not designed for such cases. In this same letter, he advised Mr. Packard to keep the facts of this transaction from all public prints, and shun all agitation of this subject in any form.

Another evidence that he had slidden back into the old selfish "policy" principle is seen in the fact that a letter was read to my court at Kankakee, from Dr. McFarland, wherein he urged that I was insane, in the form of a certificate, which

Mr. Packard could use for my incarceration in another Asylum. This did not harmonize with the pledges he had given me in the Asylum that he would be the defender of my personal liberty.

Another evidence that he has backslidden, lies in the fact when I met him in June last, in Jacksonville before the State's Investigating Committee, at the Dunlap House, he made a most strenuous effort to make me out an insane person, for the purpose of invalidating my testimony as a witness against the evils of that Institution. After an examination and a cross-examination occupying nearly seven hours at a single session, with the aid of his attorney and the Trustees, he failed entirely to produce this conviction on the minds of the audience, if Ex-Gov. Hoffman's testimony is a representation of others present which I have reason to think is the case; said he to me at the close of this tedious session, "Mrs. Packard, I believe you to be a perfectly sane person, and moreover, I believe you always have been."

Thanking him for the comfort this announcement gave me, I felt better fortified to meet a most cruel and wanton attack Dr. McFarland then made upon my moral character, while he knew, better than any other man, that my character was stainless.

Looking at Dr. McFarland's character from these various standpoints, I am forced into the unwelcome conviction that he is a most unprincipled man, and on this ground is unworthy of confidence as a man, and much less as a public servant. I have done all I knew how to do to raise this man, from the low level of selfish policy to the higher platform of Christian principle; but all in vain—I now herewith pass him over into the power of that State, whose public servant he is, hoping and praying that this power may be able to do for this man's benefit what "woman's influence" has failed to accomplish. And if the State will not receive him, I then leave him with his own worst enemy—I leave him with himself.

If any of my readers wish to know what has been my destiny from the time of this discharge. I would refer them to my "Three Years Imprisonment for Religious Belief," wherein they will find this part of my experience delineated, affording a fearful exhibition of the abuse of marital power, which every married woman is liable to suffer, in her present position of legal disability to defend herself.

LXXXV.

Jacksonville Insane Asylum a Type of other Insane Asylums.

It was my original intention in compiling this volume, to include between its covers the statements of other competent witnesses, who have suffered a term of false imprisonment in Insane Asylums in other States, and thus demonstrate the fact that Jacksonville is no exception to the treatment generally bestowed in such Institutions.

For this purpose, I had already obtained statements from highly educated individuals, occupying the first ranks in social position, and in public confidence, as men and women who are capable of defending their own sanity and the facts they testify to, before any legislature or impartial court, which I should esteem an honor to present to the public, did not the limits of this volume forbid it.

These individual statements represent, 1st. The Insane Asylum of Pennsylvania, at Philadelphia. 2nd. The McLean Insane Asylum at Boston, Mass. 3rd. The Retreat for the Insane, at Hartford, Ct. 4th. The Insane Asylum at Concord, N. H. 5th. The Insane Asylum at Columbus, Ohio. The representatives from these Institutions afford a most invincible argument, that the "Prisoner's Hidden Life" in all these Institutions, is but a type of what it is at Jacksonville, as herein delineated by myself and my coadjutors.

I therefore infer from these representations, that this book fairly represents these Institutions wherever found. But if the public wish these documents printed in confirmation of this assertion, I hold myself in readiness to meet this demand.

I will also state that so far as my own observation extends, I have not in this volume presented one third part of the journal I kept while at Jacksonville, feeling confident that the full and ample report of the Investigating Committee renders my doing so superfluous. Thus having ample testimony on hand to confirm and authenticate what is already published, and having the Illinois Investigating Committee's Report to back up my statements already made, so far as the representation of Jacksonville Asylum is concerned, I can assure the public they need no longer be blinded in relation to the truth; for in this volume they have the curtain view of one Asylum, and there is no reason to doubt but that this is a fair representation of others, generally.

This being the case, the need of a universal and radical reconstruction of principles in this department of humanitarian reform, is a self-evident fact, which should at once command the attention of every philanthropist.

LXXXVI.

A Note of Thanks to the Rail Road Companies, and the Press of Illinois.

It is with feelings of sincere gratitude that I am permitted to acknowledge the favors so gallantly bestowed by the gentlemanly Superintendents of the Railroad Companies of Illinois, in passing me over their roads on "Complimentary Tickets," while in the performance of this public mission for the benefit of this State. I am happy to state that no Superintendent has yet refused to give me a pass, but on the contrary, all have passed me with the most cheerful promptness whenever I have made personal application for this favor.

My grateful acknowledgements are also hereby tendered to the Hartford, New Haven, New York, Harrisburg, Pittsburg, Fort Wayne, and Chicago Railroad Companies, who passed me from Hartford to Chicago with equal cheerfulness, upon learning the object of my mission.

Indeed, special thanks are due the Superintendent at Hartford, who, self-moved, was the first to offer me such a favor, and who also gave me a letter of introduction to the New Haven Superintendent, recommending him to pass me to the New York Superintendent, and so on. By a sound and lucid argument, he convinced me of the reasonableness and propriety of asking such favors of public officers, while on a mission of public utility, prosecuted at my own expense, and working at the same time, without money and without price.

To the Press of Illinois do I feel under special obligations for the aid they have so kindly and generously afforded me in the prosecution of my mission, by allowing the columns of the papers of the various parties and sects of this State, to be used in aid of this humanitarian cause.

Both the Tribune, and the Times, of Chicago, have rendered me most valuable service, thus demonstrating the pleasing fact, that both of the political parties of this State can unite in this cause of common philanthropy.

The example of these noble pioneers has been followed by nearly all the other papers of Illinois, and thereby they are all deserving my most grateful thanks, which I do hereby freely bestow.

I am under special obligations to the Springfield Register, for their efficient and timely aid, during the session of the legislature of 1867, by allowing their columns to be used as a means of bringing the need of this reform before that body, the result of which was the appointment of the Investigating Committee.

LXXXVII.

An Appeal to the People of Illinois for a Redress of my Wrongs.

It is the State of Illinois whom posterity will hold responsible for my false imprisonment, for it was under their laws this conspiracy was shielded. I have suffered the penalty due the State, for licensing such a persecuting power against their defenseless married women.

Because of being a married woman, I have been a defenseless victim of one of the most cruel religious persecutions the page of history has had to record; and so far as the law is concerned, I have still no *right* to the home from which I was so cruelly ejected eight years since. *I am homeless*—simply because I choose to worship God according to the dictates of my own conscience, rather than my husband's; and it is because my husband, instead of the government, has the control of my personal identity, that this marital usurper has decreed that I shall never be allowed to have the guardianship of my own children, so long as I cherish my present views of truth and duty.

This usurper says, "The home is *mine* by law, and I shall protect you in it, or drive you from it, just as my own sovereign will dictates." He also says, "The children are all *mine* by law, and as their guardian, I shall not allow them to be contaminated by their mother's religious errors."

I feel that I have been deeply wronged, and injured, by this usurper's power, and I now turn with woman's trusting confidence to the manly government of this Republic, and ask you to protect me in my home as my *right*—that you protect me in the guardianship of my children, as my maternal *right* —that you protect me in my *right* to worship God according to the dictates of my own conscience, without molestation from this marital power.

I do not ask for the right of "secession" from the marriage union—I simply ask for the protection of my inalienable rights, as an individual, while in the union.

And I stand not alone in these ranks of the persecuted. Nay, verily, I am only a single representative of a large class of married women in America, who are bound by these chains of married servitude, to a soul bondage worse than death. Now that the negro slave is emancipated, there is no citizen of this Republic, who is not legally protected in their right to worship God according to the dictates of their own conscience except the married women of this *free* Republic!

Many of this class have reason to fear from the bigotry and intolerance of their husbands—their masters in law. Often has the remark been made to me by such sufferers, "Mrs. Packard, I believe just as you do, but I dare not utter my opinions for fear my husband will say I am insane, and then bring me before a Jury for trial, which will expose me also to imprisonment! Therefore I am compelled to act the hypocrite and pretend to believe what I do not!"

'Tis true the social rights of the married women are *more* imperilled than those of any other class—for her identity is so merged, or lost in that of her husband, as to render her utterly helpless, by way of self-defense from this marital usurpation. Now since the position of legal nonentity is an insuperable barrier to her receiving legal protection of her rights of religious belief, except it come through her husband, why will not our government emancipate us from our slavish position, so that we may be as well protected in the exercise of our religious belief, as our husbands are in their own?

We do not ask this recognition of our individuality, or identity for the purpose of usurping any of our husband's rights, but simply for the protection and defense of our own, from marital usurpation.

My case demonstrates the sad truth, that there are cases where the husband does usurp the rights of the wife, instead of protecting them as his marriage vow requires him to do. Now what can be the harm in allowing the wives of such usurpers a legal right and power to defend themselves when needed?

Do you say that it gives the wife a double guard of defense —the protection of the marital and legal power both? Yes, so it does, we admit, and we grant too, that it is only in such extreme cases, like my own, that the wife needs legal defense from this marital power. But we do not like to be exposed to this *liability*. Such men need the force of law to compel them to protect their wives, for the higher law of manliness slumbers within, and needs to be quickened into life and action by the lower law of human enactments.

But the objector may say, "There is no need of law to protect the married woman, for public sentiment will hold the husband to be true to his marriage vow, as the protector of his wife." Why then did not this influence hold my husband to his responsibility in this respect? And why did not the public deliver me out of my prison-house of unjust captivity? Simply because there was no law back of these influences to depend upon in making a defensive attack.

Now had this power existed, my husband would not have dared to risk the attack, and thus the evil I have suffered, might have been prevented. It was my very defenselessness which tempted him to risk public sentiment, even when he knew it was against him, trusting to the law to shield him, in open defiance of this influence.

Again—the law is made for the exceptional cases; it is not intended for the masses, who are a law unto themselves. For example, the penalties against theft are not made to restrain the masses, but the thieves of society—the exceptions. These penalties do not imply that *all* are going to steal, but since some do, and will, even in defiance of the higher law, a human law is needed for the restraint of this class.

So in asking for the protection of law to the married woman, we do not imply that the masses of men need the force of law to compel them to protect their wives—we only mean that there is, occasionally, an extreme case, where the marital power needs the restraint of the law for the protection of the wife's identity. Therefore, to meet these exceptional cases, we need a legal identity of our own, independent of our husbands. We must therefore, be emancipated, so that we can protect ourselves, as married women, in cases where our husbands will not prove true to the marriage vow.

Rev. Theophilus Packard, one of Illinois Presbyterian clergy, is a guilty man—Dr. Andrew McFarland, Illinois Superintendent of Jacksonville Insane Asylum, is a guilty man—Trustees of Illinois State Asylum at Jacksonville, are guilty men—and the State of Illinois has been ignorantly guilty in shielding all these criminal officials from punishment due them, for bringing such a deep stain upon the honor of their proud State.

To this State do I, the representative of this deeply injured class of Illinois citizens, now turn for an honorable redress of these wrongs. I do not ask you to punish these guilty conspirators, who by your own laws are guilty of no crime(!) in thus incarcerating one of her married women for religious belief. Therefore the avenging of these wrongs must be settled at a higher than an earthly tribunal. I have entered no prosecution against them, neither do I seek for such a redress.

But all the redress I have already sought, has been most cheerfully granted by Illinois Legislature of 1867, in the passage of the "Personal Liberty Bill." To secure its passage has cost me eighteen months of toilsome labor in traveling throughout the limits of the State, to awaken the torpid, blinded public to the need of this reform. I have borne my own expenses on this mission, and have worked without asking pay or charity.

I have had many obstacles to overcome. My character has been assailed by those who ought to have defended it. But in the name of right and justice I have struggled on, determined that an upright course of self-sacrificing benevolence should silence the tongue of the slanderer, and put to shame all those who would defame my stainless character.

It may perhaps under the circumstances, not be improper to state, that I have assumed pecuniary responsibilities which still demand a large share of energy and perseverance to meet.

At about fifty years of age I have been compelled, in consequence of the unreasonable position the law assigns me as a married woman, to begin life's struggle alone, and unaided, having no other capital to depend upon, but my good health and education. With the aid of this capital alone, I have paid the entire expense of printing and selling eighteen thousand books, by my own efforts entirely.

Encouraged by the sale of my books, I have ventured to assume the responsibility contained in the following letter I dropped into the Post Office, on the 25th of Dec. 1867, directed to Rev. T. Packard, South Deerfield, Mass.

A CHRISTMAS PRESENT.

Whereas, in the Providence of God, my own dear family have become objects of charity, and are now dependent, either upon public or private charity, for their support and education— And whereas, by the favor and smiles of a kind Providence, my personal efforts to secure for myself a maintenance have been so abundantly rewarded and successful, as not only to secure for myself a competency, but also justifies me, as I view it, in now assuming the pecuniary responsibilities of my own dear family.

Therefore, in order that society and their friends be relieved of the burden of their support and education, I, the wife and mother of this family, do, hereby, of my own free will and choice, bestow upon my family, viz: Rev. T. Packard, Elizabeth, George, and Arthur Packard, this offer of a home, support and educational advantages, upon the following conditions—viz:

The property used for this purpose being the avails of my own hard labor, shall be retained in my own name, and shall thereby be subject to my own control.

The location of this home must be near some college, where males and females can both receive a collegiate education at the same institution.

The State and Town where this home shall be located may be chosen by my family to whom this offer is made.

It would be my decided wish and highest pleasure to make this home a home for myself also; still I do not make this a condition of its acceptance, but willingly leave it to the decision of my family, whether this desire of my heart be granted or not.

This offer, if accepted, can be bestowed upon my family by October, 1867.

E. P. W. PACKARD.

Thus the thinking public can see the facts of my experience demonstrate the truth, that a married woman is as capable of self-support as a married man. Therefore, for a redress of my wrongs I now appeal to the people of Illinois for *emancipation from my slavish position*—that of a legal nonentity, or a non-existent being, to that of an entity, or existent being, before the law—so that I, *as a married woman*, may be as well protected in my rights as a woman, as my husband is in his rights, as a man.

Thus will Illinois become, as her honor now demands, the banner State in raising married women to that plane of existence, which the intelligence of the nineteenth century demands.

A Bill to this effect is to be presented to the Illinois Legislature of 1869, and may God grant that Illinois' stain may then be obliterated by the passage of this Bill.

MRS. OLSEN'S NARRATIVE

OF HER

ONE YEAR'S IMPRISONMENT,

AT

Jacksonville Insane Asylum:

WITH THE TESTIMONY OF

Mrs. Minard, Mrs. Shedd, Mrs. Yates, and Mrs. Lake, all corroborated by the Investigating Committee of the Legislature of Illinois.

COLLECTED AND PUBLISHED

BY MRS. E. P. W. PACKARD.

CHICAGO:
A. B. CASE, PRINTER, 139 MONROE ST
1868.

Entered according to act of Congress A. D., 1868, by
MRS. E. P. W. PACKARD,
In the Clerk's office of the Dist. Court for the Northern Dist. of Illinois.

A. B. Case, Printer, Chicago.

MRS. PACKARD'S COADJUTOR'S TESTIMONY,

APPENDED TO HER OWN

"PRISON LIFE."

CONTENTS.

Introduction, ... 9

CHAPTER I.
Reception at the Asylum, ... 11

CHAPTER II.
False Colors, ... 17

CHAPTER III.
Seventh Ward Experiences, ... 22

CHAPTER IV.
A Storm Approaching, ... 31

CHAPTER V.
Dangerous Experiments, ... 40

CHAPTER VI.
Breakers Ahead, ... 43

CHAPTER VII.
The Fifth Ward, ... 46

CHAPTER VIII.
Purgatorial Experiences, ... 55

CHAPTER IX.
Satan's Representative, ... 59

CHAPTER X.
The Resurrection, ... 64

CHAPTER XI.
The Reign of Terror, ... 73

CONTENTS.

CHAPTER XII.
Reign of Terror ended, ... 77

CHAPTER XIII.
Wives and Husbands, ... 89

CHAPTER XIV.
The Insanity of Orthodoxy, ... 92

CHAPTER XV.
How to make Incurables, ... 97

CHAPTER XVI.
Departure of Mrs. Packard, ... 102

CHAPTER XVII.
My Departure, ... 106

CHAPTER XVIII.
Reports—Visits of Trustees, ... 112

CHAPTER XIX.
Fallacies, ... 115

CHAPTER XX.
Influence of Insane Asylums upon their Victims, ... 118

CHAPTER XXI.
Testimony of Mrs. Sarah Minard, of St. Charles, Ill.... 122

CHAPTER XXII.
Testimony of Mrs. T. F. Shedd, of Aurora, Ill., ... 128

CHAPTER XXIII.
Testimony of Mrs. H. H. Yates, of Chicago, Ill. 133

CHAPTER XXIV.
Testimony of Mrs. C. E. Lake, of Aurora, Ill., ... 136

Note to the Reader.

In publishing Mrs. Olsen's Narrative, I feel called upon to state some facts, which she has (for reasons best known to herself) withheld in her statement. She states that she went of her own accord to the Asylum, and this fact is corroborated by the testimony of her family relatives. But *why did she go at all?* is a question the reader has, in my opinion, a right to know. Therefore I will take the responsibility of stating that it was because of the unreasonable and cruel treatment she was receiving from her insane husband, which treatment, for her husband's sake, she wished to conceal from the world. These influences led her to prefer going to the Asylum herself, instead of consenting to his going, as had been proposed by some of her neighbors. And in the opinion of some, it may be considered as an insane act in Mrs. Olsen's thus offering to go to the Insane Asylum under such circumstances. But Mrs. Olsen, being by her organization, one of the most benevolent and self-sacrificing of her sex, it was not, *for her*, an unnatural or insane act.

Again, her sympathizing heart had long beat in unison with the sufferings of the insane, and she desired to look behind the curtain of Jacksonville Insane Asylum, to see for herself how the insane were treated there; and therefore she consented to go on the terms stipulated in her narrative.

It may be a satisfaction to the readers of this volume, to know that the facts here stated by my coadjutors have been authenticated and corroborated by the Illinois Investigating Committee, appointed by the Legislature of 1867, to investigate and report the result to the Governor, which they did on the second of December following. In this report, Mrs. Olsen, Mrs. Minard, Mrs. Shedd, myself and five others, are named as witnesses on whose testimony, in their opinion, the public may safely rely.

MRS. E. P. W. PACKARD.

Chicago, May, 1868.

PART II.

INTRODUCTORY.

"TRUTH is mighty and will prevail," says an old adage. Those who feel impelled by some strong moral motive, to express it, are often obliged to meet and combat errors and stern opposing influences. But the earnest advocates of truth will not be disheartened by such obstacles. They know that truth has in itself a vitality, a cogency, which though long suppressed, clouded by error, and opposed by its enemies, will yet by its own innate power, win its way to the ultimate recognition of all human intelligences.

Impressed by these convictions, I have ventured to write this humble work for the public. In doing this, my object has been solely to exhibit and to diffuse the truth upon the now much contested subject of the "Insane Asylum of Illinois." In detailing my own experience and observation there, I have employed no artificial coloring. The pencil of the artist, and the graphic pen of the poet can be better employed than by attempting to heighten the color of scenes which need no painting. These scenes have been related just as they occurred before my eyes; my own reflections having been given as they spontaneously arose.

I spent more than a year there, and had the most ample opportunity to make observations in each of the female departments. There I saw the mild and peaceful, the wild and furious, the profane and indecent, and the wretched victims of a cureless insanity caused by the indulgence of the most horrible vices. Twenty days I spent in the lowest prison, or, as they term it, the *Fifth Ward*, that universal, indiscriminate slaughter-house of human life, and of human affections! Sickness, in all its terrible and most revolting forms, was witnessed in this abode of human woe. Death also there appeared, in the beautiful exemplifications of Christian martyrdom, when the smile upon the heaven-illuminated features spoke only of forgiveness, peace, and love! I saw the fearful work of death, too, in the suicidal hand; which, prompted by the fears of a life more to be dreaded, cut short its brittle thread, and precipitated its miserable victim into an uncalled eternity. I have witnessed in the Lunatic "Asylum," the brightest specimens of human loveliness and beauty, the richest gems of thought; illustrations of imperishable genius; the triumph of soul and spirit over the mortal tenement, visions of unearthly beauty, records of undying affection, the most heroic self-abnegation over the most sublime fortitude and long enduring patience,—all have here been indelibly engraved upon my memory and my heart.

In the midst of such ample opportunities, and from such rich materials have these pages been compiled; and perhaps I need only add that my present convictions on the subject of Lunatic Asylums are not indebted to the influence either of prejudice or passion nor to any mental condition calculated to distort my vision or my judgement.

This I trust will fully appear in the following pages, which are now respectfully submitted to the candid consideration of an enlightened public.

MRS. SOPHIA N. B. OLSEN.
Wheaton, DuPage, Co., Jan. 15, 1868.

I.

Reception at the Asylum.

"I will a round unvarnished tale deliver."

During the ever-memorable month of August, 1862, I had acquired from debilitated health, in consequence of long watching over my sick husband, and a great variety of other duties pressing heavily upon me, a state of mind which he thought was either insanity, or bordering upon it. In consequence of nervous exhaustion, by this over-exertion, both my physical and mental condition had acquired an unusual degree of activity, such as often results by losing much sleep, accompanied by excessive trouble or mental anxiety. This was the only way in which my condition of mind at the time of which I speak, varied from its ordinary channel; and rest and recuperation of health were all that was needed for my perfect restoration. My reasoning powers were not in the least impaired; nor was I indisposed or incapacitated as to the performance of a single domestic or other duty.

It was but a very few days after my husband had indicated his fears of my sanity leaving me, that he proposed our removal from Chicago to St. Paul, in Minnesota. In arranging for this, he left me to perform all the duties of taking care of our property and preparing to follow him. He thought best to go a few weeks in advance, and previously gave me many directions respecting the disposition of our domestic affairs; to every one of which I diligently attended, scrupulously consulting his interest and pleasure in the most minute particulars.

When he returned from St. Paul, in just one week, he found me confined in one of the city prisons in consequence of unfounded rumors originated by himself, of my assumed insanity! This most cruel and unnecessary action was performed by one whose name, in mercy to himself and his family, I will spare, and in the absence from the city of all my relations, except one who had no power to protect me from this most unexampled injustice. This nefarious business transpired, not because I had either done or attempted the *least posible harm*, but because it was feared that I *might!*

This shows the state of feeling existing in consequence of a falsely educated public sentiment on this subject. A person is reported insane; the first thing is to deprive him of all proper sympathy and of all human rights, lest he should injure some one! He is harmed, to keep others from being harmed; and very often too, upon the strength of some ungrounded suspicions promulgated by straggling reports. But it is hoped the day is not far distant when people will learn that it is better first to examine the facts of a case, instead of hastily acting upon flying rumors, when the dearest rights of human beings are at stake; when they will also learn that prisons were made for criminals, and not for innocent and feeble women!

Instead of weeping or complaining or raving in my prison, as I think many less disciplined in the school of affliction would have done, I remained perfectly quiet and self-possessed, calmly awaiting the hour of deliverance which I instinctively felt was near; and in this tranquil condition, my husband found me the next day. The keys of the Armory were instantly turned in another direction.

He had been cautioned to say but little to me, as I inferred from the mysterious taciturnity of his manner. He evidently thought my supposed malady would be increased by the "excitement" of conversation; and under the influence of this fear, forbore the proper means for investigation which would have dissipated his delusion at once. An open review of the facts would have elicited a correct understanding of affairs, and made us mutually happy on the spot, instead of plunging us into all the losses, the sorrows and the sufferings which have subsequently resulted to us both. Rumors were soon circulated among my transient acquaintances to the effect that I was insane, and that arrangements were in progress to deprive me of my liberty! It is remarkable that not a single person ever took the least pains to investigate the occasions for these rumors. Had they done so, far different would have been the result. But it is a fact, however inconsistent it may seem, that the very suspicion that a person is insane scares away cool reason from all his friends. Often with the merest trifle for a foundation, it is solemnly whispered from one to another, that "some one is insane!" The report circulates with every circumstance of exaggeration which the terrified imagination of the narrator can affix to the same, until it assumes a most terrible importance. The accused is watched in every motion; every look, every tone of the voice becomes an object of the severest espionage. Even the distress of mind all must feel when environed by such a crushing scrutiny, is construed into additional evidence of unmistakable mental derangement. Thus the suffering victim of so much folly is worried, excited and hurried along through scenes of increased and repeated excitements, until the ever-hungry jaws of the Lunatic "Asylum" so called, are opened to complete the tragical drama.

There were some circumstances which made me willing to go unresistingly to the "Asylum," but I did not wish to go as a patient; but there were reasons of entirely another character, which will be developed in the course of my history, which reconciled me temporarily to go there. It may well be inferred that the circumstances from which could spring so singular a resolultion, were of an exceedingly afflictive character; indeed such as to try every tender chord of woman's delicate nature. I watched myself with the severest scrutiny, to keep calm in this severe ordeal of my affliction, and strove to evince by my deportment, more than usual kindness and deference to those around me, and by attending strictly to the performance of all my duties, to dissipate all prejudice. But it was too late; my single-handed efforts were unavailing.

Our parting I shall not attempt to describe. We had lived together more than five years, during which it had ever been my study to promote his comfort, happiness, and interest by every way in my power, according to my best intelligence. He was dearer than my own ease or my own life; for his sake I had resigned the former, and nearly sacrificed the latter. And now for the first time, we were to be separated, by his own wishes, on the basis of *suspicions* that I was, or might become insane! A dark cloud was over my spirit as I dimly foresaw the consequences to our future life of such a separation. It seemed as if all the fountains of grief I had ever experienced were now welling up anew to overwhelm me. He exhorted me to be of good courage, assured me our separation should be but transient, and promised to pray daily for our happy reunion. I draw a veil over our final scene of separation; it is too sadly sacred for the world to gaze upon. We parted,—and forever.

He had employed my youngest brother to take me to the "Asylum;" and when he left me in charge of the latter, and stood in the street bowing and waving, with his hat, his final adieus, it seemed that my very heart itself was left behind me. I could not now restrain the blistering tears which rolled in torrents down my face. My kind brother saw my emotion, and had the good sense not to speak to me, aware that words could prove but the veriest mockery of consolation.

August 6th was the fatal day in which the formidable doors of that institution, the world calls an "Asylum," were locked upon me, and I found myself indeed a prisoner. Finding it inevitable, I submitted with cheerfulness. This submission however was given under a very mistaken idea of the doom impending over me.

It was understood by a special arrangement between myself and the Superintendent, that I was to have a comfortable room all the time; free from the noise of turbulent pa-

RECEPTION AT THE ASYLUM. 15

tients, where I could write; and that I should enjoy an *unrestricted epistolary correspondence* with my husband and other friends all the time I remained there. How far the Doctor fulfilled his pledges, we shall see in the sequel.

I was of course admitted to the Seventh, the most pleasant and highly privileged of all the wards. There my brother left me with my own consent, being assured in my presence, by the officers, that everything should be done for my comfort and for the resuscitation of my exhausted health.

I was now pleasantly initiated in what I supposed would be an "Asylum" to me in my weak and exhausted condition of body, and very cheerfully surrendered myself to the two attendants of that hall, both of whom appeared to be pleasant and amiable ladies. Firmly resolving to obey every rule of the institution, I candidly and kindly told Dr. McFarland this my determination.

I particularly desired to make myself agreeable to my attendants, not only by sparing them all unnecessary trouble in attending to my wants, but by anticipating their own wishes, and rendering them unhesitating obedience in all their requirements of me. That I faithfully adhered to this resolution all the time I was in their hall, and that I ever treated them respectfully and kindly, they did me the justice to bear me ample witness, a short time previous to my leaving the institution. It was my wish to convince my friends, especially my husband, that my industrious habits were not in the least impaired by my supposed "insanity." Therefore, my next object was to obtain some yarn, which I wished to knit for myself, that being necessary; next, for my husband, and after that, I wished to knit a quantity of hosiery for the soldiers.

I supposed the matron, Mrs. McFarland, would be willing to sell yarn to me for these useful purposes; but in this I had made a mistake. Had I done this proposed knitting, and some other work I sought, it would have come into collision with some of their plans, one of which was to have me, as do most of their victims, work unpaid for the "Asylum;" or in case I would not willingly do this, (for no one is absolutely compelled to do so,) to exhibit me as an idle insane woman. This will be more fully shown in the progress of my narrative. I however obtained, though with much difficulty, yarn sufficient to knit for myself one pair of stockings, after which I could never persuade the matron to let me have any more.

I assiduously cultivated the acquaintance of all the patients; many of them were very amiable in manners, and of a high grade of intelligence; and all, or nearly all, facile and ladylike in deportment, and easily won to conversation. They at once recognized a friend in me, and confided to me their tales of suffering, and much of their previous history. From my acquaintance with these most interesting people, I acquired a deeper knowledge of the human heart, and of human experience than I had ever learned before. It is not superfluous to say that I found them all unhappy, except those who were expecting soon to leave the place. The rest were all extremely unreconciled to the fact of their being forcibly detained in that place, when it was their choice to return to their homes.

But *my* greatest unhappiness arose from my anxiety respecting my husband. I knew, better than any one else, the peculiar bent of his mind, and how much he needed some one to soothe those agitations which I knew would occasionally sweep over his spirit. Who, like myself, could or would attempt to "hush the storm and soothe to peace?" Who should be the companion of his lonely hours? Who nurse and solace him in the trials of despondency and sickness, as I had ever delighted to do? Who would stand between him and the shafts of malice and evil tongues, and who, with tireless care, guard his happiness and life from all that could imperil the existence of either, as I had never ceased to do? Ah! these were queries which I could not solve. I could solace the disquietude of my mind only by daily committing him to the care of a merciful God, whose unslumbering eye is over all his children. This I never ceased to do, and thus found a balm for my deeply wounded spirit.

I kept constantly employed in reading, writing, and working, and in cultivating the acquaintance of my companions in bonds. An intense desire, and one which I never lost sight of, was to try to alleviate the sufferings of those around me. This field of labor had *no* limits.

II.

False Colors.

"It is a truth that must be told
That all that glitters is not gold."

For a few days, all went on very well with me. There was much to approve, and much that was calculated to impress a stranger, for such I now was, favorably towards the Institution. Some of these appearances were the scrupulous cleanliness of the halls, and the ventilation, by means of many doors and windows. The beautiful domain of thorougly cultivated land, the ample expanse of flowers which exhaled their rich fragrance in clouds of balmy perfume, causing the immediate atmosphere outside the building, to be exceedingly fragrant, and the whole scenery all but Paradisical.

I pass from this to another subject less pleasant, for my reader will remember that I am presenting life here as it is, and not as it *ought* to be. A few days after my admission, a lady came from the sewing room, and advancing with a very supercilious air, and a superabundance of smiles, said to me, "*Darling*, would you like to come with me, and a few other ladies, into the sewing room?" She was a foreigner, and had not learned the proper accent of English words,. I understood her to say *swing* room, and then for the first time, discovered, as I supposed, that there was a place of amusement, a place indeed much needed. I gladly assented, but found to my surprise, that it was no place of amusement, but one of toil.

The garments of the gentlemen, and some of the ladies who cannot make their own, are there manufactured. She invited me to take a seat, and presenting me with a part of a garment, began to instruct me how she wished me to proceed with it. Instead however of obeying *her* implicitly, as I always obeyed the attendants, I presumed to prefer that my own reason, instead of her commands, should be my teacher. I asked how much she *paid* the ladies who worked for her, and whether they worked by the piece, or by the hour, or how, or what were the conditions. I wished to ascertain respecting the terms, before consenting to work in her employ. Her replies were entirely evasive and ambiguous, leaving me however unequivocally to understand that we were to be paid only by the general advantage of working to keep ourselves from the discomforts and miseries of idleness. But why can we not work for ourselves, and our families at home, said I? that would equally well keep ourselves from idleness, and benefit our friends at the same time. She evidently did not like the spirit of my queries, and referred me to the fact that this was not a talking room but a sewing room. But I failed to see the advantages of working unpaid for others, while they were receiving the profits of such labor. Nor can I say that I have ever since become aware that it is either a privilege or a duty for an insane or a sane patient, to labor for a Superintendent without pay, while he already receives an enormous salary.

But it appeared that this estimable lady did not trouble her busy mind with moral considerations. This was not in the programme of her duties. So, as I still hesitated, instead of going to work, she proceeded with all the logic of her eloquent tongue, to inform me gravely that exercise was good for me; that I needed something "for amusement," etc. Poor Soul! did she suppose she was giving me any information? I knew all these things long before she was born.

But as she urged me very earnestly however, I civilly replied that if Mrs. McFarland, the matron required me to labor for the "Asylum" without pay, I was ready to do so, because I had voluntarily engaged to obey every rule of the Institution; but if this was not the case, I should certainly decline the honor of thus giving away my services. Besides, I added, that I was a wife, and thought it my duty to labor for my own family rather than for strangers.

On observing the cool and decided manner with which I uttered this, she persisted no longer, but opened the door and offered to escort me back to my ward. I told her I should like to remain while the other ladies remained. But a person who had uttered such obnoxious sentiments, in defence of natural rights, it cannot be supposed was allowed thus to do. Had I continued in thus expressing my ideas of justice, in the presence of the victims of *injustice*, it would not have encouraged their gratuitious toil. So I bowed to the ladies, wished them all good morning, and followed their task-mistress to my own ward. My readers may be sure that this most affectionate lady never again called me "darling!"

I was however comparatively contented in this ward for a few weeks, while allowed to write to my friends, and never supposed that I was to stay there more than two months, unless I wished to do so, this being the distinct understanding when I went there. Dr. McFarland also expressly agreed to permit me an unrestricted epistolary communication with my friends. I therefore never imagined that my letters were to be read by the Doctor and detained by him after such a sacred pledge, and when so much suffering of mind was the price of its breach.

My husband had promised to write to me once a week at least; several weeks had passed, since I had received any tidings from him, I therefore began to suspect that my letters had never reached him, indeed that they had never left the "Asylum!" Several patients also had whispered to me, that the Doctor had intercepted their letters, which had caused them great anxiety and grief. I was surprised on hearing this, as I knew that he had caused much dissatisfaction while Superintendent in the New Hampshire "Asylum" for the same offence I believed, that seeing the trouble it gave, and also as it could not effect the least possible good, he would not here pursue his old course in thus disappointing and grieving those distressed and suffering minds, so sacredly confided to his protection and compassion. The complaints by several, here alluded to, were confirmed by others, and upon closer inquiry, I at last discovered that it was only a privileged few who were allowed free communication with absent friends!

This heartless Doctor never gave me any reasons for breaking his promise to me. He is not in the habit of giving reasons for his actions.

This treatment, thus coolly violating a promise on which he knew I relied, was not calculated to allay the suffering of my mind, nor did it beget in me any respect or confidence in one who could thus deliberately falsify his own word. Many of the ladies in the Seventh ward, told me that was the way in which it had been his uniform practice to treat them, and that, though they confided in him at first, yet they had long since ceased to do so. "We don't pretend now," said more than one, "to tell him our wishes. It is of no use. He don't care anything about us. He don't pretend to notice us, but goes right out of the hall as though we had not spoken to him."

But it seemed to be a tacit understanding with all the ladies in that ward, to conceal from him the profound contempt they felt for him. They therefore were usually respectful, though never candid in their demeanor to him; thus being forced as a method of self protection, to use the resort of hypocrisy. This affords one illustration of the morality of Lunatic "Asylums." But I shall have occasion in future chapters to speak more at large of the influence of these institutions upon the morals of their victims.

Many of the ladies in this ward were so quiet, so industrious and ladylike, in short, so very much like other people, that I could not at all distinguish them except by the superiority of their patience and some other rare virtues, from the community outside.

One evening a ball was held in another hall to which I was invited, I observed a very dignified and intelligent looking gentleman, by whose appearance I inferred him to be one of the attendants. On being introduced to this gentleman I remarked. "I presume, Sir, you are one of the attendants?" "No, I am not an attendant," he replied with emphasis. "But you are not a patient here," rejoined I, "surely you are not deprived of your liberty?" "They call me a patient, he replied, but I do not call myself one, as nothing is done for my health." This was the late Mr. Wells, of Chicago, formerly editor and proprietor of a popular commercial paper in that city. He proceeded to speak very freely to me, while the rest were dancing.

He said he had been ill treated by a landlord, and that his indignation on the occasion had been construed into insanity, and that his wife being frightened, was influenced by others to take him to the "Asylum" where he had remained in a condition of great physical discomfort, and mental suffering. I asked him if he was not well treated by Dr. McFarland. He answered unhesitatingly in the negative, affirming that he was uniformly cold and frigid in his deportment to him. I endeavored to console him as well as I could, referring him to those general principles of justice, which I believed would ultimately be carried out, and work emancipation to all the suffering. I said nothing disrespectful of Dr. McFarland, as I did not wish to confirm the views of Mr. Wells, or add to his unpleasant feelings in that direction; but said briefly all I could suggest in favor of the Doctor, reminding Mr. Wells how difficult it must be to do justice to every one, in a position involving such weighty responsibility. I cannot forget the look he gave me, as he turned away in apparent disgust. "If you are the apologist of McFarland and his iniquities, I don't covet your acquaintance," he exclaimed with much emphasis. I apologized for having inadvertently wounded his feelings, and quietly withdrew to another part of the hall. In the course of the evening, we met again. Feeling reluctant that he should have an erroneous impression respecting my conversation, I made some bland remark about the festivity of the evening. Quite reinstated in his good humor, he replied very politely, and again we entered into conversation. I asked him if he did not dance on these occasions. "I have danced sometimes," he replied, but I shall never dance in these halls again. I cannot dance—I am thinking of my lonely young wife—my little babes, thus deprived of a father's protection, I am all but dying to see them." He spoke of his wife with the deepest tenderness; said she was ever true and forever kind to him; he did not at all blame her for his imprisonment, but severely blamed those who had been her advisors. "No," he repeated, as he cast a rueful look again upon the dancers, "no, no; I shall never dance in these halls any more."

Soon the ball was ended, I bade him good evening, and we parted. One week later another ball was held in the same hall, to which again a few of the patients myself included, were invited. I looked around for my friend, but looked in vain. Upon inquiring, I was informed that Mr. Wells was very sick. His prediction proved true; he had indeed danced his last. Grief and suffering had brought on a disease, which could not be cured, at least by the cold ministrations of careless hirelings. They were dancing. He was dying!

III.

Seventh Ward Experiences.

"Full many a gem of purest ray serene
The dark unfathom'd caves of ocean bear;
Full many a flower is born to blush unseen,
And waste its sweetness in the desert air."
—GRAY'S ELEGY.

A great interest was elicited by the patients in the "Asylum," by the sudden death of the highly respected Mr. Wells, and many were the prayers that ascended for his deeply afflicted family. Much sorrow was expressed that his wife was not sent for when he so much wished to see her. Some thanked God that our fellow sufferer was now free;—where his ears would not, like ours, be tortured with the daily grating of locks and keys; others wished it had been their lot, instead of his, to die, rather than longer be afflicted with a doom worse than death—that of dying by inches. Our friend was gone; his eloquent voice forever hushed on earth!

If my limits allowed, I should like to describe many of the ladies there, but this is impossible. They have drawn bright and ever enduring pictures upon my mind,—pictures of virtues rarely equalled,—never surpassed. Such industry, such long suffering patience, such forgiveness of injuries—so inflexible a regard for truth and honor I never saw outside that Institution. I will name but two examples in this hall, and I distinguish these from the rest, on account of their having suffered there so long.

Mrs. Maria Chapman was a lady of unparalleled industry, and great refinement and dignity of character. She was a pattern of neatness and good order. It was truly refreshing to visit her room, of which she took the whole care. Never unemployed a moment, her ever busy fingers were always engaged with book, needle or pen. She commands universal respect. She has been there more than six years. I wished to know why this estimable and highly intelligent lady is excluded from society. I asked her attendants in what her insanity consisted, but found them as uninformed as myself upon the subject, though she had been in this ward all the time. I believe however the crime for which she has lost her sacred liberty, is that of being a Swedenborgian! This I presume is ranked among the "popular delusions" to which Dr. McFarland refers in his most edifying "Seventh Biennial Report." But I only wish the sapient Doctor was as popularly deluded as she is, and then perhaps he might follow some of her good examples so nobly set before him in her lonely captivity.

Of Mrs. Minard, of St. Charles, I could give a description very similar to that of the amiable Mrs. Chapman. Mrs. Minard also was remarkable for her never ceasing industry, and for the truly elegant appearance, not only of her room and person, but of every work which passed through her skillful fingers. She did much sewing, and was often consulted in matters of taste, in fine needle work, by her attendants; both of whom entertained for her a very great respect. She has been absent from her family nine years, and the crime for which it seems she ought to be excluded from civilized society, and confined against her own wishes with the State's lunatics is, that she believes in the ministry of angels, or as some express it, Spiritualism!

If all Spiritualists must be confined in "Lunatic Asylums," we shall soon want Uncle Sam to give us an unlimited quantity of Government land upon which to erect them! Poor Mrs. Minard! my heart has ached for that lovely woman many times, as I beheld her placid countenance, and the premature marks of age upon her head, which grief, not years had caused, as day by day I witnessed her cheerful piety, her long suffering patience, and exemplary fortitude, I wished that many who enjoy all the blessings of which she is so unjustly deprived, could witness the same. I once asked her when she expected to go to the home of which she had often very freely spoken to me. "When the right Spiritual governs Dr. McFarland," she replied. "But you seem very cheerful and even happy," I once ventured to say to her, as by her permission I had been examining her house-plants which she tended with daily care. "No," replied she, "do not imagine it; I am not happy, though I may seem cheerful. I am thinking of my family at St. Charles, and of my long separation from them. I have about concluded I shall never be permitted to go home. As for happiness, while in these circumstances, it is out of the question." Yet she, —and I found the same true of Mrs. Chapman and several other ladies—is so strictly conscientious, so fastidiously honorable, that they will use no clandestine measures to get away.

They are wearing out their precious lives, waiting for their doors to be legally opened—in short, as some of them express it, waiting for "the right spirits to reign," and when "the right spirits" do reign, it is my conviction as well as theirs, that they will all go home to liberty and happiness. Ichabod, will then be inscribed upon the abandoned door posts of their pseudo "Asylum." Oh ignorance! how powerful thou art! how canst thou persuade the friends of such, earth's loveliest spirits, thus to cast away the choicest treasures of their own homesteads?

But it is time that I relate how I came to leave this the best, and by far the most highly privileged of all the wards in the Institution.

I had become very unhappy in consequence of my ever increasing anxiety about my husband. He had told me, previous to my leaving him, that he never could be happy till my return. I had as yet, received but one letter from him, and he said nothing about how he was prospering in all the details of our home life, in which I had so long been his only companion. In his letter he earnestly exhorted me to "put no trust in man," (this was sensible, for how can a wife trust in any man, when her own husband has forfeited her trust?) but to "trust in God," and "pray daily for the happy moment of our reunion." But that "reunion" was indefinitely protracted, and with no visible reason. What was I now waiting for? To "be cured!" Cured of what? My opinions, my affections, my mental proclivities and peculiarities were without exception, the same as they had been, allowance being made for the change in external circumstances. My executive faculties were suffering no impediment, save that of locks and keys, to their healthy normal action. All my time was industriously devoted to vigorous employment of some kind, except when confined to my bed by illness.

After my declining to assist in the work-room was reported to Mrs. McFarland, the matron, she steadily refused to let me have any facilities (except a small quantity of yarn) with which to work for myself. Then the ladies of the ward (patients "insane" of course) knowing this, gave me many little pieces of their own garments, also needle and thread, with which to busy myself for amusement as I thought proper.

The kind and amiable Mrs. Minard was the first in these acts of kindness and sympathy. With these remnants, I carefully constructed many articles for my own and my husband's comfort. Some of these with which I had spent much labor, were afterwards taken from me by stealth, and others by force, by the wildly insane of other wards, in which I was subsequently confined. But I still retain several of the larger and more valuable articles, and value them much, reminding me as they constantly do, of the love and sympathy of my beloved sisters in bonds. These pleasant employments were of much service in keeping away despondency.

Time passed on, and I could in this ward have been comparatively contented for a time, if my letters had not been intercepted, and if I could have slept at night. The Fifth and Sixth wards, immediately below the Seventh, were occupied by the noisy and furious, and the screaming and raving of such at night were so plainly heard from the open windows, as to put quiet sleep out of the question.

From this I suffered so much inconvenience, that at last, I mentioned it to the assistant, Dr. Tenny. He offered very kindly to make a change of the patient in the Sixth ward, whose room was directly below mine, and to put her in another part of the hall, and a quiet person in her place. Reflecting a moment, I sincerely thanked Dr. Tenny, for his proposed kindness, but decidedly objected. "There may be other patients in that hall, even more feeble than myself. If you remove the noisy one who keeps me awake, nearer to their rooms, she may be liable to injure them in the same way. Now as I came here voluntarily, I ought bravely to face the effects of my own action, and with your permission, will persevere in doing it." This did not quite satisfy the Doctor, who urged in reply the duty devolving on me as a Christian to take the best possible care of my health, thus acting in concert with the best arrangements he was able to make for my comfort. Dr. Tenny further urged that since this arrangement was proposed by himself and not by me, if it did injure the other patients, the fault would not be mine. But

I could not feel that I had any right to cause, by my selfish complaints, anything to be done that could possibly injure those sufferers, who, by this time, I could not help thinking, were sufficiently injured before. The Doctor desisted, and I prevailed.

In a few days however, I began to think the reasonings of Dr. Tenny were better than my own. I had become so much enfeebled by want of sleep, that my health sunk rapidly. Violent and frequent headaches distresed me daily, and, as so much was going on all the time in the hall among so many, I could neither sleep, except a very little, either day or night. One night, after about three hour's sleep, I was awakened by a violent noise below. A voice directly under my open window, screamed out in tones of thunder—"God d—n McFarland's soul to hell!" This was several times repeated with terrific emphasis, with many similar expressions.

The day after, I was again visited by my friend Dr. Tenny. Observing the unusual paleness of my face, he kindly inquired for its cause. I told him with much reluctance, that I was now convinced of the propriety of some change, but could not bear to increase in any possible way the sufferings of the other patients. I wished him to give me some very powerful soporific to compel sleep even in the terrible noise. He declined doing this. Then he called and consulted one of my attendants; the result was an arrangement for me to sleep in the dormitory, and try the result of such a change. The dormitory was small but had several beds in it. But as all who slept there were perfectly harmless in the daytime, I did not fear being locked up with them at night. I retired, and congratulated myself that Dr. Tenny's plan for my rest was the best that could be devised. I looked upon the pale quiet sleepers around me, and then fearlessly attempted for the first time in my life, to sleep locked up in a room with those the world calls "dangerous" and "unfit for society." But I had made a mistake in supposing rest possible there. In the middle of the night, one of the patients arose from

her bed, and coming to mine by moon light, brandished her
arms fiercely over my head, and looking very fierce, exclaimed, "have you come here to kill me?" at the same time,
she seized my person, firmly holding me in her grasp, as if
she intended to kill me. Had this scene occurred in the day
time, I should have had no fears; but being locked up with
her, knowing her strength and my own weakness, I confess
I did tremble for my safety. I dared not resist, nor make a
noise, knowing she would be only the more dangerous, if she
knew I was afraid of her. So I looked steadily and calmly
into her face while yet in her grasp, saying—in reply to her
question if I intended to kill her—"Oh no, not at all; I am
not going to harm you; just look at me. I only came here
to sleep to-night, I never hurt any body, and you don't either,
do you?" This somewhat pacified her; she withdrew her
grasp from my person, but did not seem inclined to return to
her bed. I knew not what to do, but finally told her I
guessed she must have had the night-mare or she would not
have thought any harm of me—I added. "we had better go
to sleep." This was intended to tranquilize her, but I knew
my danger too well to go to sleep, and remained on the defensive till the door was unlocked, and much to my relief
came the light of day. I informed the attendant of this
night's experience, and Dr. Tenny never again proposed that
I should sleep in the dormitory. This patient was soon removed from our hall, and Dr. Tenny, of whose sincere friendship for me I was now more than ever convinced, removed
from below me the noisy patient.

I now had a better opportunity to sleep than before. Yet
as day by day, I still heard nothing from my friends, my natural supposition was that some great calamity had occurred
to them. I feared the worst, and did not restrain the expression of these fears. Nor could I possibly solve the mystery of my being detained under such circumstances, I wished
to know how my supposed insanity manifested itself to others;
and respectfully questioned both my attendants, in reference
to this matter.

To the credit of these ladies, I will say that they both frankly and honestly confessed that, as yet, they had seen nothing in my appearance indicating insanity, or that was not both ladylike and kind. The names of these ladies were, Miss McElvie, and Miss Johnston. I was in the ward with them, in all, about four months, and I never found any fault with them, nor they with me, to my knowledge. On the occasion I now refer to, these ladies added to the testimony above alluded to, that I had always complied readily with their wishes, and given them no trouble. They further added that the business of deciding the sanity of the patients did not belong to them, and therefore politely begged of me not to apply to them for any information or assistance, that from their position, they had no power to give me. I felt grateful for so polite and frank an avowal of their feelings, and resolved more than ever, to treat them, as I had ever done, with deferential attention to their wishes.

I wish here to say something respecting Mr. Jones, the Superintendent of the farm. The same honest avowal was made by that gentleman, as by these attendants. Mr. Jones frequently took the patients to ride, when they were permitted that luxury. He was always present at the balls, and often had occasion to come into our hall on errands. It was on these occasions that I became acquainted with him. He seemed to be much respected, indeed a general favorite in the "Asylum." Having had, on the occasions I have named, many interviews and brief conversations with him, I once ventured to ask him, if he had ever seen or suspected any insanity in me, or any irregularity or impropriety of deportment. He declared unhesitatingly, "No, I never have, Mrs. Olsen." On learning from me, that none of my friends had ever visited me, he expressed his conviction that if they were to see me as he saw me, they would have me removed without delay. I then asked him if he should feel free to express that opinion, if he knew that Dr. McFarland would know it? He replied, in substance, "I am, indeed, in the employ of Dr. McFarland as an overseer of the "Asylum" farm, but I never sell my opinions or my conscience, either to him, or to any body else. I shall always respect myself, by freely expressing my honest convictions on all occasions." I exulted in the nobleness of his reply.

Now as I daily saw to my unspeakable regret, and disappoinment, that my communications were entirely intercepted from the outside world; and that no one could be found, who either could or would explain to me why this was done; also when my garments, one after another, were literally robbed or stolen by some of the numerous servants through whose hands they were allowed to pass—and that my health was greatly suffering, and moreover when I saw that all attempts I made by respectful remonstrance, for the alleviation of these disagreeable conditions, were not of the least avail, as the Doctor often would not take the least notice of what I said—when a certainty of these things was forced upon me, I lost all confidence in his honor, his fidelity, and in his word! From that time, I ceased making any requests of him, as himself had thus taught me to do. He saw the change in my deportment, and though I continued coolly civil, when he deigned to notice me, there were no longer on my countenance my former indications of confidence in himself. He did not evidently intend to be "conquered by a woman." And I may add that this redoubtable M. D. was not "conquered by a woman," and probably never will be; but I will venture the prediction that before he arrives to the end of his race, he will find himself both conquered and sadly whipped,—not by a woman, nor by a "conspiracy of women," but by Dr. Andrew McFarland himself.

IV.

A storm approaching.

"The combat deepens! on ye brave!"

All this time, with little interruption, I had reposed confidence in Dr. Tenny. I was glad to learn that he was from New Hampshire, since this fact would give me an opportunity to appeal to his local patriotism. We had something in common to remember, to venerate, to love, and about which we could converse. His native "Fatherland," its magnificent mountains, hills, rivers and forests were also my own; mine too that wealth of thought suggested by their ever present and most precious memories.

The peculiar educational influences of a New England life—the Sabbath School—all indeed that mark the experience of a genuine Yankee, were dearly cherished by our memories alike.

I learned from Dr. Tenny himself that I was the only patient in the Asylum from New Hamshire. This fact also, I thought, would indicate to him, a peculiar reason why, in absence of all other available friends, and thus sick and alone among strangers, he should be my especial protector and friend. This thought I once ventured to express to him, telling him that it was now impossible for me to have any confidence in the Superintendent. For this I explained the reasons to Dr. Tenny. I then procured the sacred promise of Dr. Tenny that he would not let McFarland know I had told him this. I added "Dr. Tenny, in view of all these facts I do most earnestly entreat that in all your influences over me as your patient, you will be governed by your own conscience, and not by that of the Superintendent. I will obey your commands in all things, on these conditions."

Dr. Tenny ended this conversation by giving me some very good suggestions and advice. He added, "I will be your father, mother, sister, and brother, friend, and Doctor." I thanked him with the deepest sincerity for the kind words and tones thus uttered, and added "I hope I may prove worthy of your brotherly kindness and sympathy."

I had on every opportunity, intensely watched the deportment of this gentleman. I noticed how he looked upon and spoke to every patient, and also how they spoke of him in his absence; in short, what impression his conduct was making on the minds over whom his influence and his power were so great.

Continually presenting itself to my mind, was the great contrast between him and Dr. McFarland. This contrast amused, astonished and pleased me. I was daily astonished, even to amazement, that so good a man as I thought Doctor Tenny to be, could remain in the employ, and subject to the orders of Dr. McFarland. I had never known Dr. Tenny to tell falsehoods, or to trifle with the feelings of his patients, but found that he possessed almost universally, their respect and confidence. Polite and urbane in deportment, he also appeared to feel a deep sympathy for the sufferings around him. To the complaints and requests of those in his charge, he lent a listening ear, when not driven too severely by the pressure of his other duties. The Superintendent was often absent on long journeys, and there was no one else to assist Dr. Tenny in visiting the numerous body of sufferers, and this immense amount of labor was quite too much for one person.

Indeed it was not the Superintendent, but his assistant, so far as I was ever able to see, that ever did any thing really beneficial for the patients. "Dr. Tenny does everything," "he does all the good there is done here," were expressions very often made by the ladies of our ward. Indeed he it was who did all the duties, he led the choir at the chapel, and did many other duties. I noticed that whenever he visited the hall, every eye was raised with respect, and it was sometimes amusing to see how the patients would throng around him with solicitations and requests; frequently so obstructing his path, that he could hardly get out of the hall. On one of these occasions, one of the patients pleasantly remarked. "We shall take you prisoner now, if you don't take care!"

It cannot be supposed that after such demonstrations, I could ever be an unobservant spectator of the scenes around me. I did feel a sympathy with the patients now, more than ever, and as hypocrisy I think is not included in the list of my faults,—could not forbear expressing that spontaneous sympathy, both by word and action.

I had now "passed the Rubicon, and burned the bridge," and consequently felt more loudly called upon than ever to find out all the wrongs of these oppressed ones from their own lips, and my own silent observation. What was thus elicited, I noted down from time to time in a private journal, and this book is the result.

My powerful enemy by this time had discovered that I was getting too intimate with some of the ladies who loved him as little as myself. Therefore, as in other wars, a prudent General sees it expedient, when practicable, to divide the enemy's battalions, in order to weaken their strength, so did *our* military commander now deem it for the interest of his campaign against the rights of psuedo "lunatics" to have me removed from this to a far less privileged and very disagreeable ward. Indeed it was now my doom to be conducted to the *maniac's ward!* the abode of the filthy, the suicidal, the raving and the furious! Dr. Tenny was assigned to do this ineffably mean business, as it appeared Dr. McFarland could not look in my face and do it himself, after the promises he had made to my brother and to me that I should be protected from danger and taken care of. No complaint whatever, as I afterwards learned by my attendants, had been brought against me, and every one in the hall, both attendants and patients knew that I had always cheerfully obeyed not only every rule of the hall, but every wish of the attenddants, and that I had been without exception exemplary and kind to them all.

The attendants therefore looked much surprised when they learned that I was to leave the hall. Dr. Tenny, in announcing his errand to me, used the blandest words possible. He evidently wished he had not been assigned so unpleasant a task. But why then did you do this Dr. Tenny? You knew that you was doing wrong, for you had repeatedly promised me in private conversations, that so far as you had the management of me, you would be governed by your own conscience, and not by Dr. McFarland's. Now I make no apology for saying to you, Dr. Tenny, that in this action you was not governed by your own conscience and by the Golden Rule of Christ, as in my distress, you promised you would be; no, your conscience never told you to add to the deep sorrows you knew that I was then suffering. You never felt that your duty to God impelled you to take me out of a comfortable hall, and put me into one where you knew that my feelings would be deeply lacerated and my feeble health still more enfeebled. You did this unjust and wicked action because Dr. McFarland ordered you to do it, and because you lacked the moral courage to refuse doing an unjust thing at the risk of your losing your place. I knew you was making work for most bitter repentance, when the day of your retribution should come, and that God would surely, sooner or later bring suffering in some way upon you for the same.

What if, instead of punishing an innocent woman, because your employer told you to do so,—you had stood up like a man, and a Christian, and said to him, "Dr. McFarland, I have seen nothing, nor have I reason to believe there is any good cause, why Mrs. Olsen should be assigned to the maniac's ward. She has done nothing to my knowledge deserving punishment, on the other hand, she is herself a great sufferer; she has appealed to me for sympathy and protection here, far from her friends and among strangers, and I must give it, as I have promised. Doctor I cannot obey you, I cannot add to the afflictions of this much suffering woman."

Had you taken this noble, this Christian stand Dr. Tenny, your own conscience would have smiled upon you. All the good would have approved your action, and you would for.

ever after have been a happier man. What if the Superintendent had turned you out of your place for refusing obedience to an unjust mandate? He could not have turned you out of your own approbation. He could not have excluded you from the kingdom of heaven.

I have hitherto given you ample credit for all the good that I saw in you, but I must also be just to truth, and though it pains me much, I cannot help writing as I think justice demands. But I forgave you Dr. Tenny, and tried to think you a good man, though a weak one, even after this sad occurrence.

With this arrangement I complied, without resistance, of course, remembering my engagement to Dr. McFarland, that I would obey all the rules of the Asylum.

I obtained permission of Dr. Tenny, to bid good bye to all the ladies in the hall. "You know," I remarked to him, "that I came into this hall like a lady, (not like a lunatic,) and in a decent lady-like manner I also wish to leave the hall. These ladies have become very dear to me by the sympathy and kindness they have invariably shown, and it pains me much to leave them. Yet I submit to the decree of the Superintendent."

On my approaching them one by one to bid them good-bye, they looked surprised and sad as they saw that I, who had ever been peaceable and obedient, was now ordered to this fearful ward. One of them said to me, by way of consolation, "Well, you will have a chance to get acquainted with Mrs. Packard there."

Mrs. Packard! that dear name! how little did I then know its import! How my heart throbs even now, at the sweet, the golden memories inseparably blended with that beloved name! This lovely, this angelic being.—I cannot speak or think of with any common emotions, nor is it possible for me to describe her with any ordinary adjectives,—this inestimable woman has proved to me the brightest star that ever shone around my dark path of life, since my lamented mother was laid away in her grave.

I must no longer now give vent to the spontaneous gushings of affection and gratitude which she has inspired; for it would carry me off in a tangent from my proposed attempt to give my bird's eye view of the horrible ward to which this most lovely of her sex, in common with myself, was assigned.

I will now introduce the reader to the highest part of the building, the Eighth Ward.

Escorted by Dr. Tenny, I was by him politely introduced to one of my new attendants,—Miss Belle Bailey. She impressed me quite favorably, seeming pleasant and kind. Indeed I will do her the justice to say that I never saw her appear otherwise to any one.

The next person who drew my attention was one of the unmistakeably insane, Mrs. McElhany. She instantly approached me, seized my dress, and attempted to raise it very rapidly, which of course made me shrink from her. I was astonished at this familiarity, but not alarmed, as Dr. Tenny sat down in the hall, and quietly made observations before leaving me.

I learned subsequently, that this most unfortunate woman was the oldest patient in the Asylum—I mean, had been there longer than any one—eighteen years—ever since the building was erected. I did not wonder that she was "an incurable" maniac. Yet she was sometimes quite amiable, often sensible and witty, but oftener quite the reverse.

She had been taken out of her room that I might take her former place in it, and she did not appear to like the arrangement. Probably she thought me an intruder, as she would every day, for several days, walk very near the room, and, casting furious glances at me, would rave and talk, and swear very loudly. What annoyed me still more, was that she was very immodest in her expression and gestures; and as I could neither quell nor divert her, I was obliged to endure the infliction.

In this hall were about thirty persons of various degrees both of sanity and of insanity. Some were mild and peaceful, others furious and raving; others deeply sad and silent melancholics, while a few never spoke at all, or did any work or manifested the least interest in any thing. Some were sick, but were all mixed up with the well, without having any proper attention paid to their wants. Some would persist in lying in bed though not apparently ill. When locked out of their rooms would lie upon the floor in the hall. Several were occasionally, exceedingly loud and ferocious, and while in this condition, it was unsafe to approach them. But I never feared any one in this hall, whatever might be their condition; because my acquaintance with such people had already taught me how to render them harmless.

I should like to present my reader with the deeply interesting histories of all these afflicted ones, but my limits forbid. I did not at this time, remain in the Eighth ward, quite three weeks, but as I afterwards returned and spent nearly eight months there, I had, at the second time, a much better opportunity to become personally acquainted. Our privileges here were far more limited than in the Seventh ward. Our evenings were all spent in darkness, except when the moon gave us that light, denied by the puny civilization of "Lunatic Asylums!"—as we were all locked up into our respective rooms very soon after supper. We had our choice there, to sit up alone without light or fire, or to retire to our often sleepless beds, as we chose. These rooms were comparatively unfurnished. A bed, with its indispensable appendages was all the furniture allotted to mine at first, but after a few days a chair was brought for my accommodation.

No books, not even the bible were allowed here by the Superintendent, but the attendants sometimes lent me books of their own, under restrictions. Dr. Tenny however gave me a privilege, denied to all the rest—viz: that of reading "Gibbon's Decline of the Roman Empire," a work I had never previously read.

I did not feel disposed to complain of the deprivation of those privileges afforded by the Seventh ward; I saw that the opportunity here afforded of studying a larger variety of mind would more than compensate the loss of my personal comforts. This being early in October, and the evenings long, I thought it better for my health not to retire directly after supper as did many of the rest; when not feeling too ill, I preferred to sit up till about nine or ten o'clock before retiring. This I presume was as pleasant to me as it would be to any one else thus to be banished to solitude for no crime but that of an excessive devotion to my husband. But it would be folly to stop and complain of this.

I always hated idleness, and much coveted employment in those long dark evenings, but I could not sew in darkness, and as Mrs. Packard had given me some nice yarn, I often amused myself by knitting. But darkness by no means implied silence in that ward, and some of the sounds I heard were agreeable. A few of my companions were pious, and used to sing in the darkness, very beautiful hymns, and often my ears would catch some very fine strains of poetry. Quite frequently, from the very forgiving, I heard prayers for their absent friends at home. These prayers from these persecuted victims of intolerance often brought tears to my eyes, so sublimely did they demonstrate the power of the Christian faith to give hope and comfort, when external circumstances forbade both. But it was oftener the case, that instead of hearing such delightful sounds, my ears were grated by "jarrings dire." I used to sit up for hours in darkness, to be entertained only by swearing, cursing, and still worse sounds from the vicious, in this ample hall.

On such occasions, I could not fail to think of my friends at home, enjoying in social circles, the blessings of fire, light, companionship and liberty. I thought of my self-desolated husband too; "how," queried I, "is he spending his evenings? What company does he prefer to mine, to cheer his loneliness? Is he thinking of me, as I of him?"

"Do they miss me at home, do they miss me?"

I once heard a wife exclaim in unreproachful agony, "husband, may you never know the doom of sorrow and of woe, you have assigned to me, who once shared your pillow!"

Then she broke out into sobbing and loud weeping, with which, as it perfectly coincided with my own feelings, I could not help sympathizing. We wept in concert, though separated by locks and keys. Did angels guard our husbands at home!—if so, what kind of angels?

One day I asked one of these banished ones, whom I had often heard lamenting the loss of her children, how many she had. "I do not know," replied she sadly, "two years ago, I had six lovely children. Oh, so beautiful, so obedient, so good! I wish you could see them. I hear nothing from them. I feel afraid some of them are dead." This was no uncommon case; many there have not been allowed to hear for many months from any of their friends, and the agony of mind thus caused, is not to be described.

I repeat with emphasis, this neglect or refusal, on the part of the friends at home, increases to a most painful degree, the anxiety and suffering of their banished ones. They have affection, as well as outsiders; it is a miserable delusion to assume that this is not the case.

When thus neglected year after year as many are, they often come to the conclusion that their friends are dead, or what is still more agonizing, that they have forgotten or ceased to love them—and often to this is added a fear, even yet more horrible—that they have been reported as "incurables," and are destined to drag out the residue of their lives, and then die there! When this last conviction, thus legitimately produced, takes possession of their minds, it rapidly accelerates the very condition they so much dread. Hope by degrees forsakes them; they no longer make efforts for their own preservation a dreadful languor ensues, inducing irrecoverable prostration and exhaustion, till death at last ends the sad drama! I have not the least doubt that this is a prominent cause of so many deaths occurring there.

I wish here to mention that the deaths are kept secret as possible. The body is carried away in the night, with no funeral, and either sent home or buried in the "Asylum" cemetery. In one of my walks, I counted eighty-seven graves in that little enclosure, which, on inquiry, I found had all been dug in less than four years,—though I had reason to believe that the great majority of those who die are not buried there, but conveyed to their former homes, in their coffins. How great the number of those who go there to find their "cure" in death, is more I imagine than is for the interest of Dr. McFarland to make public.

Then hurry on some cheap shroud—hustle them into a cheap coffin—don't stop for a funeral—where are the mourners? Take them from their cells to the dead-room—step quickly but carefully—make no noise—go out in twilight when no one sees; throw up the turf with hasty spade—and then by the trembling moonbeams aid, or "the lantern dimly burning" bury them darkly at dead of night! No minister—no weeping—no matter, *they are insane!*

> "Rattle their bones over the stones,
> They are lunatics that no one but 'Jesus owns!'"

V.

Dangerous experiments.

> "Whoever injures a man,
> Binds all men to resistance."—Dr. CHANNING.

One day I saw a woman in a room adjacent to my own, who was a melancholic, sitting on the bare floor, sewing for the "workroom," and looking extremely dejected and hopeless. I spoke to her, in the way I usually did to such, and coming quite near her, discovered that she had only one garment on. It was a very clean pink calico dress, and her naked feet were drawn up under her body, closely as possible, trying to get a little warmth. It was late in the season, and the weather cold and damp. I asked her why she did not wear suitable clothing. She replied, with great meekness, "they do not give it to me, and I don't know as I ought to ask for it." I then asked her, why she sat on the cold floor, being painted and uncarpeted, I thought it unsuitable for one so pale and sickly as herself. She replied, raising her eyes a little, but still sewing. "I haven't got any chair."

I stepped into my own room, and brought my chair, offering to lend it. She objected, not wishing "to rob" me. "Oh, as to robbery," I replied, "I have no robbery to complain of; I am excused from working for the Institution, while it seems that you are not. I am better clothed, and don't need a chair so much as you do, for when I wish to sew or write, I can sit upon my bed." With evident reluctance, she at last accepted the loan of my chair. "Now you are not a cat, but a woman," said I, "sit up in a chair then, like a woman, and I will try to have them get your clothing for you."

This lady Mrs. Gleason, of Chicago, was one of those extremely humble ones, who will give up their rights, because they feel unworthy to enjoy them. On looking at her head, I discovered a very obvious necessity for a comb.

"Why dont you comb your head? I think it might be useful."

"Do you think it is right to kill any thing that lives?" faintly interrogated this almost crushed-to-death victim.

"I think," replied I, "that if my head had become a pasture for such animals, I should kill them, soon as possible, without stopping to discuss the moral considerations." I said this with such a peculiar air and tone, that, in spite of herself, she actually stopped sewing, looked up from her work and half laughed. "Reason is not quite dead here, but it is evidently a good deal sick!" was my reflection.

I reported her condition to her attendants, but had reason to repent having done so, as I was told it was "no business" of mine. I replied that, "it did not appear to be the business of any one to take care of Mrs. Gleason, as no one attended to her except to set her to work, and I never could see the defenceless suffer, without trying to defend them."

One day I walked out, and by especial liberty, plucked a few flowers to carry to my room. On passing a window of the gentleman's "lower ward," I saw a pale gray-haired aged man, stretching out his thin hand, between his iron grates to me. "How do you do ma'am?" said he, very respectfully, but in a weak and rather tremulous voice. "You have been getting flowers; Oh, how beautiful they do look!"

"Yes father, do you never go out in the fresh air and get flowers!"

"No," he replied sadly.

What kind of a conscience, queried I, has he who thus can deprive an aged afflicted man from God's free gifts of air and the unbarred light of heaven? One too, whose "tedious days and nights of grief," are to be spent, like those of a criminal, within bolts and bars and prison walls? But no thought of this kind was expressed by me to him, but I cheerfully gave him all my flowers. His look of joy and surprise, as tears glistened in his aged eyes, I shall never forget! His fervent ejaculation, "God bless you!" was answered on the spot; for I was more happy thus to afford one gleam of joy to the lonely heart of this pale sufferer, than if a shower of golden coins had fallen on my path for my possession.

But again I had transgressed; again had been minding, I cannot say other people's since it was not other people's business; had it been so, I should not have made it mine.

Leaving my aged friend in rapture over his flowers, I hurried back to my hall. But I could not smother the boiling indignation with which I thought over this scene. I soon saw our protectress Mrs. Packard, at tea, and told her all about it. She said little, but from her intelligent eyes, I inferred that she thought I had gone too far for my own safety, in my demonstrations of sympathy for others. She was right; she knew better than I did, how far it would do to provoke our Superintendent by showing mercy to his suffering victims.

My health declined more rapidly here, than in the Seventh ward. It was impossible to have any refreshing sleep in the midst of so much noise, and in the sight of so much misery. My anxiety also increased to agony, as now a long time had elapsed since I had heard from home. I entreated Mrs. Mc-

Farland with tears of anguish—in the name of all that was sacred in human affections—to intercede with her husband, to restrict his severity, and let me send one letter at least, to mine. She cooly turned to one of the attendants and remarked—"If Mrs. Olsen gets troublesome, I think she will have to go down."

"Great God! what did I hear? Is it possible that a woman can thus treat my reasonable anxiety; has she no sympathy for my distress of mind? Will she punish me for the spontaneous expression of this suffering, by putting me down still lower in these gradations of torture? Can she think I do not suffer sufficiently in the maniac's ward?

The expression "going down," here means something well understood by negro slaves a few years since, who were sent "*down South* to Georgia."

Mrs. McFarland after this inhuman response to my entreaties, very suddenly rose and walked to the door. Before she had time to unlock it, I had quietly followed her, for seeing her still unrelenting, I could not restrain my weeping; it burst out in spite of myself. I promised the most perfect obedience to her own and the Doctor's slightest request of me so long as I remained, if she would persuade him to let me send just one letter home. I told her they might both read my letter, and they should see that I would not find fault or reproach them, &c. But she deigned no more replies, but pushed through the door slamming it heavily into my face, I sank powerless on the floor, in unutterable, silent, intense agony.

VI.

Breakers Ahead.

"But where's the passage to the skies?
The road through death's black valley lies."

In all my bitter experience at the Asylum, I never thought myself excused from duty. Though by a most calamitous series of misfortunes, cut off from the exercise of my social duties at home, and deprived of all society that had power to remove or abate my sufferings, yet I could not but see, all around me, the most irresistible calls for my sympathy and assistance. I could not sit idly dreaming, while so many were crying, with tearful eyes, "Oh, can not you do something for me?" I could not but respond to such thrilling calls, without ignoring every obligation which allied me to humanity. Here, indeed, was an open field; an opportunity I had long coveted, of trying to do good.

I now proceed to relate how I came to be again degraded; or in other words, "put down."

One afternoon, as Mrs. Packard was returning to her own hall in the same ward, I followed her in the public entry, a step or two, wishing to speak to her. I had not the slightest idea of giving offence to any one, or overstepping the bounds of my liberty. All of a sudden, Miss Mary Bailey, one of my attendants, came to me, and violently catching hold of my dress, dragged me away from Mrs. Packard. In utter astonishment, I asked Miss Bailey why she did this.

"You needn't speak to Mrs. Packard."

"But I was saying no harm whatever; and as the rest all speak to her, I supposed I had equal privileges. Why is this distinction made?"

She gave me no explanation whatever, but used insulting and abusive language, and on several occasions after this, dragged me about from room to room, as though I were a bag of potatoes, or some other commodity of mercenary speculation. Indeed I think I *was* a commodity of mercenary speculation.

Soon after this, there was a ball announced. I had always been allowed to attend the balls—indeed, freely invited; and not to my knowledge, had the Superintendent ever given orders to the contrary. I was not a dancer, but was very fond of attending those balls, because they afforded an opportunity to see much pleasant company from all the wards, and gave us a temporary diversion from our scenes of strife and misery. But on this occasion, Miss Bailey ordered me to "go to bed," while some of the ladies were engaged in preparing to go to the ball. I, of course, demurred; she caught me with fierce violence, dragged me to my room, and locked the door. I was astonished, for I had always treated her well, and with the kindest deference to her wishes. Her sister had never treated me ill, and I could not imagine why she should. I reflected a moment; then feeling that I could not endure such injustice, I said to her, in a pretty decided tone, through my lock and key:

"Mary Bailey, you know I have always been peaceable and kind to every one in the hall, both patients and attendants. I have daily assisted you in your duties gratuitously. I have taken the whole care of myself and of my room, and, even more than I have been able, have assisted others in their toils, and you are paid for the same. I have never been either disrespectful or unkind to any one, but always the reverse, as you well know. But you are daily abusing me, and treating me in a heartless manner. You have even torn my clothing, and I shall never mend it till I have shown it to Dr. Tenny, or to some of the State authorities. And now you are presuming to deprive me of privileges that I have always been allowed, and have never forfeited. Mary, I have borne your insolence till I can bear it no longer, and I am resolved to expose you; if within three days you do not apologise for this abuse, and atone for it by better conduct, I will make public the abuse you have shown to me."

Miss Bailey did not make any reply, though I had undoubtedly made myself heard. This was my first collision with an attendant. The next day I atoned for the speech I had made. She had reported me to Dr. McFarland, as an "unmanageable, mischief-making patient." On the strength of this edifying intelligence to that dignitary, he, without at all examining the matter, ordered Dr. Tenny to put me down into the lowest prison, or Fifth ward!

I had previously expressed a wish to Mrs. McFarland, to go and visit that ward, in order to become acquainted with its management. Her reply was very remarkable, and for a very especial reason, I wish the reader to remember and mark it.

"The Fifth ward," said she, "is very well managed. We have only females to take charge of the patients. They are very good girls, and take good care of them."

How these "very good girls" took care of their responsibilities, will appear in my next chapter.

VII.

The Fifth Ward.

" Hail horrors! hail infernal world!"

If the inhabitants of the Twentieth century should ever have the real condition of this terrible prison described as it now exists, and be informed of the purposes to which it is applied, they will not only see the perfect propriety of my quotation at the head of this chapter, but will regard this prison with the same feelings as we now do the Spanish Inquisition and its abettors and apologists.

As, under the guidance of the ill-fated Dr. Tenny, I descended the three long flights of stairs leading to this charnel house of human woe, I felt a dizzy heart-sickness which almost deprived me of the power of articulation. Was it a prescience of those "coming events," which "cast their shadows before," that affected me thus? I could not tell, but was only conscious of a faintness and weakness which nearly deprived me of the power of locomotion. I asked Dr. Tenny to give me a formal introduction to the attendant, having never seen her. He complied, and though her countenance had an expression of stern repulsiveness, I determined, if there was any goodness in her, to find it out. I would, by the patience and assiduous kindness of my own deportment, awaken and develop all of goodness and humanity that might possibly be found smouldering beneath the icy surface of her heart.

Perceiving that she was Irish, I remarked "Oh, you are an Irish lady; I love the Irish dearly; many of them have shown me much kindness. I know your people are kindhearted. Well, you may be sure that I shall give you no trouble. I always obey the rules, and try to help my attendants; indeed, Miss Bonner, I think you must have much work to do here, with so many to take care of, and perhaps I may be able to assist you some in your labor."

I thus attempted to conciliate, and enlist her kind feelings. But slander and hatred had taken fearfully the start of me. She replied, as I had said I should give her no trouble, "Indeed yee'd better not make me any trouble, it won't be well fur ye if ye do."

I confess I was "taken back a few miles!"

She continued, "yee's no better'n the rest on em; yee'r all jist alike here, un ye needn't ixpict iny better treatment un the rest on um git. Now ye jist set down (pointing to a hard stationary bench) un mind yer business. Yer the wust un the crazyest on em all in the hull Institution; yees a nuisance."

After this most amiable delivery, she stopped to take breath, and fearing she might again start on a fresh "heat," I immediately obeyed her, by sitting down in silence on the bench she had assigned me. I began to doubt my power over the insane. Here indeed I saw "the insane" without mistake, but I then thought, and never afterwards changed my opinion, that Lizzy Bonner was more insane than any one in her care! I did not fear them, with all their fury; but I confess I did fear her, with her much wilder fury! I had always some expedient by which I could easily disarm her very wildest maniacs, but I never could disarm or tame their far more ferocious keeper?

Beside me, sitting, or rather crouching on the same bench, were a few silent and very filthy women, with their one garment indecently torn, and a puddle of unfragrant water on the floor under their feet. Some, in more remote parts of the hall, were screaming fearfully, at which I did not wonder. If I had been a screamer, or at all nervous, I should doubtless have swelled the concert, so full was this pandemonium of every imaginable horror!

The faces of many were frightfully blackened by blows, received, partly from each other in their internecine conflicts, but mostly, I subsequently discovered by their attendants! One very fat old woman who could not speak in English, was sitting on the floor with a perfectly idiotic expression upon her face. One pale girl sat weeping bitterly, and shivering upon a bench with very thin clothing. Several were silent and appeared to take no notice of anything. These were melancholies in nearly the last stages of despair. One, in quite the last stage, as I inferred, was tied to her hard bench with her arms and chest tightly confined by a straight jacket, and attempting to commit suicide by fiercely beating her head back against the wall. The sight of this poor young female, in her frantic attempts to rush from an obvious hell into the untried scenes of an undiscovered future, was too appalling for me to gaze upon. I turned away my eyes with a sick horror, but still heard her pounding her bruised head.

No one here was working, for all capable of being made to work, were at this time engaged in some of the numerous toiling departments of the establishment. Some were lying on the floor, exhibiting the most indescribably indecent appearances.

The windows were all open; I was shivering with cold, being at this time, in the incipient stages of fever and ague. This disease was probably acquired by inhaling the "mephitic exhalations" of the Eighth ward. I drew my woolen shawl closely about my person, covering my head and eyes, from these terrific sights and sounds, and sat in dumb amazement. Is this, I silently ejaculated, the destiny to which I am doomed for an indefinite period? Oh, the insufferable anguish of those moments of horror! Language cannot portray it; it is utterly powerless. Every faculty of mind was intensified to the utmost, in those few moments of dumb tearless agony. It seemed as if my palsied heart must cease its beating. The past, the present, and the future all appeared in startling imagery before my spirit's eagle gaze, and the burning lines of Byron rose up uncalled, before my contemplation.

> "Feel I not wroth with those who placed me here
> In this vast lazar house of many woes?
> Where laughter is not mirth, nor thought the mind,
> Nor words a language, nor ev'n men mankind:
> Where cries reply to curses, shrieks to blows,
> And each is tortured in his separate hall—
> For we are crowded in our solitudes—
> Many, but each divided by a wall,
> Which echoes Madness in her babbling moods;—
> While all can hear, none heed his neighbor's call—
> None, save that one, the veriest wretch of all,
> Who was not made to be the mate of these.
> Feel I not wroth with those who placed me here?
> Who have debased me in the minds of men,
> Debarring me the usage of my own,
> Blighting my life in best of its career,
> Branding my thoughts as things to shun and fear?
> Would I not pay them back these pangs again,
> And teach them inward sorrow's stifled groan?
> The struggle to be calm?"
> —"*Lament of Tasso*," by BYRON.

Yes I did "struggle to be calm," and succeeded, in outside appearance, but "the iron entered into my soul," and still remains there. Oh, Mary Bailey! Dr. McFarland! If there is a just God, be sure that before you die, there is retributive sorrow in store for you, for the infliction of this unprovoked abuse upon one who never even attempted to injure you! Is it thus, proceeded my torturing queries, that I am rewarded, for having on all occasions here been the promoter of good order, of truth, and of peace—for having so often restrained the fury of the unmanageable, supported the weak, and tried at least to "comfort the mourner?" Is this the way in which the Superintendent of this " Asylum " fulfils his promises? If, as alleged, I am a victim of insanity, is this the way to *cure* it? No, no; and a thought of agony, such as words can never describe, shot like burning electricity through my paralyzed frame, " no, this is the way to make people insane, this is the way my tormentor has planned to make me insane."

At this crisis of advancing despair, hope suddenly came, and the inflexibly just poetry of Lord Byron was superseded by an extract of one of a more forgiving and tranquilizing tone—

> " Let not despair nor fell revenge,
> Be to thy bosom known;
> Oh, give me tears for other's woes,
> And patience for my own."

Here indeed were plenty of "others' woes," and plenty of " tears " in reserve for me to shed over them ! " Fear not," again whispered a sweet, secret voice, " when thou passest through the waters, they shall not overflow thee." "Yes, I will trust in God, there is now no one else to trust. Even Dr. Tenny has deserted me, I am indeed abandoned by every one on earth. But I will not sink, I will not die here; I will by virtue of the sublime omnipotence of will, conquer my enemies and retain my sanity, and self-possession too! Galileo did not die in his prison ; he said of the world "it still moves," and I know the world moves, and will yet move me to a better destiny. I cherished these consoling suggestions, ascribing them to him, from whom cometh "every good and every perfect gift."

But these pleasing and joyous contemplations were soon interrupted by the coarse voice of Bonner, screaming loudly from the opposite end of the long hall. She was obliged to scream very loudly, in order to be heard above the rest of the screamers.—" Miss Coalspit, come here."

Not supposing myself addressed, I did not move from my seat; she repeated, " Miss Coalspit I tell ye come here !"

Still I moved not, and began to wonder that neither did

any one else, in obedience to this imperative mandate. Observing me still motionless, she yelled out yet more furiously,
'You woman that's a settin there, with yer shawl all over yer head, I tell ye come here this minute.'

This last was a "trumpet" with no "uncertain sound!" I rose immediately, walked down the hall to where she was standing, and said in a low voice "Excuse me, Miss Bonner, I did not know you addressed me, as my name is not Miss Coalspit, but Mrs. Olsen."

"We call folks anything here, jest as happens; we don't stan' about bein' polite here to any on yees," she replied in a stormy voice.

So I perceive, but for myself, you will please excuse me from following this fashion. I have no more politeness than I need, I cannot dispense with any, but must use all I have, as I perceive politeness is rather needed here; what do you wish of me Miss Bonner?"

"I wish ye to take off that are shawl, ye don't need it here; the rest on em don't wear shawls, un you shan't."

"I am very cold—have taken the fever and ague, the chills are upon me now, and I fear sitting still with the windows open, as you say I must do, would in this very damp air, cause me to take cold; I should prefer to keep my shawl upon me for the present, if you please, Miss Bonner."

"I don't want any of yer talk; take it right off this minute, ur I'll save yees the trouble—folks have to mind here, I tell ye,—so be quick."

Seeing her fiercely approaching me, I immediately gave her my shawl, walked once more to my seat, and again sat down still, as she had ordered me to do. In this prison was exacted the most immediate and uncompromising obedience to rules and requirements which a slave holder would have blushed to inflict upon his human chattels. Our own preferences were never consulted. "You must do this because I want ye to," was all the reason given.

Does the public think this a good way for lost sanity to be regained? Alas, what has the public hitherto known about it? There is absolutely no escape from obedience here, no matter what is required. I have many times, seen even tardy or reluctant obedience punished with fearful severity; I have seen the attendant strike and unmercifully beat on the head, her patient's with a bunch of heavy keys, which she carried fastened by a cord around her waist; leaving their faces blackened and scarred for weeks. I have seen her twist their arms and cross them behind the back, tie them in that position, and then beat the victim till the other patients would cry out, begging her to desist. I have seen her punish them by pouring cold water into their bosoms, a pailful at a time, leaving it to dry without changing their wet clothing, the remainder of the day, several hours; I have seen her strike them prostrate to the floor, with great violence, then beat and kick them. At other times I have seen Elizabeth Bonner after throwing them down, their faces to the floor, pull them back and forth by the hair, and beat the noses and faces repeatedly upon the floor; I have seen her kneel upon their bodies and strike and pound them, till by struggling and crying, they became too weak to make resistance, then dragging them to their rooms, would lock them up for many hours, leaving them alone. I have seen her do all this too, without any proof that they had been guilty of what she had accused them. And even when others had accused them, she was always more ready to believe the accuser than anything the accused could say in self-defence. In this way, this Jury, Judge, and Executive of her own laws, went on using the powers her position as head attendant gave her under the direction and command of Dr. Andrew McFarland! "our accomplished Superintendent!"

It was not rarely and occasionally, but hourly and continually, that these brutalities occurred. There was not a single day, of the twenty days I staid there, that I did not witness scenes of this character. Sometimes it appeared that I must turn away; that I could not endure to see human beings thus abused. But the next thought was one of self-accusation for being thus tender to my own feelings. "If these sufferers can bear to feel it, I can and will bear to see it said I, for if I do not see these things, I cannot testify that I did. So I will even look on." But this resolution I confess did sometimes break down, for I was often so much shocked that I had to turn away my eyes, and many times I stuffed both my ears as full as possible, with locks of cotton to deaden the noise of demoniac shrieking of these victims when under torture.

One day I became so indignant that I summoned courage, and told Mrs. Bonner that if she did not stop abusing the patients in this way, I should tell Dr. McFarland of it. "Dr. McFarland knows all about it said she, I don't do anything here, but what he knows it all, and he tells me to manage the patients here by my own judgment, and I intend to do as he tells me. So you can mind your own business."

I silently resolved on that occasion that my "own business" should be to gather up in memory, and then, when the right time came, sooner or later, to bring to light, all these "deeds of darkness." And this dear reader, is the way I am minding my "own business" even now.

But I told her then that I should talk matters over with Dr. Tenny when I could get a chance to see him, and intimated that I should give him some edifying information of how matters went on. Also that in due time Mrs. Packard should be informed of these affairs.

"You shan't tell Mrs. Packard, she's a lady, and you're a nuisance; you ain't fit to speak to her."

"But she loves me," said I, "if I am a nuisance, she gave me this chain," pointing to a beautifully wrought white chain which I then wore upon my neck. "She gave me this to wear as a pledge of her attachment to me, and I shall wear it every day, for her sake."

Lizzy "looked daggers," at this discovery, and had it not been for the great popularity of Mrs. Packard there, I think she would have robbed me of this beautiful ornament, as I have seen her rob others of gold ornaments. At that moment, I was wearing garments which Mrs. Packard had lent me in the Eighth ward, as my own under garments had been stolen from me, and divided among some of the employees in the Asylum. As soon as "Liz" knew I was wearing borrowed garments of Mrs. Packard, she compelled me to take them off and give them to her, to be returned to Mrs. Packard, saying that it was against the rules for one patient to borrow of another. I said "I wish it was against the rule, to let the servants steal the clothing from the patients." But this I said in my own heart, not vocally.

The loss of these garments, added to the robbery of my shawl, caused me to shiver continually. In a few days, the fever and ague was so established, that I became at last nearly prostrate. When again I saw Dr. Tenny, I told him how I constantly shivered for the loss of my clothing. He ordered Lizzy to restore my shawl immediately, which she did; my stolen garments were not returned. After this, Lizzy appeared to hate me with a bitterness that was truly appalling. She tried in many ways, to provoke me to ill temper, as I supposed, in order to frame some complaint against me, or to have some excuse for abusing me. But I determined she should have not even the semblance of justification for the wanton insults with which she first met, and almost uniformly ever afterwards treated me, especially while in the lowest prison ward. I resolutely governed my temper, persevered in obeying instantly her slightest commands; and always addressed her with tones of mildness and conciliation. She never in the Fifth ward, used any violence with me, but assured me, of her readiness to do so, in case I dared to disobey. As she saw to her sorrow, that there was some danger of Dr. Tenny protecting me, she was obliged to refrain from actually striking me, but calmed off occasionally some small portion of her ever boiling fury, by shaking her fists, and annoying me with all the little petty persecutions possible.

VIII.

Purgatorial experiences.

"You will never mend till more of you are burned."

In my dialogue with Lizzy Bonner, already referred to, I had given her to understand that I should lay these matters before Dr. Tenny the first opportunity. She replied, that if I interfered, I should "git the same treatment the rest on 'em git." I was so closely watched, however, that no opportunity occurred for a long time, in which to tell Dr. Tenny. Dr. McFarland seldom came into the Fifth ward, and when he did, would pass directly through the hall, without ever, to my knowledge, stopping to show the least sympathy, or the least attempt to relieve the sufferings so dreadfully apparent in every face. We used to say that Dr. McFarland's nose was too delicate; he didn't seem much to enjoy the *smell* of the Fifth ward. We didn't blame him for that; we only blamed him for making us endure it.

Once, and only once, he insulted me by coming into my room. He gazed at me with a kind of an oyster-like expression; and, at last, when he had gazed sufficiently, said, in a tone of affected wonder and commiseration, "Mrs. Sophia B. Olsen!" I stood erect before his gaze, and deigned not to speak a single word, but *gave him a look of reproach and defiance*, which I intended should say, "You have not hurt me, and now it is too late to hurt yourself in my credit." I then looked significantly at the door, and for once he did a sensible thing, which was to immediately take himself out of my sight. I could bear the looks of even Lizzy Bonner, with all her hateful ferocity—could even speak kindly to her; but after the repeated demonstrations of heartless treachery I had received from her master, McFarland, I could not endure the looks of him for a single moment. Indeed, for nearly two months, I avoided him as I would a snake; it seemed as if his very presence in the hall would throw me into convulsions.

Mrs. McFarland used frequently to visit the ward, and sometimes would sit down and talk with me, and with others. She was generally pleasant, and used to laugh a good deal. I very rarely saw any indications of either pity or sympathy in her. She used to say, "Oh, I hear so many stories; one has one trouble, another, another trouble. I can not help it. I didn't bring you here, and it is not I who keep you here," &c. I think Mrs. McFarland is not naturally cruel or heartless; but she was not free then; she was a subordinate as well as the attendants, and had very little power over the patients. She would often say, when earnestly appealed to, "I have no power to grant your wish; ask the Doctor. It isn't as I say about things."

My own unconquerable pride would not permit me ever to tell her how I suffered in that prison, and with what intense abhorrence I regarded all the *modus operandi* there. I affected a stoical indifference to my fate, and never made the least complaint to her, or expressed any desire to return to the Eighth or Seventh wards. I thought of the apostle Peter in prison, who said, "Let them come themselves and fetch us out." But I did not feel thus with respect to my fellow patients; but plainly told Mrs. McFarland just what I have here been telling the public, about the brutalities of "Lizzy" Bonner. I also tried to appeal to her feelings of sympathy for her husband's honor, which I thought was in danger of some "trifling discount," when these things would be, as they surely must be, made known to the world. I used every argument, every possible persuasion I could summon, to induce her to curtail or end the power of Lizzy there. But my efforts with Mrs. McFarland proved as powerless as they had ever been with her indomitable husband.

I could now do nothing more than to spend my utmost care for the preservation of my life and sanity, and to learn all I could, by observing the phases of life around me.

One day I noticed, in one of the small rooms, a very pale and quiet young lady sewing. She was neatly dressed, and her room very clean and tidy. She was stitching on a very fine shirt bosom. I was much surprised to see her in prison. Observing me lingering at her door, she very politely invited me to walk in, which I was glad to accept. It was a relief to get out of the noisy hall, and my own room afforded me no quiet. I soon entered into conversation with this young person, and found her highly intelligent and ladylike in her manners. I was glad to keep up her acquaintance, and by her invitation, visited her every day in her room. I found rich treasures in her mind, fully repaying all the attention I gave her. She had been left an orphan in infancy, and had been always a child of poverty and sorrow; yet the nobility of her nature had ever inclined her, with a yearning aspiration, towards "the good, the beautiful, the true." She possessed warm affections, and had met with sad disappointments, sometimes, in the object to which this confiding love of her pure nature was directed. She related her sad history to me very freely, though without the least attempt, apparently, to throw herself upon my sympathies. She expressed no reproach, or even dislike to any one; made no complaints of the sufferings or deprivations of her present forlorn condition. She was never allowed any amusement or relaxation; never attended chapel prayers, balls, walks, or rides. But every day, not even excepting the Sabbath, with her ever busy fingers, it was "stitch, stitch, stitch, from weary morn till night."

She would even, when the bell rang to call us to meals, sew to the last minute, then actually run down the hall to the dining hall, swallow her meal hastily, then run back to her room, catch up her needle, and continue her work till day was done and twilight had darkened. By sewing thus rapidly and incessantly, she accomplished an almost incredible amount of work for the Institution. I asked her her motive in toiling so incessantly, expressing my fears that her health would suffer by such application. She replied, "Mrs. McFarland is going to pay me for making these shirts."

"How many have you made? Do you keep an account of them?"

"Oh no, but I suppose they keep account, and I suppose 'twill be all right."

Poor child! She had been deluded into the belief, that by thus constantly toiling for the "workroom," she had been laying up a fund for herself that would hasten her removal, for she was very desirous to leave the "Asylum." I did not undeceive her, feeling that the opposing influences were too strong against us both. This unfortunate person was indeed "laying up a fund," but it was a fund of future sickness, of sorrow, and bitter disappointment. This course of life, also did, indeed, "hasten her removal," but it was a removal from earth!

In one of my interviews, she asked if I could not obtain some books for her. "Oh, it is so long since I have seen any kind of a book! I do so long to get hold of something to read, if its nothing but an old almanac; do try to get me something, won't you?" I responded, "I am not now allowed to read myself; my last book has been taken away, but I will watch every opportunity, and if possible, will bring you something to read." She thanked me fervently.

I felt deeply distressed for the unhappy doom of this lovely young person, and much feared that a continuation of Dr. McFarland's present "treatment of her case," would terminate in an "incurable" insanity. In the course of a few months, my worst apprehensions were realized in the most fearful manner. I once asked her attendant why Miss Hodson never went out of doors. She replied, "because she used to be so ugly when we let her go out; she wanted to go off, and once undertook to run away, and now she ain't a goin' out any more. It's too much trouble to git her back."

How strange that she wants to run away! Do you think, my reader, that in such circumstances you would not wish to run away? Do you think you could be contented to go and stay there? If so, I pray you, then, go and stay there The world can spare you.

IX.

Satan's Representative.

"Remote, unfriended, melancholy, low."

Among those which are the most "remote" from human sympathy, the most "unfriended" and "melancholy" of all the sons or daughters of sorrow, I certainly consider the victims of the Jacksonville "Asylum" prison. Of these, I shall now briefly describe a few:

The first on my list, a little child—there known as "little Dilly," only about nine years of age. Even the young "lambs of the flock" (I wonder whose flock,) packed into this abode of torment! She eats, drinks, exists and sleeps in companionship with these dreadful beings. She had learned of her companions the elements of the most demoralizing education—taught by our noble State authorities, through their most "accomplished Superintendent." This little child has learned to curse, to swear, and to use obscene expressions with a volubility that would shock a sailor or a pirate! I heard she had a bad temper, and had learned to swear before she went there. Indeed! then why was she not sent where she might have a chance to reform, instead of having such manners confirmed, and made irreclaimable?

If a farmer has in his flock a diseased sheep or other animal, does he confine it with other sick ones in some small pen? No; he knows better how to take care of even the brutes. I wish the State of Illinois knew better than thus to maltreat and "pen up" the bodies and souls of helpless childhood! I expressed a wish to be permitted to have "little Dilly" a short time with me each day that I might teach her to read, but could not get the least attention to my request. They would not trouble themselves, so much as to give a decent refusal, but spurned my proposition with contempt. Is there not an old-fashioned and very unfashionable Book, somewhere, that speaks about "taking away the key of knowledge, neither entering in, nor suffering others to enter?" Is this the way to "suffer little children" to come to Christ?

Mrs. Hays.

My description of this prison would be very defective, if I neglected to describe this person. She was one of the most remarkable specimens of humanity I ever saw. Active, bold, furious, frantic in the extreme; profane, indecent and horrible in all those actions which justify such adjectives, equally in the extreme. Yet, anomalous as it may appear, this singular individual would at times, evince a disposition of kindness and benevolence, so strongly marked, so tenderly expressive, as often to excite in my mind the sincerest admiration as well as astonishment. She was so active and apparently strong, she would run, and dance, and jump along the halls with the dexterity of a bounding deer. We used to say she actually flew.

Her attendant kept her almost constantly at work at the coarsest drudgery. But she would find time every day to visit every one of the patients in the hall. She fancied herself the supervisoress; and as such would examine their condition and clothing to see what was needed. This of course she did on her own responsibility, as, though she was very skilful in finding out the wants of the rest, she was not equally skilled in supplying those wants. I was willing she should visit me, for she really supplied me with many comforts, and by her wonderful adroitness, procured many privileges; had it not been for her timely aid, I should have suffered much more than I did. But, unfortunately, she was much addicted to using tobacco, and would eject the superfluous perversion of the gastric juice all over the floor, and the walls of her room, with a liberality, which, to a decent woman, must be truly appalling. It certainly appalled me, when, to my utter consternation I discovered that this room was assigned to me!

In this most filthy place, I could not breathe without nearly strangling, but I was assured that the room was "good enough fur yees." Sick and enfeebled as the ague had made me, I yet felt more able to scrub and clean, than to breathe and sleep in this terrible Pandora's box as it was. I very mildly asked of my attendant the privilege of procuring from the washroom a pail of hot water and soap, with which to clean this room. She granted this favor, and I was overjoyed, having feared that I was to be locked in here as it was. I began my task, proceeding gradually as my strength allowed, to scrub and make clean this filthy room, so far as I was able to reach the walls upward. The remainder I was obliged to leave unfinished. But the floor I made quite clean, with abundance of water and soap scrubbing, so that before night the room was really quite tolerable. One of the insane, who was allowed to go out, had the kindness to bring a nice boquet of beautiful flowers, which I accepted gratefully, and placed in my partly darkened window. I looked upon these beautiful expressions of good-will with real pleasure,—a pleasure bestowed by the sweet ministrations of our gentle mother nature.

What a poor fool I was, to imagine for a moment that such a privilege would be allowed me! As soon as Lizzy came along, she rushed up to my flowers, jerked them out of the room in an instant, without saying a word, then giving the door a bang with her keys, vanished out of my sight. I dared make no remonstrance "lest some worse thing might come to me." The next day, lo, a worse thing did come! Seeing how tidy and clean I had made the room, she informed me she wanted that room for another patient. Before I had time even to look up in astonishment, I was jerked out of it, with as little ceremony as had been my unfortunate flowers the previous day. Opening another door, into another horribly filthy room, she said "this is to be your room now." I shall not attempt to portray my feelings on this occasion!

With much abated strength, and now rather waning hope, again I procured soap and other etceteras, and repeated the cleaning process of the previous day.

I was allowed only two days to *enjoy* (?) this room before I was again driven into one still worse! These "petty persecutions" continued till the attendant saw that I had no strength left with which to scrub. Then she put me into a "screen-room" as it is termed, and there I remained the time I staid in this ward.

One day I heard a dreadful noise, worse by far, than any I had previously heard. It appeared that for some trifling offence, disputing with an attendant I believe, Mrs. Hays had incurred the anger of Lizzy Bonner, who now was punishing her. She tore off, one after another, every single article of clothing from her victim. She did this with so much haste, that she tore the under woolen garment into several pieces, and threw the pieces about the floor. Then when perfectly nude, the attendant kicked her body till she had crowded her quite under a stationary bench, when Mrs. Hays curled herself up in a heap, so to speak.

Lizzy's back was turned to me; she did not know I was "taking notes." I stood paralyzed on witnessing these barbarities, silent and motionless, transfixed with a cold creeping horror, "Oh God." exclaimed I, "in the deep abyss of my soul, "while with dumb lips I quailed." Is it thus that thy children must suffer? "how long, Oh Lord, how long?" The screams of the sufferer were so terrific, and the blows she received so much more terrific, that at last I turned to leave the scene, feeling that I could no longer endure to see it. But in one instant,—as if more than mortal strength come to my aid,—I thought, "if this sufferer can bear to feel them, I will train my selfish nerves to look on. Because, if I do not see these things, I can never say that I saw them, and as they do exist, I wish to be able to testify." I silently prayed that death would come to the suffering Mrs. Hays, and relieve her from further torment. But she did not die, for her time had not come. Neither did I die, "for my time had not yet come." We both had an errand to this earth which had not yet been finished. Mrs. Hays after this did many acts of kindness for me which I have not time to here describe, and notwithstanding the bad points I have named respecting her. I must in justice say that I am not certain but she really saved my life.

After Lizzy had beaten, and pulled her hair, and kicked her, to her perfect satisfaction, she dragged her across the hall, into an empty room, and after telling her that "she shouldn't have any supper," left her entirely naked, locked up alone. Mrs. Hays made no reply; she seemed evidently much weakened; I had no idea that she could live till morning, for I did not then know how far the endurance of human suffering could be carried. I said nothing to any one. A heavy cloud like the gloom of a funeral in a stormy day was upon my spirit. I felt as though the power of human language had left me, and I quietly glided back to my screen-room. I saw at supper time while passing her door on my way to the dinning hall, that two other very insane women had now been locked up with Mrs. Hays. Their door was only half a door, the upper part being an open iron frame like a window frame, so that one on passing, could see all within. Indeed this was just like my own door at this time, so that I had no protection, not even that of a whole door to defend me from the horrid sounds, sights, and smells of this **truly** Purgatorial abode.

"But why are these three dangerous women locked up together," was my query. I believe it was done so that in case the black spots which the blows of Lizzy had made upon the face of her victim should not disappear in comfortable season, their infliction might be ascribed by the attendant to the two fierce patients locked up there with her! I went to my supper table sadder than I had ever felt. The terrible sights I had seen followed my vision and destroyed my appetite. I managed to steal a buscuit from the table, intending to slip it through her bars to the suffering Mrs. Hays, as I passed her door on returning to my own room; but Lizzy, who I believed suspected something of the kind, followed me closely, drove me into my room, and locked my door for the night.

X.

The Resurrection.

"If I ascend up into heaven, thou art there."

It is time to conduct my readers out of this horrible ward, and I am sure they think so too. I might write a large volume, describing scenes of cruelty and injustice quite equal to any here detailed, but my limits will not allow.

My health had now become extremely enfeebled; I could not sleep except when utterly prostrate from long wakefulness, nature could hold out no longer. It was my practice to stuff cotton into my ears to deaden the sounds of the terrible shrieks which came from all directions. This cotton was furnished by Mrs. Hays voluntarily; she used to procure it by stealth, telling me to put it into my shoes to keep my feet warm. But the cotton had not power to solace even one brief hour, for the dreadful sounds would find avenues to my ears. I thought I must either become insane, from the long pressure upon my brain, caused by these influences, or must die of brain fever, so terrible was the pain in my head.

As a last resort, in my persistent endeavors to counteract these influences, and thus protect my sanity, I used to rise in the night, from my recumbent position, and sit up with these large wads of cotton bound tightly about my ears, at the same time vigorously pressing my head and face downwards to divert the blood from the cerebral veins. I had already begun to experience symptoms of congestion of the brain. One night while much distressed by such apprehensions, an unusual lassitude crept over me, and ere I was aware, was actually lost in the sweet unconsciousness of slumber. I was not in heaven, though, in this enviable hour of rest, I dreamed I was there, but in the midst of my rapture over the thought that such a lingering death as I had been suffering, was now indeed "swallowed up in victory," lo! a fierce and rapid succession of far other sounds than "the songs of the redeemed," convinced my reluctantly waking eyes that I was not yet, as I had hoped, "on the other side of Jordan!" "Oh God! Oh God! let my tormentors be swallowed up forever in the lake of fire and brimstone," shouted with terrific loudness, a sufferer of about twenty years of age. Her room was but a few feet from my own. She continued with vociferations of this character, as long as she had breath. Before this song was ended, it had awakened and excited another patient opposite, who, angry to have her temporary sleep thus disturbed, screamed out, "Yes, I mean to send McFarland's soul to hell; there it shall be roasted and burned for thousands, millions, millions, trillions, trillion years." This too was many times repeated, as she emphasized and prolonged the first syllable, m-i-l-l-ions m-i-l-l-ions.

Thus this aged woman and the young girl, the fiercest in the hall, tortured my brain, and in the same way almost every night of my stay in this ward; till in my iron determination *not* to become myself insane, I actually discovered a method of effectually fighting against Dr. McFarland's seeming decree that my sanity should become annihilated!

I relate it for the benefit of any readers who may possibly be placed in similar circumstances. Finding that sleep was out of the question, with such a jargon about my head, I resolved to neutralize the effect of such sounds by reversing the current of their ideas; by calling to my aid with a violent effort of will, opposite ideas. Sitting up, erect in my bed, with as loud a voice as I could possibly command, to help to drown these opposite voices, I repeated passages of the most beautiful and attractive poetry I had ever learned in former years.

These daily distractions, added to the intense mental exertions of these my midnight labors, had now perfectly prostrated my health. At last I was unable to rise from my bed. I can not find words to express the intensity of feeling with which I wished my friend Mrs. Packard might be allowed to come from the Eighth ward and visit me. But I knew better than to ask this indulgence. I would as soon have asked any of my key-holding "powers that be" for liberty to rap at the gate of heaven, to call down the angel Gabriel to see me—I should have had no less probability of success. Indeed, if by any mortal or immortal agency, Mrs. Packard had been allowed to "descend into hell" to visit me at that time, I hardly think, so intoxicating must have been my joy, that I should have known any difference between herself, and an angel from heaven!

But I was now really sick and helpless. What could I do? I had a fever, but knew no one to do anything for me. Dr. Tenny was absent much of the time, but when he did visit the hall, my ever busy tormentor, Lizzy Bonner, would generally contrive to take up the whole of his time directing him to other scenes, in order to keep him away from me. Besides I had a suspicion all the time that he felt guilty for having allowed his better nature to bow to McFarland's most wicked command for my imprisonment there. It was my impression that Dr. Tenny did not wish to give me an opportunity to give him that just reproach that he well knew he deserved. But he did not understand my nature. I did not feel like reproaching him, though he had betrayed the great confidence he knew I had reposed in his honor, I felt too much grief to entertain reproach or revenge.

My attendant that morning, missing my presence at the table, called to my room, and said, "Ain't ye up yit?" "I am sick, Elizabeth," replied I. "Please excuse me, I can not go to the table, and do not wish to eat." Perceiving my inability to rise, she brought me a plate of baked pork, and hot biscuit! I thanked her, but declined, telling her it was impossible to eat it. She seemed angry, though my manner to her was perfectly gentle as it had ever been. She hastily responded, "The rest on 'em don't complain; its good enough fur 'em they think; un it's good enough for ye too, so ye'll eat that or git nothin." I preferred to "git nothin." I then very mildly asked her if she would bring me a cup of weak tea without sugar, or, if that was not convenient, a glass of cold water. She replied, "If yee's too good to eat sich as the rest on 'em cat, I won't bring ye nothin more." So shutting my half-door with a bang, she left me.

But as it seems "my time had not yet come to die," I rallied, and in two or three days, became able again to leave that bed of pain, and go out into the hall. But as neither rest nor safety was to be found there, I again went to my room. Here, being so weak, the intrusion of the noisy was more annoying than ever; being now unable to either amuse them or attract them out of my room, as I had often done before. They would persist in pulling over everything in the room, then, in the same manner, would examine my person, put their hands into my pocket, and feel of my head, making themselves, in spite of the best efforts I could make to get rid of them, most disgustingly familiar. They would overhaul the work, which even here, I still tried to do; often taking away parts of it, causing much disturbance. In other moods of mind, they fancied me their enemy, and would inflict punishments like Lizzy Bonner, on their own responsibility. Sometimes they would strike me suddenly, knock me down, and often spit upon me, either in my face, or upon my hands or garments, as suited their convenience. Sometimes they annoyed me still worse by trying to pull my clothing from my person, declaring it was theirs, and I had stolen it from them.

These, as I subsequently learned, were not the ordinary specimens of "insane people," but rare and extraordinary specimens of distorted humanity; no less indeed than the State's incendiaries and thieves who had been brought from the State's Prison and from the Penitentiary of Illinois! Who can wonder that Elizabeth Bonner thought they were as good as I was, and entirely appropriate companions for me, when Dr. McFarland had assigned me to their companionship! She was only a tool in his hands to carry out his purposes.

But now in my present condition of weakness, I ventured to humbly ask her to lock me up alone in my room in the day time, explaining how they annoyed me, and promising if she would comply with my request, that I would help her again about her work all I could, as soon as I was well. But she refused, saying, "what business had ye to be here then? ye ain't crazy, un ye must have been ugly, or yur friends wouldn't put ye into sich a place as this, I ain't a goin tu run round ahter ye, un ye needn't be complainin iny more to me. If they kill ye, 'tis likely ye deserve it." So I concluded that though locks and keys were always ready to be used against me, yet never could they be used for my protection or advantage.

Therefore, as now I could not defend myself from their fury while sitting up, and feeling very sore and lame, from their blows, I felt no longer able to fight so unequal a battle, and now retired to my bed in the day time covering myself as closely as possible, to protect my head from the danger of their blows. My attendant did not allow such indulgence long, but soon ordered me to "git up, and not muss up the bed in the day time." I rose mechanically, and once more, with but half an armor, endeavored "to win my desperate way." So, on and on I struggled daily, never for a moment losing sight of my original determination to learn all the mysteries of "Lunatic Asylums!"

Day after day, three times each day, did the great "Asylum" bell summon us to take our meals for the protraction of wretched existences. Such a crowded table! More than seventy women in all degrees of sanity and of insanity, of virtue and of vice, and of every gradation between these extremes,—promiscuously huddled,—jammed, literally crammed together at these tables! All wanted to have "their say,"· except a few silent ones, who rarely spoke at all. I was, on these occasions generally silent, in order the better to observe the practical application of "our accomplished Superintendent's" method of applying the "Physiology of Dietetics" to the restoration of diseased intellects!

His system was directly at war with those systems of the present age that are most approved by those enlightened reformers who have made the laws of health a special study.

None of these, I believe recommend the abundant eating of pork for feeble and sickly people. They do not recommend eating supper of hot biscuit in the quickest possible haste, and then rushing immediately to bed. But this was practiced there, always in the Fifth ward. We were often commanded to "hurry! hurry up! I want to clear the table, then take your biscuit to your room and finish it there." Sometimes I have seen half a dozen or more at a time running with a half-munched hot biscuit in hand to their bed-rooms, while the attendant was behind, impatiently swinging her keys ready to lock them in.

Perhaps Messrs. Fowler, Wells and others had better employ Dr. McFarland to write a series of articles in their popular health journal, describing the benefits of his new system of dietetics. I think he might throw some light which never on this subject has illuminated their pages! The Doctor is a scientific man, and of course acquainted with the laws of health. Now, I want him to explain to "the dear people," the peculiar benefits of suppers of hot biscuit, with tainted butter being "hurried" down the throats of diseased patients; then, of their going to bed in a small room full of miasma from all manner of noxious exhalations, oppressed with every emotion of disgust, anger and grief, that such a system can impose. Let him describe their impotent attempts at slumber, and their frequent nightmares. The public ought to know the peculiar benefits of such a system, and I am aware of none so well calculated to show these benefits as " our accomplished Superintendent."

Whenever I walked from my "screen room" to my meals; to the wash-room, indeed any where, I had to "watch therefore" how I should step, in order to escape some of the "dangers" which, in the language of a well known religious poet, "stand thick o'er all the ground, to push us to the tomb." If I went too near an old lady, Mrs. Triplet, who always sat in one place by which I was obliged to pass on my way to meals, she would brandish her arms and curse and swear loudly threatening to kill me. If, in my attempts to escape her, I came too near another on the opposite seat, (both of whom spent most of their time, sitting on their seats) the latter would discharge a load of spittle, which she had previously prepared for my reception, into my face, or about my person. So I was each moment, obliged to study how to so adjust my steps as to escape this Scylla and Charybdis. I found it necessary also to appear to be careless, and to conceal from all the fact of my using such vigilance. I did literally walk in a straight and narrow way.

My position here constantly reminded me of that locality, so graphically described by Bunyan, the "Valley of Humiliation," where Christian, at every step encountered "gins, traps, pits and snares." These were ever menacing my progress, and often caused me internally to exclaim, "Why am I made to possess months of vanity, while wearisome nights are appointed unto me." But "there is an end to all earthly things," it is said, and I here add my testimony that there is also an end to some unearthly things. According to previous arrangements, of Mrs. McFarland and Lizzy Bonner, it was now officially announced in the hall, that the latter was to take about fourteen of her patients up to the Eighth ward in a few days. This of course created a great sensation, and the query became general "who is going?" "Is it I?" So, while yet unable to sit up all day, I joyfully emerged with the rest, and in due ceremony, we were conducted to the very highest part of the building. The room assigned me was in the north end of the hall. It was a very cold room, exposed to the winds, and far from the fires, all of which were in a cellar below all the halls.

It was well for me that I could not then anticipate the suffering which the coming winter had in store for me. I had no expectation of being obliged to spend the winter there.

In this hall I could work; so my former employments were again resumed, but I suffered so much from chills and fever, it was comparatively little that I was able to do besides taking proper care of my room, and keeping my clothing in good repair. I soon saw Dr. Tenny, and prevailed upon him to let me resume the study of Roman history, which had been interrupted while in the lowest prison ward. He again brought me "Gibbon's Decline and Fall of the Roman Empire." The only way I could preserve this book from being taken from me by some of the wilder ones in the hall, was to keep it constantly about my person. I made a strong bag for the purpose, tied this to my apron strings, and when not reading always placed the book in it, carrying it to my meals and every where I went, when obliged to leave my room. In this way I managed to read five volumes of that immortal work, and found it productive of much pleasure by giving an agreeable diversity to the sadness of a prison life. I name these circumstances to show how difficult it is, in such a place, to cultivate or improve, or even benefit one's mind. Yet this is supposed to be a place where even disordered minds are restored to order. Oh humbug! what is thy name? where is thy representative?

Our ascent to the Eighth ward occurred in the morning. When the dinner hour arrived, and I again saw the tranquil beaming face of my beloved friend, Mrs. Packard, I longed to throw myself into her arms, and weep with joy upon her bosom.

She was affected in the same way as were many others respecting the abusive treatment to which the patients were subjected. Yet she did not see the worst forms of this cruelty. The attendants dared not in her presence perpetrate these. She honestly expressed her feelings both to them and to the officers on this subject. When her eloquent, yet intensely gentle and tender voice was raised in the defence of the suffering ones around her, every other voice was hushed. We all knew she "was a host" in herself, and many of the "insane," possessed yet sufficient sanity to recognize in her their future deliverer.

The hand of this our dear friend was ever ready to administer acts of beneficence, so far as her restricted privileges would permit; her voice to soothe, to cheer and to sustain;

to encourage the desponding and indolent to energetic activity and self respect, and to intellectual and moral elevation. The sick delighted to grasp her hand, when she was permitted to visit them, and deep were the murmurings when this privilege was not allowed.

Such an ardent lover of truth, so heroic a defender of principles, dear as her own life, I never saw outside these walls. The boldness with which she reproved tyranny, and the thrilling eloquence with which she defended the cause of suffering humanity, were truly "a terror to evil doers!"

No one was so popular in the whole institution. Without ever being intrusive, she drew all eyes, all ears, in every circle. At balls the most aerial dancer; in labor, the most industrious, in all public gatherings or private circles, "the observed of all observers." The wonderful power she possessed over the minds of others drew all to her ample heart, with an irresistible magnetism. When she came into our hall, every hand, eye and heart, were open to receive her. I never saw one, who took the least notice of anything, who, after having seen her once, did not wish to see her again. When we suffered any unusual abuse, it was very often said, "I'll tell Mrs. Packard of this." We knew our rights would find an able advocate in our firm and gentle friend.

Doctor and Mrs. McFarland were much annoyed by these demonstrations of the fact that Mrs. Packard was so much more popular than themselves; and this annoyance was undoubtedly the reason, that shortly after the accession of the patients from the lowest prison, to her ward, the privileges of Mrs. Packard were materially abridged. The restrictions to which she was condemned, were very severe; sufficient to exasperate the gentlest mind. Yet they could not ruffle her undaunted spirit, or change to a frown, the sublime tranquillity, of that heaven-sustained soul.

XI.

The Reign of Terror.

"Strike till the last armed foe expires."

To my astonishment and joy, at dinner, the day we entered the Eighth ward, Lizzy Bonner said to me, "Mrs. Olsen, you can have your seat at the table next to Mrs. Packard." I did not dare even to thank Miss Bonner, or to show any demonstration of my joy when this most delightful decree was announced, but quietly took my seat. Here, for a few weeks, I had the privilege of eating without fear that my brains would be knocked out, or that any other episode from dinner, such as some one's upsetting my plate, or laying her hair into it, or crowding or sneezing, or anything of the kind. Mrs. Packard and myself conversed in very low tones, so as not to disturb any one, and not to permit our attendant to suspect that we were particularly happy. Our meal hours were the most pleasant hours I enjoyed, for with my sweet friend by my side, I forgot that the potatoes were always cold, the meat often tainted, and butter no longer visible. I forgot the immodest and profane conversation that was common with a certain class of women, who, though they evidently, had a long time had the privilege of " go thy way," yet as evidently had omitted to recognize the force of the divine mandate to "sin no more!"

About this time, some changes had made impressions on some minds which looked very ominous. It was whispered that our ward was to be broken up, and some of us put into the Sixth ward. I trembled at the thought that I might be included among the number, for I had heard that the Sixth ward was not much better than the Fifth, and I could not bear to again "go down." These changes however did not affect me.

It had been so long since I had heard from home, that I supposed, very naturally, that all who had formerly known and loved me, had become accustomed to the idea that I was "incurably insane," and consequently incapable of appreciating letters from them! Bitter indeed was this apprehension; yet I derived some consolation, by thinking that if indeed it should be my destiny to die there, which now, as my health had become so feeble, was very probable, my friend, Mrs. Packard, would surely vindicate my sanity to my friends at Chicago, as soon as it should become in her power to do so.

Mrs. McFarland now avoided Mrs. Packard as much as possible; not only declining to show her the least sympathy, but utterly refusing to speak to her. Though the latter could never be accused of ever breaking any of the thousand and one rules of our key-holders, and yielded, no less than myself, implicit obedience to all their commands, yet, she was accused by the matron and one of the most obsequious of the attendants, of being "very troublesome!" I believe she was "very troublesome," to some of Satan's kingdom; since she persisted so firmly, not only in giving no cause for offence, but in exhibiting, so far as the most blameless life could do so, all the "peaceable fruits of righteousness." But it troubled the adversary much to know that she spent nearly all her time writing in her own room, some "mischief," they had reason to fear, might come of it, "Othello's occupation" might become endangered.

It had been discovered by the powers that be, that her alliances were becoming quite too numerous for the enemies' forces. She was now securely entrenched by fortifications erected by the warm friendship of numerous partizans; and the daily accessions to her party were a signal of defeat to the enemies' forces. Indeed we all felt that we had been drawn into a regular civil war with the Institution!

All the seventy patients in the Eighth ward who took the least interest in anything, sympathised with Mrs. Packard; and, so far as I could learn, every attendant, both male and female, in the Asylum, defended, and very highly respected Mrs. Packard. This state of affairs created increased apprehensions in the camp of the enemy. Something must be done. Our potent commander, after holding a war-council with several of his allies, the chief of whom was Bonner, the Prime Minister, now issued officially from his "sanctum," a new and startling Proclamation. It was this:

"All intercourse between Mrs. Packard and the inmates of the west division of the Eighth ward, must be prohibited except under strict guard of an attendant! Mrs. Packard must not be allowed to go into the hall, except when accompanied by an attendant. She is to hold no more prayer-meetings, lend no more books, and those she has lent must be immediately returned."

This Proclamation was met in our hall with silent hisses of execration. Some, however were far from being silent. A few swore loudly on the occasion, and prayed very loudly for a fresh instalment of curses upon the head of Dr. McFarland. As for me, I wept more bitter tears than any I had ever shed there, knowing that now my life was to be deprived of almost its only earthly solace. In a very few days, I was suddenly ordered to leave my seat at the table next Mrs. Packard, and take a seat at another table in the same hall, by the side of an old lady who was known to be the fiercest and most dangerous of all the female patients in the Asylum! She had been recently conducted from the prison below.

I met this terrible order without trembling, but with a deep and inexpressible indignation, that of course was voiceless. I left my table immediately, without a word of demurring, and took a seat, as ordered, by the side of this fierce woman.

About this time all our rules were rendered much more severe than ever. We were seldom permitted to go out of the house at all; some were never allowed to go, but were kept constantly in close confinement. These were harmless patients too. One was Miss Hodson, the industrious sewer that I spoke of in the Fifth ward. Rides were also prohibited. The balls were suspended, and only a very few were permitted to attend the chapel services. Company was also kept out of our ward for a long time. We were not allowed private conference with each other, and all who did not render instant obedience were severely punished. I often saw Lizzy Bonner pull patients into their private rooms, and shut the door after them. Then I would hear her beating them, and the latter screaming, and in a choking stifled voice begging, "Oh, don't kill me, don't kill me." I did not let the attendant know I heard this.

This was indeed a "Reign of Terror!" "No matter," thought I, "so that it proves the prelude of a "Revolution." A revolution, I inferred, could not but make our prospects better, since I could hardly imagine how they could be worse. I heard and saw many unmistakeable portents that a storm was coming of an unusual character.

One patient had become so disgusted with life under such circumstances, that she determined to destroy it by starvation. She had been a long time in close confinement in her own room alone. I many times knew that Lizzy was using violence upon her person, throwing her heavily upon the floor. She persisted in her resolve on suicide till she became emaciated almost to a skeleton; for many weeks taking neither food or drink except by force. Her resolution thus to die was at last overcome by fierce pains of hunger. She now was glad to eat, and a terrible reaction ensued. Her long abstinence had made her so fiercely hungry that it seemed she would devour every thing she could reach. After eating as much as was assigned to the rest, she would clutch the food from the other patients, and devour it with the most terrible voracity. But all were glad to see her eat, thinking she had now abandoned the idea of suicide. She now came constantly to the table with the rest, and behaved so mildly for several days that all were confirmed in the hope that she might yet live and recover.

One day at dinner, she startled every one at the tables, by suddenly seizing a knife and cutting her own throat! Oh I will not attempt to describe the terror of this scene! The wound, however, was not so deep as she intended to make it; the knife was immediately taken from her bleeding throat,

and she was led to her room and again put into a straight-
jacket in solitary confinement. But no one, as yet, had ever
heard her speak a word in that hall. This was the first attempt at suicide I had seen at Jacksonville. There were
many others, some successful, in different parts of the house
as I heard by attendants and others, but I am only describing
scenes that fell under my own observation.

Another unfortunate actually threw herself from a high unbarred window in the work-room, four stories from the ground,
and was taken up dead from the pavement. She had been
there only a few days, and it appears had no knowledge of
the place. I saw her when she arrived, she was mild and
gentle, conversed intelligently of her husband, and of the
home she had left; expressed a strong desire to return to it
again. Every thing she saw seemed so very strange to her,
and the severe restrictions so mysterious to her frightened
sensibilities, she thought herself in a worse house than she indeed was, if such a thing is possible. They wanted her to
increase the number of gratuitous laborers in the work-room;
took her there, and required her to go to work with the rest.
She sat down and looked distressed, at last rose up suddenly,
exclaimed with a voice and look of terror, "Oh, what kind
of a place have they brought me to?" then rushed suddenly
head foremost from the window, into eternity! Oh, reign
of terror! reign of terror!!

XII.

Reign of Terror ended.

"My soul be on thy guard."

Scenes of tumult and terror now so frequently succeeded
each other, that no one felt that life was safe. With nothing
to afford hope,—no avenues to the world—no amusements to
relieve the ever thickening horrors of such a destiny, a look
of fixed discontent now sat on every countenance. Our an-

niversaries came and left us, with nothing to give us either joy or change, except a slight change at dinner.

Thanksgiving! Oh what thrilling memories of my New England life were awakened by the arrival of this brightest, best, most joyous of all New England days! Oh New England! when will these charms, engraven on my deathless memory, no less than the bold and glorious pictures of thy rocks and hills and everlasting mountains, upon my fadeless vision, when again will these realizations return with all their golden glories unmarred by the horrible discord of these grating locks and keys? And now Thanksgiving has come and gone, but the tormenting specters evolved by busy memories have not left us!

Winter has come, yet the heart sickness, which arose from hope deferred; the sense of utter loneliness which clung to every aching heart; the utter isolation of spirit, the slow wearing away and undermining of every tie that bound us to earthly existence; oh this it was that made up the deepest, darkest, heaviest gloom of that cold December, the saddest month of the year. Hour after hour wore away, in the unblest monotony of that dim, shadowy spectral semblance of life! Deeper and still deeper grew the sadness on the many silent faces of these daughters of affliction. They were thinking, thinking, thinking.

At last this reverie was broken by the loud summons of the supper bell, which announced that we were now to take our last meal in the year. We once more congregated around our unsocial board; but little was said; yet the faces of all silently but eloquently spoke the burning thoughts within. After supper, we were immediately remanded to our rooms, and locked up as usual, to spend the long evening as best we might, in darkness, cold, and silence. I muffled my shawl around me, and sat several hours that memorable evening, brooding over the mournful past, and querying vainly of the unprophetic future. The bell heavily chimed out its last hour! and another year had departed forever.

The New Year came—the New Year! that day so full of

inspiration and rejoicing to every place on Christian earth, outside of prison walls! to us it brought only a protraction of our reign of terror! the same revolting scenes were daily and hourly repeated; the same restrictions, the same everlasting espionage, the same threats, and disgusting horrors!

At this time, one, bolder than the rest, by some means escaped, and attempted to run away. The alarm was given, and the "watch-dogs" were out. By these she was speedily overtaken, forced back to the Asylum, and condemned to solitary confinement as her punishment.

Two others ran away not long after this scene. One was a widow, a young and very beautiful lady of excellent talents and a very cheerful disposition. She was not insane as I could discover at the time, though much dejected by grief for the death of her brave and much loved husband who had died in the army. Soon after hearing this afflictive intelligence, she became ill with a fever, and this was probably, as is often the case, accompanied with temporary delirium. Her friends, not knowing how to treat either the fever or its consequent delirium, which they thought insanity, found a convenient way of getting rid of their responsibility, by handing her over to the care of "our accomplished Superintendent," to receive her three hundredth share of his attentions. (There are three hundred in the Asylum.)

Here it had been her destiny to remain for many months; and feeling very anxious for the welfare of her children at home, and moreover, being indefinitely put off by the most silly excuses, and reprehensible delays, she at last assumed the responsibility of asserting those rights, which nature had given her of finding and taking care of her own babes.

She was accompanied by a kindred spirit, another widow, whose husband had also laid down his life upon our bleeding country's sacrificial altar. Neither was this person insane that I could discover; I believe she was several times the subject of some harmless trances. But I think she did a very sane action in trying to free herself from bondage. Their plan succeeded so well, that, after traveling six miles they were overtaken by a kind hearted teamster, who by the request of the now much wearied travelers, took them into his conveyance, and listening sympathetically to their truthful tale of distress, carried them on their way until overtaken by their remorseless pursuers.

On their return, one of these was sentenced to one of the lower prison wards, and the other brought to our hall in the Eighth ward. Hers was a most courageous spirit; she even smiled on entering our hall, determining to disappoint her victorious captors by showing herself unrevengeful, and in no wise bowed in spirit, or humiliated! Therefore, instead of complaining that she was deprived of all her privileges in the privileged Seventh ward, and sentenced to the noisy tumults of the maniac's ward, she daily evinced the most pleasant and cheerful deportment. Mrs. Davis was very beautiful and musical, and withal a decided wit; so benevolent too, so unaffectedly kind that she would often relate some amusing story, or use her most musical and enchanting voice by singing for the entertainment of the desponding, when her own heart was full of unutterable sorrow for her own griefs. If this cheerful and most noble-hearted woman was "insane," I wish every woman in the land possessed such an "insanity!"

But with all her heroic attempts to throw off the benumbing influence of affliction, she did suffer most keenly in mind at her disappointment in not being permitted to see her darling children. This feeling, together with the over-exhaustion of so long a walk, soon brought on a fever. I used every morning, and many times in the day to visit her, that I might assist her if possible, and also learn from her those beautiful lessons taught by her trusting faith and hopefulness. As she lay, day after day, on her bed of suffering, surrounded by the noisy and filthy, of whose annoyances I never knew her to complain, I had never beheld a more perfect example of patience. But I burned with indignation at the ignorance of a community, in the very country her husband had fought and died to protect, that his beloved young wife could not herself be protected from such shameful abuses as those she suffered here.

A few weeks after her recovery, she went home. Could she have gone at the time she had started, or previously, instead of being punished in prison for thus braving danger for the love of her children, she might have escaped the fever. Our reign of terror augmented to such a degree, that I did not deem it safe to enter the dining hall, even when the door was left open, for a glass of water for the suffering Mrs. Davis, without humbly asking liberty of Lizzy to do so! We all felt ourselves hotly pursued by the enemy. Only the wild and reckless scarcely dared to breathe. They indeed, like the mad Saul of Tarsus, in his fruitless attempts to destroy Christianity, dared to "breathe out threatenings and slaughter," not against Christ, or any of his followers, but against our Asylum prison-keepers and their abettors in the unjust embodiment of State Legislation!

In this our painful emergency, we could not appeal to Dr. Tenny. He was absent on some mission, and we had long since ceased to hope for the least assistance from any other officer.

At every opportunity, we banded together in little secret societies, in earnest, agonizing consultation. One proposed that all who were reliable should combine together, and when the attendants were out of sight, and the Superintendent in the hall, we should unite upon an agreed signal in an attack upon himself. We were to form around him; then one of the strongest in our number was to confine his mouth by her hand, to keep him from calling for aid; others, on each side, were to secure his limbs, and then we were to demand our liberty at the peril of his life. Several of the bolder wished at once to act upon this programme; others objected; so we decided to adjourn for further consideration. At our next meeting the infeasibility of this plan was eloquently presented by one of the speakers, and the final fate of this bill was to be unanimously voted down. We knew if so bold a scheme should fail of practical success, we should be subjected to the most fearful tortures as punishments. 4A

At last one of our number, a very intelligent married lady, discovered after much painful thought, an expedient which did much to alleviate our sufferings, by causing to be essentially relaxed the fierce discipline to which we were subjected. Let those who may blame us for acting upon this, remember that we were fighting for our lives. Compelled as we were to inhale the poisonous gases from so many diseased bodies while sleeping so near each other, and the still deadlier exhalations arising from typhoid and other fevers, ulcerated lungs, and fetid sores, all confined in one hall; we felt, that between the above influences, and the sudden blows and violence which all the time menaced us, by the fierce maniacs and their fiercer keeper, that our lives were most essentially imperilled. Our liberty, even the liberty of speech and writing had all been taken away, and we wished for emancipation from this inexorable thraldom with an agony of desire that none but the victims of such a bondage can ever appreciate.

The proposition now under consideration, was, that we should make a general onslaught or campaign against the State's property, and in various ways, destroy all we possibly could, without discovery. Thus we should make apparent to our persecutor, that this most desperate movement was but the natural and legitimate result of his own extreme severity to his victims—that it was the complete desperation of our circumstances which evolved this "military necessity." The plan was presented to me for my individual sanction—I did not advise the measure; always maintaining that it was better to suffer than to do wrong, and that it was wrong to waste or destroy property; that I did not believe in doing evil that good might come. They then asked me—as I did not see fit to join in the enterprise—if I intended to expose those who saw fit to do so. "No," replied I, "depend on my honor; I do not advise such proceedings, nor will I join in them; yet neither will I betray you, whatever injury you may inflict upon the property of the State, provided you will be sure, in your depredations, not to hurt any person."

They were satisfied; plans were now all arranged, and I observed as the plot thickened, so did also the affected tranquillity on the faces of the plotters become more apparent.

Sunday was the day this military strategy reached its developement in action. The attendant went to church, leaving but a slight guard in her place. And now, when unobserved, the exploit began—bed-comforters, blankets, and nice expensive bed-spreads were torn into long narrow strips, and these strips dexterously coiled or wound up on the finger, and then, one by one, squeezed into little openings through some of the ventilating vacancies, or some other tight place, whence they could not "return to tell the tale." Sheets, towels, and bed ticks followed in the rear of destruction. Pillows were ripped open, and their contents emptied from the window in a brisk gale of wind. The person who did this, called me to see the edifying spectacle. The wind was an auxiliary, and so scattered the feathers, like the flakes of a coarse snow storm, that no outsider could tell from which of all the numerous windows the rejected feathers were cast out.

When our attendant reappeared, as she gradually discovered what had been transpiring in her luckless absence, it was equal to a theatrical performance to witness her consternation. She fluttered around from room to room, shaking her ominous keys, and slamming the doors, as she vainly sought to discover the authors of the "raid." She stormed and raved; then raved and stormed, and threatened; the fury in her eye indicating that she was longing to strike somebody; but alas, on this emergency, she didn't know who to strike, the most vigilant inquiries she was able to make only eliciting that nobody knew anything about it. At last, she came to the conclusion as she vexatiously expressed it, "I believe the divil's at the bottom of it all."

The reply elicited by this remark with most provoking coolness by one of the patients was, "You must be right, in your conjecture Lizzy; I think, undoubtedly, that the devil is indeed at the bottom of it all."

Poor Lizzy! she did not know how much we enjoyed her distress! Monday morning came, and soap was in requisition. "Where's the soap?" roared Lizzy, but no one deemed it expedient to inform her that its use had been misapplied, and diverted considerably from its appropriate function. Many bars had mysteriously disappeared; and this reminds me that I have read in agricultural papers that soap suds when mixed with other enriching substances proves an excellent fertilizer!

Respecting the fate of the nice new blankets, on Lizzy's earnest inquiry of the very person who destroyed them, the latter very gravely informed her that the devil appeared to her in the night and carried them away! Skeins of expensive sewing silk, and spools of thread next vanished mysteriously from the work-room, and were found tangled up in inextricable confusion. "Spirits," were accused of abducting them away.

One day, a large quantity of brooms had been purchased, and deposited in a closet connected with the wash room. I once saw one of "the initiated" go to these brooms with a pair of scissors, and cut the strong threads, used to bind the broom together. This was effected so adroitly, that nothing unusual was discovered, and broom after broom was made the object of this destructive operation, while keen eyes were watching to be sure that none of the "powers that be" were in sight. At last the mischief was completed upon the unresisting brooms, with no sign left to tell the tale. But by all the observers, who in those watchful days were not few, it was noticed, that while used in sweeping, behold these new brooms evinced a strong disposition to scatter themselves in liberal disintegrations over the floor. Some remarked that these last new brooms must be a cheat,—were very badly made. These unfortunate brooms, thus voted below par, I fear did not bring much credit to their manufacturers, since, without living out half their days, they were rapidly becoming smaller and beautifully less until quite demolished. A new supply was soon ordered, but whether from the same establishment as were their unfortunate predecessors, deponent saith not.

After the completion of this exploit, an attack was made upon glass and crockery. This required more circumspection, but for this new freak of madness, there was on hand a new method! In order to give the destructive smash to these doomed articles, they would take opportunity, either when the great Asylum bell was ringing, or when some of the screamers were blowing their blast, or on some other of those noisy occasions which so frequently occur, and then, just at the right signal, the deed was accomplished.

In this manner, windows, looking glasses goblets, and crockery, were dashed upon the floor, at different times, on all possible safe occasions. Tea-spoons, knives and forks, were stealthily taken from the table, and thrown out of the window; clothing and curtains torn and mutilated, doors were smashed, cushions opened, the walls were scratched and strange literature in conspicuous places written there! It was astonishing how many opportunities they had in which to effect their plans, in triumphant defiance of all our vigilant guardians. Lizzy, when obliged to leave the hall, would never re-enter stealthily, to give us a horrible and ghastly surprise, but always with a kind of flourish of trumpets, that warned us, in timely season, of the edifying magnetism of her presence. The noisy furor of her ever clattering keys, and the clamorous bang of the great ponderous doors, were of the character of those ancient trumpets, which certainly did not give an uncertain sound! These preliminary circumstances, always accompanying Lizzy's advent, were very skilfully turned to account in the service of the very ones they were meant to intimidate, giving them a chance to leave the scene of military activity. and glide quickly to a remote part of the hall. There they would assume an expression of most unedifying ignorance, as though the very possibility of doing mischief were as foreign from their minds, as the thought of "thy servant's being a dog," was to Hazael of antiquity.

These events kept our unfortunate attendant in a most unenviable condition of mental derangement! In her search for the authors of the mischief, she at last applied to me. "This mischief," said she, "can't all go on without your knowing something about it. I know you can tell, if you're a mind to say; do you know who broke that glass?" "I did not break it myself," said I, "and if I knew who did, certainly should not report them, and thus subject them to punishment. They suffer enough now." She declined questioning me further, and pushed her researches in all other directions, but with no better success. As the case had now become intolerable, the whole proceeding was at last reported to the matron.

She received the intelligence with much consternation. "This will never do" said she, "this must be stopped or the State will find it out, and find fault with us. You must find the guilty ones, and have them sent to the Fifth ward." Again I was questioned, "Mrs. McFarland," I replied, "I do know who has done these things, but do not intend to expose them. I would sooner be sentenced to the Fifth ward myself than bring such a doom on any of these patients, so please do not question me, for I do assure you, I will not inform against these defenceless sufferers." She importuned me no further, but ordered all the attendants to keep up the most vigilant watch over all our motions. This was done, but still the disorders continued with scarcely any abatement, and so adroitly was it consummated, that not the slightest clue could be obtained to these mysterious "under-ground railroad" operations. I saw hundreds of dollars worth of property destroyed, but did not I also daily see far worse sights in the destruction of health, of liberty, of reason, of life and of human rights, caused directly by the power of our misguided State over the helpless victims of its would be beneficence. I could not remedy these far more deplorable evils, therefore the existence of an incomparably smaller evil, the destruction of the State's property, I confess gave me little uneasiness. Dr. McFarland himself, by his fierce restrictions and severities, was the only one really responsible in this case, therefore I should have been guilty of the deepest baseness had I caused his helpless victims to suffer a punishment which I felt that he alone deserved.

It was discovered at last, that these depredations were committed in consequence of the desperation to which the sufferers in that hall were reduced, to extreme trials caused by the tyranny of our keeper! The Doctor saw his mistake in drawing our reins so tightly, and fearing they might snap entirely, saw it for his own interest and safety to relax them. Orders were suddenly given that walks might again be allowed, company again permitted to visit us, and that in several other particulars more lenity should be shown. Doctor Tenny at last returned, and a general amnesty ensued, at least we felt that we were reinforced. Hope began to revive and the mischief at last ceased.

After the expiration of our reign of terror, the leader of the mischief confessed it herself to the authorities, and promised voluntarily that she would do nothing more of the kind. She expressed her willingness to be punished, but would not expose one of the rest to share her fate. If a particle of humanity had been alive in our Superintendent, he would at least, have put her upon trial; but instead of a pardon or a reprieve, behold a straight-jacket was brought with imperative orders that it be put upon her, and she forthwith assigned to the Fifth ward! One of the patients rushed to me, with eyes filled with tears, and told me of this fearful decree. I could not believe it, till I went into the hall and saw its execution! There stood Bonner, extending the jacket, while she informed the victim of her doom. We expected to see resistance and one of the terrible staight-jacket battles. But this heroic woman prevented this by saying, "I will not resist you, I will go. Don't pinion my arms. I will do it myself." She then put on the jacket as readily, and with as much apparent cheerfulness as if it were a comfortable garment, instead of an instrument of torture, then turned around for Lizzy to lace it up behind. Bidding us good-bye with a kind and cheerful tone, she asked us to pray for her, and calmly and courageously followed her attendant to her dreary Fifth ward prison!

I have read of Columbus in chains before the monarchs of Europe; of Socrates in prison by order of the dignitaries of ancient Greece; of Luther before the Diet of Worms, defending in the face of the world the principles of religious liberty; of Galileo in his cold prison declaring, "it still moves;" but I believe the heroism of these martyrs was excelled by that of this most noble woman, who rather than expose her fellows to punishment, cheerfully took it upon herself, knowing well that a doom of horror there awaited her.

Her departure caused a general gloom in the hall. Her health was suffering, and we feared she would not be able to survive the treatment, and the deadly malarious atmosphere of the Fifth ward. In a few days she became very sick with fever, and having no proper care, she lingered several weeks in great suffering. She expressed a wish that I might be allowed to visit her, but this of course, was not permitted. She was one of the kindest hearted persons I ever saw. If some of our modern fashionable christians, who in times of revival have so much to say about coming out from the world and taking up the cross, would visit the sufferers of that Fifth ward, they would there learn by some of its inmates, what "coming out from the world" and taking up the "cross of Christ" really means.

The very bold measures taken by this heroine, destructive to property as they were, were prompted by benevolence. This was not her first attempt at redress. She had reasoned and remonstrated, and begged and implored both Doctor and Mrs. McFarland that they would show mercy and lenity to the patients in their care. She had in my hearing, exhausted all efforts of this kind that could be applied, before she counselled or perpetrated any mischief to the property of the State; this was done as a last resort. She concluded as all other means had failed, she could scare the Doctor into milder measures, and indeed suceeded to thus procure for us a restriction of severities, and a much more ample latitude of privileges. As her punishment for thus benefitting us, it was her doom to languish in, that revolting purgatory for many weeks, with a suffering borne, as even her attendant admitted, with uncomplaining patience! She was not allowed to send any intelligence to her husband who was all this time kept in ignorance of her condition. But he visited her at last, and had the good sense to remove her at once. He told me he should never, under any circumstances, take his wife to a Lunatic Asylum again. He found the nice little sum of fifty dollars charged for the destruction of property of which I have spoken, but as I heard Mrs. McFarland say, he said he wouldn't pay a cent. Glad of it! If our State is willing its property should be wasted in that way, I think it not out of place to let the hard working taxpayers know it.

XIII.

Wives and Husbands.

"Wives and husbands there must part."

Returning from a walk one day with others, I observed, on coming up the long flight of stairs, a scene which gave my feelings a severe shock. The attendant evidently did not wish us to see this, for she kept hurrying us along to our hall, but the circumstances were such we could not help it. A husband who that morning had made a brief visit to his wife, was then taking leave of her. She failed to recognise the propriety of being left, and wished to return to her home with her husband. She entreated him, with tears that ceased not flowing, to let her go home and see her children. "Oh husband dear, do let me go home; I don't want to stay here any longer, it don't do me any good. I must go, O I must live at home with you and my children. Dear, dear husband, do not leave me here!" The husband hesitated, looked at her streaming tears, then at the door; he lingered; there was an evident struggle in his mind. Perhaps he thought of his courtship life, of all her youthful charms ere her toiling fidelity to him had faded the early beauty from that now pale cheek and tear-dimmed eye. Perhaps he remembered love's promises, his marriage vow of everlasting protection and union of home and interests. Perhaps he thought of God's injunction "they twain shall be one," perhaps—ah! I know not what cogitations were in his mind. The agitated wife perceiving his indecision, seizing the advantage, took his arm within her own, and embracing him, exclaimed again, in tones of agony, "O husband, I must, I must go home with you, do not, do not leave me here!"

Several of the officials of the Asylum were standing near, the husband had evidently been receiving instruction from them instead of his own conscience; then with one violent effort, he disengaged himself from the trembling grasp of the pleading wife, left her and walked hastily down the stairs. In her anguish she sank down powerless upon the floor, and was dragged by two men, still gazing after her husband's receding form, to all the horrors of locks, keys, and imprisonments!

We all returned to our hall in sadness and silence, the attendant soon left. When we found ourselves unwatched, one said, "O, how could that man have the heart to leave her, when she so begged to go with him?" Another replied, that "he had been befooled by the Doctor who had told him it would not be safe to take her home." Said a third, "what a fool a man must be, to let another man judge between himself and his wife! he ought to have known himself whether she should have gone home. If he wanted to go and attend to his affairs, he ought to have considered that she had the same right, for his home duties and her own were the same." Another spoke with apparent disgust, in her turn, to the last speaker. "Do you think such husbands possess the faculty of consideration! I don't agree with you, it appears to me that all their own consideration, all their faculty of independent thinking, has become weakened if not destroyed when they give up to the stupid prejudice that another man can better guide a woman than her own husband!" Said another voice, "now they will call this poor woman noisy and excited, say it hurts her to have her friends visit her, because she can not help crying and grieving about his leaving her; then they will put her down into a lower ward, where of course she will grow worse, and may become incurable. Yes, this is the way they do here; I wish the public knew it."

"My God!" echoed yet another hitherto silent voice, "it makes me shudder to think how many splendid minds are made incurable lunatics, or worried into a sickness which ends in death, by just these barbarous means!"

At this stage of the colloquy, our attendant re-entered the hall. The conversation here ended, but our thoughts did not end. The stupid thoughtlessness with which a husband can commit to other hands, the wife of his bosom, when distracted or enfeebled in body or mind, is utterly unaccountable. No one would trust a valuable horse to be stabled without knowing something of the treatment he would be likely to receive. Would you, farmers, commit one to strangers of whom you knew nothing beyond the fact that they are public stable-keepers! Would you send even a horse to a stable, and permit him to remain for months and even years without visiting, or at least sending some one to visit the animal! Would you not fear he might be cheated out of the proper quantity of oats or other food—that he might be exposed to contagious diseases from other horses in his vicinity, or that in some way, his value might be diminished? Would it be a safe experiment thus to commit even a horse to the mercy of fortuitous influences? How is it then, that you give less care to your tender wife?

Did you tell her, when a lover, that you could not engage, in all future circumstances, to give her as much attention as your animals should receive? Was it among your lover's vows, in your sacred moonlight rambles, that if she became insane, you would desert her—that you would love and cherish her, and share her destiny "till death us do part," on condition that she would retain her youth and beauty unimpaired; but that, if these, or if health or reason should fail, you would consign her to some other man? O, no, such was not your sacred vow! What did you promise her? I was not there listening under the hedgerow; I did not witness your sacred vows before marriage; I only witness how you fulfil them afterwards! But you know what you did promise, and she knows, and God knows.

XIV.

The Insanity of Orthodoxy.

"A guilty, weak and helpless worm."

Another lady who interested me much was a Mrs. Brown, who belonged to a peculiar class of minds. She was a melancholic. Her insanity consisted in an excess of piety. I do not mean by this expression, an excess of Christian principle, for I know not how any one can possess the calm, self-balanced and benevolent disposition of Jesus in excess. But I mean an excess of those internal emotions that an erroneous system of theology had taught her to consider essential to salvation. She was a victim of ultra orthodoxy. Mrs. Brown was able to converse intelligently on all other subjects with which she was acquainted, but when religion was alluded to, she would be filled with doubts and fears, and overcome with the most distressing apprehension in view of the sins of her own heart. If any sins were cherished there, nobody I think outside of herself had discovered it. She was a pattern of the strictest honesty, conscientiousness and fidelity, and very affectionate and kind to every one. Never repining or complaining of her own sufferings, but ever ready with words and deeds of kindness to others, she had become very dear to me, as also to many others. Yet this most exemplary person looked upon herself as the chief of sinners, and upon her own heart, as the centre and nucleus of depravity and emnity to God sufficient to justly sink her soul to everlasting condemnation! Every morning, for many weeks, she would come to my door and rap; then, with streaming tears and a voice trembling with a sense of her unworthiness, would entreat me to pray for her, and to say something comforting "to strengthen her faith" as she expressed it. She came so frequently upon these errands, that I confess it sometimes annoyed me, especially, when suffering, as I often did, from headache.

But I never permitted her even to suspect that she was troublesome, fearing it would increase her sense of her overwhelming guilt and sins of heart! She would present her requests in a form like this, "Do you think there can be any mercy for me? Can you think of any comforting verse in the bible that will apply to my case?"

"O, yes, Mrs. Brown, 'come unto me, all ye that labor and are heavy laden, and I will give you rest—I love them that love me—and those that seek me early shall find me.'"

"Well, but can you suppose that such an unworthy sinner as I love God?"

"Certainly you do; you love God better than I do, and better than most people, else you would not care whether you pleased him or not. And you seek him early too. You are up every morning even before light, and before you are half dressed seeking how to find Christ, even of poor unworthy me. Surely you love God and seek him early too, therefore it is clear to my mind that these comforting passages do apply to you case."

She thanked me, smiled through her tears, and returned to her own room to dress for breakfast. Similar scenes occurred every morning, only less and less easy did they become to me, for, as she expected a fresh instalment of comfort, in the shape of another new verse, I sometimes began to fear that my memory would be exhausted of the requisite supply. I ne day said to her, "Doctor Tenny is a good Christian, nd some of the attendants here, I hope are so too. why don't you go to them for comfort—perhaps they could more readily reach your case than I can."

She hesitated, then said, "O, it seems as if you understand me better than they do. O, you are certainly going to heaven! but I—" here she broke down completely and wept so inconsolably, that I determined never again to give her the slightest repulse whatever my own condition might be. The next morning before I had had time to quite dress myself, she came to my room and began to apologise and begged to know if I could suggest any consolation for the trials of mind she had suffered all night. "When thou passest through the waters I will be with thee, the mountains shall depart, and the hills be removed, but my kindness shall not depart from thee." At another time, "Fear not, for I am thy God."

"Are you sure this is for me?" she queried in a voice of tremulous agitation.

"Perfectly sure, else I should not have so readily thought of it." Again she went away rejoicing, and promised by my request, to apply those verses, every time her doubts and fears arose. So I labored with her daily, and found, wearying as this often was, in my weak health, that it afforded much benefit to me. It partially diverted my mind from my own sorrows to see others with far more distressing woes than my own. I did not expect to be punished in an eternal hell after death, while this poor sufferer did. So I could not help trying all possible ways to relieve such apprehensions.

On one occasion, when this afflicted woman seemed unusually cast down with her imaginary bundle of sin, I said to her, as I saw her approaching "O, Mrs. Brown, let not your heart be troubled." "Our light affliction, etc."

"Did that verse come to you for me?" she eagerly asked.

"Certainly, it came right into my mind just for you, for I thought of it the instant I saw you. And now every day, so soon as I see you coming, I think of some similar verse; it comes without studying for it." This last was an essential point with her, as she construed it into an evidence of her acceptance.

After a while, her visits became more frequent; she would several times a day obtain permission of her attendant to come into our hall on these errands. Sometimes she would come to my door and linger and hesitate, as if fearful of being annoying; if I did not anticipate her wishes, she would say, "You know what I want, can't you give me a little consolation?" I was often put to my wit's end to do this, yet, as I did not mean that any impediment should baffle me in my thorough investigation of the philosophy of insanity and of its cure also, I tried again, this time changing my tactics somewhat. I once said to her, "Mrs. Brown, you are deceived respecting me; I am far from being so good a Christian as you suppose. Now let me tell you of my condition. I am a poor miserable sinner, you can not imagine what a sinner I have been at home, and how terribly sinful my heart is here, only I have not the power to act it out. Why I behave so badly at home, that my poor husband can not live with me, and I trouble my other friends so much, that they cannot endure my society either. Now do you think there can be any mercy for such a sinner as I am, Mrs. Brown."

She forgot her own enormous load of guilt, and stared at me with the utmost astonishment. This diverted her mind, and this was just what I wished to do. Then, having fairly aroused her curiosity, I went on describing the longest and most terrible catalogue of short-comings, back-slidings and coldness in duty, all terrible sins to her, that I could possibly make out against myself, and wound up the tale by asking her again if she thought it possible that I could ever be forgiven!

She hardly knew what to say; but I found to my great pleasure, that, before we had finished this colloquy, she was actually suggesting consolation to me!

Now, I mentally soliloquized, if these methods, instead of the Lunatic Asylum system of compulsory obedience, fearful punishments, and unreasonable restrictions, could be allowed to prevail; that is, if a system could be devised by which the minds of the patients could be diverted from their own insane ideas, by calling to aid other and long dormant faculties of mind, the result must be that a new channel of thought would be awakened, and by this process being perseveringly applied, the insane ideas would be starved out for want of any thing to feed them, and the new process of thought thus brought to bear upon demented intellect, would in short, cure insanity! This was my theory, and I acted upon it successfully in every case, so far as I had the power.

But I noticed with pain, that whenever it was discovered that I was trying experiments so contrary to their own, they would invariably interfere, and thus my attempts were frustrated.

One day, when the gentle and pious mind of Mrs. Brown had been greatly distressed by being compelled to witness the terrible scenes of abuse and oppression so constant there, she came to me with her griefs. She made no complaint of the abuse to which she was witness, but was suffering much under a fresh exhibition of the sins of her own rebellious heart. "My grace is sufficient for thee," said I, "blessed are the poor in spirit for they shall be comforted. Don't you think these are comforting words Mrs. Brown?"

"O, yes, if they only applied to me how can you be certain that they do?"

"Every good and every perfect gift is from above," I replied; now a good thought is a good gift, so that proves it is from God; and it is for you, I know, because it came to me the moment I saw you. Now I am impressed from the same good Spirit to tell you that you must be happy all day, on the basis of these consoling verses sent so directly to you. You must not suffer yourself again to sink down into the Slough of Despond.

She would always express gratitude and go away in smiles, or at least with a very comfortable degree of tranquility. I have not the slightest doubt that I could have seen much more perfected fruits of my theory of curing insanity exemplified, could I have been allowed to prosecute my scheme, uninterrupted by the conflicting system of the Superintendent. Yet disturbed as I was, there occurred daily sufficient to convince me that reason is better than authority applied to minds already groaning under an overdose of the latter, while the former has been sadly wanting.

Now I wish to ask what in the terrible discipline to which Mrs. Brown, was subjected, was calculated to erase from her mind these dread forebodings? I believe its tendency was to confirm them, for she evidently looked upon the revolting scenes surrounding her, in contrast with the abundance, peace and comfort of the dear home she had left, as the just deserts of her terrible sins. She often said she deserved nothing better, and had no reason to complain

XV.

How to make Incurables.

"I have battled with my agony."

One day a patient received a letter from her aged mother, in which the latter entreated her to write. "Let me know" wrote the mother, "without delay, if you are alive. I hardly know if I have a daughter, it is so long since I have heard from you."

The daughter addressed, showed this letter to me, and with overflowing tears, besought me to use my influence with the Superintendent, that she might be permitted to answer this letter. I told her I had no influence whatever with the Superintendent, but would try to procure the consent of Doctor Tenny to let her write. I also exhorted her to be watchful over her own conduct, and try to control the occasional vagaries of her mind; in short, to use every possible endeavor to preserve her sanity and her patience. She made the most commendable attempts to do this for several weeks, and my hopes were sanguine respecting her. I first saw her in the Fifth ward. She was walking the hall, pale, haggard, hopeless, and constantly biting the ends of her fingers. Her dress was ragged, her hair uncombed, and her whole appearance indicated a mind on the verge of despair.

In this condition I first tried to open to her the avenues of hope. In the absence of our attendant, at stealthy conversations, I discovered that she possessed excellent talents, was a good scholar, and had formerly moved in an elevated sphere of life. She was the only daughter of a physician; had in early life married a man of wealth and ambition, with whom she had lived happily for several years, and who had loaded her with comforts and luxuries. Subsequently, the tide of her fortune was reversed; misfortune came with swift and heavy shocks, upon her devoted head. Her affectionate father was laid in the grave. She lost her husband, to whom she was most tenderly attached, by the most terrible of all deaths, the death of his affections to herself.

Won by the fascinations of another, in an evil hour, he had deserted her forever, leaving three helpless babes upon her care, with no means of support. One by one these lovely children had all been laid in their graves, and the mother was left in the terrible loneliness of the heart's deepest desolation. No wonder the energies of her mind at last gave way; that the haunting images of her heart's lost treasures were ever before her eyes. Her health sunk, she was unable longer to combat successfully the tide of her terrible calamities. In this crisis, her own brother, instead of being her comforter, blamed her for not retaining the perfection of her energies, and turned against her in the most heartless manner. She now became unable longer to baffle adversity, and having no pecuniary resources left, was reduced to the necessity of accepting a home in a miserable county alms-house. Some time after leaving the "Asylum," I went into the vicinity where these events occurred, and after diligently inquiring, found all the statements of her history she had made to me, corroborated.

In my first interview with her, observing how she had lacerated her fingers by constantly gnawing them, in her agony of mind, I suggested "now let me wrap up your fingers, and

I want you to promise me not again to put them in your mouth. Will you solemnly promise this, and keep your word?" She complied, and I soon procured some rags, and bound up her bleeding fingers.

"Now," said she, "I want you to make a promise to me."

"What is it?" said I, "most happy should I be to do anything possible to relieve your condition."

"O, promise me," she entreated with earnest emphasis, "that you will never speak to me, nor take the least notice of me in the presence of Lizzy Bonner."

"Why should I promise this? you possess an intelligent mind, an immortal soul, you have been a great sufferer, and still remain so. I dislike to treat you with disrespect or neglect in the presence of any one."

"If Lizzy sees you trying to make me happy, she will feel reproved because she has never done so herself. She will hate and ill treat you worse than she does now; and more than that, she will separate us, and thus deprive you of all opportunity to carry out your kind intentions respecting me."

I saw in this response, so much sanity, and gratitude; so much in her mind worth cultivating, that it confirmed my determination to benefit this most deeply suffering woman if possible.

I can not here recount the experiments I tried, to aid her in bringing back to its full triumph, her wavering reason and self-control. My success astonished myself; I felt almost certain she would recover. Respecting the letter Mrs. G— so earnestly wished to write to her mother; with much difficulty, I had procured a sheet of paper for my own use; this she begged of me, and wrote upon it a very sensible and affectionate letter to her mother. No fault was found with the "Asylum," or with the fact of her long sufferings there, but she gave the idea that though she had been much disordered in mind, she hoped she was now improving; that she trusted she had acquired a good degree of self-control, and thought she could now return to her mother and make both happy. Doctor McFarland soon after appeared in the hall. Leading Mrs. G—— to him, I ventured to say, in a very respectful tone, "Doctor McFarland, I am happy to believe this person now fully clothed in her right mind. She has desired me to present a request to you, in behalf of herself and her mother, but I think her better capable of stating her own request, if you will please to listen to it." I then withdrew a little.

Mrs. G—— modestly advanced, and said in a very deferential tone, "O, Doctor dear, will you please be so very kind as to let me send this letter to my poor feeble mother, if after having read it, you think it proper. She is now getting quite old, and I am afraid, may not live the coming winter through. I have caused her much grief, and now if I could only be with her, I do think I could do much to make her happy. Please Doctor, grant my request, and I will be grateful to you as long as I live."

The Doctor barely deigned to hear this humble supplication, then turned his back, without a word, and left the hall. I had so often witnessed such replies to similar appeals, that I felt not the least surprise, but I much feared the effect of such a repulse upon the sensitive mind of his patient. She had for several weeks, been making the most energetic effort to govern her own mind. She had struggled nobly and successfully to repress the natural rising of indignation, when she had been abused by her keepers, tasked, beaten and reproached for not being able to quite fulfil the severe exactions in the toiling drudgeries every day assigned to her. With unrepining patience, this child of grief had borne all these indignities, supported by the hope that she should again taste the sweets of liberty and affection with her beloved mother. I had watched with the greatest pleasure, the progress she was making in the few hours of leisure that were allowed her in reading and needle-work. But now, a shock too great for her to sustain, was given by the Doctor's most heartless repulse.

A few days subsequent, a marked change for the worse came visibly over her mind and manners. She saw how fruitless were all the efforts she had been able to make for her own recovery, and again sunk into gloomy discouragement. She now laid aside her needle and her book, neglected her personal appearance, began to pace the hall in morose silence, tearing little bits of paper, and again biting her fingers. In vain I remonstrated; in vain attempted to rally the now departing gleams of reason. She seemed to have a perfect consciousness of her own peril; indeed told me she knew she was on the road to destruction. I sought in every way I could think of to divert her mind, urged her by every possible motive to try to recall hope, and still cultivate patience.

"No, no, it is all in vain," said she, with a look of tearless despair. "You can not raise me, so little power as you have here. They keep me working most of the time in the wash and ironing rooms, I've made up my mind now, that they mean to keep me here forever, I shall never see my mother any more; never again know the joy of liberty. O, I wish I was dead."

Her descent was rapid; a short time after, she tore to shreds every article of clothing upon her person. Her attendant put her at once into solitary confinement. This did not mend the matter, she broke the glass, mutilated the furniture, broke the crockery in her room and with the sharp fragments attacked her attendant, and wounded her severely in the arm. Lizzy quickly locked her door and ran to me, holding up her bleeding arm, requesting me to bind it up for her. I did so, but pitied her victim, more than herself. As soon as she dared, she again opened the door of Mrs. G—— and called me to look at the scene. O, what a spectacle! Never saw I more complete debasement! or more perfect abandonment of all decency in human conduct! She was shouting, swinging her arms, laughing triumphantly and horribly; swearing, dancing and screaming alternately. She was led to the wash-room, beaten and washed, then straightjacketed and tightly bound by cords to a stationary bench, in the public hall. While sitting here upon the bare floor, she kept constantly uttering the most profane, blasphemous expressions against herself and all around her, against God and nature, heaven and the universe! The young patients stared in perfect horror at her terrible transformation. Her words rolled in perfect torrents from her mouth so long as she had power of utterance. Then she foamed at the mouth, which was followed by gesticulations and motions so indecent, as to forbid all attempts at description. She became so intolerable, that every patient left that part of the hall, and huddled back into the remotest places, unable longer to endure her vicinity. Her room was close to my own. Her nights like her days, were spent in raving and shouting, "O, curses, curses on Dr. McFarland! O, my mother, my mother! O, my ruin! my ruin! etc."

These were the noises with which I was tormented all the long hours of those terrible nights! Again I feared for the continuance of my own sanity, so almost impossible was it to obtain any sleep. Every particle of decency and of humanity now seemed to have forsaken my once hopeful friend. Her countenance in its contortions had wrought out of itself almost every human feature. It was remarked by one of the patients, that she now looked more like a baboon than like a human being. In a few days, she was removed to the Fifth ward. She is doubtless now, if living, ranked among those who have by such a process been manufactured into incurables.

XVI.

Departure of Mrs. Packard.

"The higher law defies all feebler claims."

The limits of this book have been such as to exclude a detail of many scenes of most thrilling interest. Among these were the arrival and departure of patients. I invariably observed that the accession of a new one caused a feeling of universal distress to the initiated. "Poor soul!" they would often exclaim, "she little knows what she must suffer before she leaves this building!" The most stirring events connected with the departure of patients, were evolved by that of Mrs. Packard.

As the circumstances of her leaving have already been given to the public in her own most interesting book, "Three Years Imprisonment," I need not repeat them here. But there were some things of which she could not inform the public, not having witnessed them.

Her departure elicited a deep interest both among the sane, and the insane. Every motion made that had a bearing on the subject became a theme of animated discussion. "Will she really leave us now? will they force her to leave before she wishes? will her husband come and force her into another prison?" were questions that echoed from hall to hall.

That the machinations of her powerful enemies might be defeated, and her own ardent wishes for liberty granted, was the spontaneous prayer of all her Christian fellow sufferers there.

I have not yet, told my readers, what may now be proper to mention about, a new commandment, that Mrs. Packard and myself had some weeks before received. It could not be called a rule of the institution, since it affected none but ourselves. It was a new commandment, manufactured as the result of a discussion between McFarland and the prime-minister, Lizzy Bonner! It was this: "Mrs. Packard and Mrs. Olsen are no longer to be permitted to speak together."

This cruel law we obeyed, being determined that they should have no ground whatever to stand upon in case they undertook in future, to base any accusation against either our deportment or our sanity. Indeed we were "stubbornly obedient," as was once remarked by one who noticed the instant alacrity with which we both invariably obeyed McFarland's mandates, and from our respective halls, we daily met at our meals in the dining-hall, without exchanging a word or even bowing to each other. Thus, as all must see, we were compelled to violate good manners. Therefore the advocates of Lunatic Asylums must also carry on a war against good manners as well as against all the principles of religion and morality!

Had Mrs. Packard and my humble self been guilty of devising "treason, stratagems, and spoils," in our mutual conversations, there would have been some justice in this procedure. But as our conversation was such as could result in harm to no one, and was a great solace to ourselves, we could not resist the conviction that such a restriction was but an unmasked exhibition of pure tyranny.

But our vigilant Superintendent forgot to make a law or even "a new commandment," that we should not write to each other. He had evidently neglected to study the motto of my present chapter respecting "the higher law laughing at jurisprudence and restraint" so, thanks to his forgetfulness! we now applied "the higher law" for our own benefit; this we could do without breaking our promise not to break his lower law.

To me it was a source of great consolation to read the tender and thrilling letters she wrote to me, in these our days of trial. Our mutual letters were conveyed clandestinely of course. I often sent mine concealed in a boquet of flowers, which by special address I could occasionally beg. At other times, I would adroitly throw my letters before her path, as she was passing to and from her meals. We never took the least pains to conceal this from the patients knowing they would not betray us.

Truly "the way of transgressors is hard," besides being remarkably unsuccessful. For this tyranical commandment did not succeed in harming us, as was intended.

The time had now come when the great question was to be settled respecting the removal of our friend from the "Asylum." This decision was officially announced in our hall by Mrs. McFarland, in reply to eager inquiries. "Yes, Mrs. Packard is to leave here to-morrow morning, whether she intends it or not. Her trunk is already packed." No flash of lightning then came gleaming into our window; no clap of thunder broke our meditations; nor did an earthquake rock the ground our house was built upon; yet if all these phenomena had really happened, I hardly think the excitement could have been greater. The raving actually forgot to rave; the swearers were held in dumb suspense, even the scarred victims of despair looked up from their blood-shot eyes! The exclamations, discussions, questions that for several hours took precedence of every other commotion, I can not describe. There was joy indeed with two or three of the attendants, who felt that Mrs. Packard's influence was a constant impediment to their opportunities of abusing their victims. They dared not use the least disrespect to herself but they dreaded the power of her atmosphere over them, it was such a damper to the operations of this very "peculiar institution."

Rev. Mr. Packard arrived in the morning, and according to previous instructions, his unresisting wife was conveyed by force in the name of the State authority, to the carriage sent to convey her away from the Asylum. O, Illinois! proud Prairie State! are you not proud of your record now among the lovers of freedom!

Our hall was now vacated by all the attendants, who in another room, were watching this operation from the windows. I heard them laughing and shouting, and clapping hands, while Bonner vociferated a loud "hurrah for Mr. Packard!" But in our hall, the scene was the reverse. Sadly, and with a throbbing heart, I saw the carriage driven away, which contained the only one except Doctor Tenny who could prove an efficient friend to me then, in my otherwise utterly defenceless position. I made no attempt to repress the fast gathering tears, nor to console others. "She has gone!" said I at last, to some in the hall who had not observed the departure of the 'bus. At this announcement, one of the insane, who up to this point, had made no demonstration of her feelings, being angry that I had so spoken, approached me suddenly, and gave me a violent blow, which prostrated me at once upon the floor!

Some lectured on the oppressiveness of husbands, others on that of State institutions; a few on "Woman's Rights," but a larger number still upon a subject with which I think they had a much better acquaintance, namely, Woman's Wrongs.

XVII.

My Departure.

"I bear a charmed life."

Having survived the horrors of the Fifth ward, and the added torments of the Reign of Terror, I very naturally adopted the conclusion quoted at the head of this chapter. Nothing in Lunatic Asylums can hurt me now. My resurrection and ascension from that dread Purgatory where so many lay down their martyred lives, is a sure proof to my mind that I have conquered death and hell, since I can conceive nothing in either of these that can be more terrible.

But I made a mistake in supposing I could suffer no more from Lunatic Asylums. Their power to inflict almost every conceivable suffering is not so easily exhausted, as I shall now show by the following scenes.

I have before alluded to my being placed at the table by the side of Mrs. Triplet, the very fiercest of all the maniac's there. Still I had no fears of her, because she had so trained me to walk in the "strait and narrow way," while in Purgatory with her, that I supposed myself sufficiently aware of her peculiarities, to be able to protect myself from the danger of her vicinity. But she frequently had a fancy, on seeing the bead in her cup that was produced by pouring her coffee, that some one had been spitting in her cup, in order to vex her. This poor creature had so frequently been made a mark of ridicule by her attendant, and by some of the patients, who had no other amusement, that she had become excessively jealous and irritable. On this occasion, observing this appearance in her cup, she looked fiercely at me, as I was the nearest to herself, and exclaimed, "Now you've been spitting in my coffee." Then suddenly, seizing my chair, as I was about sitting down, and knocking me down prostrate with the same, she proceeded to pound and beat me with such violence that now even Lizzy interposed, and pulling her away, assisted me to rise from the floor. I limped back to my room, and did not recover for many days. Lizzy was heard to say she believed Mrs. Triplet would kill me if I had to sit so close to her, so she gave me another seat. Surely this is a Lunatic *Asylum!* Is not this a place of *rest!* This was about the tenth time I had been chased about in a similar manner by fierce patients with whom I was obliged to eat!

My charmed life was yet again jeopardized more than ever, by a young girl, there known as "screaming Mary." She was perfectly quiet and mild in her appearance all the time, except about twice in twenty-four hours, she would have fits of suddenly screaming like a panther. Then she would be quiet till the next attack. I discovered she had never been taught to read, and thought I would spend some of my leisure in teaching her. In this I was assisted by another lady. One day as I was teaching her, she all at once, sudden as a flash of lightning, struck me with a violent blow on the head, which prostrated me at once to the floor; then holding me down with one hand, with firm pressure she tore the hair from my head by handfuls, and furiously beat me on the head, till I was nearly unconscious. I thought myself dying at the moment, so intense was the pain. My fellow patients, seeing my danger, sprang instantly to my rescue. They instantly seized Mary, gently but firmly, and after having with difficulty loosened her grasp from my hair, dragged her away, and held her till the attendant, then absent from the hall, heard the noise, and came to see what was the matter. Seeing the state of the case, she laughed heartily at the scene, said she did'nt care, I might mind my own business! My business then, so soon as I could walk, was to go to the washroom, and cleanse away the blood, and bathe my head in water. I was not then allowed to do this, for the dinner bell rang at the moment, and I was compelled to go to the table in this plight, my net completely demolished, my hair dishevelled and standing out in all directions. More than seventy women with their attending officials, saw me in this horrible plight! Unable to swallow food, I crawled rather than walked back to the wash-room alone, where I gently bathed my head in water to relieve the pain. I reclined upon my bed, and the thought came, surely "I bear a charmed life!"

Some time after, I asked Mary why she did this, when I was trying to teach her to read. Her reply was that she "s'posed" I would be like her former teachers, at the New York Orphan Asylum, where she had formerly been, who when she could not get her lesson, used to strike and beat her. On this occasion she had found a hard word, and being afraid that I should also strike her, concluded it was best to kill me to prevent it.

Of my own experience, little more need be said. It was but a repetition with little variation, of the preceding scenes, I have faintly delineated. Weariness, home-sickness, heart-sickness from hope deferred, and constant disgust and abhorence of the deceptions and oppressions I constantly witnessed, these were the objects of my daily thoughts.

In the same hall with myself, attracting my attention every hour, are four furious maniacs, whose presence is always dangerous, unless one is constantly on the watch. These are allowed to walk the halls unconfined at pleasure, to come into my room, and other rooms as they please, while there are others here quiet and perfectly harmless whose feeble unresisting limbs are daily confined with straight-jackets and bound with strong cords! Why such glaring injustice? Because our Superintendent neither knows nor cares for the condition of half his patients. He leaves Lizzy Bonner to "cure or kill them," to influence their minds, and train their various sanities and insanities as her own convenience or caprice may dictate!

One woman is now trying to kill herself by beating her head with all her might against the hard wall. Why don't they put her into a chair and place it so far from the wall that she could not hurt her head when throwing it back? She has been beaten with such terrible severity by her attendants, that now she undoubtedly thinks an addition by her own hands, would beat quite out the lingering spark of life, and end her suffering.

On the occasion to which I now refer, she had been again most shockingly beaten by some of the wild ones in the Purgatory, and from this place had recently been brought up.

This treatment had maddened her to desperation, and caused her as I thought, to make this renewed attempt at self-destruction. Lizzy applied a straight-jacket shortly, to which she made not the least resistance, but with an appealing glance which I can never forget, she looked up to me and said with slow accent, and with deep emphasis, " *Jesus is my witness!*" Yes, O, sufferer! Jesus is indeed thy witness, he will hear thy dying prayer! She said no more, and was immediately removed to the Fifth ward.

Not far from this time, one of the keys of the hall was missed. Lizzy suspected Miss Hodson, the industrious sewing girl from the Fifth ward, and questioned her. She denied having taken the key, but was not believed. Then commenced the most shocking scene of injustice I had ever beheld. Lizzy insisted Miss Hodson was guilty of the theft, and commenced searching her room, in every nook and corner. She scattered the bed all over the floor seeking the key. It was all in vain; it was nowhere to be found! She next accused Miss Hodson of having secreted the key about her person. This was also denied. Lizzy then hastily tore off all her clothing, till the helpless victim of such diabolical indecency, feeling a just indignation, wrought up to the highest climax of rage, fought the attendant with most terrible desperation. Seeing the contest doubtful Lizzy shouted for reinforcement; her fellow attendant came instantly to the rescue. Then both seized their victim, the one holding her arms, the other actually kneeling upon her body and beating her furiously, vociferously shouted, "now tell us where you've hid that key?"

Lizzy then pounded her on the bowels and head, kicked her furiously, and in the progress of the battle, tore out her hair, and beat her nose heavily against the floor, raising her head up and down rapidly by the hair! The sufferer now ceased all resistance; she became speechless and as I thought, insensible. Lizzy, to extort the expected confession, then ordered the other attendant to bring a pail of water. I looked on in dumb horror as I then saw those two attendants plunge the bruised head of that motherless orphan into the water, and hold it there till she strangled convulsively gasping for breath. She was now speechless, motionless and naked, they then applied a straight-jacket to her unresisting arms, locked her into a room and left her!

I beheld this whole scene without daring to remonstrate, having been many times punished for trying to excite pity for the victims when under these modes of torture. These injuries of Miss Hodson I think were incurable.

She never, while I remained, did any more work for the Institution, but would sit or lie on the floor of her own room mostly, brooding over her unrequited wrongs, in melancholy silence. After the terrible scene I have related, she never was known to converse socially with any one. By swift degrees, she appeared to lose all hope; at last she became a furious maniac. I think they have made her an incurable, if indeed she is living.

I ought to add, that a few minutes after the perpetration of this outrage, the lost key was found in the shoe of a Mrs. McClay, a patient who had made several attempts to run away. The attendants did not give Mrs. McClay the least punishment. I thought it was because they were too much fatigued in fighting Miss Hodson! Justice!! I did not tell the Doctor of this scene. Why should I? I knew that he perfectly well knew that similar scenes were every day occurring in different parts of the *Asylum!*

My brothers now began to think vigorously on the subject of my leaving the "Asylum." They saw that my husband had confided me entirely to the disposition of Dr. McFarland, and they had serious misgivings about the propriety of letting me remain longer in such hands. So they concerted together as to what plan could now be adopted for my liberation.

They were not satisfied with the way I was being managed, and now took the business into their own hands. By what authority they acquired the power to release me I never cared to inquire. Lawyers were consulted, letters without number written, and plans discussed. More than six months passed in these tiresome negotiations and delays before they were able to shape a way by which my deliverance could be effected. If they had known that all this time, my health was going to ruin, that I was literally dying by inches, they would not thus have protracted my lingering misery. But such was their confidence in Dr. McFarland, and in his most fallacious reports, they presumed all was going on right, only my long detention gave them uneasiness. I longed beyond all expression, to have some rest. O, I was so weary, weary; I longed for some Asylum from "Lunatic Asylums!"

One morning Dr. Tenny came to my room and announced the thrice welcome intelligence, that my brother had come to take me away! Was I in a trance; was liberty again to be be mine? I knew not how to express my joy. I was free! free!!

My limits will not permit me to relate the scene of parting with my sisters in bonds. It was such as to confirm my affection and devotion to them and to all who bear the dreadful name of Lunatic, forever. I leave you, my sad suffering sisters, in your "bonds and imprisonments;" but most deeply unworthy should I prove myself of the sacred boon of liberty, if I fail to remember you in bonds as still bound with you.

Be not discouraged my sisters; "learn to labor, pray and wait," I was about to add, but this would be absurd in your cases, who have already sufficiently learned these cross-bearing lessons. But learn rather to hope and to expect what I confidingly believe at no distant day awaits you, that "the day of your redemption draweth nigh."

XVIII.

Reports—Visits of Trustees.

There is nothing which the Superintendent, and others in the pay of "Lunatic Asylums" so much dread, as the diffusion of truthful intelligence on the subject of insanity, and the manner in which it should be treated. Hence the exceeding brevity of their "Reports," and the adroitness with which they will dodge the main subject on which the people most desire information in those "Reports."

I refer especially to the "Reports" of Dr. McFarland. In these we find much said about the outside arrangement and management, improvements and need of more improvements in the external machinery and accessories of the "Asylum." The attention of the reader is carefully kept aloof from a correct view of the internal movements and influences of this most complicated machinery, by the most consummate policy in the skillful writer. By presenting a dazzling view of the outside, he undoubtedly infers that his reader, without exacting the minute details, will naturally suppose that all is right within. And too many of his readers confirm him in that conclusion, by the credulous eagerness with which "our most accomplished Superintendent's Report," with all its fallacies is accepted.

The writer of these documents treats his readers very much as he does the Trustees, when they visit the Institution. He detains nearly all their time outside the building, where they examine the steam apparatus, the laundries, cook-room, the horse-stable, cow-stable, pig-pens, hen-roosts, wood shed, gardens, flowers, and shrubbery. All these, of course, are found in the most admirable order and perfection. After such a fatiguing excursion, these gentlemen are politely escorted to the banqueting hall, where an elegant dinner is just the thing to confirm their good nature, and prepare them to be pleased with every thing that subsequently invites their attention. After these most important essentials are all attended to, these gentlemen are politely escorted through the numerous halls by the Superintendent and his officials. There, a few brief minutes are spent in glancing at the hundreds of human beings who are suffering the deepest and most varied woe that mortals can suffer. To them the Trustees present themselves, bowing and smiling, full of pleasure and good nature; give them a bird's eye view, about as they would examine buildings seen from a railroad car in rapid motion!

Very rarely speak these hasty gentlemen to any of the patients; and when they do, the latter know this is no time, in such brief public visits, for any adequate knowledge respecting their condition to be divulged. They well know, that if they tell the truth to the Trustees respecting what they suffer, either that it will not be believed, or that its expression will be construed into an indication of insanity. Besides, what they might report of their real condition, would not agree with the ostensible appearances seen all around them. They also well know that if they tell the truth, they will be punished for doing so, as soon as the visitors are out of sight. They possess sufficient sanity to know that "discretion is the better part of valor."

How have I wished, after these flying visits of the Trustees, that they could immediately return, and in a condition of invisible presence, hear the conversations I have heard among the patients, on these periodical occasions. It would be as follows: "I wish they would treat us with as much respect as they do the cattle on these premises; I noticed their visit to the stable was much longer than to our hall."

"I presume," responded another, "they think we are of less consequence than the beasts; for they see to it that all the wants of their nature are attended to, while our most urgent necessities are regarded as unworthy of attention." "But what good results from their coming at all?" queried a third, "we are not benefitted by such visits; our condition is really made worse, for these deceitful outside appearances indicate to them that we are happy, while the most miserable are locked up in some secret place, and not permitted to be seen at all, lest the abuse they suffer should be seen on their countenances. At the same time, these visitors, who look only upon the surface, and judge only from what they see, and that, too, varnished up for the occasion, go away and report favorably. Thus are these Institutions 'kept up.'" Another asserting voice replied, "I wish these Trustees never would call again, since their visits, managed as they are, produce not only no benefit, but much harm to us."

But I commenced this paper by adverting to the evident wish, on the part of the Superintendent, to keep people in ignorance on the subject of the real philosophy of insanity, and the proper method of its cure. There is an abundance of facts to confirm this conjecture, for books, papers, etc., have been many times taken away by his orders, which conveyed intelligence on this subject. The works of some of the best authors on the laws of health, water cure, etc., have been carefully excluded from circulation in the "Asylum;" and though some of the privileged are allowed to read such works, when sent by friends, they are strictly forbidden to lend them to their companions. The same is true of the Doctor's own "Reports." Not one of them is allowed to be read by the patients. Why? Were he conscious of having told the truth thoroughly, then why not let it be proclaimed in all places, even on the house tops? Will not the truth bear a just revelation? What can we trust, if not the truth? Have falsehood and fallacy superior claims to our confidence?

But there is an obvious reason why these officers should be in such a tremor when the truth is likely to peep out from some of its coverts. They well know that if their "Peculiar Institutions," and the subject of insanity which they envelop with so much mystery, should be boldly and thoroughly investigated, their deceptions would be exposed, and consequently the "craft" by which they have their wealth, essentially endangered.

XIX.

Fallacies.

Of all subjects which interest or agitate our social life, I know of none so indistinctly understood, or around which cluster such utter vagueness of conception, such fallacious reasoning, as the subject of insanity and its real or supposed victims. It seems that we content ourselves with less investigation, less thought upon that, than upon any other subject; though nothing in all the enterprises of human benevolence calls more loudly at the present time, for clear, independent, and earnest thought. The suddenness with which people in all conditions of life are said to be attacked with insanity, the alarming multiplication of lunatics, the increased and imperious demand made upon our State Legislatures for large sums of money to be expended in the erection and endowment of "Lunatic Asylums," seem sufficient considerations to justify the assertion that we are quite too superficial in the data upon which we are accustomed to base our conclusions respecting the wants of the insane.

There exists quite too great a disposition to transfer individual responsibility to public and popular institutions; hence there naturally arises a great temptation to the officers of such institutions to abuse and greatly magnify the power so freely confided to them. Therefore I contend that instead of employing these public officers to think for us, to manage for us the disordered intellects of our insane friends, "a more excellent way" would be to arouse and awaken our own thoughts, and look the subject in the face, instead of becoming needlessly alarmed, and stupidly consigning often the dearest ones of our family circle to the very doubtful tender mercies of hireling strangers.

But now, as "Lunatic Asylums" are sprinkled so liberally all over our broad land, and "the cry is still they come," taxing the masses and swelling the pyramid of false national pride, what have the people to do but to fill up these receptacles with those superfluous members of a family, who are temporarily the sufferers of something unusual about their minds, which for want of another name, is at once called "insanity." This is the everlasting hobby; this the fulcrum of a great moral lever which, I believe, is one of the greatest causes of domestic discord and distress.

Does any one in the family circle evince symptoms of unusual conditions of mind, for which we cannot readily account; this is the ready epithet all manufactured to order for the startling emergency. Has a woman become excessively exhausted by weary vigils over the sick bed of some beloved one, so that for a time, she fails to step as swiftly, or smile as sweetly as usual, but flags a little in the race of her life; she is forthwith denounced insane, and punished accordingly by being sentenced to that horrible abode the " Lunatic Asylum !" If some blundering ignoramus of a Doctor, instead of curing a fever, throws it into the head, so that the patient becomes the victim of a temporary delirium—which the Doctor knows how to produce, but not how to cure—here is another victim of " insanity" to be carried off to the " Asylum !"

If a person is afflicted with neuralgia, or has lost the control and ordinary use of some of his limbs, he too, is " insane," and off he must go to that great groaning and gorged receptacle of bleeding humanity ! If a man or woman choose to adopt some of those systems of religious belief, which in one of Dr. McFarland's reports is termed " popular delusions," and it so happens that the " delusion" in question conflicts too severely with the ultra orthodoxy of the patient's friends; this also becomes at once a conclusive evidence of " insanity," and the conscientious but helpless victim must pay the severe penalty of mental independence, by an imprisonment in the self same notable Lunacy-curing (?) establishment. If a too sensitive young lady loses her lover, either by his death, or by desertion, so that her crushed affections vainly wander for some object to rest upon; the pale cheek, the sad eye, and the unhealed grief evincing the heart's deep disappointment, are construed by her fond, but lamentably ignorant parents as evidences of insanity; and yet another victim is hurried into the terrible jaws of that ever hungry monster the "Lunatic Asylum!" If a young but too trusting heart, ensnared by some serpent in human form, has taken that "one false step" which "forever blasts her fame," and her proud parents see thereby, occasion to wish to put her out of sight, it is easy to call her insane; and here very emphatically does this most accomodating institution exemplify its power in giving a convenient shelter to the pride of parents.

One more secret I must tell in a whisper. If a man becomes tired of living with his wife, and finds his affections being alienated from her because she has outlived her beauty and grown prematurely old, and her health has decayed in her arduous labors for himself and for their children—it is easy for such a husband to treat her with coldness and tyranny, which causes her that heart-breaking anguish which she can not control—it is a very easy matter for such indications to be construed into insanity; and again the ponderous doors of that great "whited sepulcher" are thrown open, to swallow up within its ample labyrinth of destruction another victim of "insanity!"

Her now freed gallant, noble husband, does not complain of the taxes and expenses incident to such an Institution. Nay, nay; he shouts "Hurrah for Lunatic Asylums! I go in for Lunatic Asylum! Noble charities! Grand institutions! they suit my case exactly. My wife is insane—the Doctor says so, bless the kind man; now I am relieved—my wife is in good hands now. Long life to the Superintendent! Glorious institutions! Jacksonville Lunatic Asylum forever!"

XX.

Influence of Insane Asylums upon their Victims.

One great objection to "Lunatic Asylums" is that they create a virtual abrogation of the marriage vow. In this, each party promises, by every sacred obligation of our nature, and by the immortal sanctions of our religion, to share all the fortunes and destiny of the other "in sickness and in health, till death do us part." Now what becomes of this sacred promise when one of the parties consigns the other to a prison, where her liberty of speech and action is impeded at every point? Instead of sharing sorrow together, one party endures a grief in which the other does not participate—the constant sorrow caused by the banishment from home and all its countless blessings. When a husband does this, instead of taking care of her as he promised, he trusts her to a great company of strangers who neither know nor care for her, and whom he does not know himself, and in most cases, has never seen. Who are those thus entrusted to "take care" of these sorrow-stricken ones? Not the Superintendent—indeed he does not even know half the time what attention they require. He seldom sees them, and still more seldom speaks to them. Not his wife—she is fully employed in other ways; but a miscellaneous horde of stupid servants mostly, who are gathered from the kitchens of hotels, or other places of service, and these too quite often, from the lowest class of English, Irish and German servants, whose principal qualification is that they are strong and willing to obey orders!

These are the ones, Oh, husbands! who you think are better qualified than yourselves to take your feeble and diseased wives, and guide their disordered minds to healthy action! Many of these servants can not write their own names, or even read. What do they know of the philosophy of the human intellect!—what of curing insanity?

I wish the public could be aroused to the absurdity of such a blind acquiescence in the supposed necessity of such "Asylums." It seems that the whole public have gone mad in their blind devotion to this pet Institution. I have sometimes thought that if all the inmates of the Jacksonville "Asylum" were at once entirely liberated, and an equal number of the advocates of that Institution, including Dr. McFarland of course, immediately confined in their places, that the State would be the gainer by such an arrangement; for on this subject I verily believe, in the language of a gifted Poet, that truth authorizes us to exclaim,

> "See Bedlam's closeted and hand-cuffed charge,
> Surpassed in frenzy by the mad at large!"

When public opinion is thus misguided, it is capable of producing an incalculable amount of mischief. These Institutions build up an absolute monarchy in the very center of our Republican government, thus creating an eternal warfare between the two. Their tendency is therefore to weaken Republicanism just in proportion to their own increase of power. The power thus conferred by our State legislation upon one individual is absolutely fearful to contemplate. His influence is greater over domestic life than that of the Governor of the State. It is not the business of the Governor to decide as to individual cases of insanity. If a man suspects one of his family is insane, he does not apply to the Governor, but to Dr. McFarland, who always finds the suspicion well-founded. On him, on his absolute will and dictation, depend the destinies and happiness of many hundred families within the State. Yea, on his *ipse dixit* it depends whether a husband and wife shall live together, as God appointed, or whether the wife, *nolens volens*, shall be separated from him and assigned a far different life from his own, in the care of a man who feels not, or ought not to feel, for her any peculiar affection. For him it is to decide whether a mother shall enjoy the privilege, given to her by God and nature, of nursing and training her own offspring, or whether the tender infants be consigned like herself, to cold and careless hirelings.

But it is objected, "the mother is not fit to take care of her children." Why is she not fit? Because she believes that spirits from heaven watch over and guide both herself and her children? Because she believes that our religious opinions ought to be free and untrammelled? Because she thinks that primitive Christianity is a better guide than its mock imitations of the present degenerate age? These are the only grounds on which a very large number of the Jacksonville patients have been confined and kept away from their homes and their families.

Witness the case of Mrs. Minard, who, for nine years was thus abused—of Mrs. Packard, who, for three years was allowed by the laws of the State, to be kept against her own wishes, from her home and family. Of many others, whose cases, though less strongly marked, come no less within the class of those whose peculiar religious belief does not at all unfit them from performing all their home duties, were they allowed to do so, in the most praiseworthy and exemplary manner.

The prejudices of a misguided public in favor of this Institution, and the power resulting, opens the way for any tyrannical and wicked husband who wishes to get rid of his unloved wife, to vex and annoy her into sickness, or some nervous, irritable, or otherwise unfortunate condition of mind, to call this "insanity," and send her away, either by criminal deception, or brutal compulsion, to these most deceptive places called "*Asylums.*"

There, by degrees, every feeling of her gentle nature is crushed and outraged. She learns, not to forget her innocent children, but, by imperceptible degrees, she does often learn to cease to love her lawful husband, and he has taught her the lesson himself by the stupid, the blind, the criminal confidence he reposes in a popular public man, called, *The Superintendent of a Lunatic Asylum.*

The Insane "Asylum" crucifies the warmest affections of the heart; resists all the spontaneous impulses and aspirations of human life, and crushes out, inch by inch, in the lacerated bosom of many a bleeding victim, the last expiring remnants of earthly hope. Is it superfluous, then, to pronounce these institutions an unqualified curse? I consider them the greatest plague spots upon our national escutcheon. "Asylums" indeed they are, but not in any sense, to that deeply afflicted class for whom, in the plenitude of its benevolence, our generous State designed. They have been corrupted—perverted, so that instead of curing lunacy, they are far better adapted to increase and render incurable, cases of but partial derangement—indeed, to create insanity where it did not previously exist.

They are "Asylums" where sin can cover its hydra-headed form with impunity; where tyranny, unmolested and unquestioned can preside.

They are "Asylums" where the most concentrated and appalling features of the veriest despotism under the sun, can prosper and flourish; where falsehood can bury its shameless front, under the insidious disguises of mock piety; where robbery, theft and murder are unrebuked.

Language is utterly powerless to describe the terrible effect of a long compulsory residence within those awful walls, upon those most unhappy beings there incarcerated. Many die outright, before the various stages of that stultifying process become completed. Those who survive, often become the victims of incurable melancholy. All hope flies away, for they feel that one by one, every tie which bound them to life is severed; that friends have proved traitors; vows, a stupid nullity; every pore of life is bleeding, and every heart-throb an impulse of agony. The climax of despair at last succeeds, and many are driven to suicide.

These victims have been taught to regard their former friends as enemies, and these very "friends" have taught this terrible lesson;

"And truest friends, through error, wound our rest."

In the wreck of human intellect and human affection thus caused, the spectacle is often presented of deformed and dethroned humanity, the contemplation of which is sufficient to "make an angel weep!"

Where then is the benefit of "Lunatic Asylums?" Echo responds,—Where?

XXI.

Testimony of Mrs. Sarah Minard, of St. Charles, Ill.

Knowing that the public are ignorant of the real character of their Institution at Jacksonville, where I have been held an unwilling *prisoner,* for the last nine years, I feel conscience-bound to give to the public the following testimony, hoping it may open the eyes of some of the deluded defenders of such institutions, to see the need of either reforming or of destroying them.

At the solicitation of friends, I consented, nine years since, to go to Jacksonville Insane Asylum, to secure a course of " medical treatment," such as they thought might be a benefit to my health. We all supposed that Insane Asylums were hospitals, where the patient received some " medical treatment," superior to what could be obtained elsewhere; and as my nervous system had become somewhat prostrated by disease, and on the principle that prevention is better than cure, I consented to go and receive medical treatment for my nervous system. But nine years of experience and observation have convinced me that this Institution is far from being the place to be benefitted by the " treatment " bestowed upon the patient.

When I first went there, I felt that I needed some medicine for my health, and told the physician so; but he not only refused to give me any, but even ridiculed me for expressing the opinion that I thought I came there to go through some course of " medical treatment !" All the medicine I took during the nine years I was there, was a little soda water, which the Doctor sent me one morning, after I had been suffering severely all one night, alone in my room, from a cholera-like attack. I was once confined three days to my bed, with an attack of what I called erysipelas; but I had no medicine administered to me during this sickness. So that so far as receiving "medical treatment" there is concerned, we might as well lie upon our own beds at home, and let disease take its course, as lie upon a bed in that hospital. It is very seldom that any one receives "medical treatment" while there. Many needed it very much, but could get none at all. I often used to hear the patients remark, "Why are we sent here, if not to secure for ourselves some kind of medical treatment? but we get none at all." And oftentimes it is the case, that when the patients are so sick as to be unable to sit up, they are not often allowed to lie down, even when they ask the privilege of doing so. "Keep them off from their beds!" is the Doctor's oft-repeated direction; and this seems to be his great and main prescription for "medical treatment!" But for the last two years, the attendants in the Seventh ward, where the patients secure the best treatment of any ward in the house, have ventured to use their own judgment in relation to this prescription, and they have allowed the sick patients to lie down when *they* thought their health required it. It is an unspeakable blessing there to be under the care of a humane attendant, who has sufficient moral courage to dare to use her own judgment, in defiance of the cruel, arbitrary rule of the house.

Arbitrary rule is the law of the house. For example, order is given to all the ladies in every ward, that they must put their clothes out of their rooms at night, before they are locked up for the night. In the morning, the ladies must all come out of their rooms into the hall to dress themselves, and the attendants must lock their doors, to prevent their returning to prepare their toilets alone in their own rooms. No reason whatever, would be assigned to the patients, why they should be subjected to this great inconvenience and mortification. It seemed to them to be only an effort to break them down into a state of abject subjection as dependent menials.

The first thing that is done to a patient, by way of "treatment," after they arrive, usually is, to plunge them into the bath-tub; and if they make any resistance to these plunges, they are oftentimes held completely under the water, until almost dead, before they allow them a chance to breathe. I have often heard patients say they thought they should die of strangulation by this treatment. This treatment is afterwards used as a threat, ever overhanging them, in case of any resistance to the will or wishes of those who rule over them.

I once saw an attendant jump upon the stomach of a patient with her knees, after throwing her upon the floor upon her back, and all she had done to deserve it, was to take a piece of bread from the table to carry to her room! It frightened me exceedingly, for I thought it would kill her, and I called upon others to defend her.

The first thing they did to me by way of "treatment," was to insist upon my going to my breakfast before my hair was combed. I asked leave to finish dressing and preparing my toilet, before I went. My attendant said I should go as I was. I refused, saying, "I shall not go to the table until I get dressed." She said, "You shall go as you are, or go without your breakfast!" She locked my door, so I could not go to my breakfast. I was always through before the rest, and they knew I should be if I took time to dress me before I went to the table. The patients were allowed to go to the table in the most untidy manner, with unwashed faces and uncombed hair, and I could not encourage such untidiness by my own example. I believe I did more to encourage order and decency, by this course, than by falling into these untidy habits myself.

I was once locked in my room because I told the *truth*. I related something which my attendant thought was not true. I told her it was true. She contradicted me, and said, "If you assert that again, I shall lock you up in your room!" I replied, "It is as I said." She then locked me up.

The patients are sometimes struck with the keys by the attendants, upon their hands and heads; and sometimes deep gashes are cut into their heads by this kind of abuse. Sometimes the attendants gave the patients a severe beating with the sole of their shoes.

A rule has recently been made, that no visitors can be admitted except on Tuesdays and Fridays, and on these days, the patients are required to appear in their best, the house is put in perfect order, and the instruments of punishment and torture are concealed, such as the straps, straight-jackets, etc., so that the visitors see only the best aspect of things. The great object of the Institution seems to be to subject the patient to the will of the persecutor.

The table fare has been extremely poor for the last two years; no fruits, no melons, scarcely any vegetables, no new milk at all, oftentimes, although twenty-five cows are kept there at the State's expense. The calves are raised and fatted on the new milk for exhibition at the State fairs! The vegetables are appropriated to the same use, at the patients' loss. Frequently they are without any butter for several days in succession, and often when it is provided, it is so poor it can hardly be eaten. The tea and coffee are very weak and very poor, without cream and without new milk. Meats they have in abundance, suited to the fare of working men, rather than a class of house invalids.

I will mention the case of Mrs. Emma Craig, of Bairdstown, whose case represents a large class of patients I saw there. She is a spirit medium, *but not insane.* She was kidnapped and put in without any trial, simply because she claims that she converses with her three children, who died a few years since; and this they call her "insanity." She shows no evidence of insanity whatever, in her conduct—it is only her opinions she is imprisoned for. She disliked to be bathed in the manner required, feeling that it injured her health. Her attendants then forced her under the water, abusing her by their rough handling, then took her to her room, and there knocked her head against the wall, with so much violence, that her false teeth flew from her mouth, when her attendants became so frightened that they left her; and thus this fortunate accident saved her from a continuance of this kind of abuse!

I, Mrs. Minard, do hereby testify, that I do not think I was insane any of the time I was there; neither do I think my friends ever had any justifiable cause for locking me up as an insane person. I know I have said and done things they could not understand, neither can I tell how these ideas came to me. I never went with the Spiritualists, nor have I read their books, but I know I do converse with spirits, and receive direction from them and instruction; but I can't tell how it comes to me. And this is what they call my insanity. But it is not insanity—it is spiritual religion. I feel that I have had a spirit guard about me, or I should have become insane, by the treatment I have experienced in Jacksonville Insane Asylum. That Asylum is a most dreadful place to put one into, as it was conducted while I was there. If that Asylum is a specimen of others, I think they had better all be destroyed, than go on as they are now conducted. No one who goes there can ever feel entirely free from the bad influences which they get while there; and when once put there, they are almost certain to be put there again and again.

I took the whole care of my room, during all the time I was there. Only once was my bed made for me, except those three days of sickness, and no one has ever complained of me for not keeping my room in good order; and no one ever did a stitch of sewing for me. I did all my own sewing, except to have a dress cut and fitted occasionally. Only one was made for me, and that was made out of the house. I did all my own washing and ironing during the last two years I was there. I was in the best ward all the time I was there, and I never was locked up in any room but my own. The attendants treated me with almost uninterrupted kindness; they have not locked my door at night for seven years, neither did they require me to put my own things out of my room at night. I was the only one who was ever allowed to enjoy these privileges during all the time of their imprisonment; and this act of partiality caused some complaints amongst the multitude of other prisoners, who were equally trustworthy as myself.

The spiritual influence which accompanied me while there, seems to have left me since my return home. I do not seem to possess those spiritual gifts I then did. I can't tell why they are withdrawn, more than I could tell why or how they were bestowed. I don't know that I have done anything wrong, to cause their withdrawal. I can trust, however, it will all prove to be for the best that it is so, for my friends might continue to call it insanity, and thus my personal liberty be exposed again; for all the world could not tempt me to be false to my own honest convictions of truth and duty. All I want, and sigh for, is *religious freedom*—that I may dare to *do right*, and not imperil my personal liberty by so doing! Thank God! my personal liberty is now protected in *Illinois*, by the passage of the "Personal Liberty Bill." Would that no other State Asylum could imprison me again without a jury trial! But I shall not dare to do wrong, however, even to prevent another incarceration, and I do hope I shall never be imprisoned again.

These Insane Asylums are the worst houses in the world in my opinion, and I do wish they might all be destroyed; and I think this would be the wish of every one, if they only knew just how they are carried on, as I do, from my nine years' imprisonment there. I wish all those who defend them could be locked in one long enough to feel and know the *truth*, as I do, for I am sure they would then agree with me in wishing them all demolished. I do hope and pray that no others will ever be built in this, or any other State, unless they can be ruled with love and kindness. These are the only reformatory principles in the universe; but abuse and cruelty only cause, increase, and perpetuate the *evils* Asylums are designed to cure.

I was discharged May 1, 1867, as the result of the passage of the "Personal Liberty Bill," March 5, 1867, without any trial. SARAH P. MINARD

St. Charles, May 9, 1867.

XXII.

Testimony of Mrs. Tirzah F. Shedd, of Aurora, Ill.

It is for the benefit of those now in Jacksonville Insane Asylum that I give the following testimony to the public, hoping it may stimulate the people to provide some remedy for existing evils.

This is to certify, that I, Mrs. T. F. Shedd, was incarcerated in this Asylum on the 7th of July, 1865. I was imprisoned there fourteen weeks. My baby was five months and a half old, when I was taken from her, and my two other little girls, and *forced* entirely against my will and protest, into this prison-house, for an indefinite length of time, on the charge of monomania on spiritualism, brought against me by my husband. True I had a mock jury trial at Geneva court house, as the statute law of 1865 requires; still I felt that justice could not be done me before such a tribunal of prejudice as existed against me on the ground of my spiritualism. And so it proved. My case was *not fairly tried* before an impartial tribunal, and therefore I was condemned as insane on the subject of spiritualism.

This decision therefore placed my personal liberty entirely in the hands of my husband, who was fully determined to use this legal power to subject my views to his will and wishes. I, of course, resisted this claim, and assured him I should never yield my right to my personal liberty to him or any other power; for so long as he could bring nothing against me but what I regarded as my religion, I claimed the protection of my personal liberty under the flag of religious toleration. Notwithstanding all my arguments, my entreaties, my prayer, my protests and my vigorous resistance, by fighting single handed and alone my six strong men captors, for forty-five minutes, I was finally taken from my sick bed, bruised and sore from this brutal assault, and carried in my undress to the cars, with the handcuffs dangling at my side, leaving my little girls screaming in agony at this unnatural bereavement of their tender, loving mother. And yet this is a land of religious freedom! It may be a land of freedom for the *men*, but I am sure it is not for the *married women!*

And although entirely sane, the heartless Dr. McFarland did receive me, when my last hope of liberty died within me, and I found myself entirely in the power of a man, whom I had sad reason to fear was not worthy of the unbounded trust and confidence he was then receiving from the people of Illinois. After I was discharged, I expressed this same opinion to him in a letter as follows: "Dr. McFarland, I gathered facts from every department of the Asylum—and your private conduct towards me, which I well understood at the time—*enough to ruin you!*" I have no confidence in that man's honesty. His policy is stronger than his principles; and I told him this opinion too, in my letter to him in these words, "You took my husband by the hand and when alone said to him, 'Mr. Shedd, this woman (meaning me) is not crazy, nor never has been, excited she may have been from various causes; but temporary derangement is not possible with such an organization, although I shall pronounce her hopelessly insane, because she will not say she has changed her mind!'"

Is not his decision that I am insane, the dictation of his selfish policy, instead of his honest conviction? It seems to me that he is willing to belie his own judgement to shield himself and my persecutors from harm. And the written advice he gave my husband, strengthens this conviction in my own mind, viz: "Mr. Shedd, you must not tyrannize over her, but flatter her with presents, and let her have her own way as much as you can." Why is this? Is he not afraid I shall become exasperated toward this party including himself, and expose them in consequence? It seems so to me, for he says it is impossible for me to become insane, and this advice did not seem to be needed for my protection or good.

I think Dr. McFarland is not fit for his place, and as I view it, the safest course for him to pursue now is, for him to resign; and I advised him to do so in my letter, viz: "All that I now ask is that you give up that position which you confessed to me you were sick of five years ago, and release those women you hold there as prisoners, under the will of cruel husbands, and others who call themselves friends." This letter from which these extracts are made, was sent back to my husband with this single sentence added to it, "Is Mrs. Shedd becoming more insane? A. M."

There were a great many spiritualists there, whom he called insane like myself, for this reason alone, seeming to fear them as witnesses against him, unless they carried his diploma of "hopeless insanity" upon them. He has been obliged to liberate many such of late, by the enforcement of the law for the "Protection of Personal Liberty," and he was very careful too to send off this class of "hopelessly insane" (?) prisoners before the time appointed by the Legislature for their jury trial, so that by this policy they were denied the opportunity of a jury trial, in vindication of their sanity. And had the jury's decision contradicted the Doctor's opinion, as it did in Mrs. Packard's case, he might have had more reason to fear their influence.

One day after I had cut and made me a neat and becoming white dress, the Doctor seeing me in it remarked, "I don't see how a man could put a lady like you away from her home." At another time, he remarked, "if you were my wife, I should want you at home." Would he want an *insane* wife at the head of his family?

I enjoyed many privileges there which others did not, and I might have used these liberties to escape; but I chose rather to remain until all my prison keepers had had a fair opportunity to see that I was not insane. I also wished to look into the secret workings of this prison, but in order to do this I knew I must first secure their entire confidence, and any attempt to escape I knew would at once circumscribe my limits of observation. By the course I have pursued the Doctor has had a fair opportunity for arriving at the candid conviction he expressed to my husband of my sanity, viz: "Mrs. Shedd is not crazy nor can she be with her organization."

The confidence my keepers had in my sanity was expressed in various ways. One was by their allowing me to have my own pen-knife and scissors during all my incarceration, which act is strictly forbidden by the by-laws; and of course it would be necessary to keep these articles from insane people. Another fact I found out through them was, that this house is used as the headquarters for the Masons to get their bountiful feasts in; and yet the prisoners have heard the Doctor deny that he was a Mason, himself! But feasting the Masons is not the only feasts the Doctor is in the habit of bestowing at the State's expense, and at the sacrifice too of the much needed table comforts of the invalid prisoners, such as fruits, berries, melons, butter, cream, milk, wines, vegetables and such like. I know the State has a heavy wine bill to pay yearly, charged for the "good of the patients;" but judging from both of the Doctors' appearance at times, I should think they made free use of it themselves, and I am sure they and their guests use far more of it than the patients do.

The prisoners are kept uniformly on the plainest and coarsest kind of fare, far better suited to a class of working men, than sick women. Even butter is not always furnished, and when it is, it is often so very poor that it is not fit to eat, and I have known meat sent to the wards so very foul that the attendants would not put it upon the table, and the boarders would have nothing left them to eat but molasses and bread. Only once a week are we allowed any kind of sauce or relish of any kind to eat with our butterless bread. It is true the prisoners have the privilege of looking through the iron grates of their prison windows at the twenty-five nice fat cows, "headed by the buffalo," on their way to and from their rich pasture; but it would afford us far more solid satisfaction to have been allowed to use some of their new milk and sweet butter, for our health and comfort. It does seem that with all the money the State expends on this Institution that its boarders ought to be decently fed. But they are not.

Great injustice is done the prisoners in respect to their clothing, by losing much of it, which the Doctor accounts for on the false plea oftentimes, that "the patients tear their own clothes." Some of the prisoners do tear their own clothes, but most of their losses in clothing, are the result of wrong conduct on the part of the employees.

I once saw Miss Conkling held under the water, until almost dead, and I feared she would never get her breath again; and I was obliged to help in doing this myself, or I might have to exchange places with her! I saw Mrs. Comb, and helped do it, held by the hair of her head under a streaming faucet, and handfuls of hair were pulled from her head, by their rough handling, simply because she would not eat when she was not hungry! I have seen the attendants strike the hands of the patients with their keys, so as to leave black and blue spots for many days. I have seen them pinch their ears and arms and shoulders, and shake them, when they felt that they could not eat; and were thus forced to eat when their stomachs were so rejecting it as to be retching at the time. There is one married woman there who has been imprisoned seven times by her husband, and yet she is intelligent and entirely sane! When will married women be safe from her husband's power? And yet, she must assert her own rights, for the government does not protect her rights, as it does her husband's, and then run the risk of being called insane for so doing! I do not think the men who make the laws for us, would be willing to exchange places with us.

This house seems to me to be more a place of punishment, than a place of cure. I have often heard the patients say, "this is a wholesale slaughter house!" And there is more truth than the people ought to allow in this remark. They bury the dead in the night, and with no more religious ceremony than the brute has. We can hear the dead cart go round the house in the night to bury those prisoners who have been killed by abuse; and their next door room-mates would not know, sometimes for months, what had become of them, because they were told they had gone home, when they had gone to their silent graves! I have heard of one case where the patient had been dead one year, before the Doctor informed the friends of the death of their relative!

The prisoners are not allowed to write to their friends what kind of treatment they are receiving, and an attemp to do so, clandestinely, is punished as an offense. The punishment for this offense is, they must have their term of imprisonment lengthened for it. I once knew the Doctor to threaten to keep one prisoner longer even for aiding another in getting a letter to her friends.

The indefinite time for which they are imprisoned renders this prison all the more dismal. If the prisoner could but know for how long a time he must suffer this incarceration, it would be a wonderful relief. Then the Superintendent could not perpetuate it at his own option, as he now can and does. These prisoners are much more at the mercy of their keepers than the penitentiary convicts. As it is now conducted I should choose the place of the convict in the penitentiary, rather than the place of a patient in Jacksonville Insane Asylum. And yet there is not one in a hundred probably, of the patients who is treated as well as I was during the fourteen weeks I was imprisoned there.

The above statement, I stand responsible for as the *truth* as it was when I was there; and I now challenge the people of Illinois to bring forward proof, if it can be found, to refute it. Indeed I court and invite the most rigid investigation, knowing that the result will only be a confirmation of this statement. TIRZAH F. SHEDD.

Aurora, May, 1867.

XXIII.

Testimony of Mrs. Horace Yates,* of Chicago, Ill.

I was entered in September, 1857. Was there seven weeks. I occupied the Seventh ward. I was just recovering from a confinement, and was deranged from nevous weakness; still I knew all that transpired as well as I now do, and have as clear conception of what I experienced and witnessed there, and can relate it, as well as any period of my life.

*Her testimony was taken, under oath, by the Committee.

I had not slept for nearly two weeks, and I found the noise and confusion of an Insane Asylum a poor place to secure the quiet, and good food I needed. Nothing was done to make me sleep. I had no kind of medical treatment whatever. My food was so very coarse, I suffered greatly from hunger. The food consisted almost entirely of bread and meat. We had scarcely any butter at all. No vegetables, except very seldom some small unpealed potatoes—only once did we have beets, and this was about all they had of any kind while I was there.

Sabbath nights we had apple sauce or raw apple with our supper. This was all the fruit we had. The attendants had vegetables, fruits and plenty of good food, but the patients got no such fare. We could see cart loads of vegetables, drive into the yard, but all our longing for them could not get the patients any share in these good things. We were hurried through our meals, so that I could not get time to eat all I needed, poor as it was; and I was not allowed to carry even a crust of bread to my room. Only once did I manage to take a crust of bread to my room unnoticed. Once I took my tumbler from the table to the hydrant to draw me some water to drink, when my attendant seized me by the shoulders and shook me so long and so severely, that I could not speak to save my life. Indeed, I almost fainted under her hands. Dr. McFarland came into the wards just after, and I told him what a shaking I had just had, and I could hardly articulate from its effects, when he simply made light of it, by saying, "O, no, I guess you are mistaken; it was only a *love pat!*" He is utterly indifferent to any complaint a patient makes. This is just a specimen of the manner he treats them.

The first thing they did to me was to *force* from me my watch and jewelry. Not understanding their intentions I resisted them—they then threw me down upon my back on the floor, and jumped upon my stomach with their knees, so violently, that it is a wonder, in my weak state, they did not kill me. Mrs. Hart, from Chicago, in the room opposite, knowing what was going on, and feeling her inability to interpose in my defence, expressed her indignation by taking a silver thimble and crushing it with her foot! I thought this rather a rough beginning on a weak sick woman, but just able to be off from my bed. But I found this was the way all were obliged to submit to just so much abuse as they chose to practice upon us. I could not defend myself, neither could the patients defend each other. Nor would the Doctor listen to our story, much less protect us from their abuse. I wrote to my husband, telling him how much I wanted to come home, but although the Doctor promised to send it, he never did.

The patients are ruled with rigor, and are sometimes tortured very severely. The worst torture I found there was the shower-bath; which is, letting water drop from a great height upon them, which must be terrible, judging from the deafening, agonizing shrieks uttered by the victim while under this torture. I never witnessed this abuse, for the patient is locked up alone at the time; but we could hear their shrieks and cries for mercy.

I think the Doctor is accountable for the abuse of his patients. He ought to be their protector, but he is not: he don't seem to care how the patients are treated. It is a most dreadful place of punishment, but is not a place to be nursed and treated like a patient at all. They have to learn to be patient under wrongs, and this is the only sense that the term "patient" will apply to them.

My husband took me to ride when he came to see me, and when the horse took a road in the direction of that dismal place, it made me shudder so that he concluded to take me me home, where I soon recovered. But had he put me back, it does seem that I should have been ruined. I told my husband that I thought all such houses ought to be burned up, and I think so still, unless they are better conducted than that was while I was there.

Mrs. H. H. Yates.

Chicago, May 25, 1867.

XXIV.

Testimony of Mrs. Caroline E. Lake,* of Aurora, Ill.

I was a patient at Jacksonville Insane Asylum three months. My husband placed me there to secure a "course of medical treatment," to cure me of what is called "religious monomania." I was just as capable of judging of my surroundings as I am now. I was put through no course of medical treatment, as my husband expected I should be when he put me there, and offered Dr. McFarland five hundred dollars to secure such treatment as would cure me.

The patients get no course of treatment for insanity at that Institution, that I could find, but restraint and imprisonment, the loss of their natural rights, and in some cases, great abuse. I did not see much physical abuse in the Seventh ward, but I believe it is practised in other wards.

But it was a course of severe treatment to me, to be put where my word is not regarded—where I could not communicate with my friends, except all my letters to and from, be read by the Doctor, and to have all my rights and privileges subject to the dictation of keepers—in short, to *be a prisoner*, and treated like a convict, is most cruel treatment to bestow upon the innocent, but unfortunate. One who has lost his reason, can ill afford to lose his personal liberty also, and with it all his social rights and privileges. I think had I been left there long, I should have become insane, hopelessly. And most fortunate for me was my husband's offer of five hundred dollars, for I think this alone was all that saved me from this terrible result, for such treatment long continued must have ruined me.

I think the treatment there, makes more insane or idiotic people, than it cures; and no place that I ever was in, should I more dislike to be returned to than that Institution; and I believe there seldom was a patient there who got as good treatment as I did, or rather, who did not get worse!

*This testimony has been before the Committee, but not the witness.

If a patient enters a complaint to the Doctor, he seems utterly indifferent to it; whether it is just or unjust, he don't seem to care. It is of no use to appeal to him, while a patient there. He seems to act as though patients had no rights which he is bound to respect at all. He gives us no satisfaction in his answers to our intelligent questions. We feel that we are a despised class, to be tolerated, rather than be respected and cared for. The rule of the house necessarily produces this feeling.

Ought not the insane to be pitied, and made to feel that they are cared for as human beings, having human feelings in common with others? I do, to this day, feel an instinctive shudder, when I think how entirely defenceless and exposed I was while there. We can't help feeling that we have no laws, nor friends to shield us there; nor can our friends shield us, for we are not allowed to write to them and tell the treatment we are under, for we know it would not be sent if we did. Therefore we must be false to ourselves, and utter lies by saying we are well cared for, or we can have no communication with them whatever. Then our friends feel sure we are contented and happy, when we are most discontented and miserable; and besides, we find it impossible to get a release from our imprisonment so long as we express any dissatisfaction with our surroundings.

We must *seem* happy when we are miserable, or we can have no chance for a release. For example, I have seen Mrs. Timmons, a sane woman to all appearance, who has been there five years, crying most bitterly to be sent to her children and friends, but on hearing the Doctor's footsteps she will hush up instantly, and try to assume the most placid and quiet appearance, lest he protract her imprisonment if he found her in tears crying to go home. And it is even so when her friends visit her, she is afraid to let them know how she does feel lest the Doctor find out that she is discontented, and then her release will be sure to be "indefinitely postponed." Thus her imprisonment has been protracted on this false pretense that she is contented and happy, and thus the Doctor secures a most splendid cook for his table, free of cost! Her friends are either deceived or blinded in relation to her state, or, in my opinion, they would take her home.

I think there are many married women put there to get rid of them, who are not insane at all, and I think their husbands are made to believe they are well treated, when the subjection and arbitrary rule of the house renders them so wretched, that they prefer death to such a hopeless, *indefinite* imprisonment. I think many of these husbands would not have sent them there, if they could have known how the Institution is conducted.

Even letter writing is punished as an offence, if it is done clandestinely for the sake of writing the truth. I knew the Doctor to threaten one of the Seventh ward ladies with an *extension of her term of imprisonment,* for writing the truth to a brother of a patient, to tell him that his sister was not insane, but falsely committed, and solicited his aid in her deliverance. This is a punishment most of all to be dreaded, but as the term of each patient's imprisonment is left wholly to him to determine, he can retain them year after year, when they ought to be at home. It is my opinion, the management of the Institution needs to be radically changed, to make it what the public generally suppose it to be; for they are blinded and deluded in relation to it.

Mrs. CAROLINE E. LAKE.

Aurora, May 12, 1867.

The husband of Mrs. Lake gave me the following, as an expression of his views on this subject. Said he, "I placed my wife in Jacksonville Insane Asylum, in September, 1862, where she remained three months, when the Doctor returned her to me as 'cured,' but she was far from being so in my estimation. I sent her east, and in two months she was cured, and has had the care of her family since. I did not pay the Doctor the five hundred dollars I offered to do in case he cured her, and she remained cured six months. As for Dr. McFarland's knowledge of insanity, I think his decision in my wife's case, shows that he is either ignorant of his profession, or he is indifferent to it. I think he has already been there too long. He has become hard-hearted, and callous to human suffering. The Institution is conducted entirely different from what I supposed. I should never consent to put another friend there under its present management. I can see no reason why the patients should not be allowed to write freely, and just what they please. Every natural social right should be protected to them, as a means of bringing them back to a natural state. I hope, Mrs. Packard, you will have all the testimony published, for it ought to be."

I have a witness that these were his words.

E. P. W. Packard.

Note to the Reader.

During my extensive travels throughout the different States of this Union, where I have already sold eighteen thousand books upon this subject, all by direct personal appeals, and by single sales, I have become by this means, cognizant of the feelings and views, of a very large class of United States citizens upon this subject.

I have become personally acquainted with, and made personal appeals to three Legislatures upon this subject. I have sold almost every book to men—and I have especially sought out the men of the very first class, in point of position and influence in society, and it has been from this class alone I have received most of my patronage, in the sale of my books.

From this standpoint of personal knowledge, I am prepared to state that I know of thousands of men, found in these ranks in society, who now sympathize with me in my views of the present Insane Asylum *System*, and this number is constantly increasing through the influence of the agitation these books are producing.

In order therefore, that these individual influences be focalized into a power which may be felt, and used to secure their overthrow, on their present corrupt basis, the writer suggests that whenever this volume falls into the wake of this influence, that some self-appointed agent copy the following Constitution of an "Anti-Insane Asylum Society," and circulate it throughout the town of his or her residence, and forward their names to my address, at Chicago, Illinois, hoping thus to form a nucleus of a humanitarian reform in this most needed department of human rights.

Constitution of an Anti-Insane Asylum Society.

Since it has become self-evident from the facts before the public, authenticated by the Illinois Legislative Committee, that our present system of treating the Insane, is a gross violation of the principles of Christianity, and of mental pathology, and therefore, can not receive the sanction of the enlightened and conscientious; and knowing that it takes a long time to revolutionize such popular institutions, sustained by State's power; we can not submit to pass off the stage of action, without leaving our protest against them.

Therefore, while the present system exists, we, the undersigned, do hereby pledge ourselves,

1st. That we will never consent to be entered into such Institutions as patients.

2nd. We will never consent to have any relative or friend of ours, entered as a patient.

3rd. If we, or our relatives or friends, should become insane, they shall be taken care of by their friends, in their own homes.

4th. This Society pledge themselves that such shall be kindly and appropriately cared for.

5th. That if the relatives of the unfortunate one are not able to provide for, and bestow suitable treatment upon them, this Society shall furnish them with the means for doing so.

6th. This fund for the protection of the unfortunate, shall be bestowed by a committee of this Society, as their judgment shall dictate, after having thoroughly investigated the whole case.   Mrs. E. P. W. Packard.

Chicago, Illinois.

Mrs. Packard's Publications.

Mrs. Packard's Prison Life.—A narrative of her Three Year's Imprisonment in Jacksonville Insane Asylum, to which is appended the Testimony of her Coadjutors, including Mrs. Olsen's Prison Life, and the testimony of Mrs. Minard, Mrs. Shedd, Mrs Yates and Mrs. Lake. The facts in the volume are authenticated by the Report of the Investigating Committee appointed by the Legislature of Illinois in 1867. It contains 450 pages large 12mo. bound in cloth. Price **$1.50**.

Three Years Imprisonment for Religious Belief.—A delineation of "Married Woman's Wrongs," showing the need of her Emancipation from her legal position of "nonentity" to that of a legal entity; so that she, *as a married woman*, may be as well protected in her rights, as a woman, as her husband is, as a man. It includes also Mrs. Packard's address to the Illinois Legislature on the passage of the "Personal Liberty Bill." It is bound in cloth back, enameled sides, gilt letters and lines, flexible, and contains 158 royal octavo pages. Price **$1.00**.

Mrs. Olsen's Prison Life.—A narrative of her one year's imprisonment at Jacksonville Insane Asylum, to which is added the testimony of Mrs. Minard, Mrs. Shedd, Mrs. Yates and Mrs. Lake; all of whom endured a term of imprisonment at that Institution, and were witnesses to what they have testified. It is confirmed by the Investigating Committee, appointed by the Legislature of Illinois in 1867. It contains 140 pages large 12mo. Price **50 cts**.

Mrs. Packard's Address to the Legislature of Illinois on the passage of the "Personal Liberty Bill, given in the State House, Springfield, Feb. 12, 1867. The result of which was the passage of the Bill. A pamphlet bound in paper cover. Price **25 cts**.

☞The above Books can be obtained either by wholesale or by the single copy, of

CLARKE & CO.,

Publishers, No. 8 Custom House Place,

MRS. E. P. W. PACKARD,   Chicago, Ill.
Chicago.

www.ingramcontent.com/pod-product-compliance
Lightning Source LLC
Chambersburg PA
CBHW021426300426
44114CB00010B/661